THE SOCIAL MEANINGS
OF SUICIDE

For the present let us remain keenly sus-pecting that the longing not to die, the hunger for personal immortality, the effort whereby we tend to persist indefinitely in our own being, which is, according to the tragic Jew, our very essence, that this is the affective basis of all knowledge and the personal inward starting-point of all human philosophy, wrought by a man and for men. And we shall see how the solution of this inward affective problem, a solution which may be but the despairing renunciation of the attempt at a solution, is that which colours all the rest of philosophy. Underly-ing even the so-called problem of knowledge there is simply this human feeling, just as underlying the enquiry into the "why," the cause, there is simply the search for the "wherefore," the end. All the rest is either to deceive oneself or to wish to deceive others; and to wish to deceive others in order to deceive oneself.

And this personal and affective starting-point of all philosophy and all religion is the tragic sense of life. Let us now proceed to consider this.

Miguel de Unamuno,
TRAGIC SENSE OF LIFE

THE SOCIAL MEANINGS OF
SUICIDE

BY JACK D. DOUGLAS

PRINCETON, NEW JERSEY

PRINCETON UNIVERSITY PRESS

Printed in the United States of America by
Princeton University Press, Princeton, New Jersey

In Memory of

WILLIAM E. DOUGLAS

1938-1959

PREFACE

My original intention in doing a work on suicide was simply to build upon what Durkheim and others had done. I had assumed along with most sociologists that the fundamental arguments against Durkheim's sociological approach in *Suicide* had been successfully answered in *Suicide* itself. I intended to extend Durkheim's argument, synthesize it with certain recent ideas in psychology, and demonstrate the validity of this slightly revised theory by using more systematic and formal statistical tests of the mass of modern statistics on suicide. Not only did my whole approach demand statistical tests of the data, but I specifically intended to construct a mathematical model of the probabilities of suicide, which would be validated or invalidated by these tests.

Intending to do as complete a job as possible, I set out to collect systematically as much information on suicide as I could from every conceivable source. After having amassed and carefully analyzed a great deal of material on suicide rates, I encountered some of the early criticisms of official suicide statistics. It came as something of a shock to me to realize that I had not given any careful consideration to my fundamental source of information about the phenomena being studied. I had always known that this was a cardinal sin (and bad strategy) in any form of scientific endeavor, yet I had found it so easy to do what others had already prepared the basic forms for that it did not occur to me to examine critically what sociologists had been doing since Durkheim. I knew the abstract rule very well, but I had not yet come to see the applications of abstract meanings to specific situations as fundamentally problematic.

My faith shaken, I began a thorough search for all available information on suicide statistics. The more I questioned these statistics, the more I came to realize that they were not what Durkheim and many others had assumed they were. In addition, and with this first problem as a spur, the more I analyzed Durkheim's argument in *Suicide*, the more I became convinced that *Suicide* was a very complex work and did not fit the usual interpretations given to it by sociologists.

In an attempt to understand *Suicide* and evaluate the statistical "evidence" used by Durkheim, I was forced to look more and more into the history of the nineteenth-century studies of suicide, especially those upon which Durkheim himself had relied so very heavily. In this way my work became partly a study of the history and sociology of "knowledge" of suicide, with a primary focus on the sociological works on suicide. Only in this way could I effectively understand and criticize these works.

After I had done this, it would have been possible to leave such considerations out of a work on suicide, perhaps to present them in a completely separate book. But this would actually greatly undermine the effectiveness of my work on suicide. Without an understanding and criticism of these previous sociological works on suicide, my own theoretical approach might simply seem to add to the other approaches rather than, as I hope to demonstrate, replace them. Besides this, it became clear to me as my own ideas about suicide began to crystallize that there is at present not nearly enough of the right kind of evidence available for me to present any thoroughly convincing proofs of my fundamental propositions. My own work would have to remain at the level of making a beginning with firm foundations, of proposing a theoretical approach which seems more consistent with what *good* evidence does exist at present, and with indicating what forms of new evidence should now be sought. For this reason, if for no other, an extensive presentation and systematic criticism of the previous, dominant sociological approaches to suicide seems to be an essential part of my own work on suicide at this stage in its progress. The integration of these two purposes has, undoubtedly, not been perfect. Certainly it will seem to some that the critical part is too extensive. But it is my own judgment that the critical task is one of the most important at this time for the simple reason that we will not work to prove or disprove the value of the theoretical approach I have proposed *unless* we are first convinced of the fundamental inadequacies of the previous approaches. It is my greatest hope that this work will so convince sociologists and other social scientists, and that they will then share in the task of accumulating the mass of comparative descriptions of suicidal events so essential for further progress in research and theory on suicide.

Many people have given me support, criticism, and inspiration which were of very great help in preparing and writing this book. Though I cannot express my appreciation to all of those who helped, or even feel sure that I remember all who contributed through those vital day-to-day conversations, there are certain people to whom my debt is especially great.

Melvin Tumin proved an untiring source of help in all ways throughout the difficult years of research and writing. I have often disagreed with some of his criticisms of various drafts of this work, but by the time I had reached the final version I had incorporated most of the important ones. His support was especially important in those moments of initial doubt when my work had led to conclusions that I knew would challenge many accepted ideas.

I also owe a great deal for continued support and valuable suggestions to Paul Bohannan, Marvin Bressler, Marion Levy, Charles Page, Frederick Stephan, and Ivan Vallier. The support of Harold Garfinkel, Ralph Turner, Melville Dalton, and Melvin Seeman were very important during the final phases of writing.

My great intellectual debt to Harold Garfinkel for some of the fundamental ideas in Part IV will be apparent. The give and take in day-to-day conversations with Harvey Sacks concerning suicide and all forms of social action were also very important to the development of my ideas in Part IV.

For critical readings and suggestions concerning various parts of the book I am greatly indebted to many people, even when we could not finally agree. Very important in this respect were Peter McHugh, Aaron Cicourel, Lindsey

Churchill, Robert Nisbet, Edward Tiryakian, Leroy Gould, Kurt Wolff, Irwin Deutscher, Ronald Silvers, William Henry, Donald Ball, and Trent Eglin. Arthur Sinchcombe, Albert Reiss, Michael Edwards, and Albert Cohen made some valuable criticisms and suggestions after reading some of my closely related works on suicide.

I am deeply grateful for the unerring encouragement and suggestions given by Gordon Hubel and William McClung of the Princeton University Press. In addition, William McClung has added greatly to the readability of the book by his intelligent and painstaking work. Their examples have taught me the importance of editors to the progress of scholarship.

I owe much to my wife for her help in the arduous labor of preparing the work for publication and, above all, for sharing with me the suffering involved in writing such a difficult book. In the same personal vein, I want to express my deep gratitude for the staunch friendship of Emory and Georgette Daugherty, without whose help I might never have written this book.

Finally, I owe a great deal to the many people, such as Irving Weinstein and Lawrence Rose, who unknowingly contributed greatly to this book by discussing with me their experiences, feelings, and ideas about suicide or, in the case of people who must remain unnamed, by simply showing me through their own actions the meanings of suicide in our society.

Jack D. Douglas
January 16, 1967
Princeton, N.J.

CONTENTS

INTRODUCTION

The theoretical treatment of suicide is one of the few classical subjects in sociology. Indeed, it was of great importance in the establishment of sociology as an independent academic discipline. This important position of the study of suicide in sociology is, of course, the direct result of Durkheim's work on *Suicide*. To this day Durkheim's *Suicide* has dominated, with only a few important exceptions, the sociological works on suicide and much of all sociological methodology.

Because of this vast influence of Durkheim's *Suicide*, a very careful, detailed analysis and criticism of this work must be the first step in any attempt to treat suicide as a subject for *fundamental* sociological analysis. For this reason Part I has been devoted to just such a careful analysis and criticism of *Suicide*. Because I do not believe Durkheim's *Suicide* can be understood adequately without putting it into the historical context of the mass of nineteenth-century European work on suicide, Chapter I is a brief attempt to do this. Chapter II, the analysis and criticism of Durkheim's *Suicide*, is undoubtedly the most difficult part of this entire work; and it will surely be one of the most controversial. This chapter is not, however, self-contained. The criticism of Durkheim's whole approach as well as of his specific ideas about suicide continues throughout this work, simply because *Suicide* is the cornerstone of the whole approach to suicide taken by almost all sociologists in the twentieth century. It is especially important to note that Durkheim's famous treatment of the definition of suicide is analyzed and criticized primarily in Part III (and in Appendix II), which is an integral part of the general criticism of the data for Durkheim's work and for almost all subsequent sociological works.

Part II is the least well integrated part of this work. It is an unfortunate historical fact that the development of sociological work on suicide has not been very systematic.

When one has studied the many works on suicide since Durkheim's *Suicide*, it is clear that there has been a general tendency to treat suicide as a subject to demonstrate some specific theory which is different from that of previous workers. Because of this it has been necessary to deal with each of the significant works in themselves, trying to demonstrate errors within each and general errors committed by those using Durkheim's approach and data. This means that Part II is important in the argument, for it will, I hope, show the clear need for an alternative, better approach. But it also means that Part II cannot be extremely systematic or compact without distorting the nature of these works. It is, however, systematically integrated with the other parts of this work by the continual themes of my general argument and by considering the various theories in an order determined by their similarity to Durkheim's approach and to the one to be proposed in Parts III and IV.

Part III, the systematic analysis of the nature of official statistics and a critique of the use of official statistics by sociologists in their works on suicide, is both the analysis of the most important error made in previous sociological works on suicide and the beginning of the presentation of my own theoretical approach to suicide. In trying to determine just how officials decide a "death" is a "suicide," one is led into the theoretical approach both proposed and demonstrated in Part IV.

Part IV is the culmination of the whole argument and, if my argument is sufficiently convincing, the beginning of a new sociological approach to suicide. This approach is not totally new by any means. Indeed, it is a fundamental part of my argument concerning the nature of Durkheim's theory of suicide that Durkheim was moving in the direction of studying suicidal actions as meaningful actions; and certainly it will be clear from Part II that many of the succeeding works have added significantly to the development of the approach. But it is new in many fundamental respects. There can be no doubt that many of the details in Part IV will prove to be empirically wrong, but I believe its fundamental approach is sound and that it can help us to increasingly approximate the truth of suicidal phenomena and of social phenomena in general.

PART I · THE DURKHEIMIAN APPROACH TO SUICIDE

Il est curieux de voir l'homme, qui s'intitule avec orgueil le Roi de la nature et qui croit régler tout par son libre arbitre, subir à son insu, plus rigoureusement qu'aucun autre être de la création, les lois auxquelles il est soumis. Ces lois sont si sagement coordonnées, qu'elles échappent même à son attention.

QUETELET, PHYSIQUE SOCIALE

I   THE HISTORICAL CONTEXT OF DURKHEIM'S THEORY OF SUICIDE

General Cultural Setting

Suicide has been an important subject in the thought of the Western world. Concern with suicide has waxed and waned, but it is certainly a subject that has been discussed by most of the prominent writers from Plato to Camus. The subject of suicide has often been involved in the focal intellectual problems of these writers.

It is undoubtedly very difficult to delineate the focal concerns of Western thought for even short periods of time, and even more difficult to do so for a period stretching over centuries. But the relations between certain focal concerns of Western thought and the Western ideas about suicide seem, as I shall try to show very briefly, to give us such great insight into the early psychological and sociological theories of suicide that at least a brief treatment of them is valuable here.

It seems reasonably clear that men of the Western world, or, at least, the prominent writers of the Western world, have generally seen social action as problematic. They have seen social action as both *theoretically and morally problematic*.[1] That is, neither the explanation of behavior nor the justification of behavior has been left unquestioned. Both have been seen as themselves requiring explanation.

Two of the perennial issues of the problem of social action have been those of: (1) free will versus determinism and (2) the rights of the individual versus the rights of God

[1] Talcott Parsons has argued that the consideration of *social order* as problematic (by Hobbes *et al.*) was of critical importance in the development of social thought that eventually led to the development of sociology. (See Talcott Parsons, *The Structure of Social Action*, New York: The Free Press of Glencoe, 1949.) Social order had actually been just as clearly considered to be problematic by Plato (in *The Republic*), by Augustine (in the *City of God*), and by many others in the early periods of Western thought.

or of the society (which in more recent centuries has been stated as the problem of individual freedom versus individual responsibility). In the seventeenth, eighteenth, and nineteenth centuries these two problems became intense concerns of most European thinkers.

At first the problem of the rights of the individual versus the rights of the society was the concern which led to a thorough consideration of the old moral question of suicide —does the individual have the right to take his own life or does he have obligations to society (or to God, or to himself) that make it morally wrong for him to take his own life? John Donne and David Hume wrote strong and influential defenses of the individual's right to take his own life—at least within certain bounds.[2] By the middle of the eighteenth century this moral question had become such an important issue that most of the philosophers of the Enlightenment took it up in one way or another.[3]

[2] In his much earlier essay on suicide Montaigne had strongly implied that, though suicide is foolish (because it takes from us our all, etc.), it is still a right of the individual to commit suicide if he so desires or, at least, it is not immoral. He argued by analogy that a man who takes his own money is not a thief and, consequently, a man who takes his own life is not a murderer. (See his essay, "Custom of the Island of Cea.")

Though we shall not be directly concerned with recent philosophical works on suicide in this work, it is important to note that this concern with *suicide as a problem* is just as great in the Western world today as at any other time. In fact, though it may have been a temporary result of the Second World War, in the last few decades suicide has been considered a more serious philosophical and moral problem than at any time in the last century. Albert Camus' great work, *The Myth of Sisyphus,* which alone is enough to justify this statement, begins with the brutal assertion that "There is but one truly serious philosophical problem, and that is suicide." For other examples see P. L. Landsberg, *The Experience of Death: The Moral Problem of Suicide,* New York: The Philosophical Library, 1953; Leon Meynard, *Le Suicide: Étude Morale et Metaphysique,* Paris: Presses Universitaires de France, 1954; and Georg Siegmund, *Sein oder Nichtsein: Die Frage des Selbstmordes,* Trier: Paulinus-Verlag, 1961.

[3] See L. G. Crocker, "Discussion of Suicide in the Eighteenth Century," *Journal of the History of Ideas,* XIII (January, 1952), 47-72. The nineteenth- and twentieth-century European literature on suicide is immense. One of the consequences of this wealth of material is that it is difficult to decide which sources are the best for any particular subject. Moreover, this difficulty is compounded by the tendency of so many students of suicide to fail to make use of what previous students have done on the subject, with the consequence that the more recent works are sometimes less adequate than earlier works. For example, on the subject of the history of European thought on

The problem of determinism versus free will was, of course, very much involved in the problem of the moral rights of individuals versus the moral rights of God or society, since it was normally seen as difficult to hold an individual responsible for something which he was not believed to be able to control. But the problem of determinism versus free will was definitely considered secondary to the problem of the morality of suicide until the nineteenth century. In the nineteenth century the fundamental intellectual or theoretical concern in the study of suicide increasingly became that of determinism versus free will. This change in concerns and the specific direction it took seem to have been due to the general development of the empirical approach to the study of suicide.

There is no simple contrast in terms of empiricism between the earlier works on suicide and the late eighteenth- and nineteenth-century works. In fact, in one important respect, that of concern for the specific details of *real* cases of suicide, it is clear that during the nineteenth century there was a significant decline in the empiricism of most of the students of suicide. But there is an important contrast between the works of these periods in terms of their fundamental concerns: the earlier works were fundamentally concerned with moral questions and with questions of ultimate causality, whereas the works of the late eighteenth and the nineteenth centuries were fundamentally concerned with questions of efficient causes, with explaining suicides in terms of observable characteristics of individuals and societies.[4]

This change in fundamental concerns can, for example, be seen in Voltaire's essay on suicide which appeared in his

---

suicide there are any number of works that one might find useful, such as those by Buonafede, Bourquelot, Staeudlin, Des Etangs, Debreyne, Lisle, Legoyt, Lecky, Bayet and Fedden. The most available of these, however, and certainly among the best, are those by Lecky and Fedden: W. E. H. Lecky, *History of European Morals from Augustus to Charlemagne*, 2 vols., New York: D. Appleton and Company, 1869; and Henry R. Fedden, *Suicide: A Social and Historical Study*, London: Peter Davies, 1938.

[4] "Efficient cause" is used here in the Aristotelian sense as Durkheim and other nineteenth-century thinkers used it. Its importance will be discussed in some detail in Chapter 2, Part I, and in Appendix I.

Philosophical Dictionary. The use of the historical case-study approach was a basic method of almost all serious works on individual and social questions in post-Renaissance Europe. Montaigne's essay on suicide made excellent use of some of the many historical cases of suicide available to the humanists, but he used them primarily to demonstrate a moral point. In the *Philosophical Dictionary* Voltaire made use of the same kind of historical case material, though, quite significantly, he also considered cases reported in contemporary newspapers. But he made use of these cases *primarily* to arrive at certain "scientific"[5] conclusions about the empirical facts of suicide and the explanations of these facts. Since these "facts" and explanations were to appear again and again as basic considerations in the works on suicide over the next two hundred years, it is instructive to briefly consider them. Voltaire concluded that: (1) suicide is more frequent in cities than in rural regions; (2) the explanation of the greater urban frequency of suicide is that cities produce more melancholia (or depression) in individuals because they have more free time from physical labor to think;[6] (3) suicide can be inherited because moral character is inherited (an idea which Morselli and many others accepted); and (4) some suicides, such as Euripides' Phaedra, commit suicide in order to get revenge against someone (an idea which gained greater importance in the twentieth century).

Throughout the eighteenth and nineteenth centuries this kind of emphasis on the need to study suicide "empirically" grew rapidly. Indeed, this assumption that the "facts" or

[5] Since Voltaire was so devoted to what he conceived the scientific method to be, and was in fact so influential in spreading the spirit of science in eighteenth-century France, it seems quite clear that Voltaire intended his essay on suicide to be "scientific" and that this treatment of suicide had a great influence on the works on suicide over the next century.

[6] This explanation is remarkably similar to Durkheim's ideas about the relations between urban (intellectual) occupations, neurasthenia, and egoistic suicide. The whole theory of melancholia and suicide had been clearly stated, even to the idea of its being caused by social isolation, at least as early as the first half of the seventeenth century when Burton proposed it in his *The Anatomy of Melancholy.* But Voltaire was one of the first and most influential French writers to exhume the whole theory and put it in the general stream of European intellectual thought that leads directly to Durkheim and beyond.

"things" are the primary concern of a scientific approach was developed into the *ideological assumption* that the "things" must determine the thoughts about the things, which, in some instances, was carried to the extreme of assuming that the things determine truth, independent of any analysis of them. Oettingen, whose work on moral statistics had an important influence on Durkheim's *Suicide*, emphatically expressed the importance to nineteenth-century social thought of this ideological assumption:

> No one can deny that the need for investigation of the facts stands in the foreground of modern scientific consciousness. Interest in this aim so predominates that neither interest nor understanding is to be counted on as soon as one dares draw the reader near philosophical abstractions or out and out theological and dogmatic deductions. "From the facts to ideas!" So commands the watchword. "Where the ideas are shattered, the facts remain unshaken."[7]

The Studies of Suicide by the Moral Statisticians

With the rapid development of medicine, especially of psychiatry, and of the various forms of official statistics in the late eighteenth century and on into the nineteenth century, moral interest in suicide increasingly took a statistical bent; and the statistics were increasingly taken to be the "empirical" data of works on suicide. The statistical study of suicide was, more or less from the beginning of such studies in the late eighteenth century, understood by researchers and theorists to be a study of morality—so much so that the statistics on suicide were included (with murder and other crimes) in the general category of "moral statistics."[8] Here, then, was a fundamental perspective on suicide

[7] Alexander von Oettingen, *Die Moralstatistik in ihrer Bedeutung fur eine Christliche Socialethik*, Erlangen, 1874, p. 1.

[8] Even Morselli's great work on suicide was subtitled *An Essay on Comparative Moral Statistics*. (See Henry Morselli, *Suicide: An Essay on Comparative Moral Statistics*, New York: D. Appleton, 1903.) Durkheim himself had published an essay entitled "Suicide et Naturalité: Étude de Statistique Morale" (*Revue Philosophique de la France et de l'Étranger*, XIII [1888], 446-463); and Durkheim's *Suicide* was reviewed in the first volume of *L'Année Sociologique* under the section entitled "Statistique Morale."
It is not possible here to go into the great complexities of the hun-

inherited from the common-sense and philosophical treatments of suicide. Suicide was assumed to be a moral problem and it was assumed, quite implicitly, by all of the students of suicide involved [9] that any theory of suicide would include the moral aspects of suicide as one of the basic factors.

This assumption by nineteenth-century statistical researchers and theoreticians of suicide has greatly affected almost all sociological research and theory on suicide up to the present day. As we shall see, it was so strong in Durkheim's thought about suicide that he steadfastly maintained it on the general theory level of analysis while contradicting it and going around it on the more specific level of analysis when his data "forced" him to do so. And the predominant American approach to suicide (at least until the last few decades), the ecological approach, assumed the moral aspect of suicide to be the most important. They no longer allowed their individual moral attitudes to intrude overtly into their research and theory, but they did assume that one could understand suicide only by considering it to be fundamentally a form of social deviance.

Implicit also in this moral attitude toward suicide was the assumption that the individual's right to dispose of his own life as he saw fit was of less weight than the rights of society to make demands on him. This aspect of the conventional moral attitude bears some obvious relation to Durkheim's ideas regarding the moral superiority of society over the individual. Durkheim's general ideas regarding the causal relations between society and individual action, however, were much more affected by the development of ideas concerning the second central issue in the conception of social

---

dreds of "moral-statistical" studies of suicide and other "moral" phenomena published in the nineteenth century. Such a difficult task necessitates another book entirely, one which the author is currently undertaking. I am concerned here simply with outlining the fundamental aspects of the moral-statistical works on suicide, especially as these are related to Durkheim's *Suicide*.

[9] Contrary to the moral attitudes of many of the *philosophes* of the eighteenth century, almost all of the researchers and theoreticians of suicide in the nineteenth century took the much more conservative attitude that suicide was immoral. Some of the more positivistic, such as Morselli and Durkheim, did, however, eventually recast this attitude in terms of "pathology."

action as problematic—that is, free will versus determinism.

As the statistics on suicide began to accumulate in the nineteenth century it became increasingly clear, at least after the first several decades, that each society and, frequently, each subgroup tended to have the same suicide rates each year. (If, as was frequently the case in the earlier half of the century, the suicide rate was steadily increasing, then the rate of increase seemed to be pretty much the same each year.)[10] This regularity of suicide rates impressed these early students of social statistics, who regarded such regularity as the stuff of which the natural sciences were made and, consequently, an ideal subject for a fledgling science of society. Moreover, this regularity seemed to some of the most influential students to be related to the old problem of free will versus determinism. They assumed that such regularity of suicides committed by any given group of individuals could only be the result of some extra-individual factor that determined the wills of the individuals in the society and, thence, the suicide rates; for, so they believed, if free will were determining the actions of individuals, there could only be gross irregularity in the suicide rates.

One of the clearest and most influential statements of this argument was made by Henry Buckle. In his famous "scientific theory of history," originally published in the 1850's, Buckle considered the whole question of free will versus determinism to be more important than any other, and he strongly argued that the moral statistics, especially those on suicide, demonstrated beyond doubt that individual actions are determined by social causes. Drawing primarily upon Quetelet's work, Buckle argued that ". . . we shall be forced to the further conclusion, that such variations are the result of large and general causes, which, working upon the aggregate of society, must produce certain conse-

[10] Especially during the first few decades of collecting suicide statistics, the suicide rate mounted very rapidly for almost all European nations. It seems obvious today that this was merely a result of better social machinery for collecting the statistics on suicide, but to most students of suicide in the nineteenth century it looked as though the actual suicide rates were going up continually. This was generally interpreted as being a grave social threat resulting from some general moral sickness in the body social. This supposed moral crisis of the age greatly increased the effects noted above of the moral concern with suicide.

quences, without regard to the volition of those particular men of whom the society is composed. . . . In a given state of society a certain number of persons must put an end to their own life. This is the general law; and the special question as to who shall commit the crime depends of course upon special laws; which, however, in their total action must obey the large social law to which they are all subordinate."[11]

More than twenty-five years later Morselli summed up the same argument in his famous work on suicide:

> By the statistical returns of suicide is disclosed then, through a long series of years, such a regularity as to surpass, as Wagner proved, the statistical laws of births, deaths, and marriages. This fact has helped to change radically the metaphysical idea of the human will, and in the hands of Quetelet, Wagner, and Drobisch, has served as a formidable weapon to deny the reality of independent human actions, and to declare that the same laws exist in the moral as in the physical world. This regularity shows itself in the repetition of the same numbers in the long numerical series, from which the ulterior phases may be anticipated with great probability. This important result of moral statistics is conclusively confirmed by the actual and comparative numbers of suicides in the principal European states.[12]

The various theorists chose different factors for this basic determinant of the rates of individual moral actions. Some thought the cosmological factors must be the most important determinants of suicides. Some thought that average personality types that varied from one society to another but were very stable within each society were the fundamental causes of the rates of individual moral actions. And, of course, some thought that some reasonably stable properties of each society (or nation) must be the cause(s) of the

[11] Henry Thomas Buckle, *Introduction to the History of Civilization in England*, Revised Edition, New York: George Routledge & Sons, Limited, pp. 12, 15.

[12] Morselli, *op.cit.*, p. 16. In the introduction to the English translation of his work on suicide Morselli remarks that Wagner, one of the most important of all the students of moral statistics, had long maintained his belief in free will, but finally had to admit that the moral statistics on suicide proved otherwise.

reasonably stable suicide rate of the society. Early in the century the most influential moral-statistical work of all, Quetelet's *A Treatise on Man*, synthesized the basic ideas of (1) social organization as the basic cause of regularity in personality types, (2) personality types as the direct determinants of regularity in the actions of individuals, and of (3) the statistical comparisons of large numbers of individual actions as the appropriate method for studying human actions:

Society includes within itself the germs of all the crimes committed, and at the same time the necessary facilities for their development. It is the social state, in some measure, which prepares these crimes, and the criminal is merely the instrument to execute them. Every social state supposes, then, a certain number and a certain order of crimes, these being merely the necessary consequences of its organization. . . .

It would appear, then, that moral phenomena, when observed on a great scale, are found to resemble physical phenomena; and we thus arrive, in inquiries of this kind, at the fundamental principle, *the greater the number of individuals observed, the more do individual peculiarities, whether physical or moral, become effaced, and leave in a prominent point of view the general facts, by virtue of which society exists and is preserved.* . . .

It is not at all my intention to propose a Theory of Man, but merely to ascertain by proof the facts and the phenomena which affect him, and to endeavor, by observation, to discover the laws forming the connecting links of these phenomena. The *social* man, whom I here consider, resembles the centre of gravity in bodies: he is the centre around which oscillate the social elements—in fact, so to speak, he is a fictitious being, for whom everything proceeds conformably to the medium results obtained for society in general. It is this being whom we must consider in establishing the basis of social physics, throwing out of view peculiar or anomalous cases, and disregarding any inquiry tending to show that such an individual may attain a greater or less development in one of his faculties. . . .[13]

[13] M. A. Quetelet, *A Treatise on Man*, Edinburgh: William and

This, then, was the long tradition of European thought concerning suicide within which Durkheim worked. The emphasis on suicide as immoral, the commitment to the study of suicide by statistical means, the conclusion from the regularities of suicide rates that suicide rates must be caused by some extra-individual forces, and, though to a lesser degree, the commitment to an explanation of suicide rates in terms of the extra-individual forces of stable properties of society—all of these ideas Durkheim received and accepted (frequently more implicitly than explicitly, since he seems to have either assumed that the educated reader of *Suicide* would already know much of this background or else was himself largely unaware of the influence of some of these assumptions on his whole approach). *Suicide* was primarily a synthesis of these ideas in the service of Durkheim's goal of establishing an independent discipline of sociology, but *Suicide* was also based on many more specific ideas which Durkheim received from the moral statisticians. It is these which we must now proceed to analyze within the specific context of Durkheim's work.

Robert Chambers, 1842, pp. 6, 8. There were many other expressions of the fundamental principles of the school of moral statistics and certainly Quetelet was not the first. (Most important of the earlier works was De Guerry's *Statistique Morale de la France*, published in 1835.) But Quetelet's statement of the principles and his empirical work were the clearest and most influential.

Durkheim's *Suicide*[1] seems to have been an unfailing source of wonder to most sociologists. It has been seen as a "model of research methods" and a "model of the integration of theory and data." In view of this it is strange that no sociologist has undertaken to publish a thorough investigation of *Suicide*, either a careful, interpretive analysis of the work itself or a careful consideration of the validity of the theory. Perhaps it is the wonderment itself which has defeated any attempt to carefully analyze the work: the object of awed devotion must be seen, but not very closely.[2]

The work itself is extremely difficult. Indeed, in many ways the work seems quite inaccessible to most contemporary sociologists who have attempted to make use of it. One of the reasons for the difficulty in interpreting *Suicide* is that the work itself is very confusing, even to the point of including contradictory theoretical arguments. But probably the most significant reason for our difficulties in understanding *Suicide* is simply that we do not share Durkheim's general frames of reference, which include specific knowledge and forms of thought. Regardless of whether one assumes that understanding is greatly determined by the socio-cultural matrix of the individual, there can be little doubt that a great many of the most important statements in *Suicide* mean something different to most sociologists today from what they meant to Durkheim and his contemporaries.

Part of the difference in frames of reference that seems

---

[1] Emile Durkheim, *Suicide: A Study in Sociology*, New York: The Free Press, 1951. This edition, translated by J. A. Spaulding and G. Simpson, will be referred to throughout this book. *Suicide* was originally published in 1897.

[2] Alex Inkeles' argument that *Suicide* became a symbol of professional identity also seems to have value as a partial explanation of the lack of critical evaluation. (See Alex Inkeles, "Personality and Social Structure," in *Sociology Today*, edited by R. K. Merton, *et al.*, New York: Basic Books, 1959.)

responsible for these differences in interpretation is simply our lack of knowledge of the many works that Durkheim continually drew upon. For example, few contemporary sociologists are acquainted with Brierre de Boismont's great work on suicide, published in 1856 and referred to in numerous places by Durkheim.[3] Ignorance of this work has, for example, quite recently led one sociologist to incorrectly criticize Durkheim for failing to provide any evidence that "declassification" (or "downward mobility") frequently contributes to suicide.[4] In fact, any serious student of suicide in Durkheim's age would probably have known that Brierre de Boismont had clearly argued that a "revers de fortune" is a very frequent cause (in fact, a "cause determinante") of suicide:

> When things have arrived at this point, the men who cannot achieve the goal, or who, having touched it, are pushed back, experience the greatest sorrow. Consumed by the violence of their desires, irritated without end by the object of their greed, not being able to resist this continual torture, a great number of them become disgusted with life and put an end to this unhappy existence.[5]

Brierre de Boismont did supply evidence to support his theory and Durkheim most likely had such evidence in mind when he wrote *Suicide*. There are many other examples that could be given of the importance of historical information such as this in arriving at a correct interpretation of *Suicide*.

The greatest difference in frames of reference, however, would seem to lie in the fundamentally different forms of thought used by Durkheim in his general argument in *Suicide*. Since these different forms of thought are of the greatest importance in understanding the nature of Durkheim's general argument in *Suicide*, we shall consider them below in some detail after first examining some more specific

---

[3] Brierre de Boismont, *Du Suicide et de la Folie Suicide*, Paris: Bailliere, 1856.

[4] Warren Breed, "Occupational Mobility and Suicide," *The American Sociological Review*, 28 (April, 1963) pp. 179-188.

[5] Brierre de Boismont, *op.cit.*, p. 121. My translation. See, also, pp. 122-126. For the supporting evidence see especially p. 122.

aspects of *Suicide* as a synthesis which are of importance in analyzing these differences in forms of thought.

Suicide *as a Synthesis*

Robert Nisbet, one of the foremost Durkheimian scholars, has recently argued that Durkheim's work must be seen as a reaction to the dominant emphasis on individualism in nineteenth-century social thought.[6] In so far as one is concerned with considering Durkheim's ideas in relation to the scientific, literary, and common-sense ideas of the age *in general*, this is undoubtedly true. But it is of fundamental importance in interpreting *Suicide* to realize that Durkheim wrote *Suicide* within a much narrower frame of reference than this and that within this frame of reference Durkheim's ideas are in no way a reaction. On the contrary, it is my fundamental hypothesis here that *Durkheim's* Suicide *was primarily an attempt to synthesize the better principles, methods of analysis, and empirical findings of the moral statisticians in such a way as to demonstrate the need for an independent scientific discipline concerned with human society.*[7] It is only in the matter of the degree of emphasis on social factors, the globalness of the theoretical approach, and in the rather arbitrary rejection of Quetelet's ideas about the average "personality types" as an intervening variable between social organization and suicidal actions that Durkheim's work was at all significantly different from the most prominent of the moral-statistical works on suicide.

Later sociologists have, presumably, failed to see how much *Suicide* was a synthesis both because they have not put it into the context of the works which Durkheim relied on for almost all of his ideas and data and because of the emphasis given by Durkheim and by themselves to the practical goal of the work, that of establishing sociology as an independent discipline (presumably within the academic structures of French and American universities). In Chapter 1 I have already presented some of the evidence of the ways in which Durkheim used the ideas and data of the moral

[6] Robert A. Nisbet, *Emile Durkheim*, Englewood Cliffs: Prentice-Hall, Inc., 1965, pp. 9-13.
[7] Durkheim was quite explicit about the general goal of *Suicide* in his "Preface" to the work.

statisticians to construct his work on suicide. But there are some further details of special importance to this argument concerning the nature of *Suicide* which must now be considered.

Suicide and the Moral Repression of Individuals by Society. As Mauss pointed out long ago, the fundamental concern of all of Durkheim's work was the relations between society and individuals. This concern is especially clear in *Suicide.* (An examination of Durkheim's fundamental theory of the relations between individuals and society is presented in Appendix I.) The study of suicide probably struck Durkheim as being an ideal subject for demonstrating the need for an independent discipline of sociology precisely because the common-sense view of suicide was that it was an intensely individual act; the contradiction of common sense would be a dramatic demonstration, just the sort of thing which scientists have always used to justify their existence to a skeptical public. Buckle had quite explicitly stated the case in this manner forty years earlier and this idea had become pretty commonplace among the moral statisticians as a whole. But the study of suicide had an immensely greater advantage: the moral statisticians and others had already published hundreds of works on suicide which dealt with this question of the relations between individuals and society and the best of these almost unanimously agreed that the causes of this "intensely individual" action must be external to the individual. Indeed, as we have seen earlier, since the work of Quetelet in 1842, all moral statisticians knew of the argument that different social organizations (or the "social systems," as Quetelet very often referred to them) were the ultimate causes of different social rates of suicide. And by the time of Morselli's work, still twenty years before Durkheim's work, the only significant disagreements were over the question of just how the moral state of society was related to the individual actions of suicide as represented in suicide rates and how other correlations with suicide rates were to be related to the basic correlations between social factors and suicide rates.

Not only was there general agreement among the moral statisticians that the moral state of society (or the moral organization of society) was the primary cause of suicide rates, but there was a more specific agreement, both among themselves and with commonsensical thought of the age, that the suicide rates of European societies had been rising steadily in the nineteenth century because the moral control or repression by society of the deviant tendencies of individuals had been decreasing, as could be seen, they believed, in the changes in various rates of social relations (divorces, etc.). They believed that man must recognize or accept a moral authority, generally considered to be either religion or society, greater than himself or else his passions will grow uncontrollably, he will tend to despair and, consequently, he will tend toward suicide. Esquirol had clearly stated this general idea in his famous work of 1839, *Des Maladies Mentales*, a work known to almost all serious students of suicide in the nineteenth century:

> If, by the aid of education, one has not at all fortified his soul by religious beliefs, by moral precepts, by the habits of order and regular conduct; if he has not learned to respect the laws, to fulfill social obligations, to bear the vicissitudes of life; if he has learned to scorn his peers, to disdain his ancestors, to be imperious in his desires and caprices; certainly, all other things being equal, he will be more disposed than all others to voluntarily end his existence, as soon as he experiences some unhappiness or some reverse. Man has need of an authority which directs his passions and governs his actions. Left to his own weakness, he falls into indifference, then into doubt. Nothing sustains his courage; he is disarmed against the sufferings of life, against the miseries of the heart.[8]

This idea was expressed again and again in the works on suicide of Cazeauvieilh, Descuret, Lisle, Masaryk, Legoyt,[9] and many others. It is, as will become clearer below, the most important and distinctive general idea of Durkheim's *Suicide*. It is the idea that lies behind the two "types of suicide" with which Durkheim was almost exclusively con-

[8] Quoted in A. Legoyt, *Le Suicide Ancien et Moderne*, Paris: A. Drouin, 1881, p. 73.

[9] For a synopsis of thoughts on the subject from many different works see A. Legoyt, *ibid.*

cerned in *Suicide*, "egoistic suicide" and "anomic suicide," which Durkheim distinguished from each other only inconsistently, and generally in terms of individual rather than social causes. But Durkheim did not even have to develop the specific ideas of "egoism" and "anomie" as the fundamental social causes of suicide in European societies (though he *may* have developed the word "anomie"). At least from the 1850's onward, the word "egoism" was increasingly used as a technical term to refer to the lack of moral (social) repression of individual passions, while the soaring of individual passions resulting from the rage for monetary gain was often distinguished from this kind of "egoism" without giving it a special name (until Durkheim did so).

In the following statement, consisting largely of long quotations from Chateaubriand, Brierre de Boismont foreshadows Durkheim's theory of the causal relations between social organization, morality, and anomic and egoistic suicide; and he leads us to see Durkheim's theory of suicide as a direct outgrowth of very widespread ideas about suicide, especially as developed by the "romanticist" Chateaubriand.[10]

[10] This rather obvious relation between the romantic ideas about suicide and Durkheim's theory of suicide seems to have been generally overlooked by sociologists and historians of ideas, perhaps because of Durkheim's more obvious relation to the positivists and his professed dislike for the romantics and those influenced by the romantics. Henri Peyre (in "Durkheim: The Man, His Time, and His Intellectual Background," in *Emile Durkheim, 1858-1917*, ed. by Kurt H. Wolff, New York: Harper and Row, 1964, p. 28) has, however, provided us with an additional line of possible influence between the romantics, especially Chateaubriand, and Durkheim:

We know from the testimony of his young friends that Durkheim, also, was a severe critic of Renan. The two men belonged, to be sure, to different spiritual families. Montaigne, Fénelon, Chateaubriand, Bergson, and Gide are Renan's brothers, while Durkheim is closer to a Pascal without Christ, to Rousseau, or to Peguy.

In spite of his frank distaste for Renan's writings, Durkheim was influenced by them more than any historian of ideas has yet shown.

Robert Nisbet has also previously suggested a close relationship between the Romantics and Durkheim's sociology. See Robert A. Nisbet, "Sociology as an Art Form," in *Sociology on Trial*, ed. by Maurice Stein and Arthur Vidich, Englewood Cliffs: Prentice-Hall, Inc., 1963, pp. 148-162.

(It is quite true that this general explanation of social events, especially of immoral events, was widespread in the nineteenth century. One can find it clearly expressed in Johann Spurzheim's *Observations*

To these moral maladies are now added others of which the new indices daily reveal only too much progress. Such is the absence of rule and of the moral sense. "The secret of the contradictions of men today, says Chateaubriand, is in the want of moral sense, in the absence of a fixed principle, and in the cult of force. Whoever succumbs is guilty and without merit. Behind the liberal phrases of the devotees of terror, one needs only see what is hidden there—success deified. Success, fortune, these are the idols of the moment. . . . The doctrine of material interests—so neatly formulated in that maxim, *Each for himself and by himself*—is the greatest obstacle to generous acts and sentiments. Profoundly rooted in the masses, it is, for a time, the guarantee of public tranquility and the incessant propagator of industrial operations; but it is also the most active dissolvent of that antique honesty which has been the glory and the pride of our nation. One would not know how to form an idea of the daily breaches which that doctrine makes in the spirit. Success, such is the magic word which sweeps away consciences. What matter the antecedents of a man, his morality, if he is useful. . . .

Success, there is the general goal. Woe to the vanquished; there is nothing left for them but to perish.[11]

That Durkheim was aware of the relations between these romantic ideas about suicide and his own theory of suicide is shown by his references to Lamartine's *Raphael*[12] as an example of egoistic suicide and to Chateaubriand's *René* as an example of anomic suicide:

While Raphael is a creature of meditation who finds his ruin within himself, René is the insatiate type. "I am accused," he exclaims unhappily, "of being inconstant in my desires, of never long enjoying the same fancy, of being prey to an imagination eager to sound the depth of

---

sur la Folie, Paris, 1818. And one can find it expressed more popularly in such works as H. de Vatimesnil, "Du Dévouement et de l'Égoisme," *Le Correspondant,* xix (1847), 481-522. But there is no evidence of direct influence of such sources on Durkheim's thought.)

[11] Brierre de Boismont, *Du Suicide* . . . , pp. 39-40.
[12] *Suicide,* pp. 279-280.

my pleasures as though it were overwhelmed by their persistence; I am accused of always missing the goal I might attain. Alas! I only seek an unknown good, the instinct for which pursues me. *Is it my fault if I everywhere find limits, if everything once experienced has no value for me?"*

This description conclusively illustrates the relations and differences between egoistic and anomic suicide, which our sociological analysis had already led us to glimpse. Suicides of both types suffer from what has been called the disease of the infinite. But the disease does not assume the same form in both cases. In one, reflective intelligence is affected and immoderately over-nourished; in the other, emotion is over-excited and freed from all restraint. In one, thought, by dint of falling back upon itself, has no object left; in the other, passion, no longer recognizing bounds, has no goal left. The former is lost in the infinity of dreams, the second in the infinity of desires.[13]

Moreover, since Durkheim refers to de Boismont's work four times in the short chapter[14] in which he refers to René, it seems probable that Durkheim was influenced by the romantics' ideas on suicide through de Boismont's treatment of them.[15]

The general structure and methods of Durkheim's argument in Suicide. A good deal of *Suicide* consists of attempts to work out these central ideas and their many implications. Durkheim was intent upon producing a synthesis, not merely a syncretism of earlier ideas and data. He had a

[13] *Ibid.*, pp. 286-287. Brierre de Boismont had clearly stated the need to consider thought *and* emotion as the two fundamental, independent variables involved in the causes of suicide or any other human behavior: "To feel and react, there are the two great levers of life, and, if an illustrious philosopher has had reason to say 'I think, therefore I am,' the following formula, 'I feel, therefore I exist,' is no less evident. It is, in effect, in the state of sensibility or of impressionability and in the mode of reaction to impressionability that one must seek the causes of the problems that motivate human actions at each instant." (Brierre de Boismont, *op.cit.*, p. 47.)

[14] *Suicide*, pp. 277-297.

[15] Morselli had also clearly argued that suicide "in our days" was primarily the result of "egoism." See *Suicide: An Essay on Comparative Moral Statistics*, p. 297.

reasonably clear, though positivistic, idea of the nature of scientific theories and he intended *Suicide* to represent such a theory and its testing. (It is even reasonably clear, as Halbwachs has pointed out, that the basic idea of Durkheim's sociologistic approach to suicide was seen by Durkheim and others as fundamentally analogous to the basic ideas of the science of thermodynamics, which was greatly advanced and systematized in the nineteenth century.)

Unfortunately, Durkheim was unable to make the work very systematic or even consistent. As we shall see in our specific discussions of the theory of suicide presented in *Suicide*, the argument very definitely changes from one place to another, though with some tendency to increasingly develop the idea that the general, shared social meanings are the basic causes of suicide rates. This unsystematic, inconsistent structure of *Suicide* has, however, rarely been recognized. Sociologists have normally been more concerned with analyzing just one aspect of *Suicide*, such as the replicative method or the integration theory of suicide, rather than the work as a whole or the theory as a whole. This concentration upon the parts has had the effect of obscuring the general structural problems.

Though I shall argue that there are many problems with the critical parts of the work, Durkheim seems to have been at his best in developing the ideas he had taken from the moral statisticians. For example, the replicative analysis of data, which Durkheim took largely from Bertillon, was certainly used better by Durkheim than by any of his predecessors, even if, as Halbwachs argues, he did overlook the basic lack of independence in his tests which resulted from the cross-cutting effects of the urban-rural dimension.

The greatest weaknesses of the work are to be found in the fundamental ideas, with which I shall be primarily concerned throughout the rest of this part, and in the general structure of the work. Halbwachs, though excusing Durkheim from fault for this weakness, long ago argued that much of the power to convince readers which *Suicide* has demonstrated has been the result of the "dialectique" of the work rather than the "statistical facts."[16] It is probably even

16 M. Halbwachs, *Les Causes du Suicide*, Paris: Librairie Felix Alcan, 1930, p. 30.

much closer to the truth to say that this power to convince has been more the result of the *rhetoric* of the work (and the commitments of the audience, since psychiatrists have rarely been convinced by the work in any way). As I shall argue at greater length below, since Durkheim knew the "statistical facts" about suicide and the theoretical ideas to be used in explaining these "facts" before he wrote the work, he could and did *adjust* these two general sets of variables to fit each other and he did so in such a way as to "demonstrate" the validity of his general proposition, the sociologistic proposition, that sociology must be an independent discipline because there is a social reality independent of the individual realities. But the validity of this argument can be seen only after many detailed considerations of *Suicide*.

Forms of Thought in Suicide

Probably because of the emphatically expressed ideal of the positivistic method in *Suicide*, Durkheim's forms of thought have been seen as basically positivistic. This has reinforced the tendency to interpret *Suicide* in terms of the forms of thought common to most contemporary sociologists. Actually, however, the forms of thought used by Durkheim in *Suicide* are in many ways unlike those common to contemporary sociologists and quite at variance with those of the expressed positivistic ideal.

Though there are many points that we shall have to consider in some detail below, it seems reasonably clear that in *Suicide* Durkheim faced up to the ageless conflict between the realists and the nominalists—and cast his lot with the realists.[17] At least, realism was his dominant tendency, though he never totally cast out nominalism. Durkheim's philosophical realism is evident in two aspects of his theory of suicide: (1) his tendency to draw conclusions about the nature of reality from his conceptual analyses; and (2) his tendency to go from the general or universal to the particulars rather than from the particulars to the general.

[17] Durkheim uses the terms realism and nominalism at certain points in his work, as any student of philosophy would do. See, for example, his attack on "historical nominalism" in *The Rules of Sociological Method*, Glencoe: The Free Press, 1938, p. 94.

In *Suicide* Durkheim frequently uses rather involved logical arguments to "prove" points that contemporary sociologists would consider answerable only by empirical investigation. Consider, for example, the following argument proposed by Durkheim as part of the proof that there are at least some suicides who are not insane:

> All cases of death resulting from an act of the patient himself with full knowledge of the inevitable results, whatever their purpose, are too essentially similar to be assigned to separate classes. Whatever their cause, they can only be species of a single genus; and to distinguish among them, one must have other criteria than the victim's more or less doubtful purpose. This leaves at least a group of suicides unconnected with insanity. Once exceptions are admitted, it is hard to stop. For there is only a gradual shading between deaths inspired by usually generous feelings and those from less lofty motives. An imperceptible gradation leads from one class to the other. If then the former are suicides, there is no reason for not giving the same name to the latter.
>
> There are therefore suicides, and numerous ones at that, not connected with insanity.[18]

Such *demonstrations of existence by conceptual analysis* are quite alien to the thought processes of contemporary sociologists.

The belief that knowledge is to be had only from an examination of the universals and not from an examination of the particulars is, of course, the core of the realists' position. Durkheim very clearly stated his view that "science does not describe the individual but the general."[19] And some students of Durkheim have certainly been aware of

[18] *Suicide*, p. 67. For further discussion of the errors in Durkheim's methods of defining and of the importance of definition in his theories, see Harry Alpert, *Emile Durkheim and His Sociology*, New York: Columbia University Press, 1939, pp. 114-119. For further consideration of Durkheim's method of defining suicide see Appendix II of this work, "The Formal Definitions of Suicide."

[19] Durkheim, "Quid Secundatus politicae scientiae instituendae contulerit," thesis, 1892, translated by Alengry in *Revue d'Histoire Politique et Constitutionnelle*, 1937, p. 414. Quoted in Durkheim, *Sociology and Philosophy*, translated by D. F. Pocock, with an introduction by J. G. Peristiany, Glencoe: The Free Press, 1953, pp. xvii-xviii.

his strong strain toward the universal. As Henri Peyre has put it:

> Durkheim himself, in his *De la division du travail social*, had revealed at the outset of his career how deeply French he was (if preferring the universal generalization to the particular detail is characteristically French) when he wrote: "Only the universal is rational. The particular and the concrete baffle understanding."[20]

These statements, however, have by no means been generally taken to mean that Durkheim assumed a realist position in *Suicide* or in any of his other works. On the contrary, the interpretation of Durkheim's works which seems to be generally shared by contemporary sociologists emphasizes the empirical nature of his work, and statements such as these have been taken to be merely assertions that science must always consist of general statements relating variables that are abstractions from particular bits of data. Such an interpretation is quite in agreement with Durkheim's continual emphasis on the need for sociologists to treat social facts as "things" and to develop one's theory out of and, therefore, *after* a careful consideration of these "things." Alpert has summed up Durkheim's avowed position on this point:

> To treat social facts as things, Durkheim explained in the preface to the second edition of *Les Règles*, means simply to adopt a certain frame of mind in undertaking to study them. It implies assuming that social data are unknown, that is, that we do not know anything about them with any certainty prior to our investigations. It requires us to be on guard against our pre-notions, prejudices, and pre-conceptions. It means that we are to distrust our personal past experience, to become wary of consulting our own consciousnesses for real knowledge and of accepting that knowledge as verified truth merely because we have found it in our consciousness. The rule, in sum, only urges us to adopt an attitude of mature skepticism with regard to what we think we already know about social facts on

[20] Henri Peyre, "Durkheim: The Man, His Time, and His Intellectual Background," in *Emile Durkheim*, ed. by Kurt Wolff, pp. 30-31.

the basis of our own sentiments, feelings, thoughts and rationalizations, and to accept as a matter of principle, and as a working hypothesis, the proposition that the phenomena we are studying have properties which we do not yet know, which we cannot possibly suspect, and which all our introspection and ratiocination cannot uncover in advance.

Thus interpreted—and Durkheim himself is the interpreter—the rule is, as its promulgator admitted, only a truism. To Durkheim it implied, however, a complete break with the type of sociologizing which was prevalent up to the last decade of the nineteenth century. This was an *a priori* mode of analysis of social life characterized by the arbitrary creation of concepts whose validity and reality were scarcely doubted, and about which deductions were made on the basis of an *ad hoc* conception of the laws of human nature.[21]

This methodological ideal, however, bears only the slightest resemblance to Durkheim's actual method in *Suicide*. Certainly there is the greatest attention to statistical data in *Suicide*, but this careful consideration of data came after the general ideas about society and suicide and, in his argumentative approach to the data, Durkheim bends the data to fit his preconceived theory.

That Durkheim's theory came before a careful consideration of the data on suicide is demonstrated by a number of factors. First, as we have already seen, Durkheim's ideas on egoistic and anomic suicide were clearly stated in the works of the romantics, in Brierre de Boismont's work, and in the works of many moral statisticians with which Durkheim was intimately acquainted. Second, in *Suicide* Durkheim specifically rejects the usual approach of science to the development and testing of theories. The usual approach is to categorize data in terms of similarities which presumably, or hopefully, have been produced by some small set of similar factors. One establishes a morphology of the data and then seeks the causes.[22] As Durkheim has put it:

[21] Harry Alpert, *Emile Durkheim . . .* , pp. 82-83.
[22] This is, no doubt, a gross oversimplification of *actual* scientific endeavors. Since there are almost always a vast number of different typologies or morphologies that can be built on the similarities of the

... it would seem to be best to inquire first whether the tendency is single and indestructible or whether it does not rather consist of several different tendencies, which may be isolated by analysis and which should be separately studied. If so, we should proceed as follows. As the tendency, single or not, is observable only in its individual manifestations, we should have to begin with the latter. Thus we should observe and describe as many as possible, of course omitting those due to mental alienation. If all were found to have the same essential characteristics, they should be grouped in a single class; otherwise, which is much more likely—for they are too different not to include several varieties—a certain number of species should be determined according to their resemblances and differences. One would admit as many suicidal currents as there were distinct types, then seek to determine their causes and respective importance. We have pursued some such method in our brief study of the suicide of insanity.[23]

Durkheim first argues that the data necessary for the construction of morphological categories of suicide is not available, so that he appears to fall back—only as a matter of necessity—on defining the categories of suicide in terms of the causes which one is going to prove are the causes of these categories of suicide:

Unfortunately, no classification of suicides of sane persons can be made in terms of their morphological types or characteristics, from almost complete lack of the necessary data. To be attempted, it would require good descriptions of many individual cases. One would have to know the psychological condition of the suicide at the moment of forming his resolve, how he prepared to accomplish it, how he finally performed it, whether he was agitated or depressed, calm or exalted, anxious or irritated, etc. Now

data, scientists are usually guided in their development of morphological categories by certain tentative assumptions, either implicit or explicit, about the most likely causes or types of causes involved. The argument here is simply that Durkheim's theory of suicide involves an extreme form of etiological definition.

[23] *Suicide*, pp. 145-146.

we have such data practically only for some cases of insane suicide, and just such observations and descriptions by alienists have enabled us to establish the chief types of suicide where insanity is the determining cause. We have almost no such information for others. Brierre de Boismont alone has tried to do this descriptive work for 1,328 cases where the suicide left letters or other records summarized by the author in his book. But, first, this summary is much too brief. Then, the patient's revelations of his condition are usually insufficient if not suspect. He is only too apt to be mistaken concerning himself and the state of his feelings; he may believe that he is acting calmly, though at the peak of nervous excitement. Finally, besides being insufficiently objective, these observations cover too few facts to permit definite conclusions. Some very vague dividing lines are perceptible and their suggestions may be utilized; but they are too indefinite to provide a regular classification. Furthermore, in view of the manner of execution of most suicides, proper observations are next to impossible.

But our aim may be achieved by another method. Let us reverse the order of study. Only in as far as the effective causes differ can there be different types of suicide. For each to have its own nature, it must also have special conditions of existence. The same antecedent or group of antecedents cannot sometimes produce one result and sometimes another, or, if so, the difference of the second from the first would itself be without cause, which would contradict the principle of causality. Every proved specific difference between causes therefore implies a similar difference between effects. Consequently, we shall be able to determine the social types of suicide by classifying them not directly by their preliminarily described characteristics, but by the causes which produce them. Without asking why they differ from one another we will first seek the social conditions responsible for them; then group these conditions in a number of separate classes by their resemblances and differences, and we shall be sure that a specific type of suicide will correspond to each of these classes. In a word, instead of being morphological, our classification will from the start be aetiological. Nor is this a sign of inferiority, for the nature of a phenomenon is much more profoundly got at by knowing its cause than by knowing its characteristics only, even the essential ones.[24]

Durkheim, however, immediately switches his tack and strongly asserts that the etiological approach to definition is not merely an unfortunate stopgap measure forced upon him by the absence of sufficient data on the particular cases of suicide to make the morphological approach feasible. On the contrary, he sees this "reverse method" as the most appropriate for the scientific study of social facts:

> In all respects this reverse method is the only fitting one for the special problem that we have set ourselves. Indeed we must not forget that what we are studying is the social suicide-rate. The only types of interest to us, accordingly, are those contributing to its formation and influencing its variation. Now, it is not sure that all individual sorts of voluntary death have this quality. Some, though general to a certain degree, are not bound or not sufficiently bound to the moral temper of society to enter as a characteristic element into this special physiognomy of each people with respect to suicide. For instance, we have seen that alcoholism is not a determining factor of the particular aptitude of each society, yet alcoholic suicides evidently exist and in great numbers. No description, however good, of particular cases will ever tell us which ones have a sociological character.
>
> If one wants to know the several tributaries of suicide as a collective phenomenon one must regard it in its collective form, that is, through statistical data, from the start. The social rate must be taken directly as the object of analysis; progress must be from the whole to the parts. Clearly, it can only be analyzed with reference to its different causes, for in themselves the units composing it are homogeneous, without qualitative difference. We must then immediately discover its causes and later consider their repercussions among individuals.[25]

In this critical passage from *Suicide* Durkheim argues that

[24] *Ibid.*, pp. 146-147.   [25] *Ibid.*, pp. 147-148.

knowledge of the part must follow from knowledge of the whole. But how is one to know the whole before he knows the parts if, as Durkheim asserts in his methodological ideal, one must proceed from knowledge of the parts to knowledge of the whole? Very simply, one cannot. He must simply assume the universal and proceed to the particular.

One might conceivably argue that previous studies of particulars had led Durkheim to knowledge of the whole society. The one possible study of this sort would be *The Division of Labor*, and indeed, Durkheim did consider problems in this work similar to the assumptions about the *whole* society in *Suicide*.

There is, however, evidence that Durkheim's approach was not something he created for the purpose of making sense of some realm of empirical evidence. Quite to the contrary, the theory of *aetiological* or *genetic* definitions and the relations of this theory to the understanding of parts in terms of a predetermined (or assumed) whole were well worked out by logicians of the seventeenth century, were common stock in trade to the French *philosophes* of the eighteenth century, and were very likely picked up by Durkheim through his study of the works of the Enlightenment. Ernst Cassirer has clearly outlined the development of this general theoretical orientation toward the study of society:

> Thus arises the theory of the genetic or causal definition, in whose development all the great logicians of the seventeenth century participated. The genuine and really fruitful explanation of concepts do not proceed by abstraction alone; they are not content to divide one element from a given complex of properties or characteristics and to define it in isolation. They observe rather the inner law according to which the whole either originated or at least can be conceived as originating. And they clarify within this law of becoming the real nature and behavior of this whole; they not only show *what* this whole is, but *why* it is. A genuine genetic definition permits us to understand the structure of a complex whole; it does not, however, stop with this structure as such, but goes back to its foundations. Hobbes is the first modern logician to grasp

this significance of the 'causal definition.' He does not look upon his discovery simply as a logical reform; he sees nothing less than a transformation of the ideal of philosophical knowledge itself.[26]

One could, of course, still argue that, though Durkheim might have come to the division of labor and suicide with his general (i.e., realist) method, still in *The Division of Labor* he had established an empirical base for his general theoretical ideas in *Suicide*. Such a possibility seems plausible when one notes the close relations between the problems considered in *The Division of Labor* and those considered in *Suicide*.[27] However, when one looks for such an empirical base in *The Division of Labor* he finds that it simply does not exist, that Durkheim went from the universal to the particulars in that work just as much as he did in *Suicide*. Alpert's statement regarding this lack of particulars in *The Division of Labor* and his conclusion regarding the significance of this method of argument for a critical analysis of Durkheim's work seems most appropriate:

Durkheim did not treat the matter systematically. He committed the serious blunder of not following his own methodological precept of specificity. Nowhere in *De La*

[26] Ernst Cassirer, *The Philosophy of the Enlightenment*, Boston: Beacon Press, 1955, pp. 253-254.

Bendix has criticized much of sociological theory on the grounds that "many concepts are generalizations in disguise." (See Reinhard Bendix, "Concepts and Generalizations in Comparative Sociological Studies," *American Sociological Review*, 28 (August, 1953), pp. 532-533.) Durkheim's concepts of "suicide types" are generalizations by explicit intention. In his later works Durkheim seems to have given up his method of proving sociological theories by the appropriate choice of causal definitions, but there is ample evidence that he did not give up the general form of reasoning of which the etiological definitions are merely one representation. Rodney Needham, for example, has noted apparently without any awareness of Durkheim's earlier penchant for etiological definitions, that in *Primitive Classification* Durkheim repeatedly *assumes* that which is to be demonstrated and that sometimes he did this by using a "single word . . . which immediately assumes that which is to be proved by the subsequent argument." (Rodney Needham, "Introduction" to *Primitive Classification* by E. Durkheim and Marcel Mauss, Chicago: University of Chicago Press, 1963, pp. xiv-xv.)

[27] Parsons has even pointed out that Durkheim's whole treatment of suicide was clearly presaged in a section of *The Division of Labor*. See *The Structure of Social Action*, p. 324.

Division do we find a picture of a specific society actually undergoing the change from a segmentary to a functional structure. Durkheim, surprisingly, and unfortunately, did not think such a specific analysis necessary for his purpose. He believed it possible to study the "general fact" of the progressive advance of the division of labor in the course of social evolution, abstraction made of the specific manifestations of the phenomenon as influenced by particular conditions of time and place.

This lack of specificity had serious consequences. First of all, it made it impossible for Durkheim to test empirically his crucial, and to many, his questionable assumptions that the division of labor mitigates the severity of the struggle for existence and that it can do so without interfering with the common and individual values enumerated in the discussion above. On these points, Durkheim either is purely conjectural or he relies on an analogy from plant ecology, citing evidence from no less eminent biologists than Darwin and Haeckel. He thus raised, but did not empirically answer the question of the relation of the division of labor to the struggle for existence. An answer, at least as regards human social life, would have required the study of a specific society in the throes of the process under consideration. Durkheim, however, did not undertake such an analysis.[28]

Talcott Parsons has previously argued that Durkheim's thought moved increasingly away from a positivistic position toward an *idealist* (or realist) position until, in *The Elementary Forms of the Religious Life*, he finally declares idealism to be "almost" literally correct when applied to the social realm of nature.[29] Parsons, however, has tried to show

[28] Harry Alpert, *Emile Durkheim* . . . , pp. 109-110.
[29] Parsons quotes the following from *The Elementary Forms of The Religious Life*: "Thus there is a realm of nature where the formula of idealism applies almost literally; that is the social realm" (in *The Structure of Social Action*, p. 144, fn.1). It should be noted that American sociologists, especially Bristol and Hehlke, had attacked Durkheim for his "social realism" long before Parsons did. However, their criticisms differed strongly from Parson's criticisms and the criticisms presented in this work in that they focused on Durkheim's *ontological realism* rather than his *epistemological realism*. They were concerned primarily with showing that society can exist only in individuals. In considering the objections of early American sociologists

that Durkheim's thought changed in the direction of idealism primarily as a reaction to the failure of his early positivistic methodology to deal adequately with the empirical evidence, such as suicide rates.[30] The evidence presented above indicates that by the time of his work on suicide, Durkheim had already taken a pretty strong realist position. It is conceivable, of course, that Durkheim first went through all of the data on suicide and from a consideration of these decided what the "causes" of suicide must be. If this were true, then the theory of suicide as presented in *Suicide* would only appear to be a realist or idealist theory

---

to Durkheim's work, Hinkle has concluded that: "Like other sociologists, Bristol and Hehlke recognize that their individualism and Durkheim's social realism are contradictory. Consequently, they reject Durkheim's conception of the group. Their objection is based on their adherence to the fundamental individualism of American sociology, which is also displayed by both Michael M. Davis, Jr., and Charles A. Ellwood when they criticize Durkheim as an exponent of medieval realism and sociological objectivism."

Hinkle further argues that in the 1930's American sociologists came to support Durkheim because of his "empirical" methods. What most American sociologists seem to have failed to note are (1) the great differences between Durkheim's *ideal* and *actual* methods of analyzing data; (2) Durkheim's methods of *analyzing* data; and (3) his methods of *interpreting* data. Had they recognized these differences in his work, they probably would have rejected him because of his epistemological realism, rather than because of the rather minor "group-mind" aspects of his work. (A major factor in the increasing acceptance of Durkheim's ideas in the 1930's by American sociologists was Alpert's argument that any hint of ontological realism in Durkheim's work was not central to his theories.) (See R. C. Hinkle, "Durkheim in American Sociology," in *Emile Durkheim*, ed. by Kurt Wolff, pp. 285-286.)

George Catlin is one of the students of Durkheim who has, at least implicitly, strongly criticized Durkheim for his *epistemological realism* (i.e., his going from knowledge of the whole to knowledge of the part): "The sole disadvantage of this procedure is that the interesting and astonishing conclusion that there is a collective consciousness, which should be reached at the end of the scientific study, is hastily postulated at the beginning of it." (G. Catlin, "Introduction" to *The Rules of Sociological Method* by E. Durkheim, p. xxvii.)

(Nisbet has recently concluded that for Durkheim "The idea, the plot, and the conclusion of *Suicide* were well in his mind before he examined the registers;" and Nisbet has argued that this was so in good part because Durkheim had previously gotten his ideas about anomie largely from the Romantics. See Robert A. Nisbet, "Sociology as an Art Form," *op.cit.*)

[30] *The Structure of Social Action*, pp. 343-344.

as a consequence of the method of presentation; whereas, in fact, the method used, but not reported, to develop the theory and to validate it would have been much more in line with the "ideal" nominalist method of the sciences. But, even if this were true and one were, consequently, to disregard the "reverse method" employed, the end product of the work, the theory of suicide, would remain a realist theory—i.e., an explanation of events in nature by the application of ideas that are not abstractions from other events, but, rather, ideas merely assumed, intuited, or derived from we know not where.[31] That this is the case can best be seen further by a systematic presentation of Durkheim's theory of suicide.

Durkheim's Theory of Suicide

In examining Durkheim's theory of suicide one can either choose to consider only what is presented in *Suicide* or one can choose to consider *Suicide* in the more general context of Durkheim's sociological work. These alternative approaches will lead to very different interpretations of Durkheim's theory of suicide as presented in *Suicide*. If one considers *Suicide* in isolation from the other works, he is apt to find it confusing and much more likely to see the theory as proceeding from the data rather than the data as being carefully presented to fit the theory.[32] One is easily led to such a nominalist interpretation of *Suicide* if he takes at face value the many protestations of using only data which is highly reliable to "draw" scientific laws from.[33] A nominalist

---

[31] Bock has recently argued that this tendency to explain "events" by "assumed" general variables or forces was characteristic of nineteenth-century social thought—indeed, of just about all Western social thought. Kenneth E. Bock, "Evolution, Function, and Change," *The American Sociological Review*, 28 (April, 1963), p. 234.

[32] Such a nominalist interpretation seems especially likely if one overlooks the adoption of the "reverse method" in Chapter I of Book II and begins the argument with Chapter II of Book II, in which Durkheim first presents evidence concerning Catholicism and suicide and then draws his first "conclusion" (*Suicide*, p. 158).

[33] Consider, for example, the following protestation: "For our own part, at least, we make it a rule not to employ in our studies much uncertain and uninstructive data; no law of any interest has in fact ever been drawn from them by students of suicide. We shall thus refer to them only rarely, when they seem to have special meaning and to offer special assurance." (*Suicide*, p. 151.)

interpretation of *Suicide* and confusion over the meaning of the work are both aided by Durkheim's initial vacillation in *Suicide* between a realist position and a nominalist position. Parsons has argued that this vacillation was Durkheim's normal approach and was the result of his attempt to reconcile a fundamental contradiction in social theories.[34] Regardless of whether this vacillation between nominalism and realism was continual throughout his works, there is obviously a good bit of vacillation between the two positions in *Suicide*. I shall argue here that the over-all tenor of the theory presented in *Suicide* is realism, but there are obviously many parts of *Suicide* in which Durkheim is quite nominalist, so that there is clearly some room for the contrary argument.

If one considers *Suicide* in the context of Durkheim's total sociological work, it is much easier to see that the theory is fundamentally a realist theory. But many proponents of Durkheim's theory of suicide would certainly argue that this would be a high-handed distortion. For this reason, and for the far better reason that at least one nominalist interpretation of *Suicide* has been very influential in the recent works on suicide, I shall present what seems to be the most plausible and influential nominalist interpretation of *Suicide*. I shall then attempt to show that this interpretation is a misinterpretation of *Suicide*, especially when we put *Suicide* into the general context of Durkheim's sociological work and present what seems to be his fully developed *sociologistic theory* of suicide.

The Externalistic Interpretation of Suicide. American sociologists have generally approached Durkheim's *Suicide* from the standpoint of his "general conclusion" concerning the relation of the degree of social integration to suicide:

> . . . suicide varies inversely with the degree of integration of the social group of which the individual forms a part.[35]

They then add the assumption that integration can become so great that suicide begins to vary directly with integration, so that the over-all relation between suicide and inte-

[34] *The Structure of Social Action*, pp. 444, 447, fn. 1.
[35] *Suicide*, p. 209.

gration is U-functional.[36] The general approach seems to be to work in both directions from this central theoretical proposition. One works backward to the definition and/or the operationalization of integration and to the hypothetical causes of integration. And one works forward in the argument by attempting to show how integration is related to egoism, altruism, and anomie. Then one tries to show how these are related to the suicide rates.

Attempts to give theoretical definitions of Durkheim's concept of "integration" or "disintegration" are quite rare, presumably because Durkheim himself did not provide a specific, explicit definition. Rather, he wrote many vague and frequently conflicting statements on "integration," "cohesion," "unity," and "vitality," all of which terms seem to be used interchangeably, yet are sometimes used in conjunction.[37] Moreover, it is frequently difficult, if not impossible, to determine whether Durkheim is giving a definition

[36] American sociologists frequently prefer to keep their works on suicide within the context of Durkheim's theory, while necessarily choosing to consider only those aspects of Durkheim's theory that fit their own theories. For example, Gibbs and Martin (in "A Theory of Status Integration and Its Relationship to Suicide," *American Sociological Review*, 23 [April, 1958], pp. 140-147) maintain that:

> While Durkheim's study provides the most promising point of departure for an attempt to formulate a theory of suicide, it must be emphasized that his assertion of an inverse relationship between social integration and the rate of suicide has never been subjected to formal test and is not testable in its present form. At no point in Durkheim's monograph is there an explicit connotative definition of social integration, much less an operational definition. It is not surprising then that there is not a single measure of social integration correlated with suicide rates. Without the specification of the empirical referents for the concept and the operations used in measuring its prevalence, Durkheim's proposition is supported not by its predictive power but by his forceful argument in its defense. Thus, Durkheim's theory is incomplete; and it is to its development that the theory of status integration refers.

They then note in a footnote that: "It should be noted that Durkheim also suggested that beyond a certain point integration is directly related to the suicide rate. This becomes a testable proposition only when a measure of integration is developed." (*Ibid.*, p. 141.) Although they do develop their "measure of integration," they do not choose to test this part of Durkheim's theory or even to consider it in a second footnote.

[37] Alpert (see *Emile Durkheim . . . , passim*) has provided many instances of terms, such as "fact," which are critical to Durkheim's theories yet which are never defined, are loosely used, and are used interchangeably with many other terms.

of "integration" or is specifying the causes of "integration." However, when attempts are made to define and/or operationalize "integration," they generally are in close agreement with Gibbs and Martin:

> Running throughout Durkheim's comments on the nature of integration is the suggestion that the concept has to do with the strength of the individual's ties to his society. In formal terms, the stronger the ties of the individual members to a society the lower the suicide rate of that society. While such a statement has only heuristic value, it is possible to restate it in terms of the stability and durability of social relationships within populations. Thus the fundamental postulate of the present theory reads:
>
> The suicide rate of a population varies inversely with the stability and durability of social relationships within that population.[38]

Though Gibbs and Martin do not refer specifically to any statements in *Suicide* to support this interpretation of Durkheim's use of "integration," it can easily be seen that their interpretation is in line with certain statements in *Suicide*, such as the following:

> But society cannot disintegrate without the individual simultaneously detaching himself from social life, without his own goals becoming preponderant over those of the community, in a word without his personality tending to surmount the collective personality. The more weakened the groups to which he belongs, the less he depends on them, the more he consequently depends only on himself and recognizes his private interests. If we agree to call this state egoism, in which the individual ego asserts itself to excess in the face of the social ego and at its expense, we may call egoistic the special type of suicide springing from excessive individualism.[39]

[38] Gibbs and Martin, *op.cit.*, p. 141.
[39] It is of interest to note that this paragraph follows immediately after Durkheim's "general conclusion" relating "integration" to suicide. Anyone taking this "general conclusion" as the starting point for a consideration of Durkheim's theory, as Gibbs and Martin do, is, then, very likely to interpret integration in terms of this statement. This might be especially true of the Gibbs and Martin work since the

This is one of the most nominalistic, and even individualistic, statements in *Suicide*. Coming immediately after the "general conclusion" relating "integration" to suicide, and coming rather early in Durkheim's general argument, it is easy to see that this statement has had a great influence in determining the directions which the interpretations of *Suicide* have taken.[40]

Most sociologists rarely concern themselves with what Durkheim considered to be the causes of social "integration" or "disintegration." When they do, however, they can easily maintain a nominalist interpretation by referring to Durkheim's consideration of the significant effects on the suicide rates of political crises,[41] economic crises,[42] and similar external, objective states of society. They could go further, perhaps drawing upon *The Division of Labor*, and argue that the ultimate, fundamental causes of all social phenomena such as "integration" are the "morphological causes," especially ecological and demographic facts.[43] These morphological causes presumably lead to a certain degree of functional differentiation and this in turn produces both a certain type and a certain degree of social "integration" or "disintegration."

Working forward from "integration" in the direction of the suicide rates, one comes first to egoism, altruism, and anomie. Here the interpreter seems to have a choice. He can consider egoism, altruism, and anomie to be merely different types and degrees of "integration" of society. In this case altruism and egoism are seen pretty much as one dimension of integration-disintegration, defined in some way as a *weighted frequency of associations (or isolation)*; and

---

"general conclusion" on page 209 is the only specific reference to Durkheim.

[40] This statement of Durkheim's is, for example, quite consistent with such highly individualistic theories relating "integration" to suicide as that proposed by Robert Faris in *Social Disorganization*, New York: The Ronald Press Company, 1955; Chapter 8: *Suicide*, p. 195.

[41] See, for example, the discussion of the Boulanger crisis and its effects on suicide in *Suicide*, p. 245.

[42] See, for example, the discussion of the number of bankruptcies and its relation to suicide rates in *Suicide*, p. 242.

[43] See Edward Tiryakian, *Sociologism and Existentialism*, Englewood Cliffs: Prentice-Hall, 1962, for a discussion of "morphological causes."

anomie is seen as another dimension of integration-disintegration defined in some way as a *weighted frequency of relative normlessness, meaninglessness, etc.*[44] One then takes some statistical measures (such as the mean) of these types of "integration" or "disintegration" for different groups and compares them with the suicide rates for these groups. Alternatively, one can choose to consider egoism, altruism, and anomie to be types of "integration" or "disintegration" of the individuals who commit suicide and compare some statistical measure of the degrees of egoism-altruism and anomie of the two groups of individuals.[45]

Regardless of the alternative chosen, the dimension of "integration-disintegration" is still merely defined in terms of egoism-altruism and anomie. One can, however, define "integration-disintegration" in terms of the *variables of*

[44] The term "anomie" has been interpreted and extended by sociologists in a vast number of ways. Merton's essays on anomie have documented many of these interpretations and extensions, but there are still a great number which have not been documented. (See Robert K. Merton, *Social Theory and Social Structure*, Glencoe: The Free Press, 1957, Chapters 4 and 5.) This vast proliferation of interpretations and extensions of this one concept is an indication of the great variety of interpretations that have been given to Durkheim's theory of suicide. The intervening-variables theory presented here is meant only to be the most plausible of such theories, so that, if this theory can be shown to be inadequate, then these many other interpretations can be reasonably discarded.

[45] Though the terms egoism, altruism, and anomie are not explicitly used, these two alternative approaches are very clear in the Gibbs and Martin work and in Austin L. Porterfield and Jack P. Gibbs, "Occupational Prestige and Social Mobility of Suicides in New Zealand," *The American Journal of Sociology*, 66 (September, 1960) pp. 147-152. In the first work Gibbs and Martin (*op.cit.*, p. 141, fn. 10) adopt the "population approach" to integration and argue against the use of an individual approach:

> The failure of existing theory and research to provide an answer to this question lies in a psychological orientation to role conflict and the manner in which it is analyzed. For the most part, studies have dealt with real or alleged conflicts among particular roles. The methods employed to identify role conflict, the techniques used to analyze the phenomenon once isolated, and the conclusions reached in these studies do not lend themselves to a theory concerning the conditions that determine or reflect the amount of role conflict that prevails in a population.

However, in the latter work Gibbs and Porterfield completely adopt the individualistic approach and attempt to compare the life patterns of suicides with the life patterns of controls. There is no consideration of possible conflicts between the two approaches.

association. One can, for example, define social integration as some combination of the following factors: (1) the number of individuals interacted with in a given time, (2) the frequency of interaction in a given time, (3) the number of qualitatively different types of relations, and (4) the degrees of intimacy involved in each interaction. One can then define egoism-altruism and anomie in terms of some variables referring to individual orientations. The different dimensions of "alienation-identification" are obvious choices and are frequently found.[46]

The final step in the argument is the proposition that suicide is caused by the degree of "integration-disintegration," either directly or indirectly through the action of egoism-altruism and/or anomie. In summary, the most frequent interpretation of Durkheim's *Suicide* by American sociologists involves the following propositions:

1. The morphological factors cause certain degrees and certain patterns of social interaction.
2. The degrees and patterns of social interaction then cause a certain degree of "social integration."
3. "Social integration," defined as either states of individuals or as a state of the society, is then defined as the "strength of the individual's ties to society."
4. The "strength of ties" is then defined either in terms of egoism, altruism, and anomie or else the "strength of ties" is hypothesized to be the cause of the given degrees of egoism, altruism, and anomie.
5. Egoism is defined as a relative lack of social or collective activity[47] that gives meaning and object to life; altruism is defined as a relatively great amount of

[46] For a discussion of the different dimensions of "alienation" see Melvin Seeman, "On the Meaning of Alienation," *American Sociological Review*, 24 (December, 1959), pp. 783-791.

[47] As noted above, Gibbs and Martin operationalize the "degree of strength" of social ties or social activity in terms of the stability and durability of social ties or relations (though they do not specify what the distinction between stability and durability might be). This interpretation is reasonably consistent with Durkheim's treatment of social ties in *Suicide*, but it should be noted that Durkheim also considered the total *volume* (or density) of social ties to be a fundamental, independent causal factor. For example, he tried to show that the male suicide rate varies inversely with the *number* of children in families.

social activity; and anomie is defined as a relative lack of social activity that acts to *constrain* the individuals' passions, which, without constraint, increase "infinitely."[48]

6. And, finally, the given balance of the degrees of egoism, altruism, and anomie is hypothesized to be the cause of the given suicide rate of the given society.[49]

This presentation of the most plausible of the common interpretations of Durkheim's theory of suicide might seem

[48] The passage in *Suicide* (p. 258) generally referred to for this distinction between egoism and anomie is the following:

Certainly, this and egoistic suicide have kindred ties. Both spring from society's insufficient presence in individuals. But the sphere of its absence is not the same in both cases. In egoistic suicide it is deficient in truly collective activity, thus depriving the latter of object and meaning. In anomic suicide, society's influence is lacking in the basically individual passions, thus leaving them without a check-rein. In spite of their relationship, therefore, the two types are independent of each other. We may offer society everything social in us, and still be unable to control our desires; one may live in an anomic state without being egoistic, and vice versa. These two sorts of suicide therefore do not draw their chief recruits from the same social environments; one has its principal field among intellectual careers, the world of thought—the other, the industrial or commercial world.

Henry and Short, for example, quote this passage as *the* definition of and distinction between egoism and anomie. (See, *Suicide and Homicide*, Glencoe: The Free Press, 1954, pp. 132-133.)

[49] Durkheim argued that there always exist some degrees of egoism, altruism, and anomie in any society and that, indeed, some degree of all three is necessary for the well-being of the society. In the presentation of his data, however, Durkheim did not attempt to show that a given balance (or interaction) of the three was the cause of a given suicide rate. Rather, he related the given suicide rate to only one of the variables, presumably because of the great difficulty, if not impossibility, of specifying what the balance was in any given society. Presumably because of Durkheim's own lapses, contemporary sociologists have generally overlooked the need, according to Durkheim, of considering the interaction of all three of the variables to be the cause of the suicide rate of any society. Powell, for example, has argued, with direct reference to *Suicide*, that the suicide rate of a society can be used as an indirect measure of the degree of anomie of that society. (See Elwin H. Powell, "Occupation, Status, and Suicide: Toward A Redefinition of Anomie," *American Sociological Review*, 23 (April, 1958), pp. 131-139.

Durkheim's idea that a balance of egoism, altruism, and anomie is the critical determinant of the suicide rate of a society is used here for the sake of being consistent with the theory presented in *Suicide*. Since, however, Durkheim and almost everyone else has overlooked this point, nothing much will be made of it here.

at first to be an overstatement. It could be argued that this presentation makes the theory much more positivistic than most American sociologists have considered it to be: it presents the external variables, the social objects (such as population) and the social behavior[50] as the only fundamental causes of suicide (or of any other social action). On the contrary, the argument would run, anomie is frequently interpreted as *normlessness* and, thence, Durkheim is interpreted as having argued that normlessness causes suicide.

If, however, one considers further such an argument relating anomie to suicide, he will generally find that the supposed causes of anomie are such external disturbances of equilibrium as depressions and prosperity. Normlessness is often interpreted as one of Durkheim's causes of suicide, but normally *Suicide* is then further interpreted in such a way as to make some external, thing-like factors the causes of normlessness. Indeed, more recent sociologists have even attacked this supposed tendency of Durkheim to externalize society as too "mechanistic."[51]

Social Meanings as the Fundamental Causes of Suicide. The hypothesis to be supported here is that this positivistic interpretation of *Suicide* is a misinterpretation, presumably resulting from Durkheim's partial ambivalence in *Suicide* and from the methodological predilections of contemporary sociologists. The basic question is really very simple: Does Durkheim, in his theory of suicide, argue that social behavior is the cause of shared sentiments and morals (i.e., of *social meanings* in general) and thence of suicide; or does he argue, on the contrary, that social meanings cause social behavior and thence suicide?[52] Since Durkheim obviously considered "society" (or the "social order," or "social reality," etc.) to be the fundamental cause of suicide, this

---

[50] The term "social behavior" is used here instead of the term "social action" (or any other term denoting the same general concept) for the simple reason that "action" is generally used to refer to behavior *plus* meaning, whereas here we want to keep the two distinct.

[51] See, for example, Merton's attack on Durkheim's work as too "mechanistic" in "Durkheim's Division of Labor in Society," *The American Journal of Sociology*, XL (November, 1934), 319-329.

[52] One could eliminate the second part of each hypothesis without changing the meaning of the argument. The fundamental question is simply whether suicide is caused ultimately by social meanings or by social behavior.

question involves whether he defined "society" in terms of behavior or in terms of meanings. The same is true of the variables social integration, altruism, egoism, and anomie: are they defined in terms of and/or caused by social behavior or by social meanings? I shall argue that the evidence from *Suicide* indicates that Durkheim considered shared meanings to be the fundamental causes of suicide.

Durkheim's continually proclaimed goal of treating social phenomena as "things" and drawing scientific theory out of scientific "fact" *seems* to be achieved in *Suicide* very largely because of his method of presenting the theory and data in *Suicide*. He presented first a general chapter indicating the directions to be followed in the succeeding chapters dealing with the data on suicide, then he followed up the chapters on the evidence with several chapters concerning the theoretical conclusions supposedly justified by the chapters on data. If one follows the progress of the work carefully he can see the shift away from the positivistic theory, which made the external social behavior the ultimate cause of suicide, and toward the theory in which the social meanings of behavior are the ultimate determinants of suicide.

Having thoroughly criticized the non-sociological theories of suicide, Durkheim begins the presentation of his own theory and its supporting evidence with the general chapter entitled "How to Determine Social Causes and Social Types."[53] In the last paragraph of this chapter Durkheim makes the following statement:

> We shall try to determine the productive causes of suicide directly, without concerning ourselves with the forms they can assume in particular individuals. Disregarding the individual as such, his motives and his ideas, we shall seek directly the states of the various social environments (religious confessions, family, political society, occupational groups, etc.), in terms of which the variations of suicide occur.[54]

[53] *Suicide*, pp. 145-151.

[54] *Ibid.*, p. 151. It might be noted that in this statement Durkheim does not specifically indicate that the "social environments" are not *causes* of suicide. One could then argue that this statement is not inconsistent with the later statements in *Suicide* concerning the causation of suicide by the shared meanings of the society. Such a meticulous interpretation of Durkheim's work, however, would seem to be

Durkheim then presents his evidence on the relations between the "social environments" of the religious confessions and suicide rates. After various considerations of these relations he states:

> We thus reach our first conclusion, that the proclivity of Protestantism for suicide must relate to the spirit of free inquiry that animates this religion. Let us understand this relationship correctly. Free inquiry itself is only the effect of another cause. When it appears, when men, after having long received their ready-made faith from tradition, claim the right to shape it for themselves, this is not because of the intrinsic desirability of free inquiry, for the latter involves as much sorrow as happiness. But it is because men henceforth need this liberty. This very need can have only one cause: the overthrow of traditional beliefs.[55]

One gets a clear idea from this statement that shared beliefs, or the lack of shared beliefs, are the ultimate cause(s) of suicide (or, at least, of egoistic suicide). A statement on the following page reinforces this conclusion and makes it seem clear that the "integration" of a society is either caused by or defined in terms of these shared beliefs:

> . . . a religious society cannot exist without a collective *credo* and the more extensive the *credo* the more unified and strong is the society. For it does not unite men by an exchange and reciprocity of services, a temporal bond of union which permits and even presupposes differences, but which a religious society cannot form. It socializes men only by attaching them completely to an identical body of doctrine and socializes them in proportion as this body of doctrine is extensive and firm.[56]

In the sentence following this statement, however, Durkheim reintroduces shared "actions" alongside shared "thoughts"

---

singularly unrewarding. As we have noted above, in references to Alpert's criticisms of Durkheim, Durkheim was very imprecise in his use of terms, even of the terms of greatest importance for his whole work (such as "integration"). Consequently, meticulous interpretations of *Suicide* that depend on one or a few words are generally misleading.

[55] *Ibid.*, p. 158.   [56] *Ibid.*, p. 159.

as components of integration,[57] without making either one the cause of the other:

> The more numerous the manners of action and thought of a religious character are, which are accordingly removed from free inquiry, the more the idea of God presents itself in all details of existence, and makes individual wills converge to one identical goal. Inversely, the greater concessions a confessional group makes to individual judgment, the less it dominates lives, the less its cohesion and vitality. We thus reach the conclusion that the superiority of Protestantism with respect to suicide results from its being a less strongly integrated church than the Catholic church.[58]

In the highly significant concluding paragraph of this first chapter on egoistic suicide, Durkheim first argues that common practices and beliefs both "constitute (or presumably, define) society." He then argues that "dogmas and rites" are both important in causing suicide (or, rather, in restraining suicide) only in so far as they support (or cause?) "collective life":

> If religion protects man against the desire for self-destruction, it is not that it preaches the respect for his own person to him with arguments *sui generis*; but because it is a society. What constitutes this society is the existence of a certain number of beliefs and practices common to all the faithful, traditional and thus obligatory. The more numerous and strong these collective states of mind are, the stronger the integration of the religious community, and also the greater its preservative value. The details

---

[57] The obviously ambiguous term "components of integration" is used here to avoid specifying whether Durkheim considered the degrees of sharedness of actions and/or beliefs to be the definition(s) or the cause(s) of integration. Durkheim was unclear on this point. It is possible that he considered the meaning of integration and disintegration to be intuitively clear from common usage. In common usage they mean roughly the same thing as order and disorder and, therefore, presumably refer to a tendency for the parts (of a society) to hold together or to move together in certain directions (such as toward the fulfillment of certain goals). On the other hand, it seems more likely that he clearly recognized the tremendous conceptual problems involved in *defining* order and disorder.

[58] *Suicide*, p. 159.

of dogmas and rites are secondary. The essential thing is that they be capable of supporting a sufficiently intense collective life.[59]

Durkheim, then, has first clearly argued that shared beliefs are the ultimate causes of suicide, then he has reintroduced the external variable (i.e., behavior) as what would seem to be an equally important, independent cause; and, finally, he has argued that both the external and the internal are important only in so far as they increase or decrease the "collective life." We have, then, a high degree of vacillation over just what the fundamental theory is. One must look further in the work to finally resolve the issue, though, already, shared beliefs (or, more generally, shared meanings) seem to be more emphasized than behavior as the ultimate causes of suicide.

Parsons has already argued at length that in *Suicide* Durkheim moved increasingly away from the idea that external factors (such as the degree of functional differentiation of a group) cause the suicide rate of a society and increasingly toward the idea that forces of a "collective conscience" are the fundamental causes of the suicide rate. As Parsons interpreted *Suicide*, Durkheim considered altruistic suicide to be largely the result of the external forces of group structure, whereas egoistic suicide was seen more as the result of the internal forces of the "collective conscience" and anomic suicide was seen as almost entirely the result of the internal forces of the "collective conscience."[60]

In the chapter[61] containing his general conclusions on the

[59] *Ibid.*, p. 170.

[60] See Talcott Parsons, *The Structure of Social Action*, pp. 330-338. Noting that as one progresses through *Suicide* "what was meant earlier by egoism is much closer to what anomie comes to mean," Parsons then maintains that this "is an indication of the fact that Durkheim's own thought was in a process of dynamic development throughout this period, and that he had not defined his terms rigorously." (*Ibid.*, p. 328.) This estimate certainly seems justified by the facts. It is, however, contradictory to Parsons' earlier statement in the same work (p. 304) that *Suicide* belongs to the "early synthesis" period of Durkheim's works; and supports the thesis presented here that in *Suicide* Durkheim's thought is already clearly in transition toward, and has already in some good part arrived at, the "new general position" fully presented later in *The Elementary Forms of the Religious Life*.

[61] "The Social Element of Suicide," in *Suicide*, pp. 297-325.

forms of suicide, Durkheim repeatedly states this proposition that society consists of (or is defined in terms of) shared meanings (or beliefs) and that these shared beliefs are, in some way, the ultimate causes of the suicide rate of the collectivity. At the beginning of this chapter Durkheim states:

> The conclusion from all these facts is that the social suicide-rate can be explained only sociologically. At any moment the moral constitution of society establishes the contingent of voluntary deaths. There is, therefore, for each people a collective force of a definite amount of energy, impelling men to self-destruction. The victim's acts which at first seem to express only his personal temperament are really the supplement and prolongation of a social condition which they express externally.[62]

The "moral constitution" determines (or causes) the suicide rate. This "moral constitution" is called a "collective force" and is, by inference, considered to be an internal "social condition" that causes the external acts of suicide. Moreover, a causal explanation proceeding from the internal factors to the external factors is explicitly considered to be a "sociological" explanation and the only type of explanation that can be valid.

In this same chapter Durkheim makes other statements that clearly indicate the meaningful nature of society.[63] But

[62] *Ibid.*, p. 299.

[63] The following statement indicates that shared meanings even constitute the "social environment" that Durkheim mentioned so much in the earlier parts of the book: ". . . the social environment is fundamentally one of common ideas, beliefs, customs and tendencies." (*Suicide*, p. 302.) It would seem, however, that "custom" adds a bit of external impurity to the concept. This external impurity is even more pronounced in a statement coming several pages later:

> First, it is not true that society is made up only of individuals; it also includes material things, which play an essential role in the common life. The social fact is sometimes so far materialized as to become an element of the external world. For instance, a definite type of architecture is a social phenomenon; but it is partially embodied in houses and buildings of all sorts which, once constructed, become autonomous realities, independent of individuals. It is the same with the avenues of communication and transportation, with instruments and machines used in industry or private life which express the state of technology at any moment in history, of written language, etc. Social life, which is thus crystallized, as it were, and

at only one point does Durkheim totally commit himself explicitly to the proposition that the *internal* factors are the only factors of ultimate concern, and, therefore, the only ultimate causes of suicide:

> We do not expect to be reproached further, after this explanation, with wishing to substitute the exterior for the interior in sociology. We start from the exterior because it alone is immediately given, but only to reach the interior. Doubtless the procedure is complicated; but there is no other unless one would risk having his research apply to his personal feeling concerning the order of facts under investigation, instead of to this factual order itself.[64]

Such a clear statement of the fundamental importance of the "interior" might seem to solve the problem once and for all, but *Suicide* does not hold any such simple or final solutions.

The statement that the only valid method is to proceed from the exterior to the interior can mean at least two different things: either (1) the "exterior" (i.e., the behavior, such as "suicide")[65] is simply caused by the interior and does not in any way at any time cause the interior or (2) the exterior is in some way at some time a cause of the interior, though the interior is subsequently the most important (independent) cause of the exterior.

The first possible interpretation can be supported by arguing that the exterior, being the effect(s) of the interior, serves as a refraction of the interior. One studies the exterior to get at the interior both because the interior cannot be treated as a "thing" (hence cannot be the object of "scientific" methods as Durkheim understood them), while

---

fixed on material supports, is by just so much externalized, and acts upon us from without. (*Ibid.*, pp. 313-314.)

These two statements show how very similar Durkheim's ideas of society or "collective conscience" were to the early catch-all conceptions of "culture" developed by anthropologists. (See, also, Paul Bohannan, "Conscience Collective and Culture," in *Emile Durkheim, 1858-1917*, ed. by Kurt H. Wolff, pp. 79-97.)

[64] *Suicide*, p. 315.

[65] By Durkheim's definition "suicide" is not all exterior. It is meaningful in that knowledge of consequences is necessary. One *assumes* knowledge of the interior. See Appendix II for a further discussion of this point.

the exterior can, and because the interior can be inferred from its external (i.e., behavioral) effects. Such an interpretation is well represented by Peristiany's conclusion regarding this aspect of Durkheim's theory:

> This does not mean that individual conduct has no interest for the sociologist, but rather that all its forms—even the most common ones—are a refraction, an ectype, of a model which cannot be reconstituted by piecing them together. Durkheim's advice to the sociologist rings clear and true. It is to study norms and not individual attitudes, social imperatives and not the reaction of the average man to the average man's picture of the social order. For the sociologist it is only in relation to the normative system of beliefs and to the sanctioned channels of action that individual conduct becomes meaningful.[66]

Such an interpretation is probably quite valid for Durkheim's work after *Suicide* and it is valid for the dominant strain in *Suicide*, especially in the latter parts of the work; but it is an overstatement of Durkheim's position in *Suicide* as a whole. In *Suicide* Durkheim was clearly moving rapidly in the direction of this position, which was to be explicitly stated in his next major publication, "Individual and Collective Representations."[67] But in *Suicide* Durkheim refused, however inconsistently, to relinquish all claim to causal efficacy for the "external" (i.e., behavioral) factors. For this reason, the second interpretation seems the more valid.

In this same chapter in which Durkheim so clearly states the causal primacy of the internal factors over the external factors, he also makes it clear that the external factors have some causal significance; and here, at least, makes the nature of this supposed causal relation between the internal and the external clearer than at any other point in *Suicide*. Probably Durkheim's most explicit statement of this position is the following:

[66] Emile Durkheim, *Sociology and Philosophy*, pp. xvi-xvii.

[67] This is the major work in the volume *Sociology and Philosophy*, for which Peristiany wrote the Introduction. It is, presumably, for this reason that his statement so strongly emphasized the "collective conscience" position of Durkheim.

To be sure, it is likewise true that society has no active forces other than individuals; but individuals by combining form a psychical existence of a new species, which consequently has its own manner of thinking and feeling. Of course the elementary qualities of which the social fact consists are present in germ in individual minds. But the social fact emerges from them only when they have been transformed by association since it is only then that it appears. Association itself is also an active factor productive of special effects. In itself it is therefore something new. When the consciousness of individuals, instead of remaining isolated, becomes grouped and combined, something in the world has been altered. Naturally this change produces others, this novelty engenders other novelties, phenomena appear whose characteristic qualities are not found in the elements composing them.

This proposition could only be opposed by agreeing that a whole is qualitatively identical with the sum of its parts, that an effect is qualitatively reducible to the sum of its productive causes; which amounts to denying all change or to making it inexplicable.[68]

Society (or the "social fact") is still seen as being the "interior," the realm of meanings (especially moral meanings) in the minds of individuals. It is made clear, however, that "society" is not merely some form of summation of the meanings in the minds of individuals. "Society" is some form of dynamic whole, some *product* of the interaction of these minds. It *exists* only in the minds of individuals, but, being more than the mind of any individual or even the minds of all individuals taken together, it exists almost entirely outside the individual and acts upon him as an external force would—even though this force can exist only internally, within individuals.

The associations (i.e., the external, behavioral relations of individuals), then, are to be studied as social facts because they alone are immediately given to sense perceptions and are, therefore, the only "facts" of society available for (positivistic) scientific analysis. *But* these external associa-

[68] *Suicide*, pp. 310-311.

tions are to be considered by the sociologist to be of causal significance for suicide rates (another "social fact") *only* in so far as the behavior noted in such associations constitutes *communication* (or interaction) between minds (or meanings).[69] As meanings interact over time they change, with both frequencies and duration of interaction being independent determinants of this change. The frequencies and durations of the interactions of meanings are partly determined, at least initially, by certain factors external to the system of social meanings (or "collective representations")—such as war, economic crises, etc.[70] At any given time one can see in any given collectivity of individuals certain pools of meanings: that is, different combinations of collective representations of different degrees of strength.[71]

[69] Against the present interpretation and in line with a positivistic interpretation of *Suicide*, one might well argue at this point that, for example, the mere "fact" of social relations (or of the stable presence of others) will act as a restraint on the individual, so he will not commit anomic suicide. Durkheim, however, repeatedly rejects such arguments and, relative to this specific argument, leaves no doubt that anomic suicide is due to the lack of certain meaningful reactions of the individual to these external associations:

> It will be objected that where marriage is not tempered by divorce the rigid obligation of monogamy may result in disgust. This result will of course follow if the moral character of the obligation is no longer felt. What actually matters in fact is not only that the regulation should exist, but that it should be accepted by the conscience. Otherwise, since this regulation no longer has moral authority and continues only through the force of inertia, it can no longer play any useful role. It chafes without accomplishing much. (*Suicide*, p. 272, fn. 19.)

[70] These factors are the "morphological causes" noted above. They *may* vary completely independently of the system of theory developed by Durkheim. He takes them as givens (by genetics, etc.) and uses them to explain rather than to be explained. These "morphological causes" constitute, at least in *Suicide*, what George Homans has called the "external system" in *The Human Group*.

[71] It can be assumed that the collective representations also vary from one society or subsociety to another. But Durkheim strongly argues that this is not true of the collective representations of critical importance in the causation of suicide—i.e., altruism, egoism, and anomie. These are, supposedly, present in every society and differences in suicide rates between one society and another are caused not by their presence or absence or even by simple differences in degrees of each, but, rather, as previously noted, by an imbalance in the interaction of the three caused by a *relatively* (to the other two) too great strength of one or two of the three:

> No moral idea exists which does not combine in proportions varying with the society involved, egoism, altruism and a certain

These different pools of meanings interact with each other with different frequencies and for different durations through the behavioral contacts (or associations) of individuals. These differences cause social change (i.e., changes in the meanings themselves) and they cause changes in the collective and individual forces within individuals which, once formed, remain rather stable within individuals and increasingly determine their actions. The patterns of changes in collective and individual forces Durkheim calls "currents of opinion" and the resulting changes in patterns of causal influence on the actions of individuals are called "genetic currents" (hence the "suicidogenetic currents").[72]

The meanings or collective representations of critical significance in the causation of suicide were, of course, altruism, egoism, and anomie. These collective representations, when out of balance, exert a force on the individual that produces individual states (such as melancholy) which,

_____

anomy. For social life assumes both that the individual has a certain personality, that he is ready to surrender it if the community requires, and finally, that he is to a certain degree sensitive to ideas of progress. This is why there is no people among whom these three currents of opinion do not co-exist, bending men's inclinations in three different and even opposing directions. Where they offset one another, the moral agent is in a state of equilibrium which shelters him against any thought of suicide. But let one of them exceed a certain strength to the detriment of the others, and as it becomes individualized, it also becomes suicidogenetic, for the reasons assigned. (*Suicide*, p. 321.)

It should be noted, for the purposes of what is to follow below, that in this statement Durkheim refers to altruism, egoism, and anomie as three "currents of opinion" and implies that when individualized they constitute a "suicidogenetic" current.

In view of this statement and many others, it might be suggested that Durkheim considered these three "currents of opinion" to be the products of the interactions of more elementary collective representations, such as individualism, rather than collective representations themselves. Such a distinction might be very important for a consideration of Durkheim's argument that the increase in individualism in the Western world over a period of several hundred years was a basic cause, perhaps through its effect on egoism, of the continually rising suicide rates. But such a distinction is not at all clear in *Suicide* and will, consequently, not be considered significant. In fact, it is pretty clear from statements in *Suicide* (e.g., p. 315) that Durkheim considered even individualism to be peripheral compared to the "moral and legal precepts."

[72] Durkheim does not use the generic concept of "genetic current," but this is an obvious and useful inference from what he does say about "suicidogenetic currents."

in turn, cause the individual to commit suicide if the individual forces (or individual representations) are not strong enough to counteract the force of the collective representations:

> It is not mere metaphor to say of each human society that it has a greater or lesser aptitude for suicide; the expression is based on the nature of things. Each social group really has a collective inclination for the act, quite its own, and the source of all individual inclination, rather than their result. It is made up of the currents of egoism, altruism or anomy running through the society under consideration with the tendencies to languorous melancholy, active renunciation or exasperated weariness derivative from these currents. These tendencies of the whole social body, by affecting individuals, cause them to commit suicide. The private experiences usually thought to be the proximate causes of suicide have only the influence borrowed from the victim's moral predisposition, itself an echo of the moral state of society. To explain his detachment from life the individual accuses his most immediately surrounding circumstances; life is sad to him because he is sad. Of course his sadness comes to him from without in one sense, however not from one or another incident of his career but rather from the group to which he belongs. This is why there is nothing which cannot serve as an occasion for suicide. It all depends on the intensity with which suicidogenetic causes have affected the individual.[73]

[73] *Ibid.*, pp. 299-300. Durkheim did not deny that the individual is important, at least negatively, in the causation of suicide. One of the clearest statements of this conflict between the collective forces and the individual forces is presented on page 319 of the chapter "The Social Element of Suicide." Part of this statement is well worth quoting here:

> Two antagonistic forces confront each other. One, the collective force, tries to take possession of the individual; the other, the individual force, repulses it. To be sure, the former is much stronger than the latter, since it is made of a combination of all the individual forces; but as it also encounters as many resistances as there are separate persons, it is partially exhausted in these multifarious contests and reaches us disfigured and enfeebled. When it is very strong, when the circumstances activating it are of frequent recurrence, it may still leave a deep impression on individuals; it arouses in them mental states of some vivacity which, once formed, func-

It is rather clear from what Durkheim says about egoism, altruism, and anomie that at least egoism is concerned with *cognitive* meaning and anomie with *affective* meaning—or with the lack of either; but Durkheim continually refers to all of them as "moral states" of society.[74] They themselves, however, are not sets of morals. Rather, they are orientations toward the (primarily moral) meanings that constitute society—or the rest of "society," since they are a part of "society" also. They seem to represent the generalized orientations toward society of submissiveness, aloofness (or superiority), and rebelliousness.[75] *All of these orientations toward society (as a system of moral meanings) are necessary for the adequate functioning of any group, but an imbalance or an upset of the equilibrium between the three leads to the production of certain types of individual states in a certain proportion of the individuals of the group and, thence, to a given suicide rate for the group.*

What, then, is it that disturbs (or maintains) the equilibrium of these forces? Or, more significantly, what causes one (or more) of the forces to increase or decrease in strength such that the equilibrium is disturbed (or restored)? This is the critical question for Durkheim's theory of suicide.

The equilibrium is the result of each force opposing or conflicting with the effects of the other two or three forces.[76] Each force, when not restrained by the other forces, leads to suicidogenetic forces within the individuals. Durkheim first takes up altruistic suicide and then egoistic suicide. Though, as we have previously noted, the meaning of ego-

---

tion with the spontaneity of instinct; this happens in the case of the most essential moral ideas.

[74] Parsons has argued that Durkheim moved increasingly in the direction of conceiving of society solely in terms of *cognitive meanings* (*The Structure of Social Action*). In this respect, as in so many others, *Suicide* seems to represent a critical transition with, consequently, many inconsistencies and much vagueness.

[75] It is at least clear that these are the orientations produced in individuals by altruism, egoism, and anomie respectively. (See, especially, Chapter 6, "Individual Forms of the Different Types of Suicide," in *Suicide*, pp. 277-294.)

[76] Durkheim specifically argues that no force can restrain itself (see *ibid.*, p. 366), just as he argues that the individual cannot restrain himself but must rely upon others for restraint.

istic suicide shifts and is, therefore, somewhat uncertain,[77] it seems quite clear that Durkheim intended these two to be the opposite ends of one social dimension of involvement in society, running from noninvolvement (or aloofness) to overinvolvement (or submissiveness). Society functions adequately, and there is no increase in suicide, when the two forces of egoism and altruism oppose each other "adequately." When, however, the equilibrium is destroyed or weakened, the suicide rate increases.

The specific question here, then, is what causes these forces to change. One possibility would be that the degree of "social integration" changes and this causes a change in the forces of egoism and altruism. Remembering, however, that social integration must be defined not in terms of the external (e.g., of number of children) but, rather, in terms of the internal, we must then ask what social meanings constitute social integration. The answer seems to be that integration might be defined as (1) the dimension of egoism-altruism (i.e., of noninvolvement-involvement in society) or, it might be defined as (2) the equilibrium of the two opposing forces; or it might be defined, in the light of our previous consideration of integration, as (3) the number of shared meanings.

The second definition seems more likely than the others, since the concept of integration can then be extended to cover the equilibrium between the two opposing forces of anomie and fatalism (which we shall come to shortly). When this is done, the general hypothesis that suicide varies directly with the degree of social integration makes much more sense within the context of Durkheim's theory than if integration is merely defined as the dimension of egoism-altruism. Though such an interpretation is in line with the general hypothesis concerning the relation between integration and suicide, it does not seem to be in line with Durk-

[77] It is also true, as Parsons has noted in *The Structure of Social Action*, that the meaning of altruism shifts from the external state of non-differentiated structure to the internal state of moral obligation. This shift of meaning parallels the shifts from external to internal states in the chapters on egoistic and anomic suicide. This is in line with Durkheim's conclusion in the chapter immediately following these three that the sociologist should start with the exterior and work in to the interior.

heim's statements to the effect that integration consists of shared meanings (and, in the earliest stages of the work, of shared behavioral practices). In the first two chapters on the types of suicide (i.e., the two chapters on egoistic suicide) Durkheim seems to be arguing that egoism causes suicidogenetic currents in the individuals and that shared meanings, or social integration, act to restrain these suicidal forces. In these chapters any meanings that are strongly held and shared are presumed to restrain the suicidogenetic forces caused by egoism.[78] It should be obvious, however,

[78] For some reason Durkheim does not specifically exclude egoism from the meanings that, when shared, restrain suicide. The reason for this might be that Durkheim was at this point still vacillating between considering the external factors of association to be of critical importance in the causation of suicide and considering the internal factors to be of critical importance.

This confusion leads to a seeming contradiction very early in the work. In his attempt to refute the theory that climate causes suicide, Durkheim argues that in the summertime there is increased (external) collective activity and that this increased activity leads to an increase in the suicidogenetic forces, presumably because of an increase in altruism or egoism due to the increased communication of these ideas. As long as one sticks to the external factors of association, this finding is in direct contradiction to the arguments concerning integration and suicide presented in the beginning of the first chapter on egoistic suicide. However, at the end of the chapter on "Suicide and Cosmic Factors" Durkheim noted that:

> Of course, we are yet uncertain how collective life can have this effect. But it already appears that if it contains the causes of the variation of the suicide-rate, the latter must increase or decrease as social life becomes more or less active. To determine these causes more exactly will be the purpose of the following book. (*Suicide*, p. 122.)

This allows one to reinterpret the subject in the light of the meanings of social relationships, which Durkheim begins in his consideration of egoistic suicide. However, he never does adequately explain how it is that for the same collectivity of people (e.g., the French) an increase in collective activity can be said to produce an increase in suicide when considering one factor (e.g., climate) and a decrease when considering another factor (e.g., marriage or religion). In this instance the pools of meaning and their patterns of distribution must be the same (in so far as we're considering all of France in each instance), so an increase in general collective activity (i.e., interaction of meanings) *should* produce the same effects on the critical meanings (i.e., on egoism, altruism, anomie, and fatalism) and, therefore, on the suicidogenetic forces and, therefore, on the suicide rates.

This is one of the few instances in which such a direct contradiction is allowed to stand. As we shall see, Durkheim generally infers the critical meanings (of egoism, altruism, anomie, and fatalism) from the data on associations and on the suicide rates. The theoretical

that these shared meanings that are to restrain the suicidogenetic currents must exclude the shared meanings that
cause the suicidogenetic currents. But, *rather than segment-
ing the internal realm of shared meanings and clarifying
the relations between some set that causes and another set
(called integration) that restrains these causes, the focus of
Durkheim's analysis shifts increasingly toward the four
critical meanings as both cause and restraint and the term
integration is replaced by equilibrium as the factor of critical importance in restraining the suicidal forces of society.*
This would indicate that the two are really the same and
refer to a balance between the four social forces that cause
suicidogenetic forces, a balance that prevents suicidogenetic
currents within individuals.

Now, just as egoistic and altruistic forces restrain each
other, so the *anomic* force has an opposite force that restrains it—fatalism.[79] This dimension is one of legitimate
discipline or control (fatalism) and the lack of legitimate
discipline or control (anomie).[80] The suicidogenetic current

---

explanation, then, is always fitted to the evidence by assuming whatever one must about the meanings involved. Since there is no independent measure of the meanings, such assumptions are impossible to
refute by demonstrating that actually the associations cause an increase in the strength and sharedness of some other meanings. This
method generally "eliminates" contradictions.

[79] See *Suicide*, p. 276, fn. 26.
It seems significant that Durkheim introduced fatalistic suicide at
the end of the chapter on anomic suicide and made a direct comparison between the opposition of these two forces and the opposition
of egoism and altruism. It seems clear from this that his general theory
of suicide has only slowly evolved throughout the first three hundred
pages of *Suicide*. This would explain the uncertainties and contradictions shown in these earlier parts of the work as opposed to the
much greater clarity and strength of conclusions in the rest of the
work, in which the general theory is presented several times.

[80] There is little doubt by this time in *Suicide* that the *meanings*
of associations is the critical factor. External force must be accepted
as *morally right* before it can adequately restrain the anomic force's
tendency to cause a suicidogenetic force in the individual. On pp.
251-252 we read:

> But like the one first mentioned, this discipline can be useful
> only if considered just by the peoples subject to it. When it is
> maintained only by custom and force, peace and harmony are
> illusory; the spirit of unrest and discontent are latent; appetites
> superficially restrained are ready to revolt. This happened in Rome
> and Greece when the faiths underlying the old organization of the

produced in the individuals by a loss of equilibrium between these two opposing forces is one of hopelessness or despair, especially agitated depression.

Our picture of the general theory, then, is much clearer: *suicide is caused by suicidogenetic currents, which are in turn caused by a lack of (or decrease in) equilibrium (or integration) between the two sets of opposing forces or by one of the sets changing its strength.* We also know, from previous considerations, that a change in strength of a social meaning (such as egoism, altruism, anomie, or fatalism) is caused by a change in the frequency and/or in the duration of the communication (through external association) of two minds possessing this social meaning. For the purposes of an analysis of Durkheim's theory of suicide we can assume that in some (unexplained) way morphological causes and/or other meanings (e.g., individualism and progress) determine the frequency and duration of (external) social associations. Since all individuals have within themselves all four of the social meanings that cause suicidogenetic currents, we must assume that communication changes the strength of one (or two) relative to the strength of its opposite (i.e., decreases the equilibrium between the forces) either because (1) there is a difference in strength to begin with and the stronger meaning grows more than the weaker with the same frequency and duration of contact or (2) *there is selective communication of meanings in any given association*—i.e., all the individuals involved have all the meanings involved, but only one (or some) of the meanings is communicated, and it grows in strength relative to its opposite. There is no evidence that Durkheim even considered the first alternative. The second interpretation seems to be the only reasonable one. Assuming, then, that the

---

patricians and plebeians were shaken, and in our modern societies when aristocratic prejudices began to lose their old ascendancy. But this state of upheaval is exceptional; it occurs only when society is passing through some abnormal crisis. In normal conditions the collective order is regarded as just by the great majority of persons. Therefore, when we say that an authority is necessary to impose this order on individuals, we certainly do not mean that violence is the only means of establishing it. Since this regulation is meant to restrain individual passions, it must come from a power which dominates individuals; but this power must also be obeyed through respect, not fear.

second alternative is the valid one, we are faced with three critical questions: (1) what determines which of the meanings will be communicated in any given association(s); (2) how do we know what meanings are being communicated; and (3) how do we measure the relative strengths of the meanings in any given society?[81] The first is, again, the question of causality, the question of what causes the *selection of meanings* to be communicated in given associations, which, in turn, causes the increase or decrease in the equilibrium of the opposing forces. The second and third questions are both questions concerning the fundamental epistemology of Durkheim's theory of suicide.

The first question itself leads into the epistemology of the work. As we have already noted, Durkheim obviously believed that all individuals possess all of the meanings, but that different meanings are transmitted in different associations.[82] Why this is so was not really an explicit question to Durkheim, but the implicit answer seems clear enough. One might first argue that different meanings are transmitted in different associations because different (external) things (such as economic failure) occur with different frequencies and intensities in different associations. And, in a way, Durkheim considered this to be so. Otherwise, why be concerned with the rates of failure and all the other things that occur in different associations? But, as we have seen, the different things that occur in the different associations are significant for the causation of suicide *only* in so far as they have meanings,[83] meanings that are different for different associa-

[81] It is necessary to know the relative strengths at least before the communication of any meanings, even if we do know what meanings are being communicated and what their effect on the strengths of the four critical meanings are, if we are to determine whether the communication of a given association is increasing or decreasing the equilibrium of the two sets of opposing forces.

[82] The three most important associations and the meanings communicated in each that are considered in *Suicide* are the following:

(1) altruism is communicated in the military career;
(2) egoism is communicated in the intellectual careers; and
(3) anomie is communicated in the business or financial occupations.

[83] The "things" called orders in the military segment of society, for example, have significance for the causation of suicide only in so far as they elicit a feeling of rightful subordination or some other meaning.

tions. We have, then, come full circle. Different meanings are communicated in different associations because the different associations involve different meanings.[84]

Though Durkheim was concerned to some degree with giving a dynamic explanation of changes in the meanings involved in any given association, for most of his purposes in *Suicide* he merely assumed, implicitly, that the meanings communicated in any given associations were more or less constant and that their causes were nothing external to the meanings of the association. The only critical question remaining is that of how one knows what meaning(s) is being communicated in any given association.

In *Suicide* Durkheim not only considered the meanings communicated in associations to be of critical importance in the causation of suicide, but *he also considered these meanings to be very clearly known to the sociologist who is a member of that society*. Again and again, for example, Durkheim argued that men and women (and men at different ages) respond to marriage (or widowhood, or divorce, or childlessness) with different actions (such as different suicide rates) because these things mean different things to the two (or to men at different ages). He then goes into great detail regarding these different meanings, even going so far as to discuss the differences in degrees of sociability (i.e., the degrees to which they are affected by the communicated meanings) between the masculine mind and the feminine mind.[85]

Durkheim did not present any evidence on public opinions as to the meanings of the different associations. Nothing could have been further from the whole nature of his theoretical approach to suicide.[86] Durkheim did not be-

---

[84] One could, of course, once again look to the "morphological causes" to explain how associations come to have more of a given meaning over long periods of time. For example, one could argue that the increase in functional differentiation (especially in the division of labor) in Western societies over the last several hundred years has caused an increase in egoism. Such an argument is very much in line with the theory presented in *The Division of Labor* and is consistent with certain statements in the early parts of *Suicide*. This, however, would still leave one with the question of how one knows which meanings are increasing in which associations.

[85] See *Suicide*, especially pp. 215-216.

[86] The position taken here is in direct contradiction to that taken by Tiryakian on this point, as expressed in the following statement:

lieve that the individual could be very conscious of the collective forces actually causing his actions. He believed that the individual representations were only echoes of the collective representations, the nature of which the individual could only be dimly aware.[87] Consequently, it would do no good to try to determine the meanings communicated in any associations by analyzing the beliefs or thoughts of the individuals involved.

Durkheim's explicit position on the question of how one comes to know what meanings are involved in the associations of a whole society is very simple. One merely studies the juridical (especially the legal) norms of the society. These are not the collective representations themselves, but they are the clear and unmistakable precipitates or refractions of the collective representations and are the only means of gaining sure knowledge of the collective representations.[88] Durkheim, then, very specifically considered the juridicial norms to be the only adequate indicators (or indexes) of the collective representations, which cause not only the juridical norms but the suicide rates as well.

Durkheim, like most of his contemporaries, was a legal "realist." He believed that the meaning and the application of the law is usually obvious, that the mores and the laws

---

"To place his attitude in perspective, it may be said that the current study of 'public opinion' is essentially what Durkheim would have termed the study of the 'collective consciousness'. . . ." (E. A. Tiryakian, *Sociologism and Existentialism*, p. 19.)

[87] This position was not too clearly presented in *Suicide*, but was fully developed in Durkheim's next significant work, "Individual and Collective Representations," in *Sociology and Philosophy*.

[88] Durkheim also added the requirement that the juridical norms be the most stable or "normal" juridical norms before they be taken as the indicators of the collective representations. The aberrations or divergences from these "normal" juridical norms were considered to be "pathological" and were simply rejected as indicators of the collective representations of a society. This whole idea has been strongly criticized by Bayet (Albert Bayet, *Le Suicide et la Morale*, Paris: Felix Alcan, 1922, pp. 6-7) and later writers (see for example, Harry Alpert, *Emile Durkheim* . . .). This particular point, just as is true of the whole argument concerning the relation of juridical norms to the collective representations, is a carry-over from the *Division of Labor*. It is quite inconsistent with all of Durkheim's attempts in *Suicide* to explain changes in suicide rates within any one society and it is quite insignificant for the general theory of *Suicide*. Consequently, we shall simply leave this point out of our considerations of Durkheim's theory of suicide.

are rarely in conflict, and that laws, consequently, can be taken to represent the social definitions of right and wrong without any independent empirical determination of the mores. These assumptions have been severely criticized many times and can hardly be accepted today.[89] Our concern need not, however, be with the acceptability of these assumptions since Durkheim did not in fact attempt in any very serious fashion to determine just what the juridical norms regarding suicide had been in Europe over the centuries.[90] And, most

[89] See, for example, Alpert's criticism (*ibid.*, especially pp. 123-138). The very best criticism is that presented by Bayet in his excellent and massive work on the development in Europe over many centuries of the juridical norms and social mores regarding suicide. See *Le Suicide et la Morale*.

[90] Durkheim considers the history of the European juridical norms regarding suicide in eight to ten pages (see *Suicide*, pp. 326-336). At the same time that he criticizes Durkheim's conception of law and its place in society Bayet criticizes (on pp. 7-8) this hasty treatment of what Durkheim *ostensibly* considered to be the most important causes of suicide rates:

> Is he [Durkheim] concerned with the number of facts? After having devoted more than three hundred pages to the study of suicide, "a social phenomenon," he devoted only ten pages to the study of the evaluation of suicide, a moral phenomenon. If he is so brief, it is because he considered the law almost exclusively. From the Gallo-Roman epoch to the Revolution, it is with the aid of canonical and juridical texts that he determined the evolution of morality. Nothing on the writings of philosophers, nothing on literature or customs. Almost nothing on jurisprudence. In total, only several facts. I know well that a law has the advantage of being an easily gotten social fact. Morality seems to be rolled up in it for the greatest convenience of sociologists and it is of the real morality of actions, since it provides for sanctions. But from the first it remains to be known if these sanctions are applied: the existence of a law is a fact, but the application of that law is itself also a fact. Jurisprudence, neglected by Durkheim, leads, in that which concerns suicide, to completely different conclusions than those of law, properly called. Moreover, a law, even applied, does not forcefully express the morality of an epoch. At the end of the 18th century there was an abyss between the criminal law of France and the opinion of the greatest number. In other epochs the divorce is less sharp, but the law registers morality only in simplifying it. All that which is nuance or diversity falls out. In restricting the number of facts studied one risks mutilating the moral reality.
>
> Are the chosen and too few facts at least well established? On this point it seems to me that the method followed by Durkheim is not rigorous enough.

Durkheim probably assumed that the best histories of suicide, which he refers to in a footnote at the beginning of his treatment

important, he did not attempt to show how one might explain the changes in suicide rates within any given society over time in terms of the "unchanging" juridical norms. Apparently Durkheim was concerned with two levels of analysis of suicide rates, though he did not clearly distinguish the two in *Suicide*. On one level he was attempting to carry out a *comparative macrocultural analysis of suicide*. On this level he was concerned with comparing the long-run suicide rates of one whole culture (such as Europe) with the long-run suicide rates of another whole culture (such as that of Japan) in terms of their fundamental social differences. This form of macrocultural analysis was similar to what Durkheim had done in *The Division of Labor*. It is really a carry-over from the *Division of Labor* and is peripheral to most of *Suicide*, which is almost entirely concerned with the second level of analysis, which we might call the microcultural level of analysis.

This microcultural analysis was partially forced on Durkheim by previous moral-statistical research and theory on suicide. As we have already seen, almost all of the moral-statistical works on suicide had involved comparisons of suicide rates between the different nations of Europe and between different regions, occupational groups, age cohorts, and so on within each nation; and Durkheim relied on these works for his methods of analysis and empirical data. The task of synthesis and the means (i.e., both the methods and the data) available to him forced him to desert his macrocultural type of analysis in favor of a more microscopic level of analysis necessary for dealing with data from subcultures.

When Durkheim moved from macrocultural to microcultural analysis he faced the problem of finding some new indicators to serve as his indirect means of knowing (or measuring) the collective representations. Since suicide rates changed rapidly, and varied greatly from one group to another within each nation, the relatively uniform and unchanging juridical norms could hardly be used as indica-

of the subject, were adequate treatments of this subject. Bayet severely criticizes this judgment, but the important point for our purposes is that Durkheim did not attempt seriously to integrate this small section of *Suicide* with the rest of the work.

tors of forces causing these differences. Unfortunately, Durkheim seems not to have been very conscious of this problem. He continued at times to argue as if the juridical norms were adequate indicators while actually, when dealing with specific problems and data, shifting to quite different indicators. These were, in part, the mores of the different groups being considered. Thus, for example, in his discussion of suicide rates relative to the different states of family relations (childless, widowed with children, etc.) he does not merely discuss the laws governing marriage relations, parental relations, etc. Rather, he goes into great detail concerning the generally accepted obligations, though not legally sanctioned, of widows, widowers, childless wives, etc. In fact, he seems to go so far as to implicitly consider the burdens of these obligations to be causally significant for suicide rates. At least in these parts of *Suicide*, Durkheim had clearly moved away from his general argument that the moral meanings are all important. Affective and cognitive meanings are given equal significance in these microanalyses. Indeed, at times the affective or cognitive meanings seem to become much more important. For example, in his discussion of the high concentration of egoistic suicide among the intellectual occupations Durkheim suggests that a great deal of thinking (or cognitive activity) relative to the amount of action makes one more suicidal, at least if the "tradition" is already weak; that is, presumably, if there is a lack of equilibrium between the sets of causally important forces.[91] Durkheim showed, in this discussion of the individual types of suicide, that on the very microscopic level of analysis of suicide he considered the cognitive meanings (or, at least, their relative amount) to be indicators of the collective representations. Moreover, he had taken the same position in one of his earlier arguments concerning egoistic suicide. This argument, which he considered fundamental to his theory, reveals a great deal about Durkheim's whole method in *Suicide*.

In the first chapter on egoistic suicide Durkheim presents

[91] Durkheim explicitly took this principle from Hartmann (see *Suicide*, p. 280), but he did add to it and put it in context so that it remained consistent with his theory—i.e., with the proposition that it is the equilibrium between the collective representations that is of ultimate causal importance.

evidence and an argument to show that suicide rates vary with respect to the three major religions of Europe, with Protestantism having the highest rate. He then tries to show that the more educated a group of people, the more suicide they will have. And finally, he tries to show that the Protestants, who have the highest suicide rate, are also the most educated. The idea, not explicitly expressed, is that both religion and degree of education are independently related to the suicide rates in Europe, but there is a strong tendency for the two factors to be related to suicide rates in the same direction—i.e., if the religion is associated with a low suicide rate, then the degree of education will also be low. But Durkheim's data presented him with a strong exception to this general argument. The members of the Jewish faith had a low suicide rate, yet they were highly educated. Durkheim might have merely given up the idea that religion and the degree of education are related to suicide rates in the same direction, then gone on to show that, though the Jews as a whole group have a low suicide rate, the more educated Jews contribute a disproportionately large share to the Jewish suicide rate. But he did not do so. Such an argument would have worked against his larger argument concerning the relations between Protestantism, the search for knowledge, and suicide. All three of these seemed to represent a break with "tradition," to be in some way "deviant,"[92] for all major European nations. It would, then, seem plausible to argue that these specific breaks with tradition (all three of them supposedly representing increases in egoism) prove that tradition in general has been weakened. (After all, why would tradition be broken if it were not first weakened?) Durkheim could then argue that the "tradition" that has been weakened and then broken by egoism had been the equilibrium between the opposing forces of egoism and altruism. (A similar argument was later followed for the opposing forces of anomie and fatalism.) The progress of the argument would, then, seem to quite admirably exemplify the method of going from the external to the internal, from the indicators (or indexes) to the fundamental

[92] This might well be the reason for Durkheim's later argument to the effect that, regardless of the temporary public indulgence today, suicide has always been and still is "pathological."

causes, or from the "things" of social phenomena to the "meanings" of social phenomena by strictly "scientific" (or positivistic) inference. Now, we have already seen that Durkheim's etiological "types of suicide" were the same types that had been thoroughly discussed in romantic literature and in the previous technical literature on suicide, a fact which must surely lead one to suspect that the causes were in some unstated way known (or assumed) before the indicators were known (or measured). When we consider Durkheim's argument concerning the relations between Jewish society, education, and the suicide rates we can see quite clearly that this is true of Durkheim's actual (as opposed to his stated) method in *Suicide*. For, to explain the high degree of education and a low suicide rate among Jews, as opposed to the high degree of education and a high suicide rate among Protestants, Durkheim argues that education has a different "significance" for Jews. That is to say, the *"things" of education* (the numbers of years attending school, etc.) *have a different meaning* for the Jews. Indeed, Durkheim makes up a principle to the following effect:

But if the Jew manages to be both well instructed and very disinclined to suicide, it is because of the special origin of his desire for knowledge. It is a general law that religious minorities, in order to protect themselves better against the hate to which they are exposed or merely through a sort of emulation, try to surpass in knowledge the populations surrounding them. Thus Protestants themselves show more desire for knowledge when they are a minority of the general population. The Jew, therefore, seeks to learn, not in order to replace his collective prejudices by reflective thought, but merely to be better armed for the struggle. For him it is a means of offsetting the law.[93]

[93] E. Durkheim, *Suicide*, pp. 167-168. (It is of some interest to note here that at the end of this statement Durkheim has implicitly argued that a group can have a low suicide rate precisely, in part, because of its opposition to the juridical norms of the society. This is quite contradictory to his theory of "legal realism" and his theory regarding the relation between the juridical norms and suicide.

In *Suicide* Durkheim creates all manner of "general principles" to prove that what seems an exception to his theory is really not so at

Because of this different meaning of education for the Jewish subculture, Durkheim implicitly argues, a high degree of education among the Jews does not constitute a break with tradition, as it does among Christians, and therefore does not lead to a high suicide rate.

There are several critical points to be noted in this example of Durkheim's method of theoretical argument in *Suicide*:

1. As we have seen in some detail, the social *meaning* of the association (e.g., the degree of education of a group) is of critical importance for the theoretical explanation.

2. The social meanings of the statistics are not *known* (or measured) by means of some other statistics; but, rather, they are supplied whole by Durkheim *after* it becomes clear that the statistics do not support the theory and some other explanation must be offered to support it.

3. The statistics on the external associations become indicators of the collective representations (i.e., of altruism-egoism and anomie-fatalism) only because *intermediary meanings are supplied by Durkheim.*

4. The meanings are supplied after the statistical relations between the data on the external associations and the suicide rates are known,[94] so that the statistical relations between the two are in each case provided with the appropriate meanings to make them commensurate with (or linguistically connected with) their assumed underlying causes.

5. Breaks in tradition (or social change of a "pathological" degree) are implicitly (and never explicitly) assumed to *indicate* a break in the equilibrium of the opposing forces of altruism-egoism and anomie-fatalism.

---

all. Lacombe was probably the first author to systematically criticize Durkheim on this point and, drawing on Lacombe, Alpert severely criticizes *Suicide* for it. See Harry Alpert, *Emile Durkheim . . .* , p. 124.

[94] Again, we must remember that even if these statistical relations had not come first in *Suicide*, they would still have come first in Durkheim's own thinking, since almost all of the significant relations he considers had been thoroughly worked out many years previous to his own work.

We have already considered the first point in sufficient detail. Most of the other points have been at least partially dealt with, but some elaboration seems to be called for before we give a systematic summary of Durkheim's theory of suicide, his method of theoretical analysis in *Suicide*, and the faults of this method.

It is, at least on the surface, very difficult to understand why Durkheim, with all of his positivistic emphasis on studying social phenomena as "things" (i.e., on "scientific objectivity"), should have failed almost entirely to even attempt to provide any "objective" evidence on the internal meanings of the external associations. It seems so obvious today that the investigator can hardly hope to know what fundamental meanings (i.e., what collective representations) the associations might be caused by (and, therefore, serve as objective indicators of) unless one knows in some way the more immediate (or superficial) meanings of the associations and has some *clearly established means of relating these more superficial meanings to the more fundamental meanings* (i.e., some pre-established means of determining what fundamental meanings the measured, more superficial meanings are indicators of). In his *actual* methods of theoretical analysis it was also, at least implicitly, obvious to Durkheim that one had to know just what the more superficial *meanings* of the associations were before one could tell what more fundamental meanings they were caused by (and, therefore, indicators of). Durkheim's big problem, in this respect, and the one which he seems to have understood least in *Suicide*, was threefold. First, as we have already seen, Durkheim believed that the meanings, both superficial and fundamental, of the associations could not be determined in any way by determining how the individuals involved saw them—i.e., the conscious meanings of the associations to individuals were not theoretically significant. Second, as we have partially seen, Durkheim's methodological position, as developed in *The Division of Labor*, led him to consider juridical norms as the only adequately measurable indicators of the fundamental meanings—for they alone were objective (or thinglike) enough to measure.[95] Third, since the juridical norms were insufficient for

[95] Durkheim could even consider the juridical norms to be quanti-

his analysis in *Suicide* (for the reasons we have already examined), Durkheim was left with no "objective" measures of the superficial meanings involved. In the place of such "objective" measures and the meanings to the individuals involved, he substituted the meanings of the associations to himself as a member of the society and as a social observer. *He relied upon his own common-sense knowledge of social action in European societies to provide most of the superficial meanings of the associations.* Bayet stringently criticized Durkheim for his reliance upon his own common sense to provide the moral meanings associated with suicidal actions:

> I believe that this table partially reproduces the reality. But I also believe that it only partially reproduces the reality. In any case, what is important is that it is necessary to take the author at his word. Where are the practices proving that Protestants "punish the suicide"? In what way is "distance" expressed toward those touched by suicide? What facts permit one to say that "the common morality reproves suicide"? Durkheim did not say. Undoubtedly he is of the opinion that the morality of his time is his and that he knows it. But one can also suppose, without any paradox, that our own morality is in one sense quite unknown to us. From the scientific standpoint, the testimony of the greatest philosopher cannot replace observations submitted to control, to criticism.[96]

Durkheim was, then, using his common-sense understanding of his everyday social experience to provide the most important part of the data to be used to test his theory. He did make many partially controlled observations of the relations between associations and suicide. But, in line with the usual positivistic misunderstanding of statistical data, he believed in general that the data spoke for themselves.[97] It was

---

tative measures of the moral meanings, since he believed it to be a general principle that the severity of punishment (as, for example, specified in years of imprisonment) for violations of the juridical norm was a direct indicator of the strength of moral feeling (or conviction) associated with the normative pattern of behavior.

[96] A. Bayet, *op.cit.*, p. 8.

[97] Morselli had stated the general positivistic bias very well in the following statement:

partially because he did not provide any controls on this voice of the statistics that the voice became that of his own common-sense understanding of social action and spoke so strongly in support of his general theory.

One could provide any number of further examples of Durkheim's reliance upon his common-sense understanding of European social action to interpret his statistics on associations and suicide. One worth mentioning is his interpretation of the different relations between non-marriage, marriage, and suicide rates for men and women. When Durkheim invoked the supposed differences between the masculine mind and the feminine mind to explain the less "constraining" effect on women of marriage, he was merely following the established practice among students of suicide. Morselli had argued, for example, that men are, by their nature, much more subject to "egoistical motives" than women:

As to other causes (physical and moral) the greatest excess of men is found in the group of vices, in that of financial embarrassments, and in weariness of life, that is to say, amongst the egoistical motives, whilst among women, after mental diseases, there predominate passions, domestic troubles, shame and remorse (especially in cases of illegitimate pregnancy). Among the causes which urge them to leave this life woman always exhibits that spirit

Statistics may be compared to a two-edged weapon, murderous to the inexperienced or malicious who wishes to use it in his own fashion; and so in the observation and classification of their data it is necessary to bring to bear practice, moderation, and prudence. It is always easy to lay down laws and then model one's own researches upon them and make facts bend to our own preconceptions and *a priori* reasoning. This Procrustean bed is not suitable to a science of observation which studies objective phenomena. Let us then have facts first and derive our laws from them afterwards, which, however, is not always easy or possible. We therefore divide this book into two parts, the analytical and the synthetic, believing with Newton that the "investigatio rerum ea methodo quoe vocatur analytica semper antecedere debeat eam quos appellature synthetica."

(Morselli, *Suicide: An Essay in Comparative Moral Statistics*, pp. 11-12.)
Durkheim would have done well to more carefully heed the cautions in this statement.

of self-denial, that delicacy of feeling and of love, which inspire all her acts.[98]

Durkheim did not dispute the greater egoistic suicide rate of men. Largely working with the same statistics on family associations and suicide that Morselli used, Durkheim found about the same statistical relations and, working in the same theoretical tradition, he agreed, in his own way, that the difference was man's greater egoism. But he then supplies a completely contrary (and very complex) common-sense interpretation of this supposedly greater masculine egoism, an interpretation that happens to fit all of the details of his own theory:

> This is also why woman can endure life in isolation more easily than man. When a widow is seen to endure her condition much better than a widower and desires marriage less passionately, one is led to consider this case in dispensing with the family a mark of superiority; it is said that woman's affective faculties, being very intense, are easily employed outside the domestic circle, while her devotion is indispensable to man to help him endure life. Actually, if this is her privilege it is because her sensibility is rudimentary rather than highly developed. As she lives outside of community existence more than man, she is less penetrated by it; society is less necessary to her because she is less impregnated with sociability. She has few needs in this direction and satisfies them easily. With a few devotional practices and some animals to care for, the old unmarried woman's life is full. If she remains faithfully attached to religious traditions and thus finds ready protection against suicide, it is because these very simple social forms satisfy all her needs. Man, on the contrary, is hard beset in this respect. As his thought and activity develop, they increasingly overflow these antiquated forms. But then he needs others. Because he is a more complex social being, he can maintain his equilibrium only by finding more points of support outside himself, and it is because his moral balance depends on a larger number of conditions that it is more easily disturbed.[99]

[98] *Ibid.*, p. 305.   [99] *Suicide*, pp. 215-216.

Even when he was aware of common-sense interpretations that were completely contrary to his own, he continued to use common-sense interpretations with complete confidence. *The only plausible explanation seems to be that he assumed the whole theory to be true, so any particulars must necessarily fit—if only the theorist will look around for the "right" interpretation.*

If we look at the simplest structure of Durkheim's theory, we can see how easy it was for him to think that the statistical relations spoke for themselves. In its simplest terms there are only three interrelated sets of factors in Durkheim's theory of suicide: the suicide rates, the statistics on associations and other group properties, and the fundamental causes of these two factors. (See Figure I.)

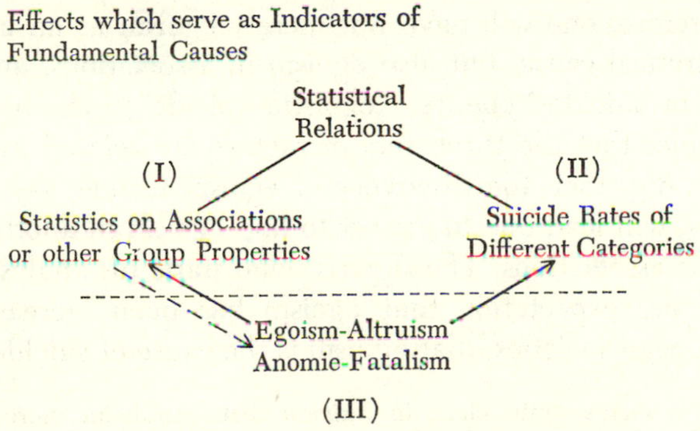

Effects which serve as Indicators of
Fundamental Causes

Statistical
Relations

(I)   (II)

Statistics on Associations   Suicide Rates of
or other Group Properties   Different Categories

Egoism-Altruism
Anomie-Fatalism

(III)

Figure I. Simplest Structure of Durkheim's Theory

Now, as we have seen, Durkheim knew pretty well what the statistical relations between I and II were before he started his work. He also expected that at least the general factors of egoism, anomie, and social equilibrium were in some way the causes of suicide and of other social phenomena (at least of *changes* in such factors as social associations). Several general aspects of Durkheim's method of analysis then seem to have led him to read into the data meanings to support his theory. The most important was his failure to provide any clear and distinct definitions of the theoretical concepts (of egoism, etc.). Next, and this is very clearly related to the problem of definitions, was his failure to provide any guidelines for operationalizing the theoretical concepts, while nevertheless actually operationalizing them.[100] Once Durkheim had failed to provide these definitions, he was free not only to move backwards from the data to the meanings of the data, but he was also free, within certain loose bounds of common sense, to invoke whatever meanings he wanted. The third critical aspect of Durkheim's method of analysis that led him to read in the common-sense meanings that would support his theory was his implicit assumption that effects of the same cause will have morphological similarities, not only with each other but with the cause as well. That is, for example, if certain suicides and certain associations are caused (at least in part) by, say, egoism, then one will be able to observe egoism not only as the force acting on suicides and associations but also within associations and suicides themselves.[101] Therefore, one will have not merely egoism as an abstract theoretical cause, but also egoism in associations, and egoism in suicides (hence, "egoistic suicide"). If, then, one assumes that the three sets of factors are related as Durkheim did, then the discovery of egoism in one, say in suicides, will lead one to expect to find egoism in another, say in the associations. The theorist who starts his analysis with a strong expectation that egoism has been increasing in European societies, that egoism is the cause of suicides, that

[100] It seems quite clear in *Suicide* that Durkheim more or less assumed the meaning of such concepts as egoism to be already known, so any European reader could be expected to recognize egoism when he saw it. It is probably for such a reason that he considered operational definitions unnecessary. We have previously seen that in his definition of "suicide" Durkheim first rejected the common-sense meanings of the term, yet went on to assume implicitly that the term suicide has a meaning independent of the theorist's definition which the theorist must get at (or discover). The same process seems to be at work in his later considerations of the general meanings of egoism-altruism and anomie-fatalism. The only plausible explanation seems to be that he thought of all of these terms as referring to fundamental *substances* (or *essences*). Only this would seem to explain why most peoples' interpretations of the terms are incorrect and yet they have meanings independent of the theorist which he must think out in some way. This verbal realism (or substantialist way of thinking) was merely one more aspect of Durkheim's general Aristotelian way of thinking. (For further consideration of this Aristotelianism, see Appendix I.)

[101] One can see rather clearly here that egoism is merely a substance (or an essence) which the three sets of factors *partake* in.

associations are causally related to these two factors, and whose analysis involves the three aspects just outlined is very likely to see egoism in his data on social associations.

Critical Summary of Suicide

Because of the central role Durkheim's work has played in most recent sociological works on suicide, it is important that certain crucial aspects of its influence and failings be briefly summarized and emphasized apart from the multitude of considerations that have gone into this chapter.

It is clear that Durkheim's general purpose, one might say his philosophical purpose, in writing *Suicide* was to demonstrate that sociology can, should, and must be an independent science of the universe of human action. *Suicide* was, then, first and foremost, intended to be a lethal weapon in a great, though limited, intellectual war of the late nineteenth and early twentieth centuries. As such, it must be expected to bear many of the stigmata of ideological warfare. And it does. There is the highly argumentative approach to alternative theories, which in places goes to the extreme of redefining the enemy's position so that it will be easier to overwhelm. There is the idealization of his own method to make it appear scientifically pure, with little or no consideration of the actual method used to arrive at and test the theory. There is the strong assertiveness about the truth of his own theory, which led Durkheim to gloss over any difficulties of definition without noting the existence of any such difficulties, to deny the validity of any evidence contradictory to his own theory, and to conceal through silence the great inadequacies of the evidence he used to support his own theory.

However, though *Suicide* was intended to be a weapon, and though many of its crucial faults are directly attributable to this intention, it must be kept in mind that *Suicide* was intended to be a weapon primarily by demonstrating, not by arguing abstractly. Durkheim believed that the need for an independent discipline of sociology could only be proved by specific demonstrations and he intended *Suicide* to be just that. However, contrary to much of the impression fostered by Durkheim's positivistic rhetoric, this demonstration was not and could not be in the "facts" about suicide to be considered in the work. For one thing, the "facts" about suicide and the relations between suicide and various other social variables (such as family membership variables, church affiliation, education) were almost all established by previous works that did not purport to be sociological and which Durkheim did not consider to be sociological. The demonstration would have to be in the *general theoretical analysis* of such "facts" and relations.

The general structure of Durkheim's theory of suicide is roughly that schematized in Figure II.

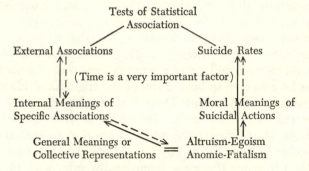

EXTERNAL SYSTEM

Tests of Statistical
Association

External Associations   Suicide Rates

(Time is a very important factor)

Internal Meanings of   Moral Meanings of
Specific Associations   Suicidal Actions

General Meanings or   Altruism-Egoism
Collective Representations   Anomie-Fatalism

(The solid arrows represent the directions of strong causal effects, the broken arrows the directions of weaker causal effects that have a stronger effect as the time of operation is increased.)

Figure II. More Detailed Structure of Durkheim's Theory of Suicide.

Early in *Suicide* Durkheim seems to be concerned primarily with the statistical relations between suicide rates and the rates of external associations (or categories of education, etc.), so that the work is still very much in the vein of Durkheim's positivistic theorizing in terms of morphological variables in *The Division of Labor*. But as the work develops it becomes clearer that he assumes these external associations to be significant only in so far as they are caused by (hence, are indexes of) the meanings involved in (or communicated in) the interactions of the persons taking part in the associations and in so far as they partially cause, at least over the long run, the meanings involved in the associations. Furthermore, Durkheim argues, these meanings of specific associations and the normative meanings of suicidal actions are significant in this way only in so far as they are caused by (hence, are indexes of) very general shared meanings of the given society, meanings which we have taken the liberty of calling collective representations even though Durkheim did not clearly develop this idea until his later works. Durkheim argued that there were two dimensions of polar-opposite forces in dynamic equilibrium in any society that are of primary importance in causing suicide, when their equilibrium is broken or shifted to a new level, and in causing the meanings of the external associations. He did not believe these fundamental meanings could be measured or even shown to exist directly. They are perhaps best looked at today as being largely intervening variables justified only by their ability to help tie together or synthesize a mass of predictive hypotheses; but Durkheim thought of them as being non-directly observable "things" with Aristotelian causal force. The reason for the statistically significant covariance of suicide rates and some rates of external associations is that both are caused by the same interaction of fundamental forces or collective representations.

Besides being out of line with twentieth-century scientific thought, Durkheim's general theory has the great fault of being adjustable in such a way as to be irrefutable. As we have argued in this chapter, Durkheim is extremely careful in trying to show exact, empirical, quantitative relations between suicide rates and rates of external associations. But when it comes to showing that the significant associations between these two sets of variables are due to some specific underlying meanings that are themselves caused by the fundamental forces (collective representations), then he merely assumes the meanings to be those that best fit his theory. He assumes the meanings that are operating in any given association to be self-evident, at least to himself, so that he does not have to provide any evidence for them. (These are generally his *petitio principii* in *Suicide*.) Moreover, Durkheim did not provide specific enough theoretical and operational definitions of his fundamental forces to make it possible to establish any adequate systematic criteria for deciding when one force is acting and when it is not.

All of these faults become more significant when we know, as I have tried to show in the beginning of this chapter, that Durkheim brought his general causal forces (his collective representations) to *Suicide*, rather than arriving at them after careful consideration of the evidence.

In view of all of this it would be unjustified to believe that Durkheim successfully demonstrated what he thought he had and what so many since have believed he did. Yet *Suicide* remains the best sociological work on suicide, primarily because of the *ideal* of scientific investigation of social phenomena which it is built on and because in the final analysis it broke with the positivistic tradition of research on suicide, the tradition which was so antithetical to the treatment of suicide as actions caused by social meanings.

PART II · THE POST-DURKHEIMIAN
SOCIOLOGICAL THEORIES OF SUICIDE

En fermant [Durkheim's Suicide] plus d'un lecteur, surtout plus d'un lecteur philosophe, a sans doute eu le sentiment que le problème du suicide ne se posait plus, et qu'on en connaissait désormais la solution. Est-ce la dialectique, sont-ce les statistiques qui emportaient la conviction? L'un et l'autre sans qu'on sût bien toujours distinguer ce qui était l'un et ce qui était l'autre. Quelquefois la dialectique plus que les faits, non par la faute de Durkheim, d'ailleurs. Mais cela présentait plus d'un inconvénient. On ne s'apercevait pas que l'édifice reposait sur des fondements qui n'étaient point partout aussi solides. Comment en eût-il été autrement? Il n'y a pas d'oeuvre scientifique que de nouvelles expériences n'obligent à réviser et compléter.

MAURICE HALBWACHS,
LES CAUSES DU SUICIDE

INTRODUCTION TO THE
POST-DURKHEIMIAN THEORIES

Durkheim's classic work was the last of the works on suicide to attempt to consider and solve most of the basic problems of the study and theory of suicide as a social phenomenon. Halbwachs' work is the only sociological work since that of Durkheim to even reconsider a number of the fundamental problems treated in Durkheim's *Suicide*. Some of the work done by sociologists in these many years has been of very high quality. Certainly Bayet's empirical study of suicide and social norms is a great work; and Halbwachs' work is a worthy successor to that of Durkheim. But compared with Durkheim's *Suicide* most of them have been more or less superficial and fragmentary, rather than fundamental and inclusive.

Perhaps Durkheim's work was itself the primary determinant of this course of events. *Suicide* has been too much of a challenge. Being so extensive and inclusive, it defied attempts at encompassment. Being in many ways a *tour de force* welding together disparate ideas and data, rather than a systematic and consistent work, it has been difficult to systematically criticize, test, and go beyond. And, being one of the seminal works in the formation of the academic discipline of sociology, it has been something of a sacred object, the status of which seemed better fitted by praise and emulation than criticism and revision.

As a result, most of the sociological works on suicide have been influenced by *Suicide*, even when the influence has simply been that of shaping the exposition so that it will be seen to fit under the broad reach of *Suicide*. This has generally resulted in these works having some obvious similarities and redundancies. But it has also resulted in different theories being added to the stem as appendages without consideration of the fundamental problems involved in either the stem or the appendage. The ultimate result has been the transmission of the stem and the proliferation of the appendages in a relatively unoriginal and unsystematic fashion.

Consequently, we cannot review these works on suicide in terms of certain fundamental categories and relations common to all. Instead, it has seemed necessary to consider each theory independently. Only a careful presentation and criticism of each system (or partial system) of theory seems to avoid the same theoretic parochialism shown by most of these theorists and leads to an inductive comprehension of the basic categories and relations involved in these works.

This does not, of course, mean that there can be no system to these criticisms. On the contrary, though it is my firm conviction that only a critical treatment of each major work as an *independent* work can constitute an adequate review of previous studies of suicide, still these works do have common weaknesses. We shall consider these major weaknesses along with the contributions of these earlier works in Chapter 11 and in Part III we shall attempt to unravel the significance of the almost exclusive reliance by these sociologists upon official statistics for their data on suicide. But to prevent confusion it seems important at this stage to provide the reader with the general criteria according to which these earlier works are criticized.

First, there are the many criticisms of these works that are founded on the generally shared criteria for "adequacy" (not simply "validity") of scientific works in general. In this respect the fundamental question is that of the adequacy of the information used to construct and test theories. The "empirical" evidence upon which the sociological theories of suicide have been constructed and tested has consisted almost entirely of the official statistics on suicide. Thus, a fundamental question to be considered in analyzing the adequacy of these theories is that of the adequacy of these official statistics. In fact, this question is so important and its answer so significant for any consideration of the adequacy of these sociological theories of suicide that all of Part III is devoted to answering it. In so doing I have considered in detail what seems to me to be the fundamental weakness of all but a few of these works on suicide. But I have also attempted in this criticism to show how we should empirically investigate suicidal phenomena, a theme which will be carried through in much greater detail in Part IV.

Besides the generally shared errors of induction these works can also be shown to have many errors of induction and deduction (or analysis) that are peculiar to a single work or to a few works that take a particular approach. These questions are of importance in considering the adequacy of each work. Consequently, much of this Part II will be devoted to such considerations.

Secondly, it is important to consider the adequacy of previous works in terms of the best alternative theoretical approach. As the alternative theoretical approach one *might* attempt to present a formal theory, the propositions of which could be shown to generate better predictions in terms of the best available data on the realm of phenomena covered by the theory. My aim, however, is quite different. One of the fundamental propositions of my argument is that almost all previous sociological works on suicide have used data (official statistics) on suicide which were inadequate for the theoretical purposes of the works; they implicitly assumed that these statistics reliably represented one thing, while actually these statistics represent many things (or, better, are the end product of many complicated social processes) and should not be assumed to represent even these things reliably. Consequently, the alternative offered could not be of the nature of a theory that better *predicts this given* set of data.

There is another reason why the alternative proposed here cannot be one that simply attempts to predict or explain the data used by previous sociological investigations of suicide. Through my investigations of official statistics on suicide and of individual case reports it became increasingly clear that suicidal phenomena in the Western world are not what sociologists have previously assumed them to be. Most important, it became quite clear that concrete suicidal phenomena do not have clear and sufficient cultural definitions in the Western world. After recognizing a number of discrepancies between the fundamental assumptions of the sociological theories and the nature of the real world phenomena it seemed clear that there was a basic weakness behind these particular weaknesses—that of *the deductive hypothetical approach*. Following Durkheim's example, sociologists had studied suicidal phenomena by defining them, implicitly assuming that the operational definitions used by officials in collecting statistics were the same as their own definitions, assuming that some general theoretical approach was correct, making hypotheses from this theoretical approach about the official statistics, and then testing to see if the statistical data validated the hypotheses. (This, of course, was the ideal behind these works. In fact, however, there is every reason to believe that the theorists almost always knew the statistical "evidence" before constructing or "deducing" any hypotheses.)

The idea that this hypothetical approach is at the root of most of the important weaknesses of the earlier sociological works on suicide leads to the assumption underlying the proposed alternative I will be making: namely, that we should begin *as far as is possible* with a study of the real world phenomena, above all with a study of the meanings of these phenomena to the social participants. Rather than giving *ad hoc* (or one's own common sense) definitions to the phenomena or taking as the definitions the unknown but assumed definitions of some unseen officials, we should begin by trying to determine the meanings of such phenomena to the people actually involved. If we are at some point to provide formal definitions, they should come only after a thorough study of the real-world patterns of actions and meanings. Making this assumption and, thereby, beginning to develop the alternative approach proposed in Part IV seems justified on several grounds: the many weaknesses of the other approaches; the presumed value of a scientific strategy of sticking very closely to observation, description, and measurement in the early stages of studying any realm of phenomena; a general expectation that *social meanings* will prove to be the critical factors in the scientific study of human actions; and the apparent value of the proposed alternative in yielding empirical generalizations, low-level theoretical generalizations (if we should distinguish between these two), and clearly defined theoretical and empirical problems whose solutions seem to promise far greater advances along the same lines. It is precisely because the proposed alternative is justified in these terms that the previous sociological works on suicide are, for the most part, to be criticized in these terms. However, since these criticisms are much less certain than the types previously mentioned, much of the burden of criticizing the earlier works must fall on the earlier types of criticisms rather than on these general justifications of the proposed alternative.

THE GIBBS AND MARTIN STATUS
INTEGRATION THEORY OF SUICIDE

Gibbs and Martin, unlike many other sociologists who have published works on suicide, clearly recognized the ambiguities in Durkheim's treatment of "social integration" and the consequent lack of rigorous tests by Durkheim of his theory of suicide.

At no point in Durkheim's monograph is there an explicit connotative definition of social integration, much less an operational definition. It is not surprising then that there is not a single measure of social integration correlated with suicide rates. Without the specification of the empirical referents for the concept and the operations used in measuring its prevalence, Durkheim's proposition is supported not by its predictive power but by his forceful argument in its defense. Thus, Durkheim's theory is incomplete; and it is to its development that the theory of status integration refers.[1]

---

[1] Jack P. Gibbs and Walter T. Martin, "A Theory of Status Integration and Its Relationship to Suicide," *American Sociological Review*, 23 (April, 1958), pp. 140-147.

It should be clear from the earlier discussion of Durkheim's *Suicide* that Durkheim did in fact give a number of connotative definitions of "social integration." The problem is really that he gave a few too many with conflicting meanings. Since the meaning of "operational" is generally vague in sociology, it is not clear whether this part of the above statement is true or not. I would argue, however, that Durkheim's many analyses of data certainly contain a clear, implicit operationalization of "social integration," though I would further argue that he could not operationalize the many different theoretical statements in a unitary fashion because they conflicted with each other. Gibbs and Martin are right about vagueness, but for the wrong reasons. (This chapter was completed before the appearance of Jack P. Gibbs and Walter T. Martin, *Status Integration and Suicide*, Eugene: University of Oregon Press, 1964. It has been left as it was because the book follows the original argument in all essentials. By using data from other countries some of the difficulties are actually compounded.)

It is, then, to the correction of this supposed lack of testing of Durkheim's theory of suicide that Gibbs and Martin direct their work. As a result, the Gibbs and Martin theory of suicide is quite similar to Durkheim's theory. The similarity consists specifically in the consideration of suicide rates relative to officially defined social categories with only implicit consideration of any significant personality or individual factors. In this respect it is contrary to almost all of the sociological works that have been done on suicide since Durkheim's work and has special importance for our purposes.

Gibbs and Martin concluded that Durkheim's concept of "social integration" would be best operationalized as the "stability and durability of social relationships" within a population.[2] But they believed that there was no evidence available on the stability and durability of social relationships, so they proposed to "utilize observable conditions that presumably reflect these characteristics."[3]

By "observable conditions" Gibbs and Martin were not proposing that sociologists study real cases of suicide or even that they read case descriptions by people who have observed real-world suicides.[4] They proposed to observe *role (or status) conflict*, which they assumed to be the fundamental determinant of the stability and durability of social relationships within a population.[5]

Gibbs and Martin, however, then decided that observing the degree of role conflict is impossible. So they decided

[2] *Ibid.*, p. 141. Gibbs and Martin give no indications as to why the "volume" or extent of relationships (the frequency of contacts, etc.) should not be considered part of the operational definition of "social integration." It is obviously of fundamental significance in Durkheim's implicit operationalization of "social integration." And most sociologists have tended to consider it a fundamental index of "social integration" regardless of the specific problem they were concerned with.

[3] *Ibid.*, p. 141.

[4] In his most recent statement on the matter Gibbs has taken a somewhat more lenient attitude toward the study of individual cases of suicide, though his position seems to have changed only to the extent that, following his work on social mobility and suicide in New Zealand, he is now ready to accept studies of status-careers as socially significant. (See Jack P. Gibbs, "Suicide," in Robert K. Merton and Robert A. Nisbet, *Contemporary Social Problems*, New York: Harcourt, Brace and World, Inc., 1961, p. 259.)

[5] Gibbs and Martin, *op.cit.*, p. 141.

that ". . . it is necessary to shift from the current emphasis on the psychological dimensions of role to its sociological correlate—the concept of status."[6] They did not in any way define "status," but their usage of the term was precisely the same as their usage of the term "role," *except* that Gibbs and Martin seemed to identify status with the usual social categories employed by officials—age, sex, occupation, marital status, etc. At least, these are the only actual kinds of status referred to in the work. Thus, they shifted from the theoretical concept of "role" to the word-labels of officials, called "status" by Gibbs and Martin and "justified" by sociologistic word formulas, without any fundamental consideration of the sociologistic position.

Gibbs and Martin then argued that the more role-conflict there is in a group, the less frequently the two roles will be occupied by a given individual, or the less often one will find the two status labels attached to him by officials. This "extent of association in the occupancy of statuses is referred to as the degree of *status integration*."[7]

The basic idea, then, is that the greater the role conflict of a given combination of roles or statuses (called a "status configuration" by Gibbs and Martin), the more frequently an individual will change to another status configuration. Thus the relative lack of occupancy of a status configuration shows how much role or status conflict there is in that configuration.

The picture one gets from the Gibbs and Martin presentation[8] is that of a role configuration filled with conflict so that individuals tend to leave it and, when for some reason they can't, they leave life by means of suicide (at least they do so with more frequency than others with less role conflict). But there actually is little justification for this interpretation of the theory. It is quite compatible with the theory to argue that the status configuration is occupied to a low degree because society demands that people not move into that configuration. For example, is not the status configuration of unmarried mother relatively (to that of married

6 *Ibid.*, p. 142.
7 Jack P. Gibbs, "Suicide," in *Contemporary Social Problems*, p. 157.
8 For a formal statement of their postulates see Gibbs and Martin, *op.cit.*, p. 143.

mother) infrequently occupied precisely because society demands that one not join it rather than that society makes conflicting demands once one is in? Gibbs and Martin seem to have implicitly assumed that there is equally free entry into and out of a status configuration. Consequently, they do not consider the rather obvious possibility that a status configuration might be occupied infrequently not because of a conflict of roles once one is in the configuration, but because for normative or other reasons the society (or the officials) restrict entry just as society can restrict exit. Officials can, for example, restrict exit entirely—e.g., there may be no divorced people because there is no divorce.

Even if, however, we were to accept the argument that status integration indexes can give us some worthwhile measures of normative conflict (in status configurations), we would not be able to agree that a status integration index is an index of the general durability and stability of social relationships in a given society. It is a *static* index of an individual's role occupancies, not any measure (even very indirect) of an individual's relations over time. Thus, unfortunately, the Gibbs and Martin theory of suicide does not actually offer a test, good or bad, of *their* interpretation of Durkheim's theory of social integration and suicide.

But this does not mean that the Gibbs and Martin theory is contrary to the fundamental idea of Durkheim's theory of suicide. In one way the Gibbs and Martin theory is more consistent with Durkheim's sociologistic ideas than was Durkheim. We have seen that in certain respects Durkheim did consider individual factors and microcultural meanings to have causal effect on the individual's suicidal actions (or, perhaps, it would be better to say on his non-suicidal actions). But Gibbs and Martin do not consider what effects role configuration conflicts might have on individuals that lead to their committing suicide. There is no mention of how role configuration conflict might be related to anything on the level of individual action. We are presented only with an abstract argument concerning the "conflict"[9] of sets of norms; we are told that this conflict is assumed to be adequately indexed by the relative frequencies of occupa-

[9] There is no definition of "role conflict" in any of the works on the status integration theory of suicide.

tion or non-occupation of given sets of norms (or official labels of supposedly existing sets of norms).[10] And then we are told that suicide rates will be significantly, inversely correlated with this index (i.e., status integration). We are not told that there exists any causal relationship, very likely because this would imply some direct action of existing things upon other existing things and without some kind of collective consciousness or individual personality there is nothing for these undefined normative conflicts (as properly indexed by status integration) to act upon to produce supposedly probabilistic actions such as suicide.[11]

But, before we get taken up with such rational, *a priori* criticism of Gibbs and Martin's work, let us remember that Gibbs and Martin criticize their predecessors almost entirely on the basis of not having produced theories that generate hypotheses that can be tested adequately with available data. This is their primary claim to significance for their own work. Indeed, Gibbs and Martin actually reject such *a priori* criticisms as these: "Once formulated, however, the modification of a theory should be based on its empirical shortcomings rather than on purely *a priori* theoretical objections."[12] Let us consider, then, the empirical basis for their own theory, that is, the adequate testing of the hy-

[10] Gibbs and Martin give no indication that the official labeling of role occupants might be different from the imputations of roles by the egos or the significant alters involved. It is clear, for example, that the official estimates of the number of marriages in a given state would be quite different from the actual number of imputed marriages, which would normally include common-law and lengthy cohabitation marriages.

One of the unfortunate consequences of the Durkheimian sociologistic approach to the study of suicide seems to be the assumption that one must look only at the big picture, which means looking only at official statistics and not considering what they might mean. There is the ever-implicit assumption, stated so clearly by Morselli, that "a corpse is a corpse." As I shall argue at great length in Part III, the big picture given by official statistics is a false image.

[11] Action at a distance might seem to be a good preliminary assumption for a theory dealing with physical bodies at great distances from each other and with no perceptible substance between them. But such an assumption seems hardly justified when one is dealing with "social norms" found by examining individuals and their concrete actions.

[12] Gibbs and Martin, *op.cit.* Actually, of course, their own criticism of Durkheim is completely *a priori*. They never attempt to show their theory to be empirically more true.

potheses generated (after many questionable deductive steps) by their own theory.[13]

First, no significant tests are presented in any form. Gibbs and Martin did publish two "demonstration tests" or, rather, the results of such tests. They computed the status integration measures for the statuses of occupation, age, sex, and color in the populations of thirty states in the United States and then correlated these status integration measures with the respective suicide rates. They reported that they got a coefficient of correlation of —.37. Their own conclusions regarding the "adequacy" of this test seems correct:

> It should be pointed out in connection with this test that these populations are not actual societies and that the measure of integration suffers a serious handicap. The measure is based on employed persons in the labor force while the suicide rate pertains to the total population. Particularly in the case of females, there may be a sizeable discrepancy between these two categories.[14]

Most importantly, one certainly would not want to call the American states "societies." One cannot expect sex roles, age roles, and color roles to be normatively defined in any uniform way in any given state. For one thing, Halbwach's criticism that such studies overlook the basic distinction between rural and urban ways of life, is quite appropriate here.

It is also important to note, as Gibbs and Martin do not, that there is no reason to expect that the measure of status

---

[13] It is unfortunate that Gibbs and Martin begin (pp. 143-144) the discussion of the testing of their own theory with a statement that undermines all of their earlier criticisms of Durkheim, *et al.*, and opens their work to their own criticisms:

> There are numerous difficulties involved in attempting to develop a measure of the degree of status integration in a population. One major problem is inadequate data. There is no existing source, in fact, for the type of data that would be needed for an ideal test of the major theorem. The dangers of using inadequate data for testing the theorem include the possibility that negative results may stem from inadequacies of the data rather than from a lack of validity in the theory. The availability of data, however, cannot be permitted to determine theory.

It seems best, however, to overlook this general statement and simply consider Gibbs and Martin's actual tests.

[14] Gibbs and Martin, *ibid.*, p. 146.

integration gotten from statuses will represent the over-all, average measure of status integration that would be gotten from considering all the statuses (or even some reasonably large number of them) of any society. The number of possible combinations rapidly becomes immense.

The second demonstration case presented by Gibbs and Martin is more instructive of the inadequacy of the testing of the theory and, most likely, of the theory itself. Gibbs and Martin presented their findings from this second test in the following manner:

> These frequencies represent the proportion of males 60-64 years of age in the United States in 1950 who occupied each marital status. The marital statuses and proportions ranked by size are married (.793), widowed (.096), single (.086), and divorced (.025). The corresponding average annual suicide rates for 1949-1951 are 36.2, 64.7, 76.4, and 111.1. Thus, without exception, the rank order of the status integration measure representing the integration of marital status and age predicts the rank order of the suicide rate: there is a consistent inverse relationship.[15]

If we translate these conclusions back into the theoretical statements of the work, we would conclude, for one thing, that American males aged 60-64 years who are widowed have more suicide than American males aged 60-64 who are married precisely because there is more normative conflict between the statuses of the widowed American male, aged 60-64, than there is between the statuses of the married American male, aged 60-64. Now, surely no one would deny that the former status configuration is less blessed (or more unhappy) than the latter status configuration. But where is there any normative conflict between these three statuses of male, aged 60-64, and widowed? Gibbs and Martin have not, like many other sociologists, considered the meanings of the role to be *problematic*: but they have gone most others one better by implicitly assuming the role has to mean whatever it must in order to support their theory. They use the label as being equivalent to the role in terms of norms. Next, if the role is a member of a set of roles associated (by populations) with a suicide rate greater than

[15] *Ibid.*, p. 147.

is another set of roles, then that role must be more con-
flictful with the other members of its set than are the roles
of the second set with each other.[16] There is, then, a great
gap, such as we found in Durkheim's *Suicide*, between their
theoretical argument and their specific, generated hypotheses, so that there is plenty of room for fitting the
findings to the theory.

The Gibbs and Martin status integration theory of suicide
is interesting because it is one of the only works on suicide
that is a theoretical extension of Durkheim's sociologistic
theory of suicide. It does not, however, seem to be a very
successful extension of the theory: it suffers from just about
all of the faults of Durkheim's work and has many of its
own. (It is obvious that this theory is not as predictive as
Durkheim's, if for no other reason than that it has such a
tight focus.) Certainly the theory has not been successfully
tested—even the supposed demonstrations are quite dam-
aging to one's hope for the theory.

[16] This second demonstration test is presented as though it were a
surprise to the authors. Actually, a general knowledge of sociology is
all one needs to know the relative frequencies of occupation of these
role configurations and the associated suicide frequencies. One would,
then, know that this second demonstration case would support the
status integration theory before he started. So we have the same
problem we found in Durkheim's *Suicide*. Predictions one knows to
be true before he makes them are very suspicious, especially when the
author can *adjust* the theory to be sure of making the right predictions.

POWELL'S STATUS AND ANOMIE
THEORY OF SUICIDE

Powell's theory of suicide,[1] like almost all of the more recent sociological works on suicide, is placed firmly in the tradition of Durkheim's *Suicide*, at least by the general intentions expressed. Powell does add a socio-psychological theory, derived largely from Erich Fromm, but for the most part Powell's fundamental ideas about suicide are consistent with Durkheim's general approach to suicide. This general consistency with Durkheim's approach, combined with the socio-psychological addition, puts Powell's theory midway between the sociologistic and the psycho-social theories of suicide.

Compared to most fundamental theories of suicide, Powell's theory is a complex one. Because of this complexity, it is helpful to briefly schematize Powell's ideal theory of suicide. This is done in Figure III.

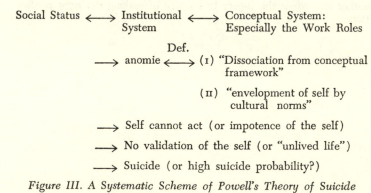

Social Status ⟷ Institutional ⟷ Conceptual System:
                    System   Especially the Work Roles

                        Def.

⟶ anomie ⟷ (I) "Dissociation from conceptual framework"

                        (II) "envelopment of self by cultural norms"

⟶ Self cannot act (or impotence of the self)

⟶ No validation of the self (or "unlived life")

⟶ Suicide (or high suicide probability?)

Figure III. A Systematic Scheme of Powell's Theory of Suicide

[1] Elwin H. Powell, "Occupation, Status, and Suicide: Toward a Redefinition of Anomie," *American Sociological Review*, 23 (April, 1958) pp. 131-139.

As is usually the case with the psycho-social theories of
suicide developed by sociologists, Powell's work considers
the psychological aspects of his theory to be *non-problematic*. It is assumed that individuals kill themselves when
they cannot validate their "selves" through the normally
approved form of status activity—or is it when they can't
"succeed" in their attempts to validate themselves by achiev-
ing occupational-economic "success"? This unexamined assumption is one form of the frustration-leads-to-suicide
theoretical assumption, but it is a very special form of the
general assumption. It assumes that the social "validation"
of the self is an absolutely fundamental goal of human
beings. But, other than telling us that "the self has its being
in the social process,"[2] Powell did not have anything to say
about the nature of the "self" and its relation to such an
(undefined) action as "suicide." Consequently, though
Powell's treatment of the psychological variables included
in his theory is not so commonsensical as the treatment of
the psychological variables in most of the psycho-social
theories of suicide proposed by sociologists (see the section
on status change theories of suicide), still his treatment of
them is not sufficient to allow one to know just what the
"theory" says about real world phenomena, such as real
cases of suicide.

Actually, Powell did not consider concrete cases of suicide
in his theory. In the Durkheimian tradition, he considered
official suicide rates for the social categories of ranked occupations (with some checks on the official designations of
occupations). His statements about the relation of the "in-
validation of self" to suicide include no indication that one
might test them by observing individuals and their actions.
He did not consider it necessary to support psychological assumptions or assumptions about the meanings of social
phenomena, such as "failure," to the social actors.

Powell did attempt to support his arguments regarding
the concentration of the two types of anomie at the two
extremes of the occupational status hierarchy, but not by
providing any evidence (or indication that such evidence
might be necessary) on the actual occupational groups involved in Tulsa, Oklahoma. Instead, he provided evidence

[2] *Ibid.*

about various kinds of status groups in the United States. As usual, there was the implicit assumption that the conceptual systems (the meanings of social statuses) are the same everywhere, an assumption that hardly seems justified in view of the cultural complexity of the country.

In general, Powell committed the same error committed by Durkheim in *Suicide*: he kept his State-Action theory of suicide loose enough to read into statuses whatever meanings he needed to support his general ideas, so that the vague and questionable data of officials on suicide became simply a positivistic justification for some complex theorizing about the nature of man, society, and suicide. One merely takes some theoretical ideas from various sources (especially from Durkheim and Fromm), chooses some official data on suicide, and fits the two together—leaving terms undefined, data unquestioned, and the methods of analysis unclear.

THE ECOLOGICAL THEORIES
OF SUICIDE

The Nature of Ecological Approaches

The ecological approach to the study of human society has been the most distinctive of American sociology. In fact, the approach has been so distinctive and its adherents so committed that two prominent American sociologists have recently argued that the ecological approach is the only fundamental sociological theory which can achieve the goals of all of sociology—i.e., the scientific, systematic analysis of "social organization."[1] This approach has been especially influential in the American works on suicide.

Though it is not relevant here to attempt any thorough analysis of the ecological approach, it will be useful to distinguish three major types of ecological theories. These are best considered in terms of the dominant emphasis of each: (1) the emphasis on the causal dependence of social action on physical environment, especially the city, of the society or social group; (2) the emphasis on the interdependence of social units (especially of populations) as a cause of social action; and (3) the emphasis on the *meanings*, especially the values, involved in social interaction as causes of social action. That is, in each ecological theory we find one of these three causes considered to be the ecological cause itself, though in the case of the number (2) emphasis (interdependence of social units) we find a strong tendency to consider the ecological approach largely as a method of areal analysis rather than explicitly as a cause. Almost all ecological theories include considerations of all three factors, or hypothesized causal relations, but one factor is normally stressed over the other two to such an extent that it becomes very largely identical with *the* ecological approach.

[1] See Otis Dudley Durcan and Leo F. Schnore, "Cultural, Behavioral, and Ecological Perspectives in the Study of Social Organization," *American Journal of Sociology*, 65 (1919), pp. 142-148.

Early Ecological Approaches to Suicide

The analysis of the ecological theories of suicide is complicated by the rather vague, multifactored structure of most of the works in this vein. The analysis is especially complicated by the frequent addition of a behavioristic theory of the "suicide process" to the ecological approach to suicide. We shall attempt to bring order into the seeming chaos of these various ecological approaches to suicide by first presenting the different forms and then proceeding to the relations between the ecological approaches and the situation-personality (i.e., behavioristic) theories of suicide included in many of the ecological works.

The first ecological works on suicide were closely related to other types of ecological studies going on at the University of Chicago. A number of the early works of the Chicago sociologists contained references to the place of suicide in Chicago. But Zorbaugh's study of the "dweller in furnished rooms" was one of the first to clearly relate suicide to physical aspects of the city and to the types of social relations supposedly caused by the physical and population factors of the city:

> In this situation of mobility and anonymity the person is socially isolated. His wishes are thwarted. He finds in the rooming-house neither security, response, nor recognition. He is restless and he is lonely. . . .
>
> The emotional tensions of thwarted wishes force the person to act somehow in this situation. His behavior may take one of three directions: He may find himself unable to cope with the situation, and attempt to withdraw from it. This withdrawal frequently takes the form of suicide. There was a bridge over the lagoon in Lincoln Park, in the heart of the North Side rooming-house district, which was nicknamed "Suicide Bridge" because of people who threw themselves into the lagoon. Because of its sinister reputation the city tore it down. A map of the distribution of suicides on the Lower North Side shows how frequently this seems the only way out to persons of the rooming-house world.
>
> . . . the cold, unsociable atmosphere of the city tends towards increasing morbid introspective tendencies which

finally lead to despair and suicide. It is remarkable how many of such individuals one meets in the psychopathic wards. It is incredible how many of them have for the first time in their lives met a friendly look and encouraging word in the observation ward, having been brought there after an unsuccessful attempt at self-destruction.[2]

Schmid, whose work on suicide was strongly influenced by Zorbaugh's earlier work on life in the great urban areas, agreed with Zorbaugh in his emphasis on the causal importance of the physical and quasi-physical (e.g., "cold, unsociable atmosphere,") environments of the individuals. Schmid, like Zorbaugh, emphasized the suicidogenic effects of the core areas of cities, and further, tried to show that the suicide rate decreases rather steadily as one goes out from the core areas toward the suburbs.

But the emphasis on the physical, ecological causes of suicide is by no means dominant in Schmid's work.[3] Schmid, Cavan, Faris, and most of the other sociologists who took an ecological approach emphasized certain population variables as the dominant causes of social disorganization, which was assumed in turn to cause suicide or suicide rates. The fundamental idea of most of these ecological approaches to suicide was quite simple. Suicide was considered immoral in the Western world. (As we have previously argued, it was assumed implicitly that morality is, for purposes of sociological analysis, the most important cause of social patterns of action.) Anything that produces a decrease in the causal effect of social values (i.e., by definition, any social disorganization[4]) will cause an increase in suicide (i.e., immoral action). The most important causes of social disorganization are the variables of mobility[5] (or is this

---

[2] Quoted in Calvin F. Schmid, *Suicides in Seattle, 1914 to 1925: An Ecological and Behavioristic Study*, Seattle: University of Washington Press, 1928, pp. 20-21.

[3] The most important of Schmid's studies of suicide are the following: *Suicides in Seattle, op.cit.; Suicide in Seattle, Washington, and Pittsburgh, Pennsylvania: A Comparative Study*, Pittsburgh: University of Pittsburgh Bulletin, 27 (1930), pp. 149-157; and "Suicide in Minneapolis, Minnesota: 1928-1932," *The American Journal of Sociology*, XXXIX (1933), 3048.

[4] Quoted from Thomas and Znaniecki by Schmid in *Suicides in Seattle*, p. 12, fn. 11.

[5] Schmid makes the following statement concerning the relation

just an index of the other two variables and thus varies directly with social disorganization?), social anonymity, and the rate of social-relations contact. (The density, absolute size, and complexity of the population would, presumably, be ultimate, social determinants of social anonymity and rates of primary and secondary relations.) Since these variables are the most important causes of social disorganization, which in turn is the most important cause of deviant behavior in general, then they must be the most important causes of suicide.

There is almost no explicit consideration in any of these works of the values and disvalues involved in using an ecological approach to suicide as compared to using some alternative approach. These students of suicide assumed the ecological approach would prove to be the most valuable, presumably because it had been demonstrated by other Chicago School sociologists to be useful. This, however, was not an obviously valid assumption. Park himself had stated that "human (or social) ecology" is a *perspective* rather than a theory and that it is, in large part as a result of its being a perspective, not found to be true by empirical testing, but rather, assumed to be valuable on very general principles.[6]

By failing to carefully consider the tentativeness of their basic theoretical "perspective" and by failing to establish critical tests of the theory, these Chicago students of suicide were able to convince themselves that their unsystematic, multi-factored approaches were really theories and that the evidence supported their theories. The fundamental weakness of their works resulting from this too ready acceptance

---

between social mobility and social disorganization: "It has been clearly shown by a number of studies of urban life that a high rate of mobility is indicative of social disorganization, the degree of disorganization varying more or less directly with the amount of instability of the population." (*Suicides in Seattle*, p. 12.) Presumably, mobility is here considered to be an index of social contact and anonymity, but such theoretical considerations are left quite vague by Schmid and others of the ecological tradition.

[6] See Louis Wirth, "Human Ecology," quoted in *Studies in Human Ecology*, ed. by G. Theodorson, Evanston: Row, Peterson and Co., 1961, pp. 72-73. For a balanced critical review of the Chicago School ecological works see Terence Morris, *The Criminal Area*, London: Routledge and Kegan Paul, 1957, pp. 85-105.

of their basic ideas was their failure to provide any significant supporting evidence for their hypotheses—i.e., that
social disorganization and suicide rates vary directly and,
more importantly, that social disorganization is a cause of
personal disorganization. Cavan and others after her clearly
recognized the nature of the *ecological fallacy* and argued
that it had to be avoided.[7] Cavan and Schmid both presented
extensive and very worthwhile ideas about the relations
between the social variables and the individual variables
causing suicide (see below); and Cavan presented some
secondary evidence regarding individual suicides. But none
of the "ecologists" of suicide presented any evidence to
demonstrate a causal relation between the "group property"
of social disorganization and the suicide rates by showing
that individuals who suffered from social disorganization
were the ones most likely to commit suicide. Cavan's secondary evidence on individual suicides showed merely that
some few individuals who committed suicide were also the
victims of social disorganization. Since she could not get
much worthwhile statistical evidence on individuals who
commit suicide, she had to rely very largely on a descriptive, case study approach. Any descriptive, case study approach to the study of social action faces the grave problem
of determining what cases are representative of the society
(or some part of the society to some degree) and what
cases are not. One can attempt positively to show that his
cases are representative—for example, by showing that
they are taken from a general, clearly perceptible pattern of

---

[7] Cavan made both general and specific references to the dangers
of the "ecological fallacy," though not by that name. The following
criticism of both Durkheim and Morselli involves a clear recognition
of the nature of the fallacy in a very concrete case:

> The lack of agreement between these two writers is not so much
> a matter of difference in statistics as difference in the particular sta
> tistics upon which emphasis is placed. Morselli emphasized the
> ones which supported his point; Durkheim, the ones which sup
> ported his. The value of the statistics in both cases is lessened by
> the fact that no direct relation can be shown between alcoholism
> and suicide. Only a study of actual cases can determine whether
> alcoholism and suicide are linked together. (Ruth S. Cavan, *Suicide*,
> p. 289.)

This statement and similar ones by Cavan do not contain any consideration of the statistical principles involved in the ecological fallacy
argument, but it clearly pinpoints the implications of the argument.

events; or he can try to show negatively that his cases are representative, generally by showing that a thorough search was made and no (or insignificant) negative instances could be found. Since the descriptive, case study approach is generally done as an alternative to rather than in conjunction with a statistical study, it is generally not possible to show positively that one's cases are representative, so one must normally rely on some evidence that the negative instances are relatively insignificant. Cavan and the other ecological theorists of suicide failed to see the need for demonstrating representativeness and, especially, they failed to try to show a lack of negative instances. (There are, in fact, many negative instances.)

Though Cavan attempted to do more with case studies of suicide than others did, her treatment of this data on the individual level cannot be considered to be anything more than suggestive. These early "ecologists" of suicide were, then, guilty of the ecological fallacy even though they recognized the dangers of the fallacy and the way out of it much more than the great majority of other sociologists who have studied suicide.

One other general criticism of these early ecological approaches to suicide is that they are even more subject to the various explanations of their data in terms of the "drift hypothesis" than is Durkheim's theory.[8] In my later chapter on the statistical data on suicide I have tried to show how Schmid himself presented all the evidence necessary to support a "drift" argument (or alternative explanation) against his own tests of his theory. Schmid probably failed to grasp this clearly only because of his prejudgment of the validity of his ecological perspective and because of the unsystematic nature of his presentation of his approach and the evidence used to test it.

[8] One of the major and most effective arguments of Achille-Delmas against Durkheim's theory of suicide is that an explanation of the same data can be given more simply and, he would argue, more in line with specific evidence on cases of suicide by hypothesizing that individuals of unbalanced personality are the ones who tend to commit suicide and that they are peculiarly distributed in societies in terms of their personality nature, such that they will tend to be concentrated in cities, be more educated, more successful in business (because of greater aggression, initiative), etc. (See F. Achille-Delmas, *Psychopathologie du Suicide*, Paris: Felix Alcon, 1937.)

Social Area Approaches to Suicide

The more recent works on suicide involving an ecological approach, of which that by Sainsbury is the most important, interpret the ecological approach largely in terms of *social* (or areal) *analysis*. Sainsbury defined the ecological approach in the following manner:

> The present study of suicide will employ this second, i.e., sociological, approach, by examining the differences in suicide rate in various neighborhoods and social groups in London and interpreting these in terms of their social and cultural structure. The emphasis therefore is ecological, as the spatial distribution of suicides, that is the neighborhood in which they occur, is stressed in relationship to human institutions. To define the ecological concept further, it may be said that the behavior of a population (in this case suicide) is ecologically determined when it is formed by the experience of living in certain areas and alters after quitting them.[9]

Like most of the ecological works on suicide, Sainsbury's is fundamentally a multi-factored approach. The focus of his work is, however, ecological. He considered social disorganization and, thus, the causes of social disorganization, to be quite important in the causation of suicide. But he emphasized the over-all effects of the *characteristic properties of populations* as the most important factors in an ecological study of suicide. In so far as he was concerned with the characteristic properties of populations resulting from interdependencies of the populations, he was still arguing within the general context of the approach used by Cavan, Schmid, Faris, and the other members of the Chicago ecological school. But Sainsbury in fact goes beyond this "neighborhood factor." He carefully considers the relations of such variables as unemployment, poverty, loss of status, etc., to suicide rates of a given population area of the city of London. These variables are grouped by Sainsbury under the general heading of "social status" and he specifically intends to compare the social disorganization and social

[9] Peter Sainsbury, *Suicide in London: An Ecological Study*, London: Chapman and Hall, 1955, p. 11.

status explanations of suicide rates.[10] There is, however, not even a presumption by Sainsbury that "social status" variables have anything to do with the various environmental (or neighborhood) factors that were considered by Cavan and Schmid to be ecological factors. Sainsbury's analysis is simply an analysis of the weightings of certain factors found to be associated with a given geographically (or areally) specified position. But the weighting cannot be shown to be due to this coordinate position on the geographical or social map, as one would have to do if he were to be justified in designating his analysis as "ecological" in the earlier sense of the term. This form of analysis, when divested of its geographical references, becomes an analysis of suicide in terms of social areas, which is merely a grouping of individuals in terms of certain social properties for the purposes of a comparative analysis of the relations between these grouped properties and some other properties.[11]

A *social areas* analysis differs from the earlier form of ecological analysis in that for the former any general population properties associated with neighborhood position (physical or social) is largely irrelevant, and is certainly not considered to be a cause of the association with the other variables. Yet the two have been very generally confused. Moreover, since the social areas type of analysis differs from a social analysis in terms of comparisons of one social category (e.g., occupation) with another only in that a social areas type of analysis compares populations in terms of several categories (i.e., populations are characterized by several variables and then compared with respect to each other), there has been a general tendency for many students of suicide to go so far as to consider a social analysis in terms of comparisons of social categories to be an ecological analysis. This step-by-step progression in the use of the term "ecological" in the works on suicide is what has led to a confusion of what was originally meant by an ecological study of suicide with the more recent social areal

[10] *Ibid.*, p. 19.

[11] The best example of a study of suicide rates that is done quite explicitly in the social areal manner is that by Aubrey Wendling and Kenneth Polk, "Suicide and Social Areas," *The Pacific Sociological Review*, 1 (Fall, 1958), 50-53.

studies of suicide—and even at times to a confusion of the general comparisons of rates (in the Durkheimian tradition) with the ecological and social areal approaches. This verbal confusion certainly cannot form the basis for an adequate presentation or analysis of the theories of suicide, so we shall simply exclude these inappropriately named types of theories or analyses from our considerations of the ecological approaches to suicide.

Individual and Social Variables in the Suicide Process of the Ecological Works on Suicide

We have previously noted that Cavan was quite aware of the dangers of the ecological fallacy in works on suicide that fall within the ecological tradition. She undoubtedly recognized that any description of individuals in terms of the usual sets of social categories, regardless of how complex these sets were made, would always leave one with different probabilities of committing suicide for individuals in different sets of the social categories, rather than with deterministic explanations which would allow predictions of individual suicides. Cavan, like almost all other recent sociologists who have done work on suicide, did not explicitly consider the problem of probabilistic versus deterministic theories, but she seems to have been implicitly opposed to probabilistic explanations of suicidal actions, regardless of how much she used statistical methods of analysis to test her theories. In her view the way to get a deterministic explanation was to give increasing emphasis to the concrete, individual cases.

The nineteenth-century theorists had brought determinism into their theoretical explanations of suicide by introducing a fundamental distinction between *predisposing factors* (i.e., factors that put individuals into high probability categories or sets of categories) and determining or *precipitating factors* (i.e., factors that determined which specific individuals from the high probability categories would be the actual suicides). There was already apparent in this nineteenth-century distinction a tendency to make further distinctions between the more and less immediately precipitating factors, between the factors that in fact merely increased one's probability of suicide and those which finally made it an absolute certainty. (The *analytic induction* approach was the implicit model for this research on suicide, except that there seems to have been no attempt to show how one could ever establish any generalizations about the immediately precipitating factors. These were always treated as highly individualistic, dependent on a mass of circumstantial factors peculiar to each individual. Because of this, no theory of suicide treated it as completely deterministic and there was always the implication that one could not hope to completely predict individual cases of suicide.)

Cavan carried this process forward by arguing that there is a whole process involved in the causation of suicide. This process, her basic model for theory construction, was not really a continuum, but it contained far more stages of causal explanation than the basically two-step models of the nineteenth-century theorists. In Cavan's model there were three stages of critical importance in the causal explanation of suicidal actions. (This number was increased by Schmid's model, which was built on Cavan's basic model. First, Cavan believed that the general socio-cultural system was of fundamental importance in the causal process of suicide. It seemed clear to her that the normative definition of the suicidal action given by the general cultural system and expressed in various social responses was significant in the causal process. Most important in this respect was the supposedly general negative definition of the act of suicide in Western societies (contrasted by Cavan with the frequently positive definition of suicidal actions in Oriental societies).[12] It is this negative normative definition of suicide that led Cavan, Schmid, Faris, *et al.*, to conclude that social disorganization must be of critical significance in the etiology of suicide in Western societies:

> It is obvious from the foregoing [considerations of various normative definitions of suicide in non-Western societies] that the prevalence of suicide is not in itself necessarily an indication of social disorganization, and in fact it seems more likely that in some cases it would mean a very effective control of its members by the society. In our Western civilization, however, suicide is

[12] Ruth S. Cavan, *Suicide*, pp. 56-76.

contrary to mores and law, and most cases of suicide are instances of individual decisions to withdraw from responsibilities of living by violation of these principles. Suicide therefore usually reflects a failure of social control over the behavior of the person, and, as will be shown in the remaining parts of the chapter, is connected with various indications of individualism and detachment. It is therefore, in our society, clearly a phenomenon of social disorganization. Our society contains various mechanisms to prevent suicide and to instill in its members the will and the sense of obligation to live out the natural span of life, and suicide reflects failure in such mechanisms.[13]

The general socio-cultural system was, then, considered to be of greatest importance in the causation of suicide in so far as it generated (or caused) social situations of disorganization (or social isolation).[14] This general idea of the causal relation of the socio-cultural system to suicide was not, however, consistently maintained by Cavan or Schmid. Cavan quite emphatically believed that an increasing spirit of individualism in Western societies had led to the development of attitudes less disfavorable to suicide than had previously existed. Indeed, at one point Cavan went so far as to argue that "There is in the United States a widespread tendency to regard suicide as a justifiable and desirable means of solving difficulties."[15] Clearly, this view is in disagreement with her fundamental view of the relation of social disorganization to suicide. The only way of resolving the conflict seems to be to assume that she felt the over-all attitude was still negative, but that the lesser degree of negativeness simply made suicide more frequent. But Cavan simply did not attempt to resolve the conflict.[16] Also, it was clear to Cavan and Schmid that this very general relationship between social disorganization and suicide would not

[13] Robert E. L. Faris, *Social Disorganization*, second edition, New York: The Ronald Press Company, 1955, p. 293.

[14] This general idea that the socio-cultural system was important in the causation of suicide because it generated, presumably in terms of probabilistic stages, certain situations of individual isolation had been less clearly proposed in the nineteenth century, had been specifically rejected by Durkheim, and was later more clearly developed and supported by Halbwachs.

[15] Ruth S. Cavan, *Suicide*. p. 178.

[16] Schmid, Faris, *et al.* did not bring up the issue at all.

have much explanatory power for suicide: almost all individuals who were "isolated" did not commit suicide. To proceed to a more determinate explanation, Cavan proposed that social disorganization would increase the tendency to suicide only in so far as it caused personal disorganization, which the following statement most clearly defines:[17]

> When the personality or interests and the life organization or means of fulfilling the interests complement each other, life tends to go on in a more or less habitual manner. But when for any reason there is a break in the reciprocal relation of subjective interests and external world, a crisis or crucial situation exists and old habits and attitudes are no longer adequate to the situation. If an adjustment cannot readily be made the person finds himself dissatisfied, restless, unhappy, and in time unable efficiently to order his life. He is then personally disorganized.[18]

It was clear to Cavan that social disorganization could not be significant in the causation of suicide unless it resulted in personal disorganization. Though it was implicitly assumed that social disorganization had a certain general probability of producing personal disorganization, presumably because of the importance of social relations for many of most individuals' gratifications, still it was quite clear that for many individuals social disorganization would not result in personal disorganization. The individual variables, generically labeled as "personal interests," had to be considered independent variables in the theoretical explanation of suicide. (There is no consideration in the works of Cavan and Schmid, and only vague consideration in the work of Faris, of the possibility that these individual variables could be considered dependent on *past* socio-cultural variables.)

Moreover, this partial independence of individual vari-

---

[17] The use of the same word, "disorganization," does not mean that there is any close similarity between "social disorganization" and "personal disorganization." This use of the same term is presumably the result of some implicit analogy between the two on the basis of a *lack of fit*. Such analogies can prove useful when examined, but unexamined they often cause confusion, as this unexamined analogy has.

[18] Ruth S. Cavan, *Suicide*, p. 144.

ables meant that there would be various crises (or personally disorganizing situations). The most important crises were considered by Cavan to be (1) unidentified craving that is frustrated, (2) the recognized wish that is frustrated, (3) the specified wish that is frustrated, (4) mental conflicts, and (5) the broken life organization.[19] These crises overlap to varying degrees and may coexist; but they all represent in specific ways the general phenomena of *blocking, at various stages, normally consummated actions.*

Not only did Cavan argue that there are various types of crises, but she also argued that personally disorganizing crises can be interpreted differently by different individuals. Cavan did not systematically pursue this suggestion that the meanings of situations to the individuals involved was of significance in determining its effect on the suicide process. Instead, she proceeded to argue that certain objectively observed variables were of great importance in determining in which direction the individual moved from the crisis situation. She argued that there are several variables which determine whether an individual will move in the direction (or have a higher probability) of committing suicide. The most important of these are the following: (1) fixity of idea, (2) lack of objectivity, and (3) aggressive (resentment, anger, hate) or depressive emotions.[20]

Cavan then proceeded to attempt to make the process completely determinant by presenting various individual responses to crises. On this concrete level Cavan was concerned with different meanings to different individuals of different kinds of crises. Moreover, and very importantly, Cavan was one of the only sociological theorists of suicide to argue that individuals within the same socio-cultural system impute different normative meanings to suicidal actions. Cavan argued that these differences in the normative meanings of suicidal actions are of great importance, especially at the last stage of the suicidal process, in determining whether an individual will commit suicide.[21]

[19] *Ibid.*, pp. 148-168.   [20] *Ibid.*, pp. 171-176.
[21] As we have previously observed, Cavan did not explicitly state this, but it seems the only reasonable conclusion from her statements about the high degree of normative acceptance of suicide in the United States. Any other conclusion leaves a fundamental conflict in her work.

Conclusion

The so-called ecological theories changed greatly over time, becoming quite diffuse in meaning and covering quite different approaches to suicide. The social areas approach is of little interest to us and need not be criticized in any detail here because of its complete reliance on official statistics, which we shall deal with in great detail in Part III. The correlation of population categories with suicide rates, which has recently been confused with the ecological approaches, also relies almost entirely upon the official statistics; and where they do not they are adequately dealt with in our discussion of Durkheim's *Suicide*. In the works of Cavan, Schmid, and Faris, which one might call the classical ecological works on suicide, the ecological aspects of the works were increasingly played down as they attempted to avoid the ecological fallacy and make their theories more determinate. As they did this they gave increasing emphasis to the importance of social and individual meanings in explaining suicide. None of them systematically developed ideas about the relations of specific social and individual meanings to suicide. None of them were very clear about the problems involved. And certainly none of them attempted to relate ideas about the social self to suicide, ideas which will form a critical part of my approach to suicide as a meaningful act. These early works on the ecological approach to suicide did, however, provide a beginning for the explanation of suicidal actions in terms of both individual and social meanings. It is unfortunate that their leads in this direction were not followed by the later sociological theorists of suicide.

7 THE STATUS-CHANGE THEORIES OF SUICIDE

Introduction

The idea that a change in social (prestige ranking) status, especially a *loss* of social status, can lead to suicide is a very old idea and a very common one. Indeed, this idea is one of the most frequently encountered common-sense explanations of suicide, especially of suicide among the wealthy.[1] As explained in Part I, this idea was common among the French Romantic novelists of the early nineteenth century, Brierre de Boismont considered "déclassement" to be one of the most frequent causes of suicide, and Durkheim had this idea in mind in constructing his theory of anomic suicide. Indeed, though not very consistently, the general idea behind Durkheim's theory of anomic suicide is that a sudden change in one's social position, of which "déclassement" is the most important form, leads to a "dérèglement," or anomie, which has a certain probability of leading to suicide.

The sociologistic approach, so closely coupled with the use of official statistics on suicide, has, however, greatly retarded the consideration by sociologists of the relations of patterns of status paths to suicide rates. Even the work of Henry and Short, which involved a fundamental assumption (or deduction from assumptions) that a loss of social status (economic ranking) will produce an increase in the tendency to suicide, is restricted to group comparisons. It is only in a few works of recent years that sociologists have attempted to show by case studies that certain patterns (or types) of status paths are causally related to suicide.

These few studies are extremely restricted in their theoretical and empirical considerations. Indeed, they are far more restricted in both respects than was the work of

[1] The widespread belief that the 1929 stock market crash led to a great wave of suicides in Wall Street is, perhaps, the most extreme example of this common-sense belief.

Brierre de Boismont over a hundred years ago; and certainly they have not involved nearly so detailed a study of the relation of status loss to suicide as have some of the psychiatric studies, such as that by von Andics.[2] But these few sociological works do represent a rudimentary assumption by sociologists of the study of the "suicide process," a study which has not progressed significantly since the publication of Cavan's work on suicide.

Sainsbury's Findings on the Relation of Status Change to Suicide

Sainsbury's work on suicide[3] contains little in the way of systematic theory, but it is one of the best group-comparisons studies of suicide. (As we have noted in the section on the ecological theories of suicide, Sainsbury's work is presented as "An Ecological Study" of suicide, but it is actually ecological only in that it involves some areal comparisons and some consideration of population variables.)

What little systematic theory there is in Sainsbury's work is well stated in one simple paragraph:

> The view must be sustained that the nature of community life, its cohesion and stability, and the opportunities it provides for satisfactory relationships, alone afford a comprehensive explanation of the variations in suicide rates of communities and other social groups.[4]

Though Sainsbury did not make explicit the connection between this general idea and his ideas about status change and suicide, it seems reasonable to assume that a loss of status, which is the only form of status change which he was specifically concerned with, is a form of social instability and is, therefore, causally related to suicide. Whether

[2] Burt expressed von Andics' general proposition in the following manner: "Life, to be worth living, means a place for the living being in the community of other living beings, a place which none but himself can fill. . . . And so, what leads most commonly to suicide is not so much a change in the outlook for the individual himself: it is rather the thought (quite possibly a mistaken thought) that he no longer fulfills a necessary place in the social community." (Margarethe von Andics, *Suicide and the Meaning of Life*, "Preface" by Cyril Burt, London: William Hodge & Co., Ltd., 1947, pp. v-vi.)

[3] Peter Sainsbury, *Suicide in London: An Ecological Study*, London: Chapman and Hall, 1955.

[4] *Ibid.*, p. 72.

instability of this form (or any form) causes suicide because it is (or causes) one of Durkheim's two forms of anomie or because it is (or causes) "social disorganization" is not considered. Unfortunately, Sainsbury seems to have believed the causal relationship existed because a loss of social status is a "burden badly tolerated." His ultimate explanation of individual actions, therefore, seems to rest on the same sort of simplistic, common-sense psychology as the explanations of individual actions proposed by Gibbs and Porterfield and by Breed (see below).

In order to determine any possible relations between poverty and suicide, Sainsbury first compared boroughs of London in terms of economic class and suicide rates. But he then made more specific comparisons (in an attempt to decrease the risk of making the ecological fallacy) by comparing the suicides with the streets on which they lived, especially by comparing the economic status of the suicide with the average economic status of the street where he lived. In this way Sainsbury arrived at the following general conclusion:

> The relationship between poverty and suicide is complex. The conclusions which may reasonably be deduced from this study are that indigenous poverty does not foster suicide. On the contrary, the suicide rate tends to increase with social status. On the other hand, poverty befalling those used to a better standard of living is a burden badly tolerated, and a factor predisposing to suicide; secondary poverty of this kind would account for the rise in the suicide rate in the upper occupational classes during the economic depression (p. 19), and the discrepant finding that the incidence of suicides living in poverty is greater when the suicide's actual economic level at the time of death is the criterion, rather than the economic status that might be inferred from occupation and neighborhood.[5]

Though Sainsbury's conclusions differ little from those of Durkheim, Sainsbury made more specific comparisons. He was still making comparisons and speculating upon the significance for individuals of the comparisons in such a

[5] *Ibid.*, p. 73.

way that the results of the comparisons can very easily be explained in alternative ways. (For example, it is quite clear that the suicides of individuals poorer than the average economic status of their streets could have been caused by "differential deprivation," rather than because of a loss of social status.) But Sainsbury had taken a step in the direction of studying the *suicide process* by studying the relation of individuals' patterns of status paths to suicide.

Gibbs and Porterfield's Theory of Status Change and Suicide

The Gibbs and Porterfield study of the coroner's records on the 955 suicides officially recorded in New Zealand between 1946 and 1951 was the next significant work on status change and suicide.[6] Gibbs and Porterfield very clearly stated their goal as being a study of the possible relations between patterns of status changes and suicide:

> Our foremost concern is with the dynamics of suicide, not static conditions surrounding the suicide at the time of his death, and we shall concentrate on his social situation from birth to death.[7]

The basic purpose of this study was to determine which patterns of changes in "prestige of occupational position" were most associated with suicide. The authors first did a "static" comparison of the suicide rates of the "upper class," "middle class," and "lower class." Then they did a "dynamic" study to determine the effects of changing status. The study does not, of course, relate any complex types of status-change paths to suicide rates. The dynamic part of the study involves merely a comparison of the proportions of suicides who had given status-change paths with the proportions of the general population who had undergone the same status-change paths. The paths were restricted to two levels—a combination of the status of the family at birth with the individual's status at death. As was true in Powell's study, status was defined solely in terms of occupational prestige.

---

[6] Gibbs and Porterfield, "Occupational Prestige and Social Mobility of Suicides in New Zealand." The authors give no consideration to Durkheim's treatment of the subject or to any of the other work in this vein.

[7] *Ibid.*, p. 147.

In general, Gibbs and Porterfield found that both upward and downward mobility were associated with significantly more suicide, but downward mobility seemed to be associated with a higher suicide rate than upward mobility. Though this association between (economic prestige) status change and suicide is very much in line with Durkheim's (individualistic) theory of anomic suicide, Gibbs and Porterfield did not choose to explain their findings in terms of Durkheim's theory.[8] Instead, they proposed two theoretical explanations of their findings. The first, presented by Gibbs and Porterfield more as an introductory theoretical statement than an explicit statement of theory, is only the rudimentary form of the theory. Though Gibbs and Porterfield never presented their theory in a very systematic form, the more developed form of their theory seems to be adequately schematized by Figure IV on page 114.

Three variables are significant in the Gibbs and Porterfield theory of status change and suicide: (1) the long-run (economic prestige) status change, (2) a relative lack of strong social ties, and (3) a personal crisis. There is implicit in their argument an assumption that there is a suicide process to be found in most of their cases of suicide: the long-run change in status causes both frustration (or tension) *and* a relative lack of social ties (i.e., social disintegration); then a crisis occurs which is not offset (or solved) by one's social relations (because of step one)[9] and the crisis thereby becomes the "precipitating event" of the suicide.

The crisis, then, is of fundamental importance in the Gibbs and Porterfield theory. Unfortunately, they provide no definition of this variable. Indeed, Gibbs and Porterfield

[8] The reason for this might be Gibb's earlier interpretation of Durkheim's *Suicide* strictly in terms of "social integration" and suicide. (See the earlier discussion of the Gibbs and Martin "Status Integration Theory of Suicide.")

[9] The crisis can be a short-run (sudden) loss of economic prestige: e.g., social status, especially in the cases of long-run upwardly mobile individuals. (The more obvious common-sense explanation of such suicide, and one that would be completely within the realm of Gibbs and Porterfield's theory, is that individuals who have worked so hard to get something and then lose it suffer extreme disappointment—or frustration. Gibbs and Porterfield probably failed to consider this possible explanation simply because of the unsystematic nature of their "theoretical" argument.)

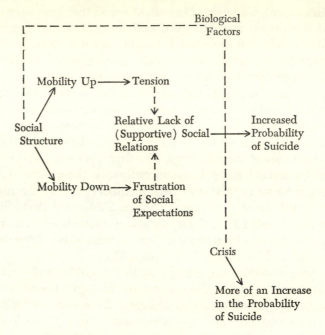

Figure IV. Schema of Gibbs and Porterfield's
Theory of Suicide

seem to have considered any immediately preceding, sudden (frustrating?) change to be a crisis, and the crisis seems to be inferred directly from the fact that suicide quickly followed the event:

> We regret that necessity precludes a description of individual cases here, and we recognize that the incompleteness of the case materials makes such an evaluation tentative at its best; but, for what it is worth, we concluded that 35 of the 50 climbers, 15 of those who "stayed put" on their father's level, and 26 of the sliders committed suicide after some precipitating event. For them the situation was a crisis.[10]

Gibbs and Porterfield also failed to note that with the lack of any non-suicidal control group it could very well be that most possible definitions of crisis (other than that of "event

[10] Gibbs and Porterfield, *op.cit.*, p. 151.

preceding suicide") would lead one to conclude that just as many (or more) non-suicidal individuals have "crises" as do "suicidal" individuals. Moreover, Gibbs and Porterfield failed to consider the possibility, which I would argue is the most plausible explanation,[11] that individuals in Western societies decide a death is a "suicide" very largely because they can find some "crisis" from which to infer motivation or, more generally, intention. Consequently, the officially designated cases of "suicide" would contain an invalidly large number of "suicides" with crises preceding the "suicides." Our general conclusion regarding the Gibbs and Porterfield variable of crisis can only be that the variable is vaguely defined and its relation to suicide undemonstrated. Probably the only values of the idea for present and future work on suicide lie in its reintroduction of the idea of "suicidal process" to the literature of suicide and its consideration of the very old idea that a given suicide is the result of a long-run situation (or sequence of situations) and a short-run situation that leads directly to the action of suicide.

Since the vast majority of individuals faced with a given socially-defined type of crisis (e.g., "death of a loved one" or "financial disaster") do not commit suicide, it is clear that such situations must have special individual meanings for the individuals who do commit suicide when faced with them. The failure to define "crisis situation" is one example of a general failure by Gibbs and Porterfield to consider any individual factors. Though the concluding statement by Gibbs and Porterfield indicates that they consider it important to determine how social-structure determines personality types, especially through socialization processes, and the relations of these to suicide, there are actually no such considerations in the work. The only psychological variable considered to be causally significant in the suicide process is "frustration" (and/or "tension"). Even this concept is not explicitly defined in terms of any states of individual affect, cognition, etc. Rather, it is simply assumed to be the *obvious* result of failure or great success in the occupational role, at least for men in New Zealand, and it is assumed to be the cause, or *a* major cause, of suicide.

[11] See Part III.

The idea that frustration characterizes suicides is not considered by Gibbs and Porterfield to be problematic because Gibbs and Porterfield did not really consider the individuals' reasons for committing suicide to be problematic. They assumed that an individual kills himself because he is unhappy about something. This is the same common-sense assumption that was partially responsible for Durkheim's decision not to consider individual reasons for committing suicide—the *general* reason (unhappiness with life) is obvious and the particular reasons (the specific crises) are too complex. The important goal, then, becomes simply specifying the social causes of the *general* individual reason for committing suicide—what social "thing" most "frustrates" individuals and makes them least able to tolerate frustration. To most contemporary sociologists it seems obvious that the most significantly frustrating "thing" is loss of social status (i.e., economic prestige ranking). Consequently, they have been concerned with establishing statistical relations between changes in economic prestige ranking and suicide. They have hardly even considered whether there might be some far stronger statistical relations between other forms of changed social relations and suicide and, even worse, whether any statistical association between economic prestige ranking and suicide might be the result of some common cause.

Many psychiatrists, on the other hand, have assumed it to be equally obvious that individuals commit suicide very largely because of a different change in social relations— that is, the loss (especially early loss) of a love object. Some of these psychiatric studies of the loss of love object and suicide have been influenced by Freud's theory of "melancholia,"[12] but most of them seem to be derived primarily from the common-sense notion that the death of a loved one frequently leads the bereaved to wish to join the dead.[13] In their research on suicide, psychiatrists have frequently reported stronger support for their theory of love-object loss and suicide than have the sociologists for their theory

[12] Sigmund Freud, "Mourning and Melancholia," in *Collected Papers*, vol. 4, London: Hogarth Press, Ltd., 1949.
[13] These psychiatric studies seem to be much more firmly based

of economic prestige-ranking and suicide.[14] Palmer found that 17 out of 25 cases of suicide had lost one or both parents by the age of 14.[15] In a study of eleven adolescents whose parents had died, Keeler found that all were depressed, there were fantasies of reunion in eight, identification with a dead parent in seven, and suicidal preoccupations and attitudes in six.[16] In a study involving comparisons with controls, Farberow found that individuals who had attempted suicides or threatened suicide were those who had lost a parent before the age of six significantly more often than had the controls.[17] Pokorny found that of forty-four suicides in a VA General Hospital, seventeen had close, and frequently early, contact with death, and two suicides had a suicide in the family.[18]

Lowenthal has reported a case of attempted suicide that gives a strong presumption that status loss was the result of the loss of a love object:

Mr. S. was admitted to the psychiatric screening wards because he had tried to commit suicide with chloroform. He was somewhat reticent about his life history, but one is able to piece together the facts that he was trained as a lawyer at an Eastern university, became a career Naval

---

[14] These psychiatric studies generally do not involve controls. On the other hand, the information obtained is probably *much* more reliable than that obtained in sociological studies such as that by Gibbs and Porterfield. (This is especially to be expected in view of Breed's findings. See the discussion of Breed's work below in this same section.)

in common sense than the common-sense sociological works on status change and suicide. Though one must expect class differences, and subcultural differences, there seems to be a much stronger expectation in our society that the death of a loved one will lead to a wish to die (and, thus, sometimes to suicide) than that the loss of economic prestige ranking will lead to a wish to die.

[15] D. M. Palmer, "Factors in Suicidal Attempts," *The Journal of Nervous and Mental Diseases*, 93 (1941), 421-442.

[16] W. R. Keeler, "Children's Reactions to Death of a Parent," in P. Hoch, *Depression*, New York: Grunne and Stratton, 1954.

[17] N. L. Farberow, "Personality Patterns of Suicidal Mental Hospital Patients," *Genetic Psychology Monographs*, 42 (1950) pp. 3-79.

[18] A. D. Pokorny, "Characteristics of 44 Patients Who Subsequently Committed Suicide," *A.M.A. Archives of General Psychiatry*, 2 (March, 1960) pp. 314-323.

officer, and sometime in middle life, for obscure reasons, was asked to resign from the Navy. At this point, he married a waitress and went to Europe with all of his life savings, some $50,000. The money disappeared quickly and the marriage soon ended in divorce. Since that time he has had innumerable jobs in travel agencies and small businesses. He currently has been trying, without much success, to give language and piano lessons. The only money he has left is $160 a month from a trust fund. Mr. S. reports that the most difficult thing he ever had to face in his life was when the doctor told him that his mother would only live for four months (he had lived with his mother until she died when he was 43, and says he has been depressed ever since).[19]

Similar cases, often with much clearer implications that the loss of a loved person was the direct antecedent of the loss of social status, have been reported by psychologists and psychiatrists. Schneider, for example, reported a case from which the following excerpts are taken:

For the rest, he had no real contact with anyone and sought to thrust himself on them by a disordered life and great expenditures. Intelligent, he became an architect and succeeded in gaining no little money, but he rapidly squandered it on drink and women. Ruined, he returned to the home of his parents, whom he hated and whom he blamed for his distress. The first attempt which necessitated his stay in a hospital is motivated by financial worries and especially by the rupture of a relationship with a woman.

Several months later, still in 1937, after proposing a double suicide, he swallowed fifteen Optalidons in the presence of a woman friend who had indicated to him that she was going to leave him. The medication made him disinhibited and he demonstrated psychomotor agitation which justified his admission to a psychiatric hospital. When he left he came to Lausanne, worked around as an architect, built himself a bizarre house where he

[19] Marjorie Fiske Lowenthal, "Social Isolation and Mental Illness in Old Age," *American Sociological Review*, 29 (Feb., 1964) p. 65.

practiced nudism, then exhibitionism, and he fell in love with a 16-year-old girl whom he overwhelmed with kind attention, then with threats which soon extended to the whole family of his sweetheart. He could not accept being abandoned and became so menacing that it was necessary to intern him again in a sanitarium.[20]

The evidence thus far presented to support the status-loss theories of suicide are less well supported than the alternative love-object-loss theory of suicide. Moreover, there is some evidence from case studies to indicate that the loss of a loved person frequently precedes the loss of social status and might be the cause of the loss of social status. The loss of social status could be causally related to suicide or it could simply be significantly (statistically) related to suicide because they are both significantly associated with the loss of a loved person.

The important point is that the sociological theorists of status change and suicide have not included any consideration of such an alternative explanation of their "statistically significant" findings. The reason for this is to be found in their fundamental approach to theory and research on suicide. These sociologists, like almost all sociologists who have done any work on suicide, have started out with the hypothetical assumption that a certain social variable, status change in this instance, is causally related to "suicide." The rest of the work is then devoted to demonstrating and refining this initial hypothetical assumption. The focus of the work is restricted to showing that there exists some significant association between the chosen social variables and official information on suicide. Alternative explanations are not considered or are discarded without any careful consideration. Consequently, one cannot tell from these works whether there are alternative theories that explain the data as well or better.

The reason for the "discovery" of statistically significant relations between social status variables (e.g., loss of social prestige ranking) and suicide seems clear enough: such

[20] Pierre-B. Schneider, *La Tentative de Suicide*, Neuchâtel: Delachaux et Nistle S. A., 1954, pp. 107-108.

variables are significantly related to an immense number of social things—death rates, ulcers, divorce rates, age of marriage, number of children, years of education and so on. Why should one not find a statistically significant relation between social status loss and suicide (or visits to the zoo)? The first scientific purpose of trying to establish a statistically significant relation between one variable and another is to discover some regularity that might have causal significance. But to establish some relatively weak statistical relation between one variable that is caused by many things and causes many things and another variable that in turn is caused by many things and causes many things, is not to fulfill this basic purpose at all.

Breed's Status-Change Theory and Research on Suicide

Breed's theory and research on economic-prestige-ranking (i.e., social status) loss and suicide[21] is one of the most recent sociological works on suicide and involves a specific reorientation of the sociological investigation of suicide both in the direction of using case studies of suicide and in leaving open the possibility of treating a sociological theory of suicide as open-ended, as something to be built up from an analysis of case studies of suicide.[22]

Breed interviewed relatives, friends, and acquaintances of 103 officially reported (to the coroner) male suicides aged 20-60 years who had lived in New Orleans for at least six months and who had died between 1954 and 1959. The first finding of Breed's interview approach was that the official reports on occupations, marital status and unemployment-employment of these 103 suicides were very much in error. In terms of employment and type of employment, there seems to have been a very significant tendency for the official reports to overestimate the social prestige ranking

[21] Warren Breed, "Occupational Mobility and Suicide," *American Sociological Review*, 28 (1963) pp. 179-188.

[22] Breed did not actually propose an open-ended approach to theory. He states specifically that in his own work ". . . the theory was developed largely after collection of data began . . ." (*Ibid.*) But the theory developed is really just a specific application of the symbolic-interactionist theory so that his theory was little influenced by the data.

held by the suicide. When one considers the strong possibility that the significant others interviewed by Breed may
have also overestimated in this way,[23] we have a strong bit
of information against the use of national official data such
as that used by Henry and Short, Powell, and most other
sociologists.

Breed's theory of the relation of economic-prestige-ranking loss to suicide is really very simple. Unlike the other
theorists in this tradition, Breed was quite emphatic in arguing that the loss of status is only *one* major cause among
many of this "complex phenomena":

> Most individual suicides are complex phenomena, in-
> volving the individual's role performance in several posi-
> tions over a period of time; the purpose of this paper was
> to highlight the relevance of the work role for American
> males, but not to insist that this is the only major factor
> involved.[24]

Presumably, Breed assumes that any psycho-social theory
of suicide must be problematic; but he did not consider any
of the problems of the general relations of individuals to
society or of a "suicidal process."

Breed did implicitly assume that actions such as suicide
are (1) deviant behavior,[25] (2) ultimately a product of
"structured strain," and (3) immediately a product of individual strain caused by a difference between a (normative?)
standard and the evaluations by ego and his significant
alters of ego's actions. Breed's "structural-interactional"
theory is roughly schematized in Figure V.

---

[23] The average number of respondents per case in Breed's study
was approximately two, but they seem to have always been people in
some close relation to the suicide. This means, for one thing, that
they will be strongly subject to the "always speak well of the dead"
value in our society.

It would be *most* interesting to compare the data given by friends
with that given by enemies and both with that given by neutrals
(such as sociologists making independent investigations of each case).
My prediction would be that there will be very great differences.

[24] Breed, *op.cit.*, p. 187.

[25] Breed draws upon the theories of deviance proposed by Merton
and Lemert to develop what he calls a "structural-interactional theory
of suicide." (*Ibid.*)

(1)

Social Structure of ⟶ Social Situations ⟶ Evaluations of
Values and Roles   that Individuals   Individuals' Role
         are in   Performances

(2)

Individual Factors ⟶ Individuals' Role + Individuals'
          Performances   Evaluations (?)

(3)

(1) + (2) ⟶ Strain ⟶ Increased Probability of Suicide
                 of Individuals

Figure V. General Structure of Breed's Theory of Suicide

There is no real synthesis of the individual and social factors, nor any consideration of such matters. And there is no consideration of what "strain" is or of how such a factor is related to suicides. As usual, Breed is relying on common-sense ideas about such factors as "strain" and about why anyone commits suicide.

The more specific structure of Breed's theory of suicide is schematized in Figure VI.

Social Structure of + Ego's Perform- + Ego and Alter Negative
Values and Work   ance of Work   Evaluations of Ego's
Roles   Role   Work Role Performance
                                in terms of Structural
                                Values

⟶ Strain in Ego   Threat of general ⟶ Significant Increase
  (Sense of   + Collapse of Life   in the Probability of
  Failure, etc.)   Organization[26]   Suicide

Figure VI. The Specific Structure of Breed's Theory of Suicide

Breed's theory of suicide is subject to most of the same criticisms we have already made of the other status-change theories of suicide. His empirical research to support his theory is greatly superior to that of most other sociologists in that he actually collected his own data on the social statuses of suicides. But his research is just as restricted in ways intended to support his statistical hypothesis as is the research in the other works on status change and suicide.

[26] Breed threw this idea in at the end of his theoretical discussion. It is reminiscent of Cavan's theory of personal disorganization and suicide, but Breed did not explain how it is relevant to his theory. This seems to be one more example of the almost haphazard treatment given by sociologists to the individual factors in suicide.

Concerning the factor of unemployment, Breed actually presented evidence that shows that more men had quit their jobs than had been fired (15 to 13) a clear indication that there *might very well* be some *third* factor causing both unemployment and suicide. Moreover, in determining the status loss of the suicides Breed accepted at face value the reports of his informants about the occupations of the fathers of the suicides. He himself had discovered that the officials, presumably acting on the basis of reports given by similar or the same informants, had made gross mistakes in categorizing the occupations of the suicides, men who had just died. Yet Breed accepted the reports on the occupations of men who had very frequently been dead for years and *who had frequently never been known of by the informants* except through the reports given them by the suicide. Considering the strong tendency among Southerners (and perhaps most cultural groups in America) to idealize their pasts, especially their lineage histories, it would seem unsafe to take at face value the reports about lineage history made by members (or close associates) of the lineage.

8 HALBWACHS' SUBCULTURE THEORY OF SUICIDE

In his Introduction to Halbwachs' *Les Causes du Suicide*[1] Mauss stated that the original purpose of Halbwachs' work on suicide had been to bring "up to date the work of Durkheim" and to indicate "in a supplementary chapter or in an Introduction what points the new facts, published after a quarter of a century, confirmed or did not confirm of his conclusions."[2] Mauss further revealed, however, that Halbwachs was slowly forced to undertake a very new work:

> M. Halbwachs felt himself forced little by little to undertake new research, to pose new problems, to present the facts under a new aspect.
> In effect a totally new book was necessary. In sociology, no more than in any science, the work of analysis is never completed.[3]

But, though Mauss had clearly noted that Halbwachs felt forced "to present the facts under another aspect," he quickly went on to argue that "the greatest part of the new facts on suicide remain of the type Durkheim had described and are essentially subsumed by the interpretation which he proposed."[4] Since Mauss considered Halbwachs' new facts to be in "essential" agreement with Durkheim's theory of suicide, he considered *Les Causes du Suicide* to be the necessary complement, the indispensable corrective to *Suicide*.[5]

In his own statements concerning *Les Causes du Suicide* and *Suicide* Halbwachs showed the same difficulty in dealing with this relation. On page three he posed the question of whether the theoretical argument of *Suicide* was con-

---

[1] Maurice Halbwachs, *Les Causes du Suicide*, Paris: Librairie Felix Alcan, 1930.
[2] *Ibid.*, p. vii. [3] *Ibid.*
[4] *Ibid.* [5] *Ibid.*, p. viii.

vincing because of the strength of the facts or because of the strength of the argument. With a great deal of objectivity, Halbwachs admitted of the master's work that it was "Sometimes the dialectic more than the facts, not by the fault of Durkheim, however."[6] He then concluded (and excused) that "There is no scientific work which new experience does not require to be revised and completed."[7] On pages fourteen and fifteen, in a general consideration of the relation of his theory to that of Durkheim, Halbwachs concluded that "Durkheim had the merit to embrace the phenomena of suicide in all their abundance and of proposing an explanation of them which could be completed and corrected, but of which the principle appears quite unattackable."[8] However, immediately after reaching this conclusion, Halbwachs stated that there were two essential points on which his work was in disagreement with Durkheim.[9] These were concerned with the relations of economic crises to suicide rates and between mental troubles and suicide. With regard to economic crises, Halbwachs concluded from his study of German economic indexes and suicide rates that suicide varied inversely with respect to the indexes and not simply with respect to economic crises. With regard to the relations between mental troubles and suicide, Halbwachs concluded that mental troubles (as well as other mental, motivational states) should be considered to be causes of suicide. Though Halbwachs considered his arguments to be quite tentative because of the need for more evidence, the general direction of his theory indicated by these two "essential points" of disagreement is in fundamental opposition to Durkheim's theory of suicide.

It is very easy to see why Halbwachs, who was such an integral part of the French school of sociology founded by Durkheim, would be unwilling to clearly state how fundamentally his work on suicide was opposed to that of Durkheim, especially when it is also noted that he wrote his work primarily for the other members of this school. But there is more to it than this. The implications of Halbwachs' work are opposed to Durkheim's theory of suicide, but these implications are generally not developed by Halb-

---

[6] *Ibid.*, p. 3. [7] *Ibid.*
[8] *Ibid.*, pp. 14-15. [9] *Ibid.*, p. 15.

wachs to the point where it is obvious that they are in opposition to the "principle" of Durkheim's work. Indeed, the most telling aspect of Halbwachs' opposition to Durkheim's theory of suicide is his relative silence (at least, until his Conclusion) concerning those aspects of Durkheim's theory which were considered by Durkheim to be fundamental. Halbwachs denied or opposed Durkheim's theory primarily by going around it. Durkheim had considered the social *meanings* (i.e., the collective representations) of anomie-fatalism, and egoism-altruism to be the fundamental causes of suicide and, therefore, the principle of his theory of suicide. To Durkheim these social causes were so fundamental that he etiologically defined his types of suicide in terms of them. In *Les Causes du Suicide*, however, we find very little mention of these social causes. We do find a great extension of Durkheim's methods of analyzing the ecological distributions of suicide and the relations of rates of social relations to suicide rates. Since this part of Halbwachs' work is so extensive, it makes the whole thing appear superficially to be very similar to Durkheim's *Suicide*. But when it came to explaining what such relations were indexes of and what caused them, then Halbwachs quietly cut away Durkheim's theoretic superstructure and imposed his own.

Since, as we have argued at some length previously, Durkheim had read his social meanings into statistical relations shown to exist between external phenomena without establishing methodological controls on such indexing and theorizing, it was quite easy for Halbwachs to simply impose or read in an alternative theoretic superstructure to explain roughly the same phenomena. There was, however, one methodological argument and series of analyses of data which Halbwachs considered to be of the greatest importance in supporting his theory and opposing (though not in principle?) that of Durkheim. Halbwachs argued that in his analyses Durkheim had overlooked the general overlap of his factors among the populations of Europe. Halbwachs argued that in Europe there tended to be high correlations between the factors of nationality, religion, degree of education, occupation, socio-economic status, family relations, and rural or urban residence.[10] Most importantly, he be-

[10] *Ibid.*, p. 8.

lieved that there was a fundamental difference between the "way of life" of urban and rural residents. He believed that differences in family relations, religion, types of occupation, degree of education, and socio-economic status were all merely *aspects* of the fundamental difference between the urban and rural ways of life.[11] And he believed that it was this fundamental difference in the urban and rural ways of life that explained most of the differences in the social distribution of suicide. Using the geographical distributions of suicide rates as an *indicator* of the social distributions, Halbwachs tried to show that the suicide rates of France decreased as one moved away from the highly populated, relatively urban river valleys toward the lowly populated, rural, mountainous regions.[12]

As we will see in our chapter on the statistical data on suicide, Halbwachs realized that statistics on suicide in rural areas were much less subject to professional controls than were those of the urban areas (primarily because in the rural areas the suspicious deaths were rarely certified for causes of death by doctors, whereas in the urban areas they generally were). It should be clear from this fact that there is far more chance for rural suicide to be excluded from the statistics on suicide. Moreover, if we accept Halbwachs' argument that the rural population is more traditionalistic, so that we can expect them to take the injunctions of the church against suicide more seriously, then we have to expect the individuals in rural areas have far more reason to hide suicides and far more chance to do so. On the basis of Halbwachs' own facts and arguments, we must conclude that any testing of his theory by the use of official statistics on suicide would be extremely biased in favor of supporting his theory. But, then, in view of our earlier arguments, we expected this, so that what we must be concerned with is Halbwachs' theory rather than his testing of the theory.

Before discussing the fundamental points of Halbwachs'

---

[11] *Ibid.*, pp. 6-8.
[12] *Ibid.*, pp. 169-197. Halbwachs was deeply concerned with establishing many statistical relations between suicide rates and various other social rates, but this relation was the one of central concern for his theory, especially in relation to Durkheim's theory.

theory of suicide, let us present a brief schematization of the general theory.[13] (See Figure VII.)

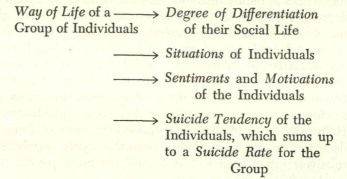

Way of Life of a ⟶ *Degree of Differentiation*
Group of Individuals   of their Social Life

⟶ *Situations* of Individuals

⟶ *Sentiments* and *Motivations*
of the Individuals

⟶ *Suicide Tendency* of the
Individuals, which sums up
to a *Suicide Rate* for the
Group

Figure VII. Halbwachs' General Theory of Suicide

As we have already noted, Halbwachs believed that the relations between rural-urban residence and suicide rates were the most important empirical relations to be explained. The fundamental principle of his theory is that the *general* cause of these relations (i.e., a direct relation between suicide rate and degree of urbanism) was a difference in the ways of life of urban groups and rural groups. Halbwachs did not very clearly define "way of life." In some contexts the term seems to include or even be defined in terms of social relations (such as types and numbers of family members). But, in general, the term is used in such a way as to indicate that Halbwachs meant something like what today we would call "culture": i.e., *meanings* that are shared and transmitted. But Halbwachs meant by the term not simply particular meanings or dimensions of meanings. He meant some system of core meanings that is related (presumably, causally) to many specific meanings (such as those of family relations) and, thence, to specific social relations. Halbwachs was clearer than Durkheim in making social meanings the fundamental category for explaining suicide rates, but his explanation was less specific than that of Durkheim, since he did not attempt to clearly delineate

[13] The best discussions of his general theory appear in *Ibid.*, pp. 5-15, and pp. 404-514.

any collective representations such as egoism-altruism and anomie-fatalism.

The second fundamental category in Halbwachs' theory, the degree of social differentiation, is conceptually related to Durkheim's analysis of the external social relations that serve as indexes of social integration. But Halbwachs specifically referred this aspect of his theory to Spencer's treatment of social differentiation.[14] There might be nothing more here than a simple statement of historical precedent, noting the source common to Halbwachs' and Durkheim's theories of social differentiation. But there seems to be more reason for the statement than this. Though Halbwachs saw the degree of social differentiation to be caused as Durkheim had proposed, the next step in Halbwachs' theoretic argument is fundamentally opposed to Durkheim's theory. Rather than proceeding simply to relate social differentiation to suicide rates, Halbwachs argues that greater social differentiation (or social complexity) causes a greater suicide rate *because* it causes certain (probabilities of?) *situations* that are more conducive to social conflicts. The social conflicts cause a tendency to depression and "cyclothymie" or disequilibrium (i.e., in general, to affective states in the individuals), which in turn cause a tendency to suicide. In his discussion of the effects of wars and similar crises on suicide rates, Halbwachs clearly stated that the external social relations remain the same, while the meanings of the relations change so that individuals are in conflict with each other less (because everyday things have less significance or cathexis?). In this argument he has compromised the independence of social differentiation as a causal factor, but has clearly stated the fundamental importance of *meanings* and of the *situated motives* of individuals in the causation of suicide.[15]

This is the break from Durkheim's theory and the reference to Spencer rather than to Durkheim seems to be a cue to this effect. At this point in his argument Halbwachs silently went around Durkheim's arguments that such a situation-personality theory cannot explain suicide rates or probabilities; he silently assumed that the basic explanatory link between the socio-cultural level of analysis and the

[14] *Ibid.*, p. 9.   [15] *Ibid.*, pp. 9-10.

personality level of analysis is that of the probabalistic situations caused by culture and society and he assumed that individual motives must be fundamental, partially independent categories in an adequate theory of suicide.

Halbwachs argued that whenever one considers the usually imputed motives for suicide he finds that they involve a common element of social isolation which he believed gave these imputed motives most, but not all, of their explanatory power.[16] This argument, of course, is one that emphasizes the social causes and aspects of individual motives. Because of this argument, which involves the often unexpressed assumption that society and culture must be considered to be the ultimate causes of motives, Halbwachs' acceptance of motives as categories in his theory of suicide is not so radically different from Durkheim's theory as is Halbwachs' assumption that the socially-generated situation of an individual is a necessary category in an adequate scientific explanation of suicide rates. This violates Durkheim's fundamental assumption that it is the operation of the whole society (or culture) that directly causes the suicide rate characteristic of a group and that a scientific explanation of this suicide rate can only be in terms of the whole social system compared to other social systems. It was this basic assumption that led Durkheim to believe, though not entirely consistently,[17] that studying individual causes (hence, "situations") was of no value for a *scientific* explanation of suicide rates. In assuming the opposite, almost without noting how radically different this is from Durkheim's approach, Halbwachs made the study of *situations* and their associated, concrete meanings a necessary part of any scientific approach to suicide.

However, other than a rather lengthy discussion of the relation of "cyclothymie" to suicide,[18] Halbwachs gave little

[16] *Ibid.*, pp. 419, 433, 434. The argument presented on pp. 12-13 concerning situated motives is somewhat more "social" than our general interpretation of Halbwachs' theory.

[17] In at least one place in *Suicide* (p. 278) Durkheim strongly implied that his method of study was dictated primarily by a lack of data on individual cases of suicide.

[18] See, especially, Halbwachs, *op.cit.*, pp. 403-449. (Deshaies has argued that Halbwachs misinterpreted the nature of "cyclothymie"; and he is probably right, though we are not really interested here in the particulars of Halbwachs' theory of the relation of personality to

attention to determining what relations exist between socially-generated situations and personality factors. Perhaps unknowingly, Halbwachs had partially integrated the situation-personality aspect of previous suicide studies[19] with Durkheim's socio-cultural theory of suicide. He had failed, like Durkheim before him, to see the fundamental necessity of *treating meanings as problematic* and in such a manner that one can determine empirically whether subcultures such as his rural and urban ways of life exist and, if so, precisely which meanings are involved to what degree in different categories of suicidal actions. Nevertheless, it is clear that Halbwachs has helped to prepare the way for a fundamental reorientation of social research and theory on suicide without throwing away the basic insights of Durkheim. It is, therefore, most unfortunate that Halbwachs' work has had almost no direct influence on the more recent works on suicide. Indeed, many sociologists who have overlooked Halbwachs' basic critique of Durkheim's work have committed the very errors which Halbwachs had so carefully analyzed.[20]

---

suicide. See G. Deshaies, *La Psychologie du Suicide*, Paris: Presses Universitaires de France, 1947.)

[19] These are primarily the psychiatric works, but Cavan's is the most important of them.

[20] The Gibbs and Martin work on suicide is a fine example of this reversion to Durkheim.

THE HENRY AND SHORT
THEORY OF SUICIDE

The most ambitious attempt by sociologists in the last few decades to explain official suicide rates is that of Henry and Short.[1] The focus of their work is on aggression rather than suicide, but suicide is considered, along with homicide, to be directly related to aggression.

The fundamental theoretic purpose of the authors in this work is to combine psychological and sociological variables to explain variations in the official statistics on suicide and homicide. Though their purpose seems to have been to present a synthesis of psychological and sociological variables, they do not achieve this goal. On the other hand, the theory proposed by the authors is not simply another multifactored approach to suicide (and homicide).[2] There is a definite, hypothesized order of interdependency between the variables such that, at least partially, sociological and psychological variables are hypothesized to cause each other in a specific sequence of stages and, thence, to cause suicide and homicide rates.

[1] Andrew F. Henry and James F. Short, *Suicide and Homicide: Some Economic, Sociological and Psychological Aspects of Aggression,* Glencoe: The Free Press, 1954. For a brief, more recent resume of this work see Andrew F. Henry and James F. Short, "The Sociology of Suicide," in *Clues to Suicide,* edited by Edwin S. Shneidman and Norman L. Farberow, New York: McGraw-Hill Book Company, Inc., 1957, pp. 58-69. There are no basic changes between the earlier and later works, but Henry and Short do place more emphasis on "vertical restraint" as opposed to "horizontal restraint" in the later work. This slight "reinterpretation" is, quite likely, intended to be a partial answer to one of the basic criticisms of their theory—i.e., that in our society lower-class individuals do not actually seem to be subject to more (general) "external restraint" than those of higher-class position. When the "Henry and Short Theory" is mentioned in this work it shall, unless otherwise specified, refer to the earlier work.

[2] Martin Gold has previously noted that the Henry and Short theory of suicide was not in fact a synthesis of psychological and sociological variables. (See Martin Gold, "Suicide, Homicide, and the Socialization of Aggression," *The American Journal of Sociology,* LXIII [May, 1958], 651-661.)

The psychological orientation is stated to be psychoanalytic and it is proposed that a combination of psychoanalytic and sociological orientations will prove most valuable in the explanation of human action. However, except for certain physiologico-psychological considerations of superego determinations of the direction in which aggression is expressed, the theory proposed has little to do with the psychoanalytic theories of suicide and homicide and does not involve any of the rather elaborate mechanisms hypothesized by psychoanalysts to explain these phenomena.[3] Rather, the psychological parts of the work are merely simple forms of the *frustration-aggression theory* which, in the simplistic form used here, are common to many of the psychoanalytic theories as well as to almost all areas of psychology concerned with drives or motivations.

The assumptions and deductions that constitute the theory of *Suicide and Homicide* are not very systematically presented by Henry and Short. There are, moreover, a number of vague points in the presentation of the theory. The theory as presented here has been made more systematic and, as will be noted, especially with respect to one fundamental assumption of the theory, an attempt has been made to clear up some of the weaker points. The reason for doing this is simply that we wish to make the frustration-aggression theory of suicide as strong as we can.

Assumption I. An increase in frustration will cause an increase in aggression, and a decrease in frustration will cause a decrease in aggression.

This is the fundamental psychological assumption of Henry and Short's theory of suicide and homicide. They do not take this assumption to be problematic. They do not consider the alternative responses to frustration that psychologists and anthropologists have shown exist, both in

---

[3] There are actually *many* different so-called "psychoanalytic" and "neo-psychoanalytic" theories of suicide. For a discussion of some of these theories see Norman L. Farberow, "Personality Patterns of Suicidal Mental Hospital Patients," pp. 11-16; Samuel Futterman, "Suicide: Psychoanalytic Point of View," in *The Cry For Help*, edited by Norman L. Farberow and Edwin S. Shneidman, New York: McGraw-Hill Book Company, Inc., 1961, pp. 167-181; and Herbert Hendin, "Suicide: Psychoanalytic Point of View," in *The Cry For Help*, pp. 181-193.

other cultures and in American sub-cultures. It is, then, entirely possible that an increase in frustration among individuals will produce no increase in aggression. It is, indeed, quite possible that an increase in frustration among individuals will produce both an increase in aggression and an increase in passive withdrawal; and it is possible that the sum of passive withdrawal responses would be greater than the sum of aggressive responses.

Assumption II. For a given population (especially a class group), an increase in aggression leads to an increase in homicide or an increase in suicide; and a decrease in aggression leads to a decrease in homicide or a decrease in suicide.

This is the assumption that homicide and suicide are both linked with aggression and that any given status group in a society will have a "preference" for either homicide or suicide, so that an increase in the mean aggression for the group will lead to an increase *either* in the homicide rate *or* in the suicide rate (and, presumably, this group preference is monotonic with respect to aggression and stable over time), but not in both rates. Unfortunately, Henry and Short do not make this assumption explicit. Indeed, they seem not to recognize that they are making such a strong assumption, but it is clear that in their tests they are. In their tests they do not determine how the suicide rate *and* homicide rate of a given status group (high or low) is varying with respect to the business cycle index. Rather, they consider *either* the suicide rate *or* the homicide rate relative to the business cycle index. Gold has criticized Henry and Short's work for precisely this and has proposed the use of a Suicide-Murder Ratio to show the existence of a *preference* for either homicide or suicide. (The great importance of this particular error in testing will become clearer as we develop below the further assumptions and predictions concerning group preferences for homicide and suicide.)

Henry and Short did not present any significant evidence to show that aggression is in fact ever associated with actions that are intended or expected to injure oneself. More specifically, they did not attempt to give evidence demonstrating that the internal, affective state called aggression is causally related to the intentional self-infliction of death.

Various psychologists, especially psychoanalysts, have, of course, argued that individuals who commit suicide have generally given definite indications of feelings of aggression. However, in one of the few reasonably careful statistical studies done on this question, Tuckman concluded from content analyses of suicide notes that only 1% of the suicides expressed inwardly-directed hostility, while 5% expressed outwardly-directed hostility—just the opposite of the Henry and Short assumption. In general, Tuckman found that hostility characterized 24% of suicide notes, while positive affect without hostility characterized 51% and neutral affect characterized 25%.[4] The suicides, then, were generally un-aggressive and when they were aggressive they expressed their verbal aggression outward, not inward.[5]

It is, of course, quite possible that the words and actions expressed aggression in opposite directions. But to simply assume such an opposition because it might be helpful to one's theory is quite unacceptable. People do sometimes "say one thing and do the opposite" (such as bark at others and bite themselves), but there is at present no evidence that this is the normal tendency.

But it is important to note that even if the available evidence showed a positive correlation between aggression and suicide or, more specifically, between internally-directed aggression and suicide, we certainly would not be justified in assuming some kind of causal relation between internally-directed aggression and suicide. This is true not only for the obvious reason that correlation does not mean causation (especially in complex organic and social systems), but also because almost none of the studies of aggression and suicide use any controls. It might well be that similar individuals (in terms of the usual social positions) put in similar tension-producing situations (e.g., financial loss) would tend to respond with the same degree of internally-directed aggression but would not show any tendency

[4] J. Tuckman, et al., "Emotional Content of Suicide Notes," American Journal of Psychiatry, 116 (1959), pp. 59-63.

[5] In Part IV I shall actually argue that the expression of positive affect can be one of the most effective means of hurting someone through suicidal actions. This, however, in no way helps the Henry and Short Theory, in which meanings are never treated as problematic.

to commit suicide. Even more important for our later treatment of suicide as a meaningful act, such studies almost never consider the situational aspects of aggression expression. Henry and Short assume that aggression is related to suicide and homicide *in general*, whereas it may very well be that only for financial-loss situations is aggression expressed by suicidal actions among the upper classes and by homicidal actions among the lower classes—perhaps because these are actions so defined as to reestablish self-esteem lost through failure, while a different expression of aggression would merely be epiphenomenal tension release.

Inference 1. Assumptions I and II lead us to infer that an increase in frustration will lead to an increase in homicide or an increase in suicide, and a decrease in frustration will lead to a decrease in homicide or a decrease in suicide.

Assumption III. An increase in general economic gains will lead to a general decrease in frustration; and an increase in general economic losses will lead to an increase in frustration.

Inference 2. An increase in general economic gains will lead to a general decrease in aggression; and an increase in general economic losses will lead to an increase in aggression.

Inference 3. An increase in general economic gains will lead to a general decrease in homicide or suicide (or both?); and an increase in general economic losses will lead to an increase in suicide or homicide (or both?).

As a general criticism of this series of Assumptions and Inferences, it should be noted that Henry and Short provide us with no evidence or argument to indicate that aggression is the only or the predominant affective-cognitive (or attitudinal) orientation produced by general economic frustration. In fact, what evidence we have on the effects of general economic loss (i.e., depression or recession) on those most affected of the lower-class (whom, as we shall see below, Henry and Short would predict would be most externally aggressive) indicates that general economic loss leads to a good deal of loss of self-esteem and withdrawal.

This is merely one form of the general failure of Henry and Short, which we considered above in the general criticisms of all recent works on suicide, to provide specific evidence or arguments to support their assumptions and/or to invalidate alternative assumptions. It should also be clear from this example that Henry and Short are guilty of the ecological fallacy throughout this work. Even if the homicide rate of the lower-class in the United States rose during economic recession as a result of frustration-produced aggression, this rise could be entirely due to some subgroup rise, rather than a rise resulting from some generally shared "class" phenomena.

Assumption IV. An individual will express (or direct) his aggression against (or toward) the object(s) to which he imputes generalized responsibility for his frustration.

Henry and Short implicitly assume that there exists some *generalized imputation of responsibility for frustration,* either outward or inward, that is *stable* over time (at least so long as one holds a given status position in society—see below, under Assumption V). This is a very big assumption. As usual, they do not consider the many arguments against such an assumption, nor do they indicate that there might be any evidence on such matters other than certain highly restricted bits of physiological evidence.

It seems plausible to argue that lower-class individuals express fatal degrees of aggression against specific alters more than upper-class individuals, not because of any *generalized* imputation of responsibility for their frustrations to the whole external world, but simply because lower-class individuals are more frequently frustrated by specific individuals in specific situations than are upper-class individuals. (That is, individuals who frustrate alters of esteem and power do so indirectly and covertly, rather than in such a manner as to elicit immediate retaliation. If this is true, then lower-class individuals may simply have highly available targets for their aggression, while upper-class individuals may be at something of a loss to find a target.) Such an explanation of high lower-class homicide rates would at least be in line with the general finding of studies of homicide (other than negligent manslaughter) that most homicides are committed as some form of immediate retaliation against the (ego-presumed) injurer.

This assumption also contains an implicit assumption that homicide and suicide are actions committed with enough central integration (or rationality) of cognitive-affective processes, perceptions, and actions to involve some uniform fitting of internal states to actions and to targets. Such an assumption, so long as it is unsupported by evidence (or even argument), seems no more acceptable than the *hypereredic* theory of frustration, rage, suicide and homicide, which hypothesizes that the opposite is true—i.e., that suicide (and homicide) is generally the result of non-directed, randomly distributed expressions of aggression. Actually, individual cases of suicide are neither exclusively characterized by non-target-directed behavior nor by target-directed behavior. There seem to be all degrees of central integration of behavior involved, but there seems to be some justification in distinguishing (for our purposes here) several *types* of suicide in this respect, such as the four types distinguished by Deshaies:

> However varied and complicated are the individual aspects of suicidal behavior in the concrete, it appears legitimate to distinguish among them four great *psychological forms*: an *automatic* form (unconscious and conscious), an *emotional* form, a *passionate* form. They have their own characteristics without being opposed to each other or excluding each other and one finds transitional forms—emotional-automatic, emotional-passionate, rational-passionate.[6]

Henry and Short tried to show that a significantly large percentage of homicides and suicides are the result of aggression expressed outwardly or inwardly as a result of a generalized imputation of responsibility for frustration to the external or to the internal. This assumption is unjustified in this general or universal form; but the idea that the *imputation of responsibility* for some undesired events is important in the action process of *some* suicides is of fundamental importance in the new theoretical orientation presented in Part IV of this work.

[6] G. Deshaies, *Psychologie du Suicide*, p. 340.

*Assumption V. The direction of the imputation of general-
ized responsibility is determined by the degree of external
restraint on the actions of the individual, such that a high
degree of external restraint will lead to the imputation of
generalized responsibility to alters and a low degree of
external restraint will lead to the imputation of generalized
responsibility to ego.*

Actually, Henry and Short include an intervening argument, which assumes that the *strength of the relational
system* of an individual is what determines the degree of
external restraint on his actions. This assumption and argument, however, merely raises too many other questions
about the meaning of "strength" as distinct from "restraint"
and about the values of such a distinction. It seems better
to circumvent these problems by excluding the intervening
step and getting right to external restraint.

Henry and Short do not attempt much of a discussion of
the theoretical meaning of external restraint. How the concept is distinct from power, a much better known concept,
is not clear. The theoretical discussion of the concept and
the assumptions involving it make it seem that the two
concepts are very much the same. It would seem that Henry
and Short are primarily concerned with a *feeling* (or a perception) of external restraint, whereas the term power is
generally not used to refer to such subjective states. But
the *feeling of powerlessness* (or powerfulness) might be a
better term. The use of the term power in any form would
very likely have led Henry and Short to see the potential
significance of distinguishing between legitimate external
restraint (authority) and illegitimate external restraint
(tyranny), a distinction which would demand a fundamental revision of their theory.

Henry and Short actually assume that external restraint
causes an individual to feel justified in directing his aggression outward. Such an assumption might possibly hold true
for a subculture with a very strong emphasis and focus on
the values of individualism, but, as a general assumption it
seems unjustified and at least highly problematic.

Assumption VI. The degree of external restraint varies inversely with the social strata.

This is one of the least founded assumptions Henry and Short make. In justifying this assumption, Henry and Short seem to identify external restraint with social power, so that they seem to be arguing that the lower the socio-economic strata of an individual the less *feeling of power* he has or the more feeling of powerlessness. But, unfortunately, by failing to clearly define the concept "external restraint" and then clearly relating it to various concepts similar to it, Henry and Short confuse (1) external restraint as a feeling of powerlessness with (2) external restraint as a *feeling of being prevented from doing what one wants to do by alters with whom one has (stable) role relationships.* Gold, for example, criticizes Henry and Short's theory for making the second assumption. He argues that it is not clear that lower-class individuals feel more restrained from doing what they want to do by their role alters than do upper-class and middle-class individuals. While noting that Henry and Short explicitly operationalize degree of external restraint in terms of achievement, possession, authority, and power, Gold goes on in the next paragraph to criticize Henry and Short for making assumption (2) about external restraint:

> A number of Henry and Short's assumptions may be questioned. It is debatable that members of higher-status categories are less restrained externally than their lower-status counterparts. For example, the behavior appropriate for an "officer and gentleman" is in many respects more limited than that allowed an enlisted man. Drunkenness off the base, for example, is apt to earn the enlisted man mild reproof but to invoke strong penalties on an officer. Similarly, eccentricities tolerated in persons over sixty-five may result in institutionalization of a twenty-five year-old. External restraints on behavior are exerted not only by persons but also by norms—norms which may apply more stringently to persons in higher-status positions.[7]

[7] Martin Gold, "Suicide, Homicide, and the Socialization of Aggression," p. 652.

This confusion seems inherent in Henry and Short's own treatment of the matter.

Inference 4. Because social status (or strata) and external restraint vary inversely, and the external imputation of generalized responsibility varies directly with the degree of external restraint, social strata (or status) and the imputation of generalized responsibility externally will vary directly. Consequently, lower-class individuals will impute general responsibility externally and upper-class individuals will impute general responsibility internally.

Inference 5. Because the external imputation of general responsibility varies directly with the expression of aggression externally, and inversely with the expression of aggression internally, lower-class individuals will express aggression externally more than upper-class individuals and the upper class will express aggression internally more than the lower class.

The only further criticism that seems worth making here of this set of assumptions and inferences has already been adumbrated by Berkowitz:

> The Henry and Short argument is an intriguing one. Their reliance on the concept of 'external restraints' might appear forced but actually is in complete accord with scientific tradition. Scientists must seek to develop unifying principles capable of showing that apparently diverse phenomena (e.g., the suicidal deaths of a wealthy person and of a lonely city dweller) are special cases of a more general phenomenon (self-blame for a frustration). The present writer does not reject the Henry-Short emphasis upon external restraints altogether but would prefer to add to this argument. High social status in our society produces more than a relative freedom from restraints. (Indeed, in many cases well-to-do families feel they have a good deal of responsibility and obligations to others. Witness the Rockefellers.) What may be more important is the greater emphasis upon self-reliance and self-accomplishment in the upper social levels. Middle-class parents frequently teach their children that a person is primarily responsible for whatever happens to him (cf. Kohn, 1959).

The lower-class individual, on the other hand, tends to see himself as the hapless victim of forces beyond his control. Thus, *since the people from the upper social levels generally regard themselves as masters of their own fate, they also must blame themselves for their social and economic failures.* In extreme cases such self-blame can lead to suicide.[8]

Part of Berkowitz' criticism of Henry and Short seems based on his failure to consider that part of their work which is concerned with the imputation of generalized responsibility. But his criticism also suggests that the *imputation of responsibility* (generalized or multi-dimensionalized) might well be the result of subculture differences perpetuated, by definition, through differences in socialization practices—i.e., upper-class parents teach their children they are responsible for what happens to them more than do lower-class parents. Consequently, we have predictions of the same thing by different theories and in such a way as to complement Gold's alternative theory to that of Henry and Short.

The rest of Henry and Short's theoretical discussion consists primarily of arguments concerning how the various social categories should be ranked in terms of social status and the specific inferences (or hypotheses) from their theoretical argument as to which of the social categories will have higher homicide or suicide rates, which categories will have their homicide or suicide rates more associated with the business cycle indexes, what directions the homicide and suicide rates will vary with respect to the business cycle indexes, and which directions the homicide and suicide rates of the various social categories will be related to the business cycle indexes. The only argument against this part of their work that seems worthwhile is that they have not graded the categories finely enough in terms of status differences. Though most of their considerations are between categories such as male-female, rural-urban, Negro-white, and various age groups, when Henry and Short do consider the more traditional status categories of

[8] Leonard Berkowitz, *Aggression: A Social Psychological Analysis,* New York: McGraw-Hill, 1962, p. 326.

socio-economic class, they consider only upper class and lower class, with no middle-class category. Their theory would predict linear relations, so that presumably, any middle-class group would be midway between the lower-class and the upper-class group. For example, the middle-class category would be predicted by their theory to have homicide rates and suicide rates in between (half-way between?) the rates of the upper-class category and the lower-class category. But, even a review of the official statistics on homicide and suicide will show this prediction to be faulty. At least for the official suicide rates, there tends to be a strong U-functional relation with respect to social class, with the upper class and the lower class having roughly similar rates (just as they have similar rates of divorce and of various other "deviant" actions) and the middle class having a considerably lower rate. This fact contradicts the fundamental inferences of Henry and Short and suggests that support for their theory on this test would only come from using dichotomous categories—if the middle class is combined with the lower class, then this category will have a much lower general suicide rate than the upper-class group. Since they do not take note of this contradictory evidence, they support their theory by the selective consideration of data.

Martin Gold's socio-psychological theory of suicide is presented as being in accord with, and, presumably, an extension of, Durkheim's theory of suicide. Quoting from *The Rules of Sociological Method*, Gold concludes the following:

> Granting the divisions among levels of generality or abstraction, each with its own reality, laws at any level of abstraction are formulated with proper regard for other levels. Just as psychological laws of perception must be consistent with what is known about neurophysiology or must bear the burden of inconsistency, so sociological laws must face up to current knowledge of psychological processes. For this reason, findings at one level are clues at the other.[1]

This, I would suggest, is a misunderstanding of Durkheim's theoretical position in *Suicide*. First, though it now seems a rather common interpretation of Durkheim's position concerning the relations of individual to social variables, it is not true that Durkheim thought of these two sets of variables as just different levels of analytical distinctions made from the same concrete data. Durkheim thought of these variables as *substantially* distinct, not merely epistemologically or analytically distinct.[2] Second, Durkheim did not mean that sociological laws or relations have to be consistent with psychological laws or relations. He did believe that psychological laws can serve as analogies, hence "clues," for the formation of sociological laws; but this is far from arguing that sociological laws must be consistent with psychological laws.

[1] Martin Gold, "Suicide, Homicide, and the Socialization of Aggression," *The American Journal of Sociology*, LXIII (1958) 651-661.

[2] This interpretation was probably greatly fostered by Parson's failure to see the strong strain of Aristotelian thought in Durkheim's work, especially in *Suicide*. (See Talcott Parsons, *The Structure of Social Action*.)

Gold argues that Henry and Short have merely provided a juxtaposition of psychological and sociological variables, rather than some kind of synthesis of the two and proposes that "Where they have dealt separately with psychological and sociological antecedents of suicide and homicide, we will suggest some child-rearing links which mediate between social structural variables and intrapersonal determinants of behavior."[3] This goal is, however, somewhat compromised on the general level by Gold's argument that the "choice of homicide or suicide . . . [is] essentially a psychological problem."[4] Gold has neglected to discuss the most fundamental problem posed by Durkheim's *Suicide*: is suicide explainable "essentially" in psychological terms or in sociological terms? And by focusing concern on the psychological variables as "essential" for a theoretical explanation of the "choice of suicide or homicide" he has given the answer opposite to that of Durkheim, while arguing that his work is in the tradition of Durkheim's.

The general structure of Gold's theory of suicide (and of homicide) is simple; and is rather immediately derivable from his few fundamental propositions. Figure VIII will provide us with an outline of this fundamental theory.

Social → *Class (Sub-* → *Lower-Class* → *Lower-Class*
Structure *culture?)* *individuals* *individuals*
Differences *tend to ex-* *will show a*
in the *press aggres-* *preference*
Socializa- *sion outward* *for homicide*
tion of *more than in-* *over suicide*
Aggression *ward while* *and upper-*
upper-class *class individ-*
individuals *uals will show*
tend to ex- *a preference*
press aggres- *for suicide*
sion inward *over homicide.*[5]
more than
outward.[5]

Figure VIII. General Structure of Gold's Theory of Suicide

[3] Martin Gold, *op.cit.*, p. 652.   [4] *Ibid.*, p. 651.
[5] Like Henry and Short, Gold distinguishes only between upper class and lower class, without considering the very definite possibility that the middle-class individuals would show very different tendencies

On the most general level, Gold's aim is to show that certain sociological variables partially determine the *choice* between homicide and suicide. The sociological variable he tries to show has this causal effect is social class (or status). However, in his argument concerning the relation of social class to the preference for the expression of aggression outwardly or inwardly, Gold merely argues that (1) the socialization of aggression is the fundamental determinant of the preference for homicide or suicide and (2) that type of socialization normally associated with the outward expression of aggression is found more among lower-class individuals than among upper-class individuals and that type of socialization normally associated with inward expression of aggression is found more among upper-class individuals than among lower-class individuals. Gold does not attempt to show that the social position of individuals has any causal effect on their socialization practices. But, it is possible that individuals with a tendency to express aggression outwardly and to socialize their children to do so are lower class precisely because of this tendency, rather than that the tendency to express aggression outwardly is caused by their social-class position. Indeed, Gold goes so far as to suggest this is the case, at least in some good part, through the linkage of these two factors with a third factor:

> Selective factors are likely to be at work here. Since a great deal of social mobility in modern America is achieved in schools, where verbal ability is a core skill, boys who have such ability have a better chance of becoming middle-class adults. Degree of verbal facility is likely to affect modes of expression, such as the parents' expression of disapproval of the misbehavior of their children.[6]

---

so that there would not be any simple monotonic relation between the variables. Gold, however, goes one step further. He specifically states that ". . . stratified data are not available to test the prediction that middle-class people are more likely than working-class people to destroy themselves." (*Ibid.*, p. 655.) He is quite wrong as far as official statistics are concerned; and the available evidence (of the same sort he accepted for his tests) show his monotonic theory to be wrong.

[6] *Ibid.*, p. 654.

Gold, then, accepted that the expression of aggression and social class position are very likely associated with each other through a third factor, that of verbal ability. Even were we to accept his argument that class and type of socialization of the expression of aggression are significantly associated, we would have to admit that, as far as Gold has been able to show us, this association could be primarily the result of social drift. We shall come back to this point shortly, but first let us consider Gold's argument concerning socialization, class position, aggression expression, and the choice between homicide and suicide.

All of Gold's evidence concerning socialization practices, class position, and the expression of aggression is concerned with minor forms of violence (i.e., physical action against a person).[7] Gold did not explicitly consider the question of

[7] It should be clear that "aggression expression" and "violence" are distinct concepts, with the former involving an inference about the internal state of the organism or person that the concept of "violence" does not. As in the case of the specific action of suicide, sociologists and psychologists who have been concerned with the concept of "aggression" and its concrete manifestations have not been concerned with what it actually *means* to the individuals involved as actors, victims or recipients, and audience. Besides any differences in the normative definitions of such actions, there are almost certainly differences in the categorizations of events, expectations of events, motive imputations associated with the events, etc., between social classes in our society (as well as between ethnic groups, regional subcultures, etc.). Wolfgang and Ferracuti have, for example, argued most cogently that homicide and other forms of physical violence are much more frequent in lower-class, urban groups than in other groups in the United States precisely because these lower-class individuals have a much greater *generalized expectation* of violence being directed against themselves in the neighborhoods they inhabit. Indeed, just about anyone entering these areas expects violence more than he expects violence in non-slum areas. The general explanation of this expectation by sociologists would probably be that there exists this expectation because there is in fact more violence in these areas, a "fact" which has to be ultimately attributed to differences in values, to Mertonian anomie, or whatnot. (Wolfgang and Ferracuti do not go into the matter of ultimate causes.) But there are two reasons why this is an inadequate refutation of the argument: (1) once the expectations are established, for whatever reason, they have *functional autonomy* (which is meant to be analogous to Allport's functional autonomy of motives) and (2) there is in fact, I would argue, a generalized belief in much of Western culture (especially in the rural areas where most of the slum-dwellers have recently come from) that the city, especially the city slum, is a *scene of evil*. I would argue that the generalized *scenic expectation* leads to defensive violence, especially to defensive violence by territorially defined, feudally

relations between frustration and aggression. It seems, however, to be an important, implicit assumption of Gold's theory that aggression is the result of frustration. There is the same implicit assumption we criticized in Henry and Short's work that there exists some monotonic relation between frustration (or whatever is assumed to cause aggression) and the expression of aggression, with suicide or homicide simply being the extreme form of the expression of aggression. There is no consideration of the distinct possibility that the extremely rare phenomena of suicide and homicide might be the result of some very special, rare kinds of socialization of aggression or of whatever is behind these actions. There is no evidence that cases of suicide are normally associated with any unusual frustrations and there are plenty of cases of suicide in which one can easily see that the presumed precipitating frustration was very minor (certainly minor by general social definition). In fact, this is so frequently the case that some students of suicide have gone so far as to hypothesize that the severity of injury involved in an attempt at suicide varies inversely with any immediately preceding frustrating experience.

We are now ready to consider three specific criticisms of Gold's theoretical argument:

1. On the general level Gold proposes to synthesize sociological and psychological variables into a theory explaining differences in group and individual preferences for homicide and suicide. He does not provide us with a discussion of what distinguishes psychological (or individual) from sociological (or social) variables and he does not consider the sociological variables most sociologists would expect to have considered. Most

---

organized groups whose primary conscious goal is that of mutual protection. There is no value in calling such defensive violence "aggression"; and there is no reason to believe that different values (held by God-fearing peasants) lead these people to be "aggressive" and to socialize their children to be "aggressive." They socialize their children (and, above all, the other children socialize them) to "take up for their own rights," etc. But, then, this expectation-socialization complex must be subject, especially over the long-run, to valuation so that values in favor of violence (not "aggression") might well become established and then operate largely independently of expectations—i.e., with *functional autonomy*.

importantly, he does not provide any theoretical argument concerning possible ways in which a social structure might generate class (subculture) differences in socialization practices (and associated values). This lack of a general argument is justified by Gold by modifying his general goal:

"Now, Durkheim tentatively regarded the choice of *anomic* suicide or homicide as a purely psychological matter, unrelated to sociological variables. In *Suicide* he writes: 'Anomie, in fact, begets a state of exasperation and irritated weariness which may turn against the person himself or another according to circumstances; in the first case, we have suicide, in the second, homicide. The causes determining the direction of such over-excited forces probably depend on the agent's moral constitution. According to its greater or less resistance, it will incline one way rather than the other.'

"Henry and Short suggest that the choice of suicide or homicide, prompted by a state of anomie, is not purely a psychological matter. While their *Suicide and Homicide* includes an insightful discussion of psychological determinants of this choice, they assert that sociological variables play an active and separate role as well, that is, external restraint growing directly out of position in the social structure conditions expression of aggression.

Our own position lies somewhere between the two. We assert that, if sociological variables condition expression of aggression, it is necessary to search for the manner in which these variables are translated into those psychological determinants which lie closer to the actual individual choice."[8]

2. We have seen, however, that this more specific goal is not actually met: Gold does not even attempt to show that individual or group social position is in any way related to socialization practices and (presumably because of this link) to the preference for inward or outward expression of aggression. He attempts only to show that more individuals who can be labelled lower class prefer outward expression of aggression (or,

[8] Martin Gold, *op.cit.*, pp. 660-661.

rather, violence?) and more individuals who can be labelled upper class prefer inward expression of aggression. Most of his argument, then, is little more than an attempt to support the hypothesis that a lower-class congeries (or categorization of individuals) will tend to show a preference for outward expression of aggression and for socialization practices (supposedly) favoring such outward expression of aggression, while an upper-class congeries will show a preference for internal expression of aggression and for socialization practices that tend to support such inward expression of aggression. The argument concerns correlations (and not very strong ones), and explanations are even suggested by Gold that are opposed to any causal relationship. The sociological part of the argument, then, is pretty much eliminated and Gold is left with the not very revolutionary hypothesis that socialization practices (i.e., social learning) affect the expression of aggression. One could, however, reconstruct the argument and seek new evidence to show that social position does have something to do with determining socialization of aggression practices and, therefore, a preference for external or internal expression of aggression.

3. One would, however, still be left with no evidence that the socialization of normal aggression has anything to do with such rare actions as suicide and homicide. At this point in his argument Gold commits an ecological fallacy of major proportions.[9]

For our purposes the significant part of Gold's essay lies in his aspiration of synthesizing sociological and psy-

[9] Gold commits other methodological errors common in the literature on suicide. For example, he treats Negro females as one group with one suicide rate, whereas actually the official suicide statistics on suicide among Negroes have tended to show a radical difference in the suicide rates of young as opposed to old Negro females: the young have a suicide rate almost equal to that of the white females, while the old have almost no suicide. (See, for example, L. I. Dublin and Bessie Bunzel, To Be or Not to Be; A Study of Suicide, New York: Random House, 1933, p. 52.) If one treated the SMR of young Negro females and of old Negro females as distinct SMR, rather than taking the average of the two, he would quite likely find one supporting and one opposing Gold's theory.

chological variables into a theory of suicide (and of homicide in his case) by establishing immediate links or bridges between the individuals' social situations and their suicidal actions. Gold looks at the relationship over time—i.e., society affects the individual's choice of suicide or homicide primarily by determining his stable personality preference between the expression of aggression outwardly and inwardly. This idea, so common in culture and personality studies and theories, fails to take into consideration the many (partially) socially determined meanings of immediate situations that are, we shall argue, so fundamental in the causation of suicide (or of homicide).

III

A SUMMARY OF THE WEAKNESSES AND CONTRIBUTIONS OF SOCIOLOGICAL WORKS ON SUICIDE

As we have seen, with the *partial* exception of the socio-logistic approaches to suicide, almost all of the works which have considered suicide to be fundamentally a social phenomenon—i.e., a phenomenon which must be explained in terms of social variables—have been psycho-social theories. Even Durkheim did not deny that an adequate scientific explanation of suicide rates would have to give some consideration to the (negative?) causal influence of individual factors. The Gibbs and Martin sociologistic theory is probably the only theory which totally excludes individual factors.

Those psycho-social theories which came before Durkheim's *Suicide* were primarily multi-factored approaches, the best being Morselli's highly influential work. Other than the general criticisms which one could level at any multi-factored theory, there are few criticisms which we have felt specific enough to these pre-Durkheimian works to take up in this work. The same factors and relations appeared repeatedly in later theories, especially in Durkheim's, which was primarily an attempt at a theoretical synthesis of the many earlier ideas and findings concerning suicide as a social phenomenon.

The psycho-social theoretical approaches to suicide which have appeared since Durkheim's *Suicide* have generally been greatly influenced by Durkheim's work and, thence, indirectly by the earlier works. Cavan and Schmid, who was greatly influenced by Cavan, were both outside the Durkheimian tradition, as we have seen. But they were greatly influenced by Morselli, so that they do have fundamental elements in common with Durkheim's work. As a consequence, there are certain elements that are common to most of these works. Some of these elements will be incorporated, though generally in a different form, in the theory of suicide I shall develop later. I have, however, been more concerned thus far with trying to show what elements in these various theories are faulty, both to show the need for a new theoretical approach to suicide as a social phenomenon and because such a concentration on errors of previous works should help us to avoid the same errors. Let us, then, systematically consider the most important and common weaknesses in the various psycho-social theories of suicide.

Common Weaknesses

One of the most general problems, to be found especially in those works most influenced by Durkheim's *Suicide,* is the use of the argumentative and casuistic-deductive methods in attempting to show one theory is better than the others because it explains or even predicts the data better. Theories of suicide have been pressed into the service of more general ideas and theories which the individual theorists *assumed* to be true before they came to the data on suicide. They then deduced what *must* be true of suicide in general if the general idea they were trying to prove was, as they assumed, true. But they have often gone one step further: they have tried to give the impression that they went from the data to the theory, that they had used an inductive method. This *positivistic rhetoric* has often given a scientific aura to these works when the actual methods used were anything but scientific.

One of the more unscientific aspects of many of these works has been an uncritical treatment of data. As long as someone called a lot of things "suicides" they assumed that they had found the valid and reliable data that would unlock the secrets of social action. (We might even go further and point out that their assumption that there ever were any "things" to which these names were applied has all along been strictly an act of faith. And acts of faith have proved notoriously bad tools of scientific research.) We shall consider this problem at great length in Part III.

A third general problem has been the generally implicit assumption that the individual or immediate causes of specific suicides are so complex that they cannot be included in any systematic theory of suicide and the conclusions from this assumption that (1) sociologists should not be very concerned with the individual cases of suicide and (2) only the macro-structure of society or culture is an adequate level of theoretical argument for explaining suicide rates. This was Durkheim's general position in his sociologistic theory of suicide. For him this assumption was directly related to the assumption that suicide must be treated probabilistically and explained in terms of the whole society acting as a unit (i.e., sociologistically). The theorists after Durkheim were not generally explicitly concerned with the assumption, but, rather, simply took the conclusions as the important parts of their arguments. The acceptance of this assumption and these conclusions by sociologists who did not accept, or in some cases understand, the sociologistic argument has been of great importance in preventing sociological investigations of the real-world cases of suicide and in continuing the uncritical use of official statistics.[1]

Just as sociologists have taken the meanings of suicide statistics to be obvious, so have they also taken the social meanings of "roles," "loss of status," and other such categories to be obvious. They have, as a consequence, been able to read in whatever meanings they find necessary to support their own particular theories. Moreover, they have assumed it to be obvious that certain groups designated by such criteria as national citizenship have a homogeneous and constant "culture" or "society." This was one of Durkheim's basic mistakes and the other theorists have merely followed him in this assumption. Durkheim gave no consideration to the problem of defining "society" or "subculture." Since his basic assumption was that it is the operation of the society (meaning, most of the time, what we today would call culture) as a whole that generates a suicide rate, it would seem obviously necessary to specify just what a society is and what individuals or groups of individuals are to be considered members of it. Halbwachs was quite right in arguing that one must consider suicide rates in relation to whole "genres de vie." In terms of Durkheim's own argument, there was simply no justification for considering the

---

[1] Certain parts of the works by Cavan, Breed, and others are strong exceptions to this criticism.

specific suicide rates of individual professions or economic groups unless one could show that there were differences between these groups in terms of their fundamental social or cultural characteristics. What he did was simply to assume that where there exist differences in suicide rates, there must exist such fundamental social differences—i.e., the theory is right by assumption.

The *assumption of cultural homogeneity* is most especially dangerous in the United States; yet this is certainly an implicit assumption of almost all works dealing with suicide in the United States. Sociologists dealing with deviant behavior and other categories of social action have been arguing that there are fundamental differences in group behavior patterns caused by the existence of sub-cultures that change the meanings of social acts. Meanwhile, the theorists of suicide have been blithely assuming that the culture of the populations they have been studying is basically the same, or, at least, that any differences are not significant for an explanation of suicide. In the Henry and Short theory there is, for example, the usual Mertonian assumption that aspirations, failure, etc., are everywhere defined in basically the same manner in the United States, so that there are no cultural differences in these matters, or in suicidal matters, between classes.

One part of the assumption of cultural homogeneity is the more specific assumption that the social norms (or any other relevant social meanings) concerning suicide are homogeneous throughout a society (or a whole group of societies that might be under investigation). Durkheim did, of course, recognize that there are differences in normative evaluations of suicide, even in one nation, and tried, most unconvincingly, to banish such facts from consideration by developing his tortured theory of normality and pathology in society.[2] It was vital for Durkheim's theory, just as for all the more recent theories of suicide, to assume that the normative definitions of suicide do not vary from one society to another—and certainly not within a society. Durkheim did assume that the ultimate causes of variations in

---

[2] Durkheim had previously developed his theory of "the normal and the pathological" in *The Rules of Sociological Method*, Glencoe, Illinois: The Free Press of Glencoe, 1962, pp. 47-75.

suicide rates must be meanings (with the strong emphasis in *Suicide* being on *normative* meanings) but these varying causal meanings were assumed to be the meaning dimensions of anomie-fatalism and egoism-altruism, rather than any meaning dimensions associated directly with suicidal actions. Now, there is an obvious methodological explanation for Durkheim's assumption of homogeneity in the culture meanings associated with suicidal actions. If Durkheim allowed the meanings of suicidal actions to vary from one comparison group to another, he would be faced with the terrible task of having to isolate the specific effects of this variable in order to control for it before he could determine the effects of anomie-fatalism and egoism-altruism. So the assumption of homogeneity would seem to be a straightforward matter of simplifying to avoid impossible complications. But there are two important reasons why this is dangerous. First, if one assumes that it is fundamentally variations in the social order, which one sees as essentially a normative order, that cause variations in suicidal actions, then the most immediate explanations of variations in the suicide rates would be in terms of the variations in the normative definitions of suicidal actions themselves. It would, then, be most unsatisfactory to simplify one's task by assuming a homogeneity of these normative definitions for no other reason than simplification—one does not arbitrarily simplify by excluding from consideration that variable which, on *prima facie* grounds, seems to be the most important causal variable. Second, we have already seen that Durkheim did not make any significant attempt to systematically control the two independent dimensions of anomie-fatalism and egoism-altruism in order to isolate their particular effects. This second fact makes it clear that Durkheim did not clearly grasp the methodological argument, so there is even more reason to reject the methodological explanation of his assumption of homogeneity of cultural (normative) meanings of suicidal actions. It would seem that Durkheim made the assumption of homogeneity for at least one major reason, and one which was not a matter of rational decision-making on his part. Durkheim's work on suicide was in the tradition of studies of suicide by the moral statisticians, who, as is clear even in their name, assumed most implicitly that suicide is necessarily an immoral action and that it must be studied as such.[3] This common-sense assumption was too basic, too implicit in the whole tradition of suicide studies for Durkheim to avoid it; but he did attempt to justify it, thereby making it more of a conscious problem and thus making it necessary for Bayet and others to give explicit consideration to the assumption and show that Durkheim had been wrong.

Most of the other sociological theorists of suicide since Durkheim have implicitly assumed either that such differences in the meanings of suicidal actions do not exist or that they are not significant. Only Bayet clearly showed the danger in Durkheim's denial of differences in the normative definitions of suicidal actions; but, unfortunately, the only student of suicide to give any significant consideration to Bayet's work was Halbwachs. Cavan did attempt to show differences in normative definitions of suicidal actions by using a simple questionnaire, though she was more directly concerned with the prevalence of suicidal thoughts than with definitions or meanings of such actions. But, this part of her work has not been followed up. Since one of the basic hypotheses of the theory to be presented in this book is that the meanings of suicidal actions differ greatly even in a reasonably homogeneous culture, this common assumption of a homogeneity of meanings of suicidal actions is here considered to be a fundamental and serious error.

Closely related to this assumption of homogeneity of normative definitions of suicidal actions in a given society has been the assumption by the sociologists that these normative definitions (or any social meanings of suicidal actions) are obvious to the sociological observer. Durkheim assumed that the juridical norms reflect the norms of a group, so he assumed that the laws against suicide in European nations meant that the norms in these societies defined suicide in a very negative manner. Such an assumption seems to have very little general value, being based on a much too simplistic view of legal institutions and social norms. However, even if one did assume this relation be-

---

[3] To study immorality as such has generally meant to search for "like causes of like effects," so that one studies immorality as such by finding immoral causes. "Evil causes evil" is the basic assumption.

tween legal norms and general normative definitions to hold, there would be no justification for concluding that European societies in the twentieth century normatively define suicide very negatively; for the simple reason that these societies have rapidly been eliminating all such legal norms against suicide. (Moreover, the homogeneity assumption would be very gravely attacked, since the rate of change has been very different in different societies.)

The assumption that the *meanings of suicidal actions* are obvious rather than problematic has most likely been the basic reason for the failure of suicide studies to make much progress. Denying the validity of something that is "obvious" to everyone is often a step in the direction of scientific progress. Whether such progress will result from the firm denial of the obvious that is at the core of the theory of suicide to be developed here is still problematic. But my denial will be extreme, for I shall argue that, rather than being obvious, the meanings of suicide are very complex and obscure, not alone to the theorists, but to the social actors involved as well.

There are many other lesser errors that are commonly found in works on suicide. For example, the ecological fallacy was especially rampant in the nineteenth century works and is present in such recent works as that by Henry and Short. To explain an exceedingly small number of suicides in terms of the external properties which these individuals have in common with huge numbers of individuals in the same society is to argue in a manner that must surely be given the most critical scrutiny. When this approach is coupled with the "statistical significance" test, which is so easy to meet when one is dealing with such complexly interdependent phenomena, it is easy to see why there are so many conflicting and theoretically fruitless sociological works on suicide.

Important Contributions

The most significant contribution of the works by sociologists on suicide has been the sociological perspective itself: the insistence on seeing suicidal actions as in some way the result of *social* factors. From the earliest works this has meant in some way the insistence on studying suicide

with respect to *social meanings*, though this has generally
been taken to mean simply the normative order of society.
As we have seen, it was generally assumed that these meanings were non-problematic or obvious, that it was the most
general, abstract values that were of fundamental importance in the analysis of the causes of suicide, and that any
meanings other than shared values were of little or no
significance.

In the more recent works there has even been some
tendency to assume that the patterns of individuals' reactions to socially defined *situations* is of fundamental importance in the analysis of the causes of suicide. There has
rarely been any suggestion that the specific, concrete interaction processes between individuals might be of fundamental importance in causing suicidal phenomena, but at
least there has been some attempt to get at the situational
factors associated with suicidal actions. (The status-loss
theories, for example, have been attempts to show that it is
not simply one's position in an abstract social structure that
determines one's proclivity or probability to suicidal actions, but that how one moves within such a structure is of
critical importance in determining this probability.)

Other specific contributions have come primarily from
works done either at an earlier time or by psychologists (or
psychiatrists) who have studied suicidal actions as social
phenomena. As we have noted, the work of Cavan (and
Schmid's work extending Cavan's) included not simply
considerations of individual factors but some consideration
of the motives most frequently imputed to suicidal individuals or actions in American society. In her detailed
presentations and considerations of the two cases of suicide
she relied largely on various common-sense and psychological ideas for her analysis; but there is also some attempt to
stick close to the meanings of the statements and actions to
the individuals involved in these suicides, especially of the
individuals who committed suicide.

Contributions of this sort, however, have not generally
been of the nature of building upon what these earlier students did. In almost all cases these students of suicidal
actions as social actions have been captives of the cultural
meanings rather than students or analysts of the cultural

meanings: they have taken such meanings as the socially imputed motives as being "explanations" in themselves or as being "mere rationalizations" (or simply irrelevant, as Durkheim argued), rather than taking them as part of the evidence about the meanings of suicidal phenomena, as phenomena demanding analyses and explanations themselves.

The consideration of contributions to the formal explanation of suicidal phenomena is not included here because of my belief that we have insufficient evidence of the sort needed to justify formal attempts at explanation at this time. But there probably are some contributions of this sort. The case of the status-loss theories provides a good example. While the idea that a loss of social status is associated with suicidal tendencies is older than any sociological work and is clearly a part of common sense about such matters in our society today, the sociologists who have proposed such an explanation have generally gone beyond the old ideas, especially in insisting in some way that the specific nature of self conceptions and the relations of self conceptions to social actions are of critical importance. This idea is not merely one shared by our theoretical approach, but the idea that one might, after much empirical investigation and determination of the ways in which meanings are constructed for suicidal phenomena and for "social status" in Western cultures, be able to find certain patterns of association between patterns of "status loss" and "suicidal" phenomena is a distinct contribution, though more in prospect than in retrospect.

PART III · OFFICIAL STATISTICS ON SUICIDE AND THEIR USE IN SOCIOLOGICAL WORKS

If suicides gave their reasons for the act in set terms, not much light would be thrown on the matter. But this is precisely what everyone who hears of a suicide tries to do. All he really accomplishes is to reduce the case to his own language, thus making it something different from the reality.

G. C. LICHTENBERG,

"REFLECTIONS," 1799

12 THE NATURE AND USE OF THE OFFICIAL STATISTICS ON SUICIDE

Throughout the Western world today there exists a general belief that one knows something only when it has been counted. Enumeration has become the cornerstone of knowledge. Though this epistemological assumption was first applied in the natural sciences, it has come to dominate Western man's thought concerning human affairs as well. Beginning with the collection of statistics on economic and artistic matters in the Italian cities in the sixteenth century, and extending from the seventeenth-century creators of "political arithmetick" down to the present day social scientists, this assumption has today become one of the most important assumptions of common-sense epistemology.

Since the eighteenth century, men concerned with systematic knowledge of the "immoral" or "deviant" actions of the members of society have relied upon official statistics for their enumerations of such actions. Considering the importance of such statistics for the formation and testing of all kinds of common-sense and scientific theories of human action, it is a remarkable fact that there is at present very little systematic knowledge of the functioning of official statistics-keeping organizations; nor is there any generally recognized need among the students of society for such knowledge.[1]

This chapter examines the information now available on the way official statistics on suicide are arrived at and the ways they have been used by sociologists in constructing and testing theories of suicide. One of the major purposes

---

[1] The most significant works on this subject are the following: J. I. Kitsuse and A. V. Cicourel, "A Note on the Official Use of Statistics," *Social Problems*, 11 (Fall, 1963), pp. 131-139; David Sudnow, "Normal Crimes," *Social Problems*, 12 (Winter, 1964), pp. 255-276; and A. V. Cicourel, *The Social Organization of Juvenile Justice*, New York: John Wiley and Sons, 1967. (All of these works have been greatly influenced by the work of Harold Garfinkel.)

of the chapter is to show that certain fundamental mistakes have been made by sociologists in their use of these statistics and to suggest the need for comparative, empirical studies of official statistics-keeping organizations and the ways their products are used.

The Use of Official Statistics on Suicide

Most of the studies of suicide by sociologists have involved the use of official statistics. Indeed, as we have previously seen, the official statistics on suicide were a fundamental reason why European sociologists turned to suicide as a likely subject for the construction and validation of scientific theories of social action. Actually, there has not been any insuperable limitation upon the observation of the phenomena that has forced sociologists to rely upon the official statistics. Even with the Durkheimian approach to suicide sociologists could have gone out to collect information on hundreds of suicides within one city, one nation, or, perhaps, even on a cross-cultural basis (though the financial problem becomes acute at this stage). A great number of European psychiatrists have used the case study method for well over a hundred years to study thousands of suicides. Most of these studies used suicides or, more generally, attempted suicides, who were brought to hospitals or whose attempts occurred in mental hospitals. But some of the more recent have used visits by psychiatric workers to the homes of the suicides or attempted suicides to get more and better information on the cases.[2] Recently, a few sociologists have begun to use case-study methods as, at least, an adjunct to the studies using official statistics.[3] Nevertheless,

[2] The best of these psychiatric studies that involve interviews in the homes of the attempted suicides or suicides is that by K. G. Dahlgren, *On Suicide and Attempted Suicide*, Lund, Sweden: Lindstedts, 1945. Dahlgren gives credit to a study by Serin, published in 1926, as the first study of suicides and attempted suicides involving interviews of the families and/or neighbors to determine life histories, emotional states preceding the suicidal acts, etc.

[3] Ruth S. Cavan was one of the first American sociologists to make extensive use of case studies. (See her *Suicide.*) Her case studies, however, were largely gotten at through newspaper accounts. Warren Breed's recent case studies of one hundred suicides in New Orleans involved interviews with friends and relatives of each suicide. (See "Occupational Mobility and Suicide.")

European sociologists frequently used case studies taken from his-all of the general theories of suicide that have been proposed and tested by sociologists have relied almost exclusively on official statistics.

The most important reasons for this almost exclusive reliance upon the official statistics on suicide seem to be the following:

1. As we have previously noted, the nineteenth-century European sociologists who started the sociological study of suicide felt strongly that the constancy of the official suicide statistics indicated that there were some lawful social phenomena involved. Consequently, the official statistics merited careful study and any theory of suicide would do well to explain them.

2. Sociologists, especially after Morselli and Durkheim, considered suicide to be largely the result of general social phenomena that could be observed only by comparing the variations in suicide *rates* between many different societies and subsocieties. This required the statistical approach, not merely as a convenience but, rather, as an essential aspect of the sociologistic approach to suicide. Over the decades this statistical treatment of suicide came to be considered so fundamental to the whole sociological approach to suicide that it has very generally come to be seen as part of the definition of *the* sociological approach:

   In this thesis suicide is approached from the sociological angle, which means that our research has been concentrated on the underlying reasons for differences in the suicide rate, viewed according to category, time and territory.[4]

torical sources, newspapers, or legal records. For example, Vito Massarotti, who was one of the first sociologists after Durkheim's work to strongly argue the importance of individual factors in causing suicide, used some case studies to demonstrate his points. (See his work, *Il Suicidio Nella Vita e Nella Società Moderna*, Rome: Bernardo Lux Editore, 1913.) And Enrique Ferri, whose earlier work on homicide and suicide greatly influenced the work of men such as Massarotti, used legal case materials extensively in his work on homicide-suicide. (See, for example, the case study of Tam, who almost died from an attempt at suicide after he had killed his sister, in E. Ferri, *Homicidio-Suicidio*, Madrid: Editorial Reviews, S. A., 1934, pp. 139-144.)

[4] Cornelis Simon Kruijt, *Suicide: Sociological and Statistical Investigations* (Summary in English, pp. 416-437), Door: Van Gorcum and Company, 1960, p. 416.

3. Especially since Durkheim's *Suicide*, sociologists have had a strong preference for general theories of suicide over the more meticulous studies that could come from the use of the case study methods.
4. Suicides were rare in all societies (thirty per 100,000 population per year being quite high). So, if one wanted large numbers of suicides to treat statistically, he would have to rely upon the only sources that covered huge populations. (To set up their own statistical bureaus for the coverage of millions of people would probably not have been financially feasible.)
5. Once the earlier sociological studies of suicide had been formulated in statistical terms and tested with the use of official statistics, it was quite the normal procedure for any new studies by sociologists to be cast in the same mold. They set a professional precedent which has been hard to break.
6. And, of course, using the official statistics was always the easiest thing to do. It is always much easier to use the great quantities of published official statistics on any subject than to go out and collect even a small part of the statistics for oneself.

In many ways the use of official statistics to test theories of suicide has become so common among sociologists in the last quarter of a century that their reason for using these official statistics might better be put negatively as, "Why not use official statistics?" Most sociologists seem to have felt that these published, official figures are the "facts" or "things" called for by Durkheim and that, as things, they do not require probing criticism or justification, but only explanation. Consequently, though American sociologists have published a great deal on the deductive problems involved in the analysis of suicide statistics,[5] there has not been a single published American work that deals primarily with the inductive problems of suicide statistics.[6]

[5] See, for example, H. Selvin, "Durkheim's *Suicide* and Problems of Empirical Research," *The American Journal of Sociology*, LXIII (May, 1958), 607-620.
[6] This paucity of commentary on the inductive problems of suicide statistics is even more puzzling when one considers the great mass of professional sociological material published on the inductive problems involved in the official statistics of other forms of "deviance," such as

From the various piecemeal comments by the American students of suicide, however, it is reasonably clear that their acceptance of the official statistics on suicide as adequately reliable and valid is based on two, generally tacit, assumptions: (1) the number and degrees of validity "errors" by officials in deciding what deaths are suicides are few, certainly insignificant; and (2) any "errors" in the designation of suicides or in the collections of the data on the rates are certainly randomized so that they do not introduce any systematic bias that would give an unreliable estimate of the relative distributions of suicides. I should like to analyze each of these tacit assumptions in the light of the arguments that can be plausibly proposed against each of them. I shall, of course, consider all of the available evidence relevant to these questions; but some of the argument will, for the present, have to depend upon careful analyses of what is most plausible. There has simply been too little empirical work done on the inductive problems of suicide statistics, and much of what has been done sheds light on these problems only indirectly. Nevertheless, there is sufficient evidence to demonstrate by careful analysis that these basic assumptions by sociologists about the nature of the official statistics on suicide are unjustified. Moreover, there is enough information available to tell us a good deal about the nature of the official statistics-keeping organizations, their methods of arriving at categorizations, the social significance imputed to suicide statistics in Western cultures, and something about the social meanings of suicide in Western societies.

Errors in the Validity of the Official Reporting of Suicides

Definitions of Suicide, Official Statistics, and Sociological Theories. One of the simplest and yet fundamental tenets of scientific thought, or, indeed, of any form of clear thought, is that one must in some manner specify the meaning of his basic terms. The scientific investigator inevitably assumes a great number of shared meanings with his reader or fellow investigators and he may even leave his basic

---

juvenile delinquency. Why, for example, have such widely applied "principles" of criminological research as "Sellin's Principle" not been used in the research on suicide?

concepts unclear for a good part of some work, fearing to commit himself too early in the game to some narrow area of investigation and theorizing by rigidly defining his concepts. But at some stage in his investigation or theory, especially before the point of testing his formal theory of the realm of data he has been investigating, he must become more specific in designating the meaning of his terms. (Whether one wants to demand something so formal as a definition of the term is best left to be determined by the specific nature of the phenomena being studied and the theory being proposed. But this is merely a question of the degree of formalization that is to be demanded of the theorist.) If he does not specifically designate what he is talking about, he must then rely upon the common-sense understanding of the term to communicate the meaning of his theory, and the testing of it must be more or less on the same common-sense level. Though it is clearly valuable at times to make do with common-sense understandings of terms rather than demanding that only one particular meaning be given to a term, a formal theory generally demands some specific designations of the meanings of one's basic terms. And if the term designates something that is to be measured, a clear specification must be made if one is to get a very good measure of it. One must, in other words, have reasonably formal definitions of the terms of a formal theory and some operational definitions if one is to test the theory by empirical means.

Most of the European students of suicide, including the sociologists, were very concerned with the formal definition of suicide. (The most important attempts at formal definitions are discussed in Appendix II.) In general, they seem to have agreed with Durkheim's position that a scientific theory should never rely upon the common-sense meanings of terms, because they believed that a theory based upon common-sense understandings can hardly hope to go beyond common sense. As we have previously seen in the cases of Durkheim and Halbwachs, these students of suicide were generally unable in fact to extricate themselves from the common-sense conceptions of suicide; but they very clearly felt a need to do so.

Most American sociologists who have done work on suicide have, on the contrary, been oblivious of the need to even consider the formal meaning(s) of the term "suicide." They have generally assumed the meaning to be given, to be known by all. The earliest American works generally considered suicide to be simply a form of *intentional or voluntary taking of one's own life*. The later works just took over Durkheim's definition. At no time have the American sociologists given significant consideration to the question of the formal definition of suicide.[7]

This lack of a formal definition of suicide in the American works is, however, less significant than might at first seem the case when one remembers that the American sociologists have, with hardly any exceptions, used the official statistics on suicide. Halbwachs long ago pointed out that Durkheim's formal definition of suicide is of no relevance to Durkheim's theory of suicide because the data being used to test the theory of suicide were not collected with this definition in mind. It is this problem of operationalizing the concept of suicide that was the central failure of the European and American sociological theories of suicide, or, rather, the central failure in the *testing* of these theories of suicide. The wedding of the sociological theories of suicide to the official statistics on suicide has made sociologists quite dependent upon the official reporters of statistics for their data, hence, for their operational definition(s) of suicide. It will do no good to make up a formal definition of suicide to be tested with data operationally defined in some very different manner.

Though the failure of almost all sociologists using official statistics on suicide to consider the differences between their own ideas on suicide and those of the people doing the categorization of suicides was of fundamental importance, there is an even more important misconception which they have

---

[7] The tendency of American sociologists to define suicide in terms of some vague "intentions" of taking one's own life is well exemplified by Cavan's very brief consideration (*Suicide*, p. 3) of the nature of suicide:

What is suicide? Superficially considered, suicide is the intentional taking of one's own life or the failure when possible to save one's self when death threatens. Within this broad definition there are types. At one extreme is the highly institutionalized form of suicide which is just passing out of the customs of oriental peoples; at the other, the equally highly individualized suicides of contemporary Europe and America.

had about the official statistics on suicide. They have believed that, though they might not know how the officials defined suicide or what their operational methods of categorization were, still *the statistics represent a reliable measure of whatever it is that they are measuring because it is relatively easy to look at a body and recognize a suicide.* (As Morselli said, "A corpse is a corpse." Generally the sociologists contrasted this reliability-because-of-simplicity-of-observation nature of the counting of suicides with the "unreliability of official imputations of motives because of the complexity of motives.")

It is not necessarily inconsistent with the best scientific strategies to attempt to measure something reliably before one knows what is causing the given measurements. For example, some progress in science can be made by discovering such a measuring device as the thermometer and using it as an objective, highly reliable measure of what in common-sense terms one calls "temperature." One does not know what causes the mercury to expand and contract (or one may even have a very mistaken theoretical explanation of the phenomena), but it still can be used in the scientific study of innumerable phenomena, providing a much more reliable measure than the subjective human sense organs. This was precisely what Durkheim and other European sociologists thought the official suicide statistics provided for the study of social forces; and Halbwachs specifically compares the official statistics on suicide with the thermometer. The official statistics on suicide were to be an objective, highly reliable measure of suicidogenetic forces. *The difficulty, however, is that one is still relying upon human judgment for the data, not simply upon sensory experience, which one also used to observe the mercury expansion and contraction against a calibrated scale, but actually upon the complex faculties of human judgments in interaction with each other.*

Failing to realize this, it is little wonder that sociologists did not try to determine the criteria upon which the judgments of officials were based. They did not at first look at the relations between the measuring instrument (the official statisticians or the expanding and contracting column of mercury) and the phenomena (the things called "suicide" by the officials or the experiences called "temperature"). Had they done so, they would have discovered that the official statistics on "suicide" wax and wane in relation to a number of different dimensions of "things" called "suicide" (called so by some people and not by others): i.e., that the measuring instruments were filled with different substances so that they wax and wane with different coefficients of expansion and in relation to different "things." They would have found that their thermometers were filled with such varying substances as steam, mercury, and liquid helium. One could not realistically expect to get reliable measures of anything by observing the expansions and contractions of such diverse substances in diverse environments. Yet this is close to what the European sociologists up to and including Durkheim did and what sociologists have continued to do up to this day. It is my aim here both to demonstrate the significances of these failings for the evaluation of the sociological theories of suicide and to determine as much as possible about how officials actually go about categorizing suicides, from which we shall also learn a good deal about the social meanings of suicidal events.

Early Considerations of the Nature of Official Statistics on Suicide. The European students of suicide, including almost all of the European sociologists, were to varying degrees suspicious of the official statistics on suicide. There were many discussions of the inadequacies of the official statistics on suicide before Durkheim. De Guerry, for example, in his work of 1835, *Statistique morale de la France*, disputed the statistical finding that suicides were increasing rapidly throughout Europe in the early nineteenth century. In 1856 Brierre de Boismont thought it quite obvious that many suicides were hidden by the victims themselves or by the families of the suicides, largely because of the shame associated with the act of suicide.[8] In 1881 Legoyt clearly outlined many of the objections to the official statistics on suicide that were to be revived with greater vigor by Krose, Halbwachs, and Achille-Delmas after the works of Morselli and Durkheim had been built on the assumption that the official statistics were adequate for the testing of a socio-

---

[8] Brierre de Boismont, *Du Suicide* . . . , p. 45.

logical theory of suicide. Legoyt even recognized the biasing of statistics along the rural-urban dimension, a bias that will later be seen to be very important in its implications for many twentieth-century theories of suicide.[9] And in 1894 Strahan concluded, largely on the basis of an analysis of the comparative rates of officially reported suicides and the rates of officially reported deaths with no causes given, that the number of suicides officially counted each year must represent about one-half the actual number of suicides.[10] Moreover, it is most important to note that throughout the nineteenth century there were some excellent works done by doctors and coroners concerning the extreme unreliability of all statistics on causes of death, some of which argued that the fundamental problems of nosology were far from being solved even for the physiological causes of death. One of the best of these was the excellent work, *On Some Fallacies of Statistics Concerning Life and Death, Health and Disease*, by Henry Rumsey, published in 1875.

Morselli was cognizant of these previous arguments against the reliability and validity of the official suicide statistics. However, he considered the official statistics of his day to be *acceptable*[11] for testing theories of suicide and for examining the breadth of the suicidal phenomena, both because he expected that any errors in them would be randomized (presumably, both within and between given societies) and because in typical positivistic fashion, he considered the sociological factors to be much more "objective" than any psychological factors.

Morselli seems not to have recognized the problem of defining suicide on the individual level. Had he done so, he *might* have seen that in each classification of a suspected suicide (or of any death that is potentially a suicide) the official categorizers of suicide are always faced with many complex decisions to be made about these so-called psychological factors. Even the decision as to whether the individ-

---

[9] A. Legoyt, *Suicide Ancien et Moderne*, pp. 112-114.

[10] S. A. K. Strahan, *Suicide and Insanity*, London: Swan Sonneschein and Co., 1894, pp. 185-186.

[11] Morselli, like the other students of suicide who used the official statistics on suicide, did not give enough systematic consideration to the problem of what constitutes "adequately" reliable statistics on suicide.

ual knew the consequences of his actions is a very difficult psychological judgment in many instances.[12]

On the other hand, Morselli might have done just what Durkheim did when faced with this problem. Durkheim obviously knew all of the objections, including those stated by Morselli in the above quotations, and he did recognize and tackle the problem of defining suicide on the individual level, proposing a general definition that is at least minimally psychological. (See Appendix II.) Yet he did not face up to the problem of the classification of these subjective, psychological factors by the official categorizers of suicide any more than Morselli did in accepting the official statistics on suicide. He did not even consider explicitly the questions of the reliability or validity of the statistics, except at those points where the official statistics in some way ran counter to his theory. Durkheim did, for example, give careful consideration to the official statistics on the motives for suicides. He took much the same position as Morselli on the official statistics on suicide motives; but he did add one consideration of these statistics that is quite interesting for the light it throws on Durkheim's general method of handling the official statistics on suicide. He presents evidence to show that the official statistics on suicide motives are remarkably consistent from one society to another and from one social

[12] It was quite likely Durkheim's realization of the great difficulty officials would encounter in deciding whether an individual knew the consequences of his actions that led him to define deaths as suicide regardless of what degree of uncertainty there might be in the expectations regarding the outcome of the actions. This definition of suicide categorically eliminated all considerations of risk-taking from a theory of suicide.

In view of the official statistics on suicide at his disposal, this definitional elimination of the complexities of the decision-making processes preceding suicidal action might seem justified. But, then, Durkheim did not bother to consider whether the officials did in fact include even this grossly simplifying assumption in their decision-making processes leading to their categorization of the cause(s) of death. Nor did he note that if they did include the factor of "knowledge of the consequences of his actions" in their definitions of suicide, then the official statistics on "suicide" would definitionally exclude most cases of "insanity," since the imputation of "knowledge of the consequences of his actions" and the imputation of "insanity" are either mutually exclusive or vary inversely. This would make Durkheim's argument, in which he uses official statistics, about relations between suicide and "insanity" either quite irrelevant or very doubtful.

group to another within the same society. Durkheim's long statement on this matter of the reliability, validity, and theoretical relevance of the official statistics on the officially designated motives for committing suicide is worth careful scrutiny:

But as Wagner long ago remarked, what are called statistics of the motives of suicides are actually statistics of the opinions concerning such motives of officials, often of lower officials, in charge of the information service. Unfortunately, official establishments of fact are known to be often defective even when applied to obvious material facts comprehensible to any conscientious observer and leaving no room for evaluation. How suspect must they be considered when applied not simply to recording an accomplished fact but to its interpretation and explanation! To determine the cause of a phenomenon is always a difficult problem. The scholar requires all sorts of observations and experiments to solve even one question. Now, human volition is the most complex of all phenomena. The value of improvised judgments, attempting to assign a definite origin for each special case from a few hastily collected bits of information is, therefore, obviously slight. As soon as some of the facts commonly supposed to lead to despair are thought to have been discovered in the victim's past, further search is considered useless, and his drunkenness or domestic unhappiness or business troubles are blamed, depending on whether he is supposed recently to have lost money, had home troubles or indulged a taste for liquor. Such uncertain data cannot be considered a basis of explanation for suicide.

Moreover, even if more credible, such data could not be very useful, for the motives thus attributed to the suicides, whether rightly or wrongly, are not their true causes. The proof is that the proportional numbers of cases assigned by statistics to each of these presumed causes remain almost identically the same, whereas the absolute figures, on the contrary, show the greatest variations. In France, from 1856 to 1878, suicide rises about 40 per cent, and more than 100 per cent in Saxony in the period 1855-1880. (1,171 cases in place of 547.) Now, in both countries each category of motives retains the same respective importance from one period to another.

If we consider that the figures here reported are, and can be, only grossly approximate and therefore do not attach too much importance to slight differences, they will clearly appear to be practically stable. But for the contributory share of each presumed reason to remain proportionally the same while suicide has doubled its extent, each must be supposed to have doubled its effect. It cannot be by coincidence that all at the same time become doubly fatal. The conclusion is forced that they all depend on a more general state, which all more or less faithfully reflect. This it is which makes them more or less productive of suicide and which is thus the truly determining cause of it. We must then investigate this state without wasting time on its distant repercussions in the consciousness of individuals.

Another fact, taken from Legoyt, shows still better the worth of the causal action ascribed to these different motives. No two occupations are more different from each other than agriculture and the liberal professions. The life of an artist, a scholar, a lawyer, an officer, a judge has no resemblance whatever to that of a farmer. It is practically certain, then, that the social causes for suicide are not the same for both. Now, not only are the suicides of these two categories of persons attributed to the same reasons, but the respective importance of these different reasons is supposed to be almost exactly the same in both. . . .

Except for intoxication and drunkenness, the figures, especially those of most numerical importance, differs little from column to column. Thus, through consideration of motives only, one might think that the causes of suicide are not, to be sure, of the same intensity but of the same sort in both cases. Yet actually, the forces impelling the farm laborer and the cultivated man of the city to suicide are widely different. The reasons ascribed for suicide, therefore, or those to which the suicide himself ascribes his act, are usually only apparent causes. Not only are the reasons merely individual repercussions of a general state, but they express the general state very unfaithfully, since they are identical while it is not. They may be said to indicate the individual's weak points, where the outside current bearing the impulse to self-destruction most easily finds introduction. But they are no part of this current itself and consequently cannot help us to understand it.[13]

This statement is worth examining in detail for what it reveals about Durkheim's methods of handling this data. First, he clearly takes a dim view of the ability of officials to adequately classify not only highly subjective matters but even highly objective matters. He notes that "official establishments of fact are known to be often defective even when applied to obvious material facts comprehensible to any conscientious observer and leaving no room for evaluation." At no point in his work does he consider *how* frequent these mistakes of fact are or what these defects imply for the use of the official statistics to test a highly complex theory of suicide such as his own. Second, he implies that the imputation of the act of suicide by officials does not involve the consideration of subjective factors such as "knowledge," which would mean that their statistics on suicide have nothing to do with his definition of suicide, and, consequently, that their statistics on suicide have nothing to do with the testing of his theory. Third, he is adamant in his insistence that the very stability of proportions of the official statistics on imputed motives for suicide is a *proof* that the officially imputed motives cannot be considered to be the causes of suicide. He argues that their stability of proportional distribution from one society to another and from one occupation group to another proves that something else must be behind them. What he fails to note is that, within the context of his argument that the stability of suicide rates for a society is evidence of the social causation of suicide, the stability of the imputed motives is *presumptive* evidence that suicide is primarily a psychologically caused action. If one always finds that the proportions of motives for suicide are constant within a group (or between groups), then surely these motives are not just accidents, are not randomized. One could argue that each motive has a certain proportion of

[13] E. Durkheim, *Suicide*, pp. 148-151.

influence over the life-and-death actions of the individuals in any Western society, so that one will always find a certain proportion of suicides are the result of each motive. Durkheim insists that such stability of imputed motives implies that there is something more basic, something causing this stability of imputed motives. But the same argument can be applied to the stability of social integration forces. What causes them? And so on. Fourth, the above three considerations leads us to suspect that what Durkheim is doing is *assuming his sociologistic theory of suicide to be correct and then explaining away any data that is contrary to it.* This suspicion is supported by his immediate jump to the social factors as the causes of suicides *and* of imputed motives. Fifth, in his treatment of the stability of the official statistics on imputed motives Durkheim fails to note that one of his reasons for using the official suicide statistics to test his theory and for considering suicide rates to be due to social causes was their stability over time, at least within each society. He felt that this remarkable stability of the statistics was in itself a demonstration of the reliability and validity of the official statistics on suicide. Yet in this section he is specifically arguing that the official statistics on imputed motives cannot be accepted as reliable or valid, even though they show remarkable stability—probably far more remarkable than the degree of stability of official statistics on the suicide rates. (As we shall argue at some length later, he did not see the reasonably obvious conclusion that if defective methods of collecting statistics on suicide motives can lead to official statistics on the proportions of motives that are remarkably stable from one society to another then surely the less remarkably stable official statistics on suicide rates can be the result of defective methods of collecting statistics on suicide.)

Durkheim must have felt that the problems involved in using the official statistics to test his theory of suicide (and of human action in general) were great; but he must have assumed that these problems had been adequately dealt with by Morselli, even though he did express greater scepticism about the statistics than did Morselli. Durkheim, for example, rejected the official statistics on the motives for suicide for more or less the same reasons that Morselli accepted them with great qualifications. Their data were similar, their methods of analysis were similar, but their emphases differed according to what theory they were trying to support. Consequently, their conclusions about the adequacies and inadequacies of the data were sometimes completely contradictory.

The issue of using the official statistics to test a "scientific" theory of suicide seems, then, to have been quiet enough when Durkheim wrote his work for him to pass over it lightly, to count on the informed reader to make the appropriate tacit assumptions—the main one being that the *relative rates* would not be affected by errors in the official statistics. However, within several years of the publication of Durkheim's work the argument was resumed with new vigor. These arguments, advanced by such researchers as Krose, Jacquart, von Mayr, Halbwachs, Achille-Delmas, and Schmid were, however, primarily arguments either against or in favor of the basic assumption of the sociological approach of Morselli and Durkheim: they attacked or supported the proposition that the rates would not be affected by any errors in the official statistics. They were, consequently, primarily concerned with the problems of hidden suicides, the systematically different methods of collecting and tabulating data on suicides and other forms of deaths in the different nations of Europe, the problems of the registration of the place of death, etc. Almost all of these analysts, however, missed the critical problem that underlies the problem of the validity of official suicide rates: the systematic variations in the *meanings* of suicide.

Social Meanings and the Operational Definitions of Suicide used by Officials. Had these students given much thought to the history of the formal definitions of suicide proposed by the many different students of suicide, they would have seen that there was a very great deal of disagreement among them. (See Appendix II.) This in itself would have been a definite indication that the meaning of suicide is by no means unidimensional, universally agreed upon, or unchanging among the various societies of Europe —and certainly not beyond the cultural borders of Europe. They would have seen that the meaning of suicide changed throughout the nineteenth century among the psychiatrists, that it went from being a form of insanity to being a form of irrational behavior and, to some, even a form of rational behavior. It went from being an act that could not possibly be intended by the person to being one that was intended. It went from being an act of whose consequences the victim could not possibly have knowledge to an act that involved a clear idea of the consequences involved. And none of these changes, or the many others that one might discover from a more thorough search of the history of the definition of suicide, were unidirectional over time or throughout the various nations of Europe.

If the formal definitions of suicide among the intellectuals were so complex, so varied, so inconsistent, so changing, what were the meanings of suicide among the many different subcultures of Europe on the common-sense level of thought at which most of the doctors, coroners, official statisticians, families of victims, etc., worked in deciding whether or not a death was a suicide? The question was not asked.[14] Halbwachs did, as we have seen, recognize that there is no way of telling how the formal definitions of the

[14] Veli Verkko, perhaps the only director of a national bureau of statistics concerned with categorizing causes of death who has published a theoretical work on suicide, presents us with an excellent example of this failure to consider the effects on official statistics of using different definitions of "suicide." Verkko specifically distinguishes between premeditated "self-murders" and non-premeditated "self-slaughters" (p. 126) and he indicates that only the "premeditated" acts are to be considered to be real "suicides." At one point he carefully compares the "self-slaughter" rate with the "suicide" rate and shows that there is clear statistical evidence that, at least at one period in the history of Finnish statistics, the "self-slaughter" rate was greater than the "suicide rate" (p. 121, fn. 8). (See Veli Verkko, *Homicides and Suicides in Finland and Their Dependence on National Character*, Kobenhavn: G. E. C. Gads Forlag, 1951.) What he *seems* to mean, however, is that the "self-slaughters" were those who died by their own hands, while the "suicides" were "self-slaughterers" who were found to have acted in a "premeditated" manner. His statements on the matter, however, are quite ambiguous. Sometimes he even *seems* to use the terms interchangeably. In any event, he fails to consider the consequences for comparative analyses of using one definition as opposed to the other. The *definition* of suicide is seen as problematic only in the sense that one must get the "real" (or Aristotelian "essential") meaning of the term. Verkko certainly does not consider whether other official bureaus of statistics use the same definition of "suicide" that he does.

theorists fit the common-sense definitions of the officials in charge of classifying deaths. Moreover, Halbwachs argued that self-sacrifices are not generally considered to be suicides, at least not in European societies, so they should not be included in the formal sociologistic definitions of suicide: one could not test for Durkheim's "altruistic suicide" with statistics that systematically exclude such deaths from the statistics on suicide![15] This argument, however, still assumes implicitly that the meanings of the term "suicide" are at least consistent among officials throughout European societies, if not consistent with some of the formal definitions of suicide.

No one has ever attempted to determine what different groups of Europeans or Americans, or even the different groups of officials who categorize deaths, mean by the term "suicide."[16] It is, then, a completely open question as to whether the official statistics labeled "suicide" statistics are measures of the same phenomena. Regardless of how reliably they measure whatever they do, and we shall see reason below to doubt that they do this well, these figures cannot be taken as either *prima facie* operational definitions of the

[15] This observation by Halbwachs was repeated and clarified by Benoit-Smullyan: "Thus he uses the ordinary statistics of suicide in estimating the total number of suicides, entirely overlooking the fact that most of his 'altruistic suicides' are not commonly considered to be suicides and do not enter into the official suicide statistics. This error is particularly glaring when he asserts that the total number of suicides decreases during a war. If cases of deliberate self-sacrifice were included, the rate might be vastly increased. He also seems to have forgotten 'altruistic suicide' in his blanket condemnation of suicide as a moral evil." (Emile Benoit-Smullyan, "The Sociologism of Emile Durkheim and His School," in Harry Elmer Barnes, Ed., *An Introduction to the History of Sociology*, Chicago: The University of Chicago Press, 1948, p. 530, fn. 37.)

[16] A few of the students of suicide who have relied on official statistics for deriving and/or testing their theories of suicide have at least tried to determine what the legal definition of "suicide" was in the society whose official statistics they were using. For example, Schmid noted at the very beginning of his work on suicide in Seattle that the criminal code of the State of Washington defined "suicide" as the "intentional taking of one's own life." (C. Schmid, *Suicides in Seattle*, p. 1) He did not consider how the various coroners of the state decided what the "intention" of an individual was, nor have any of the other students of suicide. And, of course, he does not consider alternative definitions used by coroners, such as the definition in terms of "premeditation"—see the above discussion of Verkko's definition of suicide.

formal concepts used by the theorists or as reliable measures of *any* consistent set of phenomena. What the term "suicide" means to the different groups of individuals, including the different officials who categorize and tabulate deaths, can be decided only by a great deal of difficult empirical investigation of these official organizations.

It is not merely the cognitive meanings of suicide that very likely vary from one society to another and from one subsociety to another. The moral meanings and the affective meanings of both the term "suicide" and any actions either actually or potentially categorized as suicide almost certainly vary greatly as well. On this point there is much more conclusive evidence than on the matter of the different cognitive meanings of the term "suicide." Bayet, in his great work on the variations in the moral meanings of suicide, found that in France there have been great variations in the moral meanings of suicide, that these meanings have changed greatly over the centuries and decades, and that there has been a consistent difference between the moral meanings of suicide found among the cultured upper classes and those found among the relatively uncultured lower classes. I shall argue below that such differences in the moral and affective meanings of the term "suicide" and the actions called "suicide" have had systematic influences on such matters as the attempts to hide suicides (regardless of the cognitive meanings of the term) and the willingness of the officials to use the term in categorizing deaths. But we must wait to consider this problem under the section on systematic biases in the official statistics on suicide rates.

The same almost total lack of concern for variations in the meanings of suicide is shown in the considerations by sociologists (and generally by psychologists) of the term "death." When they do consider the problems of formal definitions of suicide, these students have generally defined it in some terms involving the concept of death, such as the committing of acts which one knows have the consequence of death for oneself. How is one to know that these individuals or the people categorizing their deaths mean the same thing by the term "death" that the theorists do? Shneidman and Farberow have argued, to the contrary, that many individuals who commit suicide do so in large part because they do *not* mean the same thing by "death" that the theorists assume most of us do.[17] Schneider and many others have argued that the individuals who commit actions that result in their physical demise, as defined by doctors, do so in order to live, and certainly not to die.[18] When some *ronin* of Japan or some Asian Buddhists perform actions which lead to what American or European doctors classify as death, we must recognize that this is a classification by Western doctors, not by the actors involved. Their linguistic expressions for such actions may be totally different from the ones Western observers use and certainly might mean totally different things to the actors and the significant observers of these actions within their own cultures. Anthropologists and sociologists have decided that one cannot very well understand the kinship systems of other peoples except in terms of their own language. How, then, can one conceivably understand something so immensely more complex as "death" in any terms other than those of the actors involved? And, though the differences in meaning might not be as great within one general cultural tradition, still, does it not seem plausible to expect that there are some systematic differences of meaning involved in the uses of the term "death" between one nation and another or between one subculture and another? It is certainly my contention here that this is the case and that no great advances can be made in the study of suicide until the researchers determine what these differences in the meanings of death are and how they influence the actions of individuals.[19]

[17] Edwin S. Shneidman and Norman L. Farberow, "The Logic of Suicide," in *Clues to Suicide*, ed. by Edwin S. Shneidman and Norman L. Farberow, New York: McGraw-Hill Book Co., 1957, pp. 31-40.

[18] See Pierre-B. Schneider, *La Tentative de Suicide*.

[19] "One cannot truly understand the deeper dynamics of suicide until he comprehends its relationship to death, and the unconscious significance and meaning which death has to us. There are cogent reasons to believe that, unconsciously, we do not consider (as most of us do consciously) death to be the end of our existence or a permanent state from which there is no returning. But, rather because of the innate, unconscious narcissism of the ego, our own demise is not considered even to be a possible eventuality. In our deepest selves we believe as did the psalmist, who said confidently: 'A thousand shall fall at thy right hand, ten thousand at thy left, but it shall not come nigh thee!' Hence, most of us do not fear death because

Problems of Categorization Criteria and Search Procedures. Besides these problems of the meanings of two of the basic terms involved in the official categorization of deaths, there are two other problems, which would be met with in the compilation and use of any statistics of this sort, but are especially great and relatively unexplored in the compilation and use of the official statistics on suicide. These are the problems of (1) the *objective criteria* used to decide how to categorize a death and (2) the *search procedures* used in determining whether these criteria are met. These two problems are closely related to the problem of the

---

on the deepest level we cannot even conceive of it. We have created a vast number of philosophic and religious systems which convince us, no less than did the ancient Egyptians, that we cannot ever cease to exist, but that instead we are merely translated from one form of existence to another. This denial of death and conviction of immortality the religious person entertains consciously, but the remainder of persons appear to entertain it unconsciously, however strongly they may protest and believe that they are reconciled to an eventual termination of their existence. . . . Can it be that death may be perceived in a different fashion by the suicide—that he is able to encompass his self-destruction because unconsciously he does not perceive death as the to-be-avoided thing which most of us so regard it? There is evidence from some of my own cases that the manifestly deprived and frustrated person, who is more prone than others to employ grandiose fantasies of a compensatory character, exalts thereby his sense of narcissistic immortality and omnipotence. Death then, by one's own hand, not only serves the motives of expiating self-guilt and inflicting it on others but is not even conceived in the usual terms of fear and dread. The possibility of his own not-being is unconsciously so distant and remote that he can entertain and effect an act of self-destruction without the sense of self-preservation horror which it so commonly induces in others." (Charles William Wahl, "Suicide as a Magical Act," in *Clues to Suicide*, pp. 26-27.)

Wahl is probably wrong in his implicit assumption that most non-psychiatrically disturbed individuals have very similar unconscious attitudes toward "death." Since the subjects whose attitudes toward death he has been able to study carefully are all psychoanalytic patients, he has no basis in his clinical studies for such an assertion. And the few good studies that have been done on the meanings of death have clearly indicated a good deal of dissimilarities in the meanings of "death," at least on the conscious and subconscious level. (See, for example, W. Bromberg and P. Schilder, "Death and Dying: A Comparative Study of the Attitudes and Mental Reactions Toward Death and Dying," *Psychoanalytic Review*, 70 (1933) pp. 133-185; P. Schilder and D. Wechsler, "The Attitudes of Children towards Death," *Journal of Genetic Psychology*, 45 (1934) pp. 406-451; and Herman Feifel, "Some Aspects of the Meaning of Death," in *Clues to Suicide*, pp. 50-57.)

varying meanings of the terms "suicide" and "death," but they are independent problems that have a great deal to do with determining the overall meaning of any official statistics on suicide.

Two men who agree explicitly on what the term "suicide" means may disagree completely on whether or not a specific case or a specific type of case should be categorized as a "suicide." The meanings of perceptual phenomena presented to the observer (official or otherwise) are *always* uncertain to some degree. And in the case of phenomena that are concerned with the causes of death this is almost always the case.[20] For one thing, one cannot even be sure that the observers agree on the nature of causality, especially when it is applied to a biospherical system moving over time.[21] Moreover, some observers may look only at the immediate mechanical causes and deny causality to everything that cannot be expressed mechanically. Some observers might well look beyond the mechanical cause but only to the *immediate* volition or intention that preceded the mechanical cause by some unspecified time-lag that might well vary from one observer to another. Other observers will insist on inferring the immediate volitional or intentional

[20] Psychiatrists who have been directly concerned with the categorization of the causes of deaths have always been aware to some degree of the problematic nature of such categorizations. For example, in his very influential work on mental illness Esquirol noted that it is sometimes very difficult to distinguish a real from an apparent suicide, as, for example, in the case of drownings. (See *Des Maladies Mentales*, Paris: 1838, vol. I, p. 575.) And, quite recently, Verkko, the director of an official bureau of statistics, pointedly disagreed with Morselli's belief that nothing is more certain than a corpse. (See Veli Verkko, *Homicides and Suicides* . . . , p. 114.)

A great deal of the medico-legal literature on suicide has been specifically concerned with the problem of defining suicide. See, especially, G. L. Williams, *The Sanctity of Life and the Criminal Law*, New York: Knopf, 1957.

[21] Schmid gives a quote from a *vital statistician* which shows clearly that the vital statistician recognized the great problem of singling out one "cause" from the complex life process as the "cause" of death:

> In recording the statistics of death the vital statistician is confronted with the absolute necessity of putting every death record into some category or other in respect of its causation. However complex biologically may have been the train of events leading up to a particular demise, the statistician must record the terminal "cause of death" as some particular thing.

(C. Schmid, *Suicides in Seattle*, p. 25.)

cause only when they can specify certain very definite external (even mechanical) situations that can be socially designated as "motives" or causes of motives. Again, some observers will infer intention only when they can specify either the external situation that is socially defined as a motive or cause of motive for such actions or when they can show a previous record of actions that were categorized (by officials or what other representatives of the society?) as attempts to commit suicide. One example of such official considerations is found in an extremely interesting statement concerning the official categorization of the cause of death and the effect of this on suicide rates. Shneidman and Farberow mention one extreme case of categorizing a death as suicide *only* when there was a suicide note:

> *Post hoc*, or "after the fact" definitions, refer to those cases in which an individual is labeled as suicidal after he has committed suicide. Statistics on suicide are, of course, based on *post hoc* definitions of suicide. The primary difficulty with such definitions is in determining whether or not the individual actually killed himself. The case of the individual who writes a suicide note and then shoots himself is a clear case, but many cases of suicide are in fact more or less equivocal or debatable. For example, in the case of an individual who "jumps or falls" from a high place or who is found dead of barbiturate poisoning the question is often raised whether the case was suicidal or accidental. The term "suicide," as a mode of death used by coroners in the certification of death, is a medicolegal term, and includes, as a *sine qua non*, the concept that the person played a major role in bringing about his own demise, and that his intention in his behavior was to die. It should be obvious that statistics on suicide can be greatly influenced (in any locale or for any temporal period) by the manner in which these equivocal deaths are labeled. For example, one major city of the United States had only a consistently low number of suicides each year because the coroner does not label a case as "suicide" unless a note is found with the body.[22]

Besides these differences in the decision-making criteria

[22] Veterans Administration, Washington 23, D.C., Department of Medicine and Surgery, *Medical Bulletin*, March 1, 1961, p. 3.

one will very likely find great differences in the weighting of these criteria by the different observers. Common-sense judgments of what is going on or what has happened in a certain situation are surely patterned to some degree; but there is always, even within one reasonably small, well-integrated group such as doctors, a good deal of leeway for the individuals involved to weight the various factors in accord with their personal inclinations. And the more ambiguous the situation, the less well socially defined it is, the more important the individual weightings will be in determining the ultimate decision made on the categorization of the cause of death. *When one considers how ambiguous the social definitions of "intention to die," "desire to die," etc., are, it becomes clear that there is a good deal of such ambiguity in these categorizations.* Consequently, one must expect a low degree of reproducibility of such categorizations. As we have already seen, Durkheim himself considered imputations of "intention" to be the most unreliable form of information. Had he simply noted that even the laws specify "intention" as necessary for a legal categorization of suicide as the cause of death, he would have realized that *even his own arguments would necessarily lead one to reject the official statistics on suicide as a most unreliable form of information.*

Besides these problems of the different decision-making criteria, there are the problems of the different *search procedures* used to determine the presence or absence of the criteria. The differences in the categorization of the causes of death that can result from differences in the degree of thoroughness used in searching for the presence of the criteria for categorization as a suicide is an obvious case in point. Some observers will go to more witnesses than others in the *search for socially defined motives for suicide.* Some will go to different kinds of sources than others; and different kinds of sources will frequently act differently in categorizing a death.

For example, one observer might go to a Catholic priest to determine whether a dead man was the "type who would kill himself." Such a source might well give a very different answer than, say, the dead man's estranged wife. The critical importance of just such a source can be seen in a coroner's report concerning the death of a young soldier from California. According to the report, he had died as a result of a gun shot wound inflicted by himself while holding the gun to his head and speaking to a friend, the only person present, about playing Russian roulette. It was considered possible by the coroner that this was a case of suicide. Consequently, he proceeded to look for evidence he considered relevant to this question. He was first concerned with the immediate scene, action, agents, agencies, and with what had taken place in what sequence. (The nature of the agency, the gun, was quite important in this categorization process. It was considered important to know whether the gun was such that the number of shells and their position was obvious.) The next concern of the investigator was to determine the character of the deceased. But what sort of character properties should one look for? It would appear from the report that this was a critical turning point in the categorization process. The investigator seemed to be swayed primarily by the testimony of the individuals who were there, either immediately present at the time of the act or the first on the scene afterwards. (We might have a very strong *primacy effect* involved in such official categorization processes as a result of the need for consistency on the part of officials. On the basis of their preliminary findings, which would come largely from the immediate scene and the immediate witnesses, they might well make a tentative judgment which they feel publicly committed to.) These immediately present witnesses presented the deceased as a "joker" and a "show-off" who was always trying to make an impression on people. It was clear that they thought of the act leading to his death as a "social stunt," just another bit of "showing-off," but one with unexpectedly fatal consequences. The investigator then telephoned the Catholic priest who knew the deceased at the army camp. The priest assured the investigator that the deceased was not "the kind of person" to commit suicide. In the next sentence the investigator concluded that this was a case of "accidental self-destruction" and not a suicide.[23] Whether

[23] It was clear that the investigator(s) had not gone into the previous relations existing between the deceased and the immediate witnesses, though there seemed to be a very great deal more to their relations. The investigator did not go into the matter of why these

or not the man writing this report actually decided the case in this sequence and for this reason is in many ways irrelevant. It seems most important that he saw this as the most culturally plausible way of presenting the argument in the official report.[24]

There are many other important differences of this kind. For example, one observer might choose to look at the personal effects or the past private life of the individual much more thoroughly than another. There are, for example, quite likely different clues for different observers that indicate a death is suspicious enough (or legally questionable enough) to legitimize a reading of the diary or the personal letters of the deceased in a search for a motive or an expression of intention to die. The "right of privacy" is evaluated differently by different individuals within a society and it is largely up to the individual observer to decide where to stop in such an investigation of an individual's personal effects or private life. (And, of course, it is quite possible

---

"friends" were presenting the deceased as an irresponsible joker, nor did he try to determine if others thought of him this way. The mother of the deceased felt that these were suspicious omissions. She absolutely rejected the possibility of suicide (in conversation with the present author), but felt strongly that the soldier who was present during the shooting was actually the one who fired the shot, probably by accident. She got statements by others who knew the deceased well to the effect that he was not an irresponsible joker, she got some hearsay evidence to the effect that the soldier present at the time of the shooting had been in trouble of various sorts, and she tried to get the officials to reinvestigate the case with these considerations as major leads to new evidence. She got trapped in the bureaucratic maze of federal and state government agencies and never got anywhere at all in her attempts to reopen the case. (She did not seem aware that she needed the expert help of a lawyer. When it was pointed out to her that this was her only hope, she was not able to pay for it.) She eventually decided that the influential family of the suspected soldier had quashed all further investigation.

[24] Coroners' reports generally include references to their sources and the types of information used. It would, consequently, be feasible to get some worthwhile information on the search procedures involved in the categorization process of causes of death by a systematic treatment of such reports. One would, however, be left with the basic problem of specifying the relation of *what is reported* about the search procedures to *what is not reported*. And what is not reported might well be more important than what is reported. Far more important, one would still not know how *post-hoc* constructions (or presentations) of events are related to what could have been scientifically observed had there been anyone there to do such observing.

that some systematic biases will result from certain patterns of shared tendencies along these lines within and/or between societies.)

In general, we can say that sociologists who have used the official statistics on suicide have erred in not recognizing that the imputation of the social category of "suicide" is problematic, not only for the theorists of suicide but for the individuals who must impute this category to concrete cases in fulfillment of their duties as officials. It must be recognized that the structures (such as the definitions of the categories, the definitions of relevant information, and the standard operating procedures used in searching for relevant information) within which officials work vary greatly.[25] And, most importantly, we must recognize that the social imputation of a category such as suicide involves the *social imputation of causality of social action*, something which depends on many factors other than the "physical structure"[26] of the events, which the positivistically inclined would have us believe are the only *significant* determinants of the imputations of the categories of "cause of death."[27]

[25] Social psychiatry is one area of study in which many of the problems of the meanings of social categories have been considered to be problematic and potentially subject to great variation dependent on factors such as the cultural and socio-economic status of the categorizer. See, for example, Henry J. Wegrocki, "A Critique of Cultural and Statistical Concepts of Abnormality" in *Personality in Nature, Society, and Culture*, edited by Clyde Kluckhohn and Henry H. Murray 2nd Edition, New York: Alfred A. Knopf, 1955, pp. 691-701; and Leo Srole, "Judgmental Bias in Psychiatric Classification," in *Mental Health in the Metropolis*, vol. I, by Leo Srole, *et al.*, New York: McGraw-Hill Book Co., Inc., 1962 pp. 48-52. Some of the social psychiatrists have considered the relevance of such problems to statistical studies of mental illness. (See, for example, H. Warren Dunham, "Some Persistent Problems in the Epidemiology of Mental Disorders," *American Journal of Psychiatry*, CIX (February, 1953), 567-575.)

[26] One of the basic ideas of this analysis of the socially problematic nature of the imputation of categories is that *the "physical structure of events" is itself part of the social process*. Moreover, it seems likely that dependence of one's *estimates* of the physical structure of events upon social processes is generally recognized by the social actors involved in making the imputations of categories (especially since this idea is generally the major justification given for our "conflict" system of determining "truth" for legal purposes) and that this "recognition" is itself a major justification for explicitly giving weight to the social factors (such as the status position of the family of the deceased).

[27] The most important considerations of the social determinants of

The imputation of the official category of the "cause of death" is very likely the outcome of a complex interaction process involving the physical scene, the sequence of events, the significant others of the deceased, various officials (such as doctors, police), the public, and the official who must impute the category.[28]

The Reliability and Unreliability of Official Statistics on Suicide

The above arguments concerning the nature of official categorizations of suicide cast grave doubt on the acceptability of such statistics to test any sociological theory of "suicide." But such criticisms of the use of official statistics to test sociological theories of suicide might well be insufficient to convince those who are committed to their use.[29]

---

the perception of causality are J. Piaget, *The Child's Conception of Causality,* translated by Marjorie Gobain, London: Kegan Paul, 1955; and Fritz Heider, "Social Perception and Phenomenal Causality," republished in *Person Perception and Interpersonal Behavior,* edited by Renato Tagiuri and Luigi Petrullo, Stanford University Press, 1958, pp. 1-22. The most important work in the field of the perception of causality, which does include some very important considerations of the social determination of the perception of causality, is that of A. Michotte, *The Perception of Causality,* New York: Basic Books, 1963.

[28] For some excellent examples of the kinds of arguments that can go on for centuries concerning whether a given death was the result of suicide see the discussion of "Suicides of Artists" in Rudolf and Margot Wittkower, *Born Under Saturn,* New York: Random House, 1963, pp. 133-149.

[29] Gibbs, for example, is one of the sociologists who has accepted as probable the hypothesis that suicide statistics are not very valid: "Concern with suicide rates has created still another problem for sociological research, the question of the reliability of official suicide statistics. Following Durkheim, suicide may be defined formally as 'death resulting directly or indirectly from a positive or negative act of the victim himself, which he knows will produce this result.' But this may not be applied by persons who compile official mortality statistics. The author finds that officials (e.g., coroners) who make such decisions are not governed by a formal definition of this kind. Thus the use of official suicide statistics in research rests on the assumptions that the commonly held conception of the act: (1) corresponds to the research definition, (2) does not vary from one population to the next, and (3) is applied consistently to all cases of death." (Jack P. Gibbs, "Suicide," in Robert K. Merton and Robert A. Nisbet, *Contemporary Social Problems,* p. 227.)

Gibbs, however, goes on in the same article to argue that the psychiatrists (whom we shall discuss further below) who have denied these assumptions about reliability have not proved their case with

If, however, it can be shown that there are systematic biases in the statistics that make them unreliable for making such tests, then the two sets of arguments combined must lead us to conclude that these official statistics cannot be expected to have any significant value in constructing or testing socio-logical theories of suicide.[30] It will be my purpose in this section to show that the official statistics on suicide are probably biased in a number of ways, often in the same direction, such that the various sociological theories of sui-cide will be unreliably supported by these official statistics.

The main arguments against the presence of systematic biases in the official suicide statistics have been the follow-ing:

1. The validity and reliability of the statistics have steadily improved over the last one hundred and fifty years so that today they must be a pretty close approximation to the real rates. At least they are close enough so that, though the official rates are undoubtedly still unreliable or invalid to some degree, the degree of invalidity or unreliability is not sufficient to significantly bias any test made with them.

---

evidence. He concluded that "All things considered, present knowl-edge precludes an adequate evaluation of official statistics. Probably they are not very accurate, but the amount of error is another ques-tion. . . . We can only conclude that the question of the reliability of suicide statistics remains unsolved. (*Ibid.*, pp. 228-229.)

Yet Gibbs implicitly assumes that the validity and/or reliability of the official statistics on suicide is sufficient to make it worthwhile to go on using them to test his own theory of suicide.

In the same book Merton states that "All sociological authorities agree that the statistics of mental illness and suicide, of crime and juvenile delinquency, of prostitution and divorce are subject to all manner of bias owing to difficulties in obtaining a thorough count of comparable units." (Robert K. Merton, "Social Problems and Socio-logical Theory," *Ibid.*, p. 702.) Yet he also implicitly accepts the use of these official statistics.

In general, these sociologists simply have not regarded the use of the official statistics on suicide to be sufficiently *problematic* to war-rant a systematic consideration of the problem. Gibbs, for example, gives only one instance of a demonstrated bias in the data (from Gargas's study of suicide in the Netherlands). He did not go into the evidence of bias unearthed by Krose, von Mayr, Halbwachs, *et al.*, of which he seems unaware.

[30] It is, of course, possible that future empirical research on the validity and reliability of official statistics on "suicide" will make it necessary for us to reject the conclusions arrived at here.

2. The relatively high degree of stability of the statistics on suicide rates supports the assumption that the statistics are valid and reliable measures of some real phenomena that occur with stable rates themselves, for rates based on invalid or unreliable observations would tend to be random, thus producing instability in the rates.

3. Though it is undoubtedly true that there are many invalid categorizations of the causes of death by the officials, it can be safely assumed that all such invalid categorizations are randomized, so that for each death wrongly left out there will be one wrongly added; and the distribution of these errors will be the same for all societies or subsocieties.

Now let us discuss each of the arguments in turn to see what merits each might have.

The Problem of Changes in the Official Statistics. In 1879 Morselli believed that the suicide statistics had been steadily improving. He was not convinced that they had reached the ultimate approximation of the real rate that they would some day, but he did believe that they had by then approximated the real rates sufficiently for his form of statistical analysis. The first extensive study of the inductive problems of suicide statistics was published by Krose in 1906[31] and went a long way toward totally discrediting this assumption made by Morselli and his successors, especially by Durkheim. Further evidence against the inductive methods of the official collection methods was published in 1916 by von Mayr.[32] Both of these works were reviewed, attacked, and supported by Halbwachs in 1930[33] and by Achille-Delmas in 1933.[34]

For most of the studies of suicide, including those of

[31] S. J. Krose, *Der Selbstmord im 19. Jahrhundert nach Seiner Verteilung auf Staaten und Verwaltungsbezirke*, Freiburg i. B., 1906; and *Die Selbstmorde 1893-1908, Vierteljahrhefte zur Statistik des deutschen Reiches*, I (1910). Krose is referred to extensively by both Halbwachs and Achille-Delmas. References made to Krose and von Mayr are derived from Halbwachs and Achille-Delmas.

[32] Georg von Mayr, "Moralstatistik," in *Statistik und Gesellschaftslehre*, 3er Band, Tübingen, 1917, pp. 258-404.

[33] Maurice Halbwachs, *Les Causes du Suicide*.

[34] F. Achille-Delmas, *Psychopathologie du Suicide*.

Morselli and Durkheim, one of the most important sets of official statistics on suicide was that of Prussia, as well as those of the other German states. Krose found that though the Prussian statistics were among the oldest (beginning in 1816), until 1868 they were based upon independent collections of statistics by the Catholic priests and by the Protestant ministers from their own constituents and by the government administration for the Jews and the non-affiliated. Moreover, in 1883 there was a reform in the methods of collecting and tabulating the statistics. In this one year the official figures jumped from 4,984 to 6,171. One could hardly compare the figures before this reform with those after the reform. A similar reform in the suicide statistics of Saxony in 1876 led to an increase in the number of suicides from 745 in 1875 to 1,114 in 1877.[35]

The same tendency for any reform in the method of keeping the suicide statistics to produce an immediate jump in the statistics was found in a number of other countries of Europe. For example, from 1819 to 1872 the suicide statistics for Austria and Hungary were kept by the priests. In 1872 there was a reform of the methods of collecting the statistics which made the department of health responsible for collecting the official statistics on suicide. A year later, in 1873, the suicide rate had increased by approximately fifty per cent.[36] Again, the Spanish statistics on suicide were so confused that Krose gave 360 per year as the official figure for the period 1896-1900, while von Mayr gave 1909 per year as the official figure for the same period; and in 1905 the official figures jumped from 367 per year to 1,250 per year.[37]

These authors do not indicate whether there were any significant reforms in the methods of collecting the statistics or in the definitions of the concept of suicide which did *not* lead to an immediate jump in the number of suicides (or to an immediate decline). A thorough study of the relations between the suicide statistics and the historical changes in the statistical methods of the different official agencies would certainly have been valuable in assessing the adequacy of these statistics. It is possible, however, that such

[35] Reported in M. Halbwachs, *op.cit.*, pp. 22-24.
[36] *Ibid.*, p. 28.   [37] *Ibid.*, p. 31, fn. 1.

a study was not feasible, since in numerous instances Krose, von Mayr, and Halbwachs seem to have found it impossible to determine how the officially reported statistics on suicide were collected—Norway is a case in point.[38] In any event, what evidence they were able to get on the effects of reforms on the official statistics indicates that the reforms had such a great influence on the statistics that they were not comparable before and after the reforms. Since the statistics seem to have always jumped upward after a reform, it is reasonable to assume that the reforms, frequently consisting of turning the collection of the statistics over to the secular officials, tended to result in the unearthing of cases of suicide that would have been hidden or simply never considered under the old statistical regime. This could mean that the new statistics were more reliable; and this is certainly the interpretation given to these facts by Halbwachs and the other sociologists. But there is no way of knowing that these changes did not result in the adoption of new rules of evidence, new search procedures, and even new concepts of suicide. Indeed, there would seem to be sufficient *prima facie* reason to believe that the clergy and the people would differ on all three points from the department of health bureaucrats or the certifying doctors. Moreover, if one reform can lead to an improvement in the reliability of official statistics by as much as fifty per cent, what might one expect from several more reforms? Though there might be some law of diminishing returns at work, one would, nevertheless, expect on the basis of past experience that such reforms would send the rates shooting up each time. The only significant question of reliability would then be whether the errors are randomized within and between societies being compared. The evidence presented so far would indicate that one must strongly doubt that the errors are randomized, for the simple reason that the "improvements" differ greatly in their impact on the official suicide rates from one society to another.

What evidence there is on the "improvements" of the official statistics on suicide seems rather strongly to indicate that there have indeed been changes, sometimes revolutions, in the methods of collecting the official statistics on

[38] *Ibid.*, p. 30.

suicides.[39] Moreover, the evidence indicates that these changes have always led to increases in the suicide rates. These changes in themselves lead one to expect that further changes would produce great changes in the official statistics. If we assume that such future changes would produce as much increase in the official suicide rates as past changes have, then we must assume that the present statistics underestimate the "potential suicide rates" by anywhere from 10% to 50%; and we must expect that the amount of these underestimations varies greatly from one country to an-

[39] The official U.S. statistics on suicide present us with a special case of changes in suicide statistics. First, the most important study of official suicide statistics in the U.S., that of Dublin and Bunzel (*op. cit.*), led the authors to conclude that there was improvement in these official suicide statistics to such a degree that "prior to 1900 our statistics were so unreliable as to have little significance" but sometime after 1900 they became reliable enough to use (*Ibid.*, p. 24). The authors do not consider why there was this "improvement" in the reliability of the statistics, nor do they try to indicate exactly when they became "reliable enough" for use or within what limits they are "reliable enough" for what purposes. Second, the population base of the official statistics on suicide in the U.S. was changing almost every year up into the early 1930's (*Ibid.*, pp. 20-21). The states that were added over time were primarily southern and western, the states with the greatest regional socio-cultural differences from the north-eastern states. One would expect that changing the population base of official statistics on suicide, or on anything else, would so affect the meaning(s) and reliability of the statistics that they would be useless without some careful considerations of the effects of this changing population base. Dublin and Bunzel agreed with such an obvious objection and, consequently, "discuss mainly the figures for the Original Registration States" (*Ibid.*, p. 21). However, the sociologists who have since used the official statistics for this period have not been quite so demanding, even though their statistical tests were very frequently much more complex and, consequently, much more subject to any systematic errors or biases. For example, the great bulk of Henry and Short's statistical tests (in *Suicide and Homicide*) of the relations between suicide and business cycles in the U.S. are based on the official statistics compiled from the U.S. Death Registration States during this period of changing population base. Henry and Short go so far as to not even consider the existence of these changes in the population base, though they do define the U.S. Death Registration States: as "those states for which data on suicide are collected by the U.S. Bureau of Vital Statistics" (*Ibid.*, p. 29, fn. 6). Indeed, Henry and Short use varying periods within this period of changing population base so that variations in the population base(s) are compounded. (See, for example, *Ibid.*, p. 170, Table 7.)

It is very hard to imagine what the justification for such statistical tests as this might be. It is even harder to imagine what the justification might be for not considering the matter of justification.

other,[40] so that we have no reason to believe that the improvements in official statistics on suicide have led to greater randomizations of errors. The contrary is just as reasonable an expectation. We know that the relative positions of the European nations in terms of suicide rates have changed greatly during the last one hundred years; and we know too that their methods of collecting suicide statistics have changed greatly, but we have very little idea of the relations between these two changes. We can expect that they are great.

Whether the statistical tests used by sociologists can be expected, on the basis of this evidence, to be biased must depend partly on how fine the differences in rates for different groups are and how fine the tests are. If the investigator is merely comparing whole nations with each other (so that the populations are in the millions) and the rate of one nation is ten times that of another, then he might feel that it is plausible to conclude that the one has a higher real rate than the other, at least if he has examined the information he can get on the methods of collecting the statistics in the two different nations and found no gross differences. But almost all sociological theories of suicide rely upon much finer analyses than this and, consequently, must be assumed to be significantly biased, unless, of course, the researcher has provided evidence that they are not. And no sociologist who has set out to test his theory of suicide with official statistics has ever provided significant evidence of this sort.

The Stability of Official Suicide Rates. Halbwachs did, of course, provide an extensive sociological discussion of the reliability and validity of the official statistics he was using

---

[40] The term "potential suicide rate" is used here, rather than the more normal term "real suicide rate," simply because it is a fundamental part of the argument throughout this work that there does not exist such a thing as a "real suicide rate." Suicides are not something of a set nature waiting to be correctly or incorrectly categorized by officials. The very nature of the "thing" is itself problematic so that "suicides" cannot correctly be said to exist (i.e., to be "things") until a categorization has been made. Moreover, since there exist great disagreements between interested parties in the categorizations of real-world cases, "suicides" can generally be said to exist and not exist at the same time, though this might seem a rather incongruous way of putting it.

to test his theory of suicide. His preliminary considerations indicated that the statistics were so unreliable that they would almost certainly bias any tests of a theory of suicide which relied upon them. So Halbwachs devised an ingenious method of internally analyzing the statistical data to determine how reliable it was. He argued that if one were to consider the official statistics on just the suicides resulting from that one method of committing suicide which lent itself most easily to the hiding of suicides, then one could determine how reliable the suicide statistics were by analyzing them for stability. If the statistics on suicides committed by this method were quite stable, then the official statistics on suicide must be reliable; if they were not stable, then the statistics must not be reliable. In general, the reliability of the statistics must vary directly with the stability of the statistics on the suicides committed by this one method.[41]

The method which seemed to Halbwachs (and to other students of suicide) easiest to dissimulate was suicide by drowning. In general, drowning, he reasoned, is about the most difficult form of death to reliably categorize. Though it is public at times, there is generally little evidence to distinguish an accident from a suicide, especially if the survivors of the deceased try to hide any notes, etc., that the deceased might have left behind that would indicate the act was a suicide. Since it is so easy to dissimulate a suicide in this way, either by actions taken by the deceased before jumping in or by his successors after he is found, it must be expected that this method of suicide will lead to the most successful dissimulations and confusions among observers about intentions, and, therefore, the greatest unreliability of the official suicide statistics.[42] If, however, there is much successful dissimulation of suicides in this manner (and/or other forms of mistakes in categorizing) so that the suicide statistics are not very reliable, then one must expect that the rates of suicide committed by this method will be unstable. The rates of successful dissimulations must be dependent on many accidental factors. Therefore, the rates

[41] See M. Halbwachs, *Les Causes du Suicide*, especially pp. 41-68.
[42] Halbwachs also applies the same argument to a number of other methods. See *ibid*.

of suicide recorded as due to this method must vary. That is, if the rates are primarily dependent on chance factors rather than on non-chance decisions by the officials, then the chance factors will result in chance outcomes and, therefore, in unstable suicide rates.[43]

This rather ingenious argument can, of course, be applied to the official suicide statistics in general; if the statistics are not very reliable, then they must be dependent on chance factors that will produce chance outcomes so that the suicide rates will not be very stable. Consequently, the suicide statistics, which are stable, must be reliable.

The basic idea behind this argument is relatively simple and an old one among students of suicide. Halbwachs reasoned that if the official statistics on suicide were the result of errors or accidents, then the sum of official categorizations of suicide would be a sum of random events, events with greatly varying probabilities of occurrences. He concluded that, since the particular events would be subject to such great variations, the sums of such events would be subject to great variations. The variations would sum up and the official statistics on suicide would, as a consequence, show great instability. If, on the contrary, one finds that even that particular form of suicide which is admitted by all to be the form most subject to error in categorization has a very stable rate in the official statistics on suicide, then, reasoning backward from stability, one must conclude that the categorizations are not very subject to error or accident. This argument, which seems to be a particular form of the old idea that like effects have like causes, is a specious one. It is the same argument that lay behind the view that, since the official statistics on suicide were reasonably stable within each large society, then the causes must be reasonably stable for any large society.

Both arguments fail to note that if one is concerned with outcomes resulting from a *large* number of "causes," then it is quite possible to vary the "causes," eliminating or adding some, for example, without appreciably affecting the probability of outcomes. (In a long series of coin tossing

---

[43] See Maurice Halbwachs, *ibid*. Achille-Delmas, *op.cit.*, strongly attacked this argument, primarily because he believed *social drift* of personality types caused such stability of rates.

experiments one can, for example, add a factor of a strong wind, which undoubtedly affects the motion of the coin in the air, and thus can be presumed to affect each particular outcome, without changing the probability of occurrence of each of the two possible events from one half.) Moreover, there would actually be nothing strange at all about having a stable rate of mistakes or accidents in categorizing suicide or in any other form of social action. Buckle long ago noted, for example, that

> we are now able to prove that even the aberrations of memory are marked by this general character of necessary and invariable order. The post-offices of London and of Paris have lately published returns of the number of letters which the writers, through forgetfulness, omitted to direct; and making allowance for the difference of circumstances, the returns are year after year copies of each other. Year after year the same proportion of letter-writers forget this simple act; so that for each successive period we can actually foretell the number of persons whose memory will fail them in regard to this trifling and, as it might appear, accidental occurrence.[44]

Halbwachs' argument is fallacious in both the particular and the general case. The reasonably stable suicide rates of most societies can equally well be explained by assuming that there are *many* different factors with varying probabilities of occurrence that determine, with varying probabilities, the responses (in terms of the categorizations of "causes of death") of the official statisticians.[45] The particu-

---

[44] Henry Thomas Buckle, *Introduction to the History of Civilization in England*, p. 18.

[45] The presence of many different (presumed) causes in the whole process is quite important. If one thinks deterministically about probabilities of outcome, then it might well seem that the more the number of causes at work, the more the unpredictability and, therefore, the more the instability of outcome. This line of reasoning seems to have been the cause of the expressed wonder of Harold Larrabee over the regularity of suicide statistics in New York: "What makes the statistical regularity of long-run conduct so striking is the fact that it shows itself in acts which are not the simple outcomes of a few mechanical forces, like the movements of spun coins, but in masses of close decisions of a very complex sort." (Harold Larrabee, *Reliable Knowledge*, Boston: Houghton Mifflin, 1945, p. 436.) This same line

lar probabilities of these two sets of probabilities will be different for each society and statistics-gathering organization, but the factors involved and the probabilities of occurrence associated with each of them will change slowly enough, except when there is some great reform in the statistics-gathering organization or other such extreme changes occur, so that they will generate about the same probability distribution of categorizations of causes of death each year. *The important thing, of course, is what factors determine the probabilistic official responses. The "real" circumstances surrounding the deaths are undoubtedly one set of the determining factors. But the factors involved in causing the attempted dissimulations, the factors determining the success of dissimulations, the factors determining the circumstances that determine the perceptions and cognitions of the deaths by the officials—all of these can generate a certain highly stable distribution of official responses quite independent of the "real" factors involved in the deaths.* So we certainly cannot assume that the officials produce a stable suicide rate because they respond in a stable manner to stable factors in the causes of deaths.

---

of reasoning was very likely the cause of the wonder felt by Durkheim, Halbwachs, and all of the earlier moral statisticians over the regularity of suicide statistics within each society.

Actually, it is the complexity of the forces at work that produces the regularity of outcome probabilities. It is Larrabee's need, shared by most non-physical scientists today, to think of the coin experiment in deterministic terms that leads him into this error of reasoning. There is nothing at all simple about the "causes" of the outcomes of the flipping of a coin and it is the complexity of the causes that produces the regularity of outcome probabilities, not the supposed "simplicity."

There is, however, another real difference between the coin experiments and the suicide experiments we are considering here. In coin experiments one assumes that the real outcome is probabilistic but that the categorizations of the outcomes are deterministic. In my considerations of suicide statistics I am arguing that, regardless of whether we consider the real suicides to be probabilistic, we must consider the categorizations to be probabilistic. I am arguing that *the probabilistic nature of the categorizations is sufficient in itself to account for the regularity of official suicide statistics in any given society* or, at least, most of the regularity. But, if the suicide deaths are themselves probabilistic, so that we have a two-stage probabilistic process (i.e., probabilities of probabilities), then we can expect even greater regularity than would otherwise have been the case. This may well be the explanation of the greater regularity of suicide statistics than the regularity of mortality statistics, which are not as probabilistic at the categorization stage.

This alternative explanation for the stability of official suicide rates within most societies seems in certain respects to be more plausible than the explanation offered by Halbwachs and others. Since the number of suicides in any large population must be assumed from all available observations to be quite a small part of the contingent of the causes of all the deaths each year, it would seem that there would be a greater variability in the number of real deaths by suicide each year than the official statistics register. If death by suicide is to have a certain probability of occurrence in each society (as Durkheim and other sociologists have argued), why should suicide, with such a vastly smaller number of occurrences than the other forms of death, have a greater stability of rate than the over-all death rates themselves (as Durkheim showed they did for European societies in the nineteenth century)? It would seem plausible that this greater stability could only be the result of there being in fact a great number of unspecified probabilistic factors determining the suicide rates, so that the normal variability associated with the small numbers of trials would not occur.

Two further factors to be considered here are the instability of suicide rates on the more local levels of the various nations and the great variations in suicide rates on these levels within each nation.

Though the suicide rates of nations tend to be quite stable, the rates of local regions, such as cities and the parts of cities, tend to be relatively unstable.[46] But what one finds in the patterns of these local statistics is not wild swings. They frequently increase or decrease by as much as a factor of two from one year to the next, but very rarely more than this. Moreover, the statistics tend to oscillate between jumps up and drops down from one year to the next. Since the great majority of local statistics have these patterns of variations, the variations tend to cancel each other out when they are summed up, so that the rate of the more inclusive population tends to remain rather stable.

Now, there is not necessarily anything about this that is contradictory to the probabilistic assumption. Indeed, this is just what one might expect to find *if* he assumes there are

[46] See, for example, the degrees of yearly variation in suicide rates for the boroughs of London tabulated by Peter Sainsbury, in *Suicide in London,* pp. 95-98.

socio-cultural "causes" producing suicide probabilistically within the over-all population. When one looks at a smaller number of "experimental trials" (i.e., of operations of the socio-cultural forces), he must expect, in terms of probabilistic theory, to find great variability in outcome probabilities.

But there are two problems with this felicitous interpretation. The first is that in these local areas of the population one gets not merely more variability, but also a reasonably stable rank-ordering of the areas in terms of their suicide rates. That is, there is variability in the rates of the local area, but within a reasonably narrow range for each subpopulation. Now, one could explain this by arguing that we have probability experiments within probability experiments: i.e., local populations have their own (stable) socio-cultural structures that generate their own probabilities of suicide, while the over-all population has its stable socio-cultural structure that generates its own probabilities of suicide, with the over-all population rates being more stable because of the greater number of trials. And this is, indeed, what Durkheim, Halbwachs, *et al.* have, at least implicitly, assumed. But it is also possible to explain the stability of suicide rates of the over-all population simply in terms of the relatively small range of variations in the local population rates and the large number of local area rates to be summed up. In this way one eliminates the assumption of (stable) socio-cultural homogeneity. Since this is an assumption that is never supported by anything but preconceptions or common-sense reasonings, and since the alternative mathematical explanation is adequate in itself, one would have to drop the unsupported and superfluous assumption that the stability of national suicide rates is due to some stable socio-cultural causes.

There is no necessary reason for accepting either of the explanations. But the alternative explanation, even if one rejects the argument concerning its greater plausibility, must cause one to doubt Halbwachs' explanation and his conclusion from it that the official suicide statistics must be reliable. We cannot argue from the stability of the official suicide rates to the reliability of the suicide rates: the officials may be counting many different things in many different ways with a relatively high degree of stability in the outcomes—i.e., in the official suicide statistics.

The Randomization of Errors. Besides the argument that the suicide statistics have gotten so much better over the years that they must now lack any significant forms of unreliability and invalidity, an argument which seems implausible in the light of the available evidence, sociologists seem to have felt the official statistics on suicide were reliable and valid enough to use in testing their theories of suicide in good part just because there did not seem to be any plausible arguments in favor of significant unreliabilities and invalidities in the data. It is my purpose here to suggest that there are several fairly obvious arguments against the use of the official statistics on suicide. I shall argue that there are at least five major forms of unreliability in the official statistics on suicide which have produced biases in the testing of sociological theories of suicide: (1) unreliability resulting from the choice of the official statistics to be used in making the tests of the sociological theories; (2) unreliability resulting from subcultural differences in the attempts to hide suicide; (3) unreliability resulting from the effects of different degrees of social integration on the official statistics keeping; (4) unreliability resulting from significant variations in the social imputations of motives; and (5) unreliability resulting from the more extensive and professionalized collection of statistics among certain populations. Let us consider each of these sources of unreliability in turn.

(1) In some societies there is more than one set of official statistics on suicide. It is not uncommon for there to be two or more sets of statistics; and there are almost always at least two different sources of official statistics available to sociologists. The suicide rates reported by these different sources or by different methods of tabulating the suicide rates from one source tend to differ significantly. Halbwachs found, for example, that in France there were two major sources of official statistics on suicide: the ministry of the interior and the criminal justice department. Comparing these two sets of statistics for the period 1902-12, he found that the department of criminal justice always gave a rate of from 10% to 16% higher than the ministry of

the interior.[47] (He did not consider whether the two different sources gave significantly different rates for the different subgroups of France. If they did, then one more source of unreliability would be added.) Again, the sociologist can generally either take the figures tabulated by some central statistical bureau or he can go to the coroners' reports and tabulate his own figures. In any event, the final figures he is faced with frequently differ significantly from each other. How is he to decide which figures to accept? Generally, sociologists have taken the higher figures since they have felt that the higher figures included many suicides that were hidden to the other group of statistics collectors. The assumption that the higher official suicide rate is the best one rests upon the assumption that the only significant source of error in the official statistics on suicide is that of hiding suicides. No justification for such an assumption is offered, simply because this assumption is so much a part of the folklore of suicide literature that it has largely become implicit. In fact, the assumption seems quite unjustified. The variations in rates are probably due to a number of factors. In line with our general argument, we would expect that the differences in rates result from one group of officials having somewhat different abstract and operational definitions of suicide, different search procedures, and being subject to less pressure from the families because of their different structural positions in the society (e.g., less integrated into the same local communities as the families).

Regardless of why there is this difference between the statistics of different official organizations, the choice by the sociologists of the higher rates assumes that one of the organizations systematically underestimates the rates by at least 10 to 16 per cent. This must imply that the set of statistics chosen is quite plausibly at fault in the same way, unless some evidence is offered to show the contrary to be the case. At the very least, the chosen statistics must be seen as suspect. When one is comparing the suicide rates of one country with another, the presence of alternative suicide

[47] M. Halbwachs, *Les Causes* . . . , p. 172, fn. 2. Gargas found a similar difference between official statistics in the Netherlands. See S. Gargas, "Suicide in the Netherlands," *The American Journal of Sociology,* xxxvii (1932), 697-713.

rates for one and not the other can be the basis for a bias in the test if one just arbitrarily chooses the higher rate for the country with the alternative figures. One should at least determine whether the use of the higher rate changes the direction of the test or its significance. Yet sociologists have not done so.

(2) All students of suicide have known that there are many individual cases of attempts to hide suicide and all students of suicide have likewise assumed that many cases are successful. The psychiatrists have generally assumed, without little systematic investigation of the question of randomization of errors of this sort, that this invalidates the sociological studies of suicide relying on official statistics.[48] The sociologists, with even less systematic consideration of

[48] Gregory Zilboorg has probably been more outspoken than any other American psychiatrist in his rejection of the official statistics on suicide and, consequently, of the sociological theories based on these statistics. He rejects them for a number of reasons, but all of his reasons implicitly assume that reliability is the basic problem rather than validity. (See Gregory Zilboorg, "Suicide Among Civilized and Primitive Races," *American Journal of Psychiatry*, 92 (1935-36) pp. 1347-1369.) George Simpson, whose primary concern has been the integration of the psychoanalytic theories of suicide with the Durkheimian theory of suicide, accepted Zilboorg's fundamental arguments against the official statistics on suicide. (See George Simpson, "Methodological Problems in Determining the Aetiology of Suicide," *American Sociological Review*, 15 (1950), pp. 658-663.) Simpson's article includes the only rejection of official statistics as "sufficiently" reliable for testing sociological theories of suicide that has thus far appeared in American sociological literature, at least as far as this author has been able to determine. (The comments by Gibbs and Merton, cited above, do *not* include rejections of the official suicide statistics as *unacceptably unreliable* for the purposes of testing sociological theories of suicide.) However, almost all sociologists who have done work on suicide since the publication of Simpson's article simply make no reference to it or to the issues involved. The most legitimate reason for this is simply that the psychiatric arguments against the use of the official statistics on suicide are, with the exception of Achille-Delmas, primarily simple *assertions*. They are very likely based on their own experience with such matters, but they include almost no systematic consideration of the question of the randomization of errors. Since they do not directly attack either the assumption of the *validity* of the official statistics or the assumption of the *randomization* of errors in the official statistics, these psychiatric arguments have largely failed to invalidate the (at least implicit) assumptions made by sociologists. The present work attacks both assumptions. (More recent psychiatric attacks on the official statistics on suicide show the same failings. See, for example, Werner Tuteur, "Statistics and Statisticians: A Timely Warning," *American Journal of Psychiatry*, 116 (September, 1959), pp. 263-264.)

the question, have equally strongly assumed just the opposite. When sociologists have considered the question, however, it has been clear to most of them that there are differences in the attempt to hide suicide which must vary to some degree with respect to certain systematic subgroup differences. Probably most sociologists have, especially, felt that there are differences in the severity of moral judgments on suicide which vary significantly from one group to another, especially from one religious group to another. Durkheim, with his usual reliance upon the juridical norms as a measure of the moral attitudes, simply assumed that all of the religious groups of Europe were equally severe in their condemnation of suicide.[49] Other sociologists have argued that Catholics tend to condemn suicide much more severely than Protestants or Jews and that, as a consequence, the Catholics will tend to attempt to hide suicide much more than Protestants.[50] Even on the level of juridical norms of the different religious groups it would seem that the Catholic church condemns suicide much more severely than Protestant churches; for the Catholic church has generally retained the law that a suicide cannot be buried with church sanction, whereas the Protestant churches have largely given up this old law.[51] Though there has not been

[49] See E. Durkheim, *Suicide*, pp. 156-157. On p. 156 Durkheim states that suicide is "too little an object of public condemnation for the slight measure of blame attaching to it to have such influence" [as Legoyt and Oettingen had attributed to the blame]. By p. 157 he had changed his mind and argued that both the Protestant and the Catholic religious systems "penalize it morally with great severity." (He might have meant to distinguish between attitudes of the official institutions and attitudes of the public. If he did, this invalidates his whole argument about effects on the suicide rates of differences in the degree of emphasis on freedom and discipline between the two churches.) Since, as we have seen in the chapter on Durkheim, Durkheim almost never collected any evidence on the *meanings* (e.g., norms) he imputed to various groups or was systematic in his treatment of these *meanings*, it was quite easy for him to change his assertions about these meanings from page to page to support whatever his argument happened to be at the time.

[50] Kruijt, for example, has made a reasonably strong statement to this effect. See Kruijt, *op.cit.*, p. 426. Simpson, in his "Introduction" to Durkheim's *Suicide*, suggests that "This in turn raises the problem whether suicides of Catholics are being accurately reported since the religious prohibition against suicide in the Catholic church may well lead to serious complications." (*Suicide*, pp. 27-28.)

[51] See Ruth Cavan, *Suicide*, pp. 12-24, 40-42; Helen Silving, "Sui-

any systematic study of the mores of different groups with respect to suicide, it seems reasonable to expect that Catholics are much stronger in their condemnation of suicides than are Protestants or Jews. Assuming this, and assuming that greater moral condemnation will lead to a greater tendency to attempt to hide moral transgressions, we would expect that Catholics will attempt to hide suicides more than Protestants.

There is no direct evidence on the relative tendencies to attempt to hide suicides by the different religious groups. There is, however, at least one study that has indirect bearing on this question of attempts to hide suicide. In a comparative study of the cantons of Switzerland, Waldstein found that the Catholic cantons had proportionately more accidental deaths than did the Protestant cantons and the Protestant cantons had proportionately more deaths by suicide. Such a finding lends itself easily to the interpretation that Catholics (at least those of Switzerland) have a higher rate of attempted concealment of suicide (or a higher rate of successful concealments of suicide or both—see below).[52]

The question of whether there is systematic bias in the official suicide statistics resulting from significantly different rates of attempted concealment of suicide for different religious or other types of groups can only be answered by empirical investigations of the attempts to hide suicides. But, considering what impressionistic evidence there is on the distributions of causes of death imputations from one religious group to another, it would seem plausible at this point to expect that there are systematic unreliabilities in the official suicide statistics resulting from differences in the *rates of attempted concealment of suicides.*[53]

---

cide and Law," in Edwin S. Shneidman and Norman Farberow, editors, *Clues to Suicide*, pp. 79-95; and G. W. Williams, *The Sanctity of Life and the Criminal Law.*

[52] Schneider specifically opposed Waldstein's findings to the assumptions made by Durkheim and Halbwachs about the validity and reliability of suicide statistics. (See Pierre-B. Schneider, *La Tentative de Suicide*, pp. 90-92.) Carefully considering all of the problems involved in such questions, Schneider concluded that what evidence he had found in his research on attempted suicides (in which he did not use official statistics on suicide), the Catholics seemed to attempt suicide more frequently. (*Ibid.*, pp. 92-93.)

[53] Besides systematic differences in moral attitudes toward suicide

As a general proposition, it seems most plausible to hypothesize that the rate of attempted concealment of suicide will vary directly with the degree of (self-estimated) potential loss to the suicide's social self (and to the suicide's significant others) involved in having the death categorized as a suicide. This leads to the hypothesis that the rate of attempted concealment will vary directly with the degree of negative moral judgment associated with the act of suicide and with the degree of negative sanctions *believed* to be imposed for violations of the moral judgments. This hypothesis then leads us to expect that there will be certain systematic biases in the official statistics on suicide.

Besides the bias in the official statistics which probably results from the systematic differences in moral judgments of suicide, there is another very important source of different rates of attempted concealment, and thus of bias in the official statistics. The degree to which an individual is involved in social activity will probably vary directly with his concern for the moral approval of the others with whom he is involved. If their moral judgments of an action are negative, then he will try to avoid such an action *or* hide the act or some of both, and his attempts to avoid the act and/or to hide his having done it will vary directly with

---

between various groups, there are frequently strong differences within groups. Deshaies strongly emphasized the importance of such differences within related groups, arguing, in effect, that it is the specific *meanings of membership* that are important in the causation of suicide and not merely the vague social imputation of membership by sociologists. (G. Deshaies, *Psychologie Du Suicide*, p. 43.)

Ferracuti, who explicitly acknowledges Deshaies' contribution, has shown that in Italy, a country that is nominally a Catholic country, there is a steady increase in official suicide rates as one goes from the South to the North *and* a steady decrease in the importance of the Catholic organization. (See Franco Ferracuti, "Suicide in a Catholic Country," in Shneidman and Farberow, *Clues to Suicide*, pp. 70-78.)

Unfortunately, as Ferracuti and Halbwachs before him explicitly note, it is impossible to separate the degree of commitment to Catholicism from urban-rural residence, industrial-agricultural economy, and the degree of education. Consequently, in line with an argument to be developed in detail below, Ferracuti's findings could simply be the result of there being more effective statistics-gathering organizations in the more urban-industrial-wealthy-educated areas of the country. This factor would, however, merely reinforce the effects of the hypothesized direct relation between religious commitment and rate of attempted concealment of suicide.

his degree of involvement. Moreover, one can expect that significant others who care most about the individual's social self will try to prevent his committing the act or will try to hide his having done so in direct proportion to his and their degree of social involvement. Since sociologists have generally treated "integration" as being the same as the social involvement of the individuals of a group, we could rephrase the above propositions in terms of integration. We would then expect that *the more socially integrated an individual is, the more he and his significant others will try to avoid having his death categorized as a suicide, assuming that suicide is judged negatively. Then, even if the degree of moral condemnation of suicide were the same throughout the society, group differences in the degree of social integration would produce systematic group differences in the rate of attempted concealment of suicides and, therefore, most likely in the official suicide rates.*[54]

It seems quite likely that the degree of moral condemnation for committing a negatively evaluated act such as suicide will vary not only according to the degree of commitments of the judges to the values against the act, but also according to the status position of the individual committing the act. There is a good deal of evidence that the relation between status and condemnation for committing a negatively evaluated action (and, hence, between willingness to commit the action) is U-functional. The lower-status and the higher-status individuals seem less concerned with conforming (and with being seen as conforming) than do the middle-status individuals; and, at least for the upper-status

[54] Some theoretical speculation along these lines may be worthwhile here. Integration and the need to conform are probably related. But there is a great difference between a need to conform and a need to appear *as-if* one is conforming. It may well be true that the degree of social integration and the degree of affect-value commitment to conformity vary directly. And it may also be that the degree of social integration and the degree of need to appear as-if one is conforming also vary directly. But the rate of increase of the two needs with respect to the degree of social integration may not be the same at all. If it is actually the case that the rate of increase of the need to appear as-if one is conforming is greater than the rate of increase of affect-value commitment to conformity, then one can expect that the rate of attempted concealment of suicide will increase more rapidly as integration increases than will the non-commission of the act of suicide, so that the official statistics would be even more biased.

individuals, there is actually less condemnation for deviating from group values: they seem to have earned or been ascribed certain "deviance credits."[55] If such relations hold in the United States and in other nations, then one would expect that the middle-class individuals would tend to commit a deviant act such as suicide less frequently than upper-class and lower-class individuals, but the relation would not be of the magnitude shown by the official statistics, since the official statistics would be biased by the greater frequency of attempted concealment on the part of the middle-class individuals. Whether this bias would be significant enough to change the statistical relations based on the official suicide statistics is clearly impossible to say at this point, but there is reason to consider it an additional source of bias in the official suicide statistics. (This will be especially clear when we add the effects of integration on the rate of successful concealment. See below.)

Indeed, there appear to be *strong class differences in both the ability and the willingness of individuals to manipulate information-giving phenomena in such a way as to produce desired choices* (of, for example, categorizations of the cause of death) *by other individuals.* Specifically, *it is hypothesized that the ability and willingness to control the communication process varies directly with increasing social status.*[56]

[55] For a discussion of the various works and problems concerned with the relations between social class, commitments, and (conformity-deviance) actions, see George C. Homans, *Social Behavior: Its Elementary Forms,* New York: Harcourt, Brace, and World, Inc., 1961, pp. 336-358.

[56] Much of the line of argument and evidence leading to these hypotheses has been excellently presented by Melville Dalton in his book, *Men Who Manage,* New York: John Wiley and Sons, 1959, pp. 253-255.

Goffman's analyses of front management are probably the best known works on this problem. (See, especially, Erving Goffman, *The Presentation of Self in Everyday Life,* Garden City, New York: Doubleday Anchor Books, 1959). Goffman's work, however, is concerned with the encounter level of analysis. He does not suggest how fundamentally important the structure and process of the society that includes the encounters are in determining the degrees of concern with presenting various fronts and in determining differences in the values of these variables from one group to another within the society. Dalton's work, on the other hand, is a brilliant analysis of *encounters*

As general conclusions of this argument we would expect to find that (a) middle-class individuals will have a higher rate of attempted concealment of suicidal actions[57] than those of the lower or upper classes and (b) they will have a higher rate of success at such attempts (for other reasons as well—see below) than lower-class individuals, but lower rates than the upper-class individuals. Though we cannot be sure of the magnitudes of such differences, one would expect, largely on the basis of the close similarity in educations and occupations of middle-class and upper-class individuals,[58] that middle-class individuals would have a much higher rate of attempted concealment than individuals of the other classes, but an only slightly lower rate of successful concealments than that of upper-class individuals, who would have a much higher rate of successful concealments

---

within social structures and processes. It is, therefore, much more significant for our purposes here.

Various other sociologists have remarked upon the much more rigid, public commitment to values made by lower-class individuals than by middle-class individuals, even though lower-class individuals seem to violate these very values much more often. See, for example, Stanton Wheeler, "Sex Offenses: A Sociological Critique," *Law and Contemporary Problems*, 25 (Spring, 1950) pp. 258-278. Assuming we are not dealing with some "ecological fallacy," we could easily explain such a difference in Dalton's terms as the result of differences in the *meanings* of values themselves, with lower-class people believing values to be absolute, non-individual properties resulting from different situational experiences produced by different structural positions.

The whole problem of the relation of social status to biases in crime reporting has for decades been a focus of conflict among criminologists. In 1936 Sophia Robison used the official statistics on juvenile delinquency in N.Y. to show the various ways in which social status and other factors lead to great biases in the official statistics on juvenile delinquency. (See Sophia Moses Robison, *Can Delinquency Be Measured?*, New York: Columbia University Press, 1936.)

[57] We generally assume here, strictly for the sake of simplicity, that the various socially defined types of *suicidal actions* differ from each other primarily in degree (e.g., of moral judgment) rather than in dimensions of meaning. This, of course, is not really true and any more detailed analyses will have to give careful consideration to such differences.

[58] In terms of Dalton's analysis, occupational experience is the most important determinant of the differences in orientations toward values and in ability to communicate what one intends to communicate, with education and family experience being the next most important factors.

than lower-class individuals. Consequently, the middle-class should have much lower official suicide rates than the other classes. This, of course, is what one almost always finds to be the case.

(3) The rate of attempted concealment of suicide cannot be assumed to bias the statistics by itself. The *rate of successful attempts to conceal suicide* is an intervening variable. The actor and his significant others must play against the officials who count and categorize the causes of death (except in those cases where the officials are significant others themselves, which we shall consider below). We must know what the *coefficient of success to failures in attempts to conceal suicide* is before we can be certain about the relation of the rate of attempted concealment of suicide to biases in the official suicide statistics. The empirical determination of such coefficients and of the causes of the coefficients will undoubtedly be of tremendous interest to the students of suicide if the social meanings of suicide should prove to be such that measurements of this sort have any meaning. (My argument concerning the *essentially problematic* nature of the social meanings of suicide would lead one to expect that there are always equally valid but different constructions of meanings for the same events, so that there are always equally valid but different measurements possible for the same events. See below.) Until they are made, however, we must rely upon plausible arguments as to the causes of the coefficient and the relation of these coefficients to the possible biases in the official statistics on suicide.

It seems clear that the specific tactics used by the significant others will be a primary determinant of success or failure in any individual case. (We have considered the importance of this factor above.) A second set of important determinants of the rate of successful attempts at concealment would seem to be the relations, either direct or indirect, between the deceased and his significant others on the one hand and the officials who are categorizing the death on the other. The wishes of the deceased (or the committer of any suicidal action) and of his succeeding significant others are more likely to influence the decisions of the officials the more the deceased and his significant others are directly or indirectly associated with the officials: i.e., the more directly and indirectly the deceased and his significant others are *integrated* with the officials. We can state a general proposition concerning these relations: *the more integrated the deceased individual is into his local community and with the officials, the more the doctors, coroners, or other officials responsible for deciding what the cause of death is will be favorably influenced, consciously or subconsciously, by the preferences of the deceased and his significant others.*

There are several reasons for expecting such a relation to hold. First, the more integrated the deceased is into the community, the greater will be the immediate and mediate interaction between the officials and the deceased or the significant others of the deceased. The greater the rate of interaction, the greater the feelings of friendliness toward the deceased and his significant others. And, the greater the feelings of friendliness, the greater the positive influence of their preferences on the decisions of the officials.[59] Second, the greater the integration of the deceased and his significant others into the local community, the greater will be the expected gains and losses involved for the officials in making a decision favorable or unfavorable to the preferences of the significant others of the deceased. Third, the greater the integration of the deceased and his significant others, the more the officials will tend to expect non-deviant behavior from the deceased and his significant others and, consequently, the more he will tend to discount any suspicions of deviant behavior such as suicide. The general reasoning behind this third relation is based on the influence of an individual's past actions in determining the meaning of his present actions. One of the important bits of information available to an official trying to determine the cause of death of an individual is his case history. If the man has been well integrated into the community in the past, this will have a great influence in determining the meaning of his present actions. Specifically, a good deal of social inter-

[59] This hypothesized relation is an *extension*, from simply *immediate* relations to include *mediate* relations, of the theory of "friendliness" and "social interaction" proposed by George C. Homans in *The Human Group*, New York: Harcourt, Brace, and Co., 1950.

action will mean that he was not lonely, that he was active in furthering the interests of the community, etc. All of this will tend to make his actions preceding his death appear non-deviant or non-suicidal to the officials. (Part of this effect is undoubtedly due to the high positive correlation between degree of integration and social status. Another part is due to the influence of the need to impute a motive to an individual whose death is to be categorized as a suicide. We shall discuss this relation further below.)

The importance for the testing of sociological theories of suicide of a bias in official statistics on suicide resulting from systematic group differences in the degree of social integration is quite obvious. All of the sociological work in the Durkheimian tradition and in the ecological tradition of the Chicago school would be affected. Such biases in the official statistics would account for the rather consistent finding that urban suicide rates are higher than rural rates. In general, it seems clear that the average degree of social integration of individuals is higher in rural areas than in urban areas. More specifically, in the rural areas the officials are especially apt to be closely associated with the deceased or with his significant others and, therefore, very much influenced by their preferences, while in the urban areas the association of officials with the deceased or with his significant others will almost always be much more indirect and, correspondingly, less of an influence on their decision as to the causes of death. It also seems likely that rural individuals will have a much more negative moral judgment of suicide than will urban individuals and that, consequently, not only will the rate of successful attempts to conceal suicide be higher, but the rate of attempts will also be higher. Regardless of any differences in moral judgment, one must expect that the greater average knowledge of an individual and his significant others in a smaller community will lead to a greater significance of the imputation of a negatively evaluated category such as suicide, so the effective *incentive* is greater to conceal any suicidal actions even were the moral judgment less severe. Since there is usually a direct relation between social status and the degree of social integration, we would also expect that the official statistics would systematically underestimate the rates for the middle and upper classes. (See above.) Since the predominant social characteristic of the individuals residing in the "disorganized" core areas of the cities is that of a very low degree of social integration (and of social status), we would expect that the official statistics would systematically underestimate the rates for the outer areas of the cities relative to their estimates for the core areas. (Those individuals living in rooming houses very generally do not have any friends who influence the officials and their identity is frequently not even known at the time of the official designation of the cause of death.[60]) Any studies using the official statistics or reports on deaths to show a relation between loneliness and suicide will be biased for the same reason. Since women seem to live by themselves far less frequently than men, we would expect that their greater social integration would lead to a systematic underestimation of their suicide rates.[61]

[60] Schmid found in his study of suicide in Seattle that of the male suicides 6.4% committed in the core area were unidentified as opposed to 2.9% unidentified in the non-core areas. (Calvin F. Schmid, *Suicides in Seattle*, p. 5.) As is usual in core areas, a *much* higher percentage lived alone and relatively anonymously. (Over 13% of the male suicides in the core area were non-residents. *Ibid.*)

Once in a while one finds totally spurious differences between the official suicide rates of urban and rural areas resulting from a combination of rigid pre-judgments and gross error in induction. Wood found such an error in the work on Ceylonese suicide by Straus and Straus: "J. H. Straus and M. A. Straus have reported suicide and homicide rates of urban areas (including Colombo) approximately double the rural rates in Ceylon for 1946. . . . The data available that year were based on place of death (not place of residence), giving spurious results owing to the urban locations of hospitals and clinics." Arthur Lewis Wood, "Crime and Aggression in Changing Ceylon: A Sociological Analysis of Homicide, Suicide, and Economic Crime," in *Transactions of the American Philosophical Society*, New Series, 51 (December, 1961), 60-61, fn. 18.

[61] Far more importantly, I would argue that the *meanings* of male suicides and of female suicides are different in Western societies. Male suicides are generally perceived as being caused by extra-familial "strains," though information on intra-familial "strains" can change this general expectation. Female suicides, on the contrary, are perceived as being caused by intra-familial "strains." When a female commits a suicidal action, then, her significant male others, especially her husband, who is seen as more responsible (i.e., more the cause) of her actions than anyone else, have a much greater incentive in this respect than a female in the same situation to attempt to conceal the suicidal action.

Indeed, because of these differences in the meanings of male and female suicide in our society, a threat of suicide by a female (or an actual attempt) is an extremely effective means of social control. The

A positive correlation between the rates of attempted concealment of suicide and of successful concealment of suicide and the degree of social integration seems very likely. Such a positive correlation would produce a fundamental bias in the testing of almost all sociological theories tested with official statistics, a bias that would result in the acceptance of most of these theories regardless of the state of real-world events.

(4) Any quick glance at a number of randomly selected coroners' reports on suicides or accidental self-inflicted deaths will show the importance the officials attach to imputed motives. There is reason to assume that they, like so many of the students of suicide, implicitly define "suicide" as self-destruction resulting from an action motivated by a desire to die. Without some evidence showing them that the individual was motivated to act in a way leading to his own death, they do not impute intention or knowledge of consequences necessary to categorize the death as "suicide." The evidence of motivation (i.e., of causation of the individual's behavior) consists generally of external events such as the individual's past life situations and actions, the immediate life situation preceding his death, his communication of internal states to others via notes or word of mouth, the sequence of actions leading up to his death, the form of dramatization or non-dramatization of taking his own life, etc.[62]

---

female in our society, therefore, may actually be able to effectively complete her communication work by adopting a less dangerous form of communication than the male can. (This will all be much clearer after the reader has read the theory of suicide as a *meaningful act* to be proposed in Part IV.)

Though this difference might lead us to expect that the official statistics on female and male suicide validly reflect the real differences in these rates, we must not assume this. What we see clearly from these differences in meanings is that there are factors strongly favoring a bias in the rates such that females will have lower official suicide rates. The suspicion is too firmly based. The official statistics on these matters cannot be accepted as reliable until evidence demonstrates the suspicion invalid or valid only within certain, specifiable limits.

[62] Again, this section will be better understood after reading the last part of this work. The theory of motives and situated actions behind the present argument was developed by Kenneth Burke in *Permanence and Change* and in *A Grammar of Motives* and *A Rhetoric of Motives*, New York: The World Publishing Company, 1962.

Most important for possible biases in the official statistics on suicide are the *socially shared imputations of motives for committing suicide.* Though no one has ever empirically determined precisely what the social beliefs (or explanations) concerning suicide are, it seems probable from the literature on suicide that most people in the Western world have for centuries believed that an individual commits suicide because he is unhappy, especially because he is depressed or melancholy. This is the internal motivational state. They have, however, also believed that there are certain external life situations that are closely associated with or causes of these internal states. These external states are, then, generally taken as presumptive evidence of the internal state, though some observers will demand specific evidence that this internal state did exist regardless of what the external states were. There is, for example, the very old belief that loneliness or self-imposed isolation tends to make one depressed or melancholy and, therefore, much more likely to commit suicide. (A lack of anything to keep one's mind and hands busy is very close to this idea.) Moreover, it is generally believed that a *loss* of love through death or desertion or whatever other cause is especially productive of depression and the urge to escape it all by death.

The inference process does, of course, work both ways. If one has categorized a person's death as suicide, then one "knows" almost for certain that the person was "unhappy," especially if he was "melancholy," "depressed," etc. (see the next footnote below). The death of Marilyn Monroe in August, 1962, presented the individuals of our society with vast problems of explanation and the search for the meaning of her death shows these processes at work. She had "everything that makes one happy," yet she died under circumstances that made it seem reasonably clear to most people that she had intended to kill herself. The psychologists and psychiatrists of the Suicide Prevention Center of Los Angeles were called in by the county coroner to help him decide if this was a suicide:

> The report, which went deeply into the life of the actress before she took the fatal dose of drugs on the night of August 4, said: 'Miss Monroe had suffered from

psychiatric disturbances for a long time. She experienced severe fears and frequent depressions. Mood changes were abrupt and unpredictable.

'Among the symptoms of disorganization, sleep disturbance was prominent, for which she had been taking sedative drugs for many years. She was thus familiar with and experienced in the use of sedative drugs and well aware of their dangers.'

The report said the actress had been taking psychiatric treatments recently in an effort to reduce her consumption of the drugs and that it was partly successful during the last two months.

The investigative team said that although the amount of drugs found in her home was not unusual, other facts supported their belief her death was suicidal.

'We have learned that Miss Monroe had often expressed wishes to give up, to withdraw, and even to die. On more than one occasion in the past, when disappointed and depressed, she had made a suicide attempt using sedative drugs. On these occasions, she had called for help and had been rescued.'

The report said that information collected about events on the night of her death indicated 'The pattern was repeated except for the rescue.'

(*Los Angeles Times*, Saturday, Aug. 18, 1962, p. 3, p. 13.)

After most people had decided that her death was a suicide, there was still a need to *understand* (to impute plausible meaning to) her actions by imputing some form of "deep unhappiness" or "misery" seen to be *caused* by some situation. The many published articles on the matter show that everyone assumed implicitly that she was "miserable," etc., but almost every attempted explanation arrived at a different conclusion regarding the situational-motive cause of her misery and, thus, her suicide. One account shows that a publication concerned with sex implicitly assumed the cause to be fear of old age and the loss of her sexual beauty:

What made Marilyn Monroe take her life? The question rang around the world one sad Sunday last August, and it echoes still. This week, a quarterly called *Eros* displays

the ill-fated movie queen in 78 pictures, some of which
give a hint, perhaps, of her state of mind toward the end.
Eros bought the photographs from top cameraman Bert
Stern, who shot them in Los Angeles last June. After
modeling clothes, for a Vogue Fashion layout, Marilyn
impulsively left the room. Returning in nothing but a
towel and a transparent top, she smiled and said: "Not
bad for a girl of 36, eh?" Then Marilyn posed and posed
and posed (photos). She posed in clothes, she posed
wrapped in a diaphanous scarf—and in one picture, which
Stern declined to release, she posed completely revealed.
When she saw the prints, Marilyn seemed delighted. Six
weeks later, the girl of 36 was dead.

(*Newsweek*, November 19, 1962, p. 67.)

Ayn Rand, on the other hand, was absolutely convinced that
her "suicide" showed how misery is caused for the great
by the rampant envy of greatness in our society:

> She preserved her vision of life through a nightmare
> struggle, fighting her way to the top. What broke her was
> the discovery, at the top, of as sordid an evil as the one
> she had left behind—worse, perhaps, because incompre-
> hensible. She had expected to reach the sunlight; she
> found, instead, a limitless swamp of malice.
>
> It was a kind of malice of a very special kind. If you
> want to see her groping struggle to understand it, read
> the magnificent article in a recent issue of Life magazine.
> It is not actually an article, it is a verbatim transcript of
> her own words—and the most tragically revealing docu-
> ment published in many years. It is a cry for help, which
> came too late to be answered.
>
> "When you're famous, you kind of run into human
> nature in a raw kind of way," she said. "It stirs up envy,
> fame does. People you run into feel that, well, who is she
> —who does she think she is, Marilyn Monroe? They feel
> fame gives them some kind of privilege to walk up to you
> and say anything to you, you know, of any kind of nature
> —and it won't hurt your feelings—like it's happening to
> your clothing. . . . I don't understand why people aren't
> a little more generous with each other. I don't like to say
> this, but I'm afraid there is a lot of envy in this business."

"Envy" is the only name she could find for the monstrous thing she faced, but it was much worse than envy; it was the profound hatred of life, of success and of all human values, felt by a certain kind of mediocrity—the kind who feels pleasure on hearing about a stranger's misfortune. It was hatred of the good for getting the goods—hatred of ability, of beauty, of honesty, of earnestness, of achievement and, above all, of human joy.

(*Los Angeles Times*, Sunday, Aug. 19, 1962, p. 2.)

And Norman Mailer saw in her suicide the obvious evidence that her misery was caused by her failure to achieve her grand goal:

> But Monroe was different. She slipped away from us. She had been slipping away from us for years. Now it is easy to see that her actions became more vague every year. I thought she was bad in *The Misfits*, she was finally too vague, and when emotion showed, it was small and unattractive. But she was gone from us a long time ago.
>
> If she had done Grushenka in *The Brothers Karamazov* the way she announced she would all those years ago, and if she had done it well, then she might have gone on. She might have come all the way back into the vault of herself where the salts of a clean death and the rot of a foul death were locked together. We take the sleeping pills when the sense of a foul and rotten death has become too certain, we look for the salt in the Seconal. Probably to stay alive Monroe had to become the greatest actress who ever lived.

(*Esquire*, November, 1962, p. 134.)

Given these relations between situations and despair, it is still difficult to see how systematic differences in the imputation of despair resulting from some loss of love objects might have biased the testing of sociological theories of suicide.[63] But there is another form of loss that has been of

[63] It is possible that the generally shared belief in Western societies that women die for love more than men do, presumably because love is seen as more important to women in Western societies, will bias the statistics. The "female suicide for love" pattern of behavior is not only well recognized, but is also both reasonably legitimate, eliciting sympathy for the woman more than anything else, and an extremely damning dramatization of the evils of her loved one. (The act is most

great importance in the imputation of motivation to commit suicide which seems to be one cause of a very important bias in the official statistics on suicide. This is the imputation of *despair from loss of social position* such as wealth or one's job. Just as Durkheim and most sociologists have felt that poverty itself is not a cause of suicide while a fall into poverty (a "reverse of fortune") is, so have most members of Western societies felt that it is a loss or a fall that causes despair and not the *stable* state of poverty or social insignificance.[64]

---

strongly associated with the evil of a lover, either legitimate or not; but the attempted suicide can also be effectively directed against such persons as a daughter who has deserted her mother.) This pattern of suicidal behavior does, indeed, involve more social-meaning loss than most other forms of suicidal action. Since it is more culturally available to women than to men, it is probably a major reason for the almost universal finding that women attempt suicide far more than men in Western society and that the peak of female attempted suicide is in the 20's when lover trouble is most socially credible. (In a study of 1,000 consecutive attempted suicides entering a Detroit hospital, Lendrum found that 46 males gave "quarrels with mate" as their motive for the suicidal acts, while 148 females gave the same motive for their acts; and 12 males gave "quarrels with lover" as their motive, while 42 females gave this as their motive. See F. C. Lendrum, "A Thousand Cases of Attempted Suicide," *American Journal of Psychiatry*, 13 (November, 1933) 479-500. For a comparative study of peak ages of attempted suicide for males and females see, for example, B. Piker, "1817 Cases of Suicide Attempts: A Preliminary Statistical Study," *American Journal of Psychiatry*, cv (1938), pp. 97-117.

Since men who attempt suicide have this pattern much less culturally available to them, they have greater reason to hide any attempted suicides. Their attempted suicide rates should be depressed by this one factor.

Since the effects on gross statistical rates of suicidal actions of such a socially meaningful pattern of behavior can be offset by other patterns, one would have to carefully study the many effects of all the different patterns to arrive at any definitive conclusions. Given our present gross ignorance about the complex phenomena involved, we can only reason plausibly from the most obvious phenomena.

[64] See the brief discussion of the history of the "revers de fortune" theory in the chapter on Durkheim's Theory of Suicide. We might add to our previous discussion the clear statement by Cavan (in *Suicide*, p. 273) on the contrasting effect of *reverse of fortune* and the stable condition of deprivation:

It seems then that while mere lack of money may not be said to be a fertile cause of personal disorganization, the loss of money and necessary change in mode of living, with perhaps a developing attitude of self-depreciation, is conducive to disorganization and hence to suicide.

Cavan almost certainly arrived at this idea independently of de Bois-

An economic recession or depression causes a rise in the rate of unemployment, bankruptcy, etc. This means that not only will a higher percentage of any random sample of the individuals in the society be unemployed, but a higher percentage of the "potential suicides" in the society will also have recently lost their jobs. The officials trying to categorize the official causes of deaths will, therefore, be presented with a higher rate of presumptive external causes of internal motives for suicide. This would give the officials a higher rate of situations that *mean* "suicide."[65] One would expect, then, that the overall official suicide rate would increase with an increase in unemployment, bankruptcy, and other forms of general social and economic loss, and decrease as these variables decrease.[66] Such a bias in the official statistics on suicide might well account for such findings as that of Halbwachs that the business indexes and suicide rates were inversely related to each other in Prussia. Moreover, since loss (and recent loss at that) is the impor-

---

mont, Durkheim, *et al.*, since she did not have much access to their ideas. Her source was very likely common-sense intuition. A recent work on suicide by two journalists includes a very clear statement of this common-sense theory:

High-status people have most to lose during a depression, and when they do lose it, they frequently seek oblivion. Those at the bottom of the social and economic ladders have much less to lose in a depression and consequently feel its impact less. This does not mean that the unskilled laborer is better off in a depression than a millionaire. It does mean that in a severe depression the change from what he was before to what he becomes is potentially much greater for the millionaire. The degree of change from bare subsistence living to perhaps near starvation is much less. Those at the bottom of the ladder cannot fall far.

(Edward Robb Ellis and George N. Allen, *Traitor Within: Our Suicide Problem*, Garden City, New York: Doubleday and Company, Inc., 1961, p. 24.)

[65] This rise in officials' expectations of suicide during economic depressions is very much to be expected in view of the almost universally shared myth about suicide epidemics among businessmen during depressions.

[66] Wood has argued that "cyclical variation" in the official suicide (and crime) statistics of Ceylon, without any significant changes in the statistics organization or its functioning, shows that the official statistics are valid and reliable. (See Arthur Lewis Wood, "Crime and Aggression in Changing Ceylon," p. 58.) The argument presented here shows how such "cyclical variations" *could* be caused by cyclical variation in the real information (i.e., situated motivations) about deaths presented to the officials regardless of the *real* causes of death.

tant variable, one might well expect that the *relative* degree of loss experienced will vary directly with the probability of categorizing a death as a suicide. If this is so, then one would expect that the official statistics would be biased in the direction of overestimating the suicide rates in times of economic recession in direct proportion to social status. They would see the upper-class individual as losing more than the lower-class individual, so they would be more apt to think the upper-class individual had a socially adequate motive for committing suicide. Such a bias could produce support for a theory of the relation between social status, economic conditions in the society, and the suicide rates such as that proposed by Henry and Short.[67]

(5) No one would doubt that organizations and individuals differ in their degree of efficiency at carrying out any task. It must especially be expected that there will be differences of great magnitude in the degree of efficiency when the individuals and organizations are faced with as complex a task as deciding what the causes of death are. As in all the other cases of possible errors in official statistics on suicide, however, the question is whether there are any plausibly systematic unreliabilities in the official statistics on suicide that result from differences in efficiency.

Halbwachs believed that one of the major sources of the reliability of the French official statistics on suicide was the verification of the causes of death by a doctor. But in looking closely at the French statistics on suicide he found that, though a reform in 1866 had made it mandatory for a medical doctor to verify the cause of death, in 1926 fully one-fourth of the deaths were either not verified or were not indicated as verified. Moreover, verification was strongly biased in the direction of the larger urban areas, with verification being quite infrequent in the rural areas.[68] The reasons for this disproportionate rate of non-verification of

[67] See Andrew F. Henry and James F. Short, *Suicide and Homicide*. It need hardly be argued that the much greater degree of statistical association between economic indexes and male suicide than between economic indexes and female suicides such as that found by Henry and Short and others (e.g., see Cavan, *Suicide*, p. 273) is precisely what one would expect if the explanation of these associations presented here is correct.

[68] Maurice Halbwachs, *Les Causes* . . . , pp. 33-34.

the causes of death were, presumably, the usual lower ratio of doctors to population in the rural areas, the greater difficulty of getting to cases in the rural areas, and, quite possibly, a higher concentration of the less professionalized doctors in the more rural areas.[69] In short, the social apparatus for verifying the cause of death was much less efficient in the rural area. If one then considers the strong possibility that the rate of successful concealment of suicides will be much higher where the rate of verification is much lower, then it would seem plausible to expect, until there is any evidence to the contrary, that the official suicide rates for rural areas were greatly underestimated relative to the estimates for the urban areas. Such a bias was, indeed, of great importance in producing support for Halbwach's theory of suicide, which was so fundamentally based on the differences in life styles between the urban and rural areas and the, supposedly, higher suicide rates for the urban areas.

Such factors as the lower ratio of doctors to population, etc., in the rural areas would seem to make the statistics keeping machines of rural areas much less efficient in general than those of the urban areas. Moreover, there are generally close direct relations between urbanism, industry, and wealth. And there would seem to be close direct relations between these variables and the efficiency of the statistics-keeping machines. In the urban areas it would not even cost as much per death to certify the cause of death because of the shorter distances to be traveled by the officials. Yet it is precisely the urban areas that can better afford the specialized personnel required for efficient collection of statistics on such matters as the causes of death.

As a general proposition, then, I would argue that it is plausible to assume that the official statistics keeping machines of the urban areas are more efficient than those of the rural areas and that, consequently, the official statistics on suicide will tend to be strongly biased in the direction of showing a much lower suicide rate for the rural areas relative to the urban areas.

The implication of such a bias for a number of Durk-

---

[69] It is also quite possible that the explanation for this finding is that in rural areas the officials such as doctors are much more frequently excluded from intrusions into such intimate family affairs.

heim's statistical tests of his theory of suicide are clear enough not to warrant specific consideration; and we have already noted the significance of such a bias for Halbwachs' theory of suicide, which specifically hypothesizes a fundamental difference in suicide rates between rural and urban areas resulting from fundamentally different styles of life. The implications of this bias for certain other more recent tests of sociological theories of suicide are, however, less obvious and warrant some specific consideration.

Porterfield has proposed a theory of suicide which hypothesizes that the fundamental differences between folk-type societies and secular-type societies will produce differences in the suicide rates of the two types of societies, with the suicide rate varying directly with the degree of secularization and inversely with the degree of folk elements present. This theory is actually a variation (if not exactly the same theory) on Halbwachs' theory of suicide, since folk means about the same thing as rural and secular means about the same thing as urban.[70] In constructing his indexes of the two types of society and in testing his theory with the official statistics on folk-secular elements and on the suicide rates, Porterfield specifically considers the urban areas to be more secular and the rural areas to be the more folk. He uses the different states of the United States as his different "societies." The folk states are, of course, predominantly the southern states and the sparsely inhabited Rocky Mountain states. These states are the least urbanized, the least industrialized, and the least wealthy. We would expect from this that they also have the least efficient statistical machines and that, therefore, they will have low suicide rates. In fact, *we would predict, in line with the general principle of statistical bias proposed in this section, that the three variables of urbanism, industrialism, and wealth will vary directly*

[70] See A. L. Porterfield, "Indices of Suicide and Homicide By States and Cities: Some Southern-Non-Southern Contrasts With Implications for Research," *American Sociological Review*, 14 (1949), pp. 481-490; "Suicide and Crime in Folk and In Secular Society," the *American Journal of Sociology*, LVII (1952), 331-338; and "Suicide and Crime in the Social Structure of an Urban Setting: Fort Worth, 1930-1950," *American Sociological Review*, 17 (1952), 341-349. See also A. L. Porterfield and R. H. Talbert, *Crime, Suicide and Social Well-Being In Your State and City*, Fort Worth: Leo Potisham Foundation, 1948.

with the official suicide rates in each state and with each smaller area of each state (such as the counties).[71] Whether the statistical covariance between such factors and the suicide rates is due to some fundamental differences in the effects on individual actions of rural (or folk) and urban (or secular) social life or is due, instead, to the bias in favor of the urban areas, can only be determined by intensive empirical investigation of the question; but we certainly cannot accept Porterfield's test as long as the question is not answered.[72]

[71] Cavan found, as we would predict, that the regional variations in suicide rates, especially between those of the North and those of the South, were predominantly due to the proportionately large rural population of the South. Southern cities with populations over 100,000 have suicide rates just slightly lower than Northern cities of the same size and these slightly lower rates for Southern cities are undoubtedly due to the higher proportion of Negroes, who have very low official suicide rates, in the Southern cities. (See R. S. Cavan, *Suicide*, p. 51.)

Also, such findings as that by Mayo that increasing industrialization is positively associated with increasing suicide rates is precisely what one would predict from the principle of bias proposed here. (See Peter Sainsbury, *Suicide in London*, p. 12.) Again, Wechsler's finding that an increasing rate of growth is positively associated with an increasing suicide rate is subject to the same explanation and criticism. (See Henry Wechsler, "Community Growth, Depressive Disorders, and Suicide," *The American Journal of Sociology*, LXVII (July, 1961) 9-17.)

This could also be the explanation for the close, direct relation between industrialization and suicide rates in the Western world over the last two hundred years.

[72] One striking bit of evidence concerning differences in the degree of willingness of officials of different societies to communicate information concerning suicidal actions warrants consideration here. In 1950 Schneider and his coworkers in Switzerland attempted to do a questionnaire study to determine how many attempted suicides come to the notice of the doctors of the French-speaking part of Switzerland:

". . . The inquiry failed and the number of responses was ridiculously small. It is useless to comment at length on the causes which led to this sorry result. Some are relevant to the essence of our research: one does not like to talk of suicide or of the attempt. This subject is still partially taboo, equally for doctors. On the other hand, we committed certain technical errors. Especially, the fundamental attitude of the Swiss-Roman doctor is frankly negative with respect to scientific inquiries by questionnaire. Now, this attitude determines more than anything else the results of research of this type whatever the errors one might accumulate. It is a question for investigation, not for criticism.

We sent nearly 2000 questionnaires and received 27 responses in all."

(Pierre-B. Schneider, *La Tentative de Suicide*, pp. 70-71.)

In other words, their rate of return was less than 1½ per cent. Several

The implication of a bias in official statistics that varies directly with the degree of urbanism (as well as industrialism and wealth) is much less obvious for the Gibbs and Martin status-integration theory of suicide, but it is significant. In general, I would argue that status-integration and urbanism vary directly. Clearly one of the oldest ideas of sociological research and theory on the differences between urban and rural areas has been that rural society involves far less role conflict than urban society; and, consequently, by the definition of status-integration used by Gibbs and Martin, status integration varies directly with the degree of urbanization. It is, then, clear that the statistical relations found by Gibbs and Martin to exist between status-integration and suicide rates could be the result of the degree of urbanization, as Halbwachs, Schmid, Porterfield, and others have argued *or* it could be the result of a bias in the statistics favoring higher rates for the urban areas.

Summary of Major Weaknesses of Official Statistics

This chapter has been concerned with many general and specific errors involved in the use of official statistics on suicide to construct and test sociological theories of suicide.

---

years later, without any knowledge of Schneider's abortive study, Shneidman and Farberow attempted the same kind of study in Los Angeles, though, possibly, with fewer "technical" mistakes: "The percentage of returns can be commented upon. Of the 6,602 letters to M.D.'s, we received over 5,000 responses (77 per cent), and of the 1,534 letters to D.O.'s, we received over 1,000 responses (66 per cent). This kind of response to a mail survey from physicians is in itself noteworthy and reflects the interest in the topic." (N. L. Farberow and E. S. Shneidman, *The Cry For Help*, p. 22.)

We, of course, cannot tell if the differences are the result of differences in the meaning of suicidal actions in the two different sociocultural systems, differences in the privacy of such matters, differences between rural and urban doctors' willingness to communicate information concerning suicidal actions, or other factors. Quite likely, the striking differences are the result of a combination of such factors. But we can be reasonably certain that information made public by doctors (and presumably, similar officials) about suicidal actions in the one society will not be comparable in any (statistical) way to that similarly made public in the other society.

One would expect to find similar, though less striking, differences between rural and urban doctors in America, even in the same region.

A brief summary of the major points of the argument will help in understanding the implications for both the criticism of earlier sociological works and the arguments presented later in this part concerning the types of information which we must make use of in developing and testing an alternative theoretical approach.

By official and general common-sense ways of thinking about such matters, suicide is an unnatural way of dying. Like other unnatural forms of death,[73] suicide is subject to police investigation and the various alternative forms of action which can be ordered by officials in the light of such investigations. The definitions of such categories of unnatural causes of death are generally given by laws. Presumably, these constitute what sociologists would consider to be *formal* or abstract definitions of the phenomena to be categorized in concrete cases by officials. Though there is some general agreement that the "intention to die" must be in some way inferable in order to categorize the cause of death as suicide, there is much disagreement between the national and local laws on how "suicide," "intention," etc., should be defined and what constitutes adequate grounds for inferring "intention." This constitutes the first clear basis for expecting that the official statistics as compiled by national organizations will be invalid: the data being compiled must be presumed, until sound evidence is found to the contrary, to be incomparable because of the influence of the formal definitions on the actual categorizations.

Regardless of the effects of the formal definitions, it is clear that coroners do in fact use different *operational* definitions of suicide. Moreover, different coroners' offices use very different *search procedures* in trying to get evidence for their decisions about categorizations of causes of death. These two facts must lead us to expect that suicide statistics are incomparable even within each local area.

In addition, there are the obvious factors of changes in the definitions, changes in the methods of certifying causes of death, changes in officials entrusted with such certifica-

[73] The whole conception of "unnatural" is, of course, a very difficult one to unravel; but the most general meaning is probably that of "any sudden death for which no organic cause is immediately observable as the basic underlying cause."

tions, changes in methods of reporting causes of death, etc. These changes have been very great in the nineteenth and twentieth centuries, and, for the most part, have not been considered by sociologists using the official statistics.

The most important error involved in the use of the official statistics, however, has been the same error as that made in the theories themselves; that is, the assumption that "suicidal actions" have a necessary and sufficient, unidimensional meaning throughout the Western world. This assumption lies behind the assumption (or argument) that the officials must be making use of the same definition as the theorists and that all of the officials must be making use of the same definition. It lies behind the assumption (almost never even made explicit) that the categorization of a death as "suicide" would mean the same thing to all social groups, strata, and individuals, so that any actions relevant to the official statistics (such as attempts to hide the facts about the death so that it would not be categorized as a suicide) would be equally distributed throughout the society being considered. Most significantly, this assumption lies behind the failure to see that an *official* categorization of the cause of death is as much the end result of an *argument* as such a categorization by any other member of society.

Future Studies of Official Statistics and Suicide

The final and most certain answer to the question of the reliability and validity of the official statistics on suicide can be given only by intensive and extensive empirical investigation of the methods, implicit and explicit assumptions, etc., of the officials who are responsible for the statistics on suicide *and* of the whole processes by which deaths in various societies are brought to the attention of various categories of officials for decisions concerning the "cause of death."[74]

[74] If one's goal is to determine the relations between various values of some social variables and values of suicidal variables, as it was of Durkheim and Halbwachs, then the problems involved in getting worthwhile "real" rates becomes immensely more difficult. Halbwachs argued that if one is concerned with the relations between society and the intention to die, then one must consider attempted suicides as well as suicides and try to determine the relations between suicides and attempted suicides. Consequently, he gathered what data he could on attempted suicides relative to suicides. (See Maurice Halbwachs, *Les Causes* . . . , pp. 69-91.) But even Halbwachs assumed that most

Such studies of the organizations and social processes that produce official suicide rates, however, will only tell us what the official suicide rates are and are not. They will not necessarily tell us much about the real-world suicidal phenomena; and, unless the cumulative implication of the many arguments against the normally assumed validity and reliability of the official statistics on suicide is mistaken, they will show us that these official suicide statistics are so greatly in error that they cannot be used for the scientific study of suicide itself.

The problem of determining "real" suicide rates will remain. And the problem will very likely remain for a long time, for the problem is by no means simple. Determining the "real causes" of a single death is, in the majority of cases, a great problem in itself. Frequently, even a team of psychiatric "experts" on suicide can only arrive at more or less rough categorizations of the causes of a single death after many days, or even weeks, of intensive investigation.[75] The problems involved in carrying out such investigations on a large enough scale to get significant samples of the deaths in a number of different socio-cultural systems,[76] in which the techniques of investigation would have to vary,[77] are quite beyond solution at the present time.[78]

---

attempted suicides would be successfully concealed, at least in the nations where negative sanctions were imposed for attempting suicide (*Ibid.*, p. 69).

If one were further concerned with studying the various forms and degrees of indirection involved in expressing a desire, intention, etc., to die, the problems involved in getting at "real" rates become excruciatingly difficult.

[75] The case of Marilyn Monroe, which was thoroughly examined by the psychiatrists with the Suicide Prevention Center of Los Angeles, is an example of this difficulty.

[76] I would argue, along the lines developed in this chapter, that a nation, especially the U.S., or even a large city must be considered to be a multiverse of socio-cultural systems. Just determining what the significant boundaries of such systems are to be would be a problem obviously far beyond the present knowledge and theoretical sophistication of sociologists.

[77] One might not even be interested in measuring the same variables from one society to another.

[78] At the present time the Suicide Prevention Center of Los Angeles is, to the knowledge of this author, the only organization in the world that has any potential for eventually producing some data of this sort for a limited population.

I would argue that these problems can be solved sufficiently for scientific purposes[79] only after the shared and individual *meanings* can be and have been determined for different socio-cultural systems, and only after many of the critical problems of getting at, describing, and measuring the individual cases of suicide have been solved. Indeed, the problem of determining what "real" rates we are interested in cannot be solved until the fundamental problem of determining meanings has been solved. Since these two general problems are closely related and *must* be, at least to some degree, attacked simultaneously, a basic reorientation of sociological work on suicide in the direction of intensive observation, description, and analysis of individual cases of suicide seems to be necessary. And, the emphasis of this research and analysis must be on the whole complex of shared and individual *meanings* of the actions involved in the suicidal process.

As will become clearer in Part IV, it is my strong expectation that such studies of the social meanings of suicide will lead us to see that the *essentially problematic nature* of such social meanings means that the idea of a "real rate" is a misconception. How many "suicides" there are in a given group at a given time is dependent on the concrete argument processes used. A sociologist might arbitrarily choose one dimension of meaning of "suicide" and attempt to construct a "real rate" for this dimension. However, such a procedure would probably be irrelevant in explaining such meaningful action as suicide. Moreover, how could one ever avoid the prior *social screening process*, which is subject to all of the essentially problematic meanings that result from an argument process? And, even if one could do this, how could one construct a "real rate" of "intention," so necessary in almost all formal and common-sense definitions of suicide and so essentially problematic itself?

---

[79] One's purposes might, of course, be "practical," i.e., *explicitly bound by presently known possibilities*, rather than "scientific," i.e., explicitly bound by *more* absolute cognitive standards rather than by present possibilities. (This is not to assume that "science" is based on explicit cognitive assumptions that are completely absolute. It is a matter of degree, not of absoluteness.)

PART IV · SUICIDAL ACTIONS AS SOCIALLY MEANINGFUL ACTIONS

An act like (suicide) is prepared within the silence of the heart, as is a great work of art.

ALBERT CAMUS,
THE MYTH OF SISYPHUS

So ist Kleists Sterben die "stärkste Realisierung seines Lebens."

A. BODENSOHN, *HEINRICH VON KLEISTS BEGEGNUNG MIT DEM TODE*

I do not say that it is cowardly to kill one-self, because that moral antithesis has always made me laugh, but I do say that there is a desire to create an impression. Believe me, my friend, I have played with the idea two or three times in my life, and when I look back it does seem to me that the hope of horrifying the spectators and arousing their pity at the denouement of my tragedy played a certain part in my resolution.

XIMENES DOUDAN, *REVOLUTIONS IN TASTE*

SOCIAL ACTIONS AS MEANINGFUL ACTIONS: FUNDAMENTAL CONSIDERATIONS OF THE NATURE OF "MEANING"

I3

> *We shall call "action" (Handeln) any human attitude or activity (Verhalten) (no matter whether involving external or internal acts, failure to act or passive acquiescence) if and insofar as the actor or actors associate a subjective meaning (Sinn) with it.—Max Weber[1]*

It is common knowledge among contemporary sociologists that Max Weber defined social action in terms of the *subjective meanings* of activities to the social actors involved and that he defined sociology as that science concerned with the study of social interaction. A sociologist defining sociology and social action in this way would, quite clearly, be concerned with studying suicidal actions as "subjectively meaningful" actions; he would, for example, be concerned with the suicidal "motives" as a ". . . meaningful complex (*Sinnzusammenhang*), which appears to the actor himself or to the observer to be an adequate (*Sinnvoll*) ground for his attitudes or acts."[2] In spite of the usual ceremonies of deference to Weber by contemporary sociologists, however, there has never been an attempt of any significant proportions to study suicide in this way.

There are, presumably, a number of reasons why, in spite of the great respect paid Weber's works by most sociologists, there has been almost no attempt by sociologists to study suicidal actions as meaningful actions. For one, as we have argued at some length in our treatment of Durkheim's *Suicide*, sociologists have taken Durkheim's approach to the study of suicide to be *the* appropriate approach, in some

---

[1] Quoted from *Wirtschaft und Gesellschaft* in Talcott Parsons, *The Structure of Social Action*, pp. 640-641.

[2] *Ibid.*, p. 642.

good part just as a matter of "traditional" authority and as a matter of a clear paradigm standing as a set of instructions on how to study suicide. But there seems to be more to it than this.

There have been, after all, a number of sociologists who have called for sociology of the type indicated by Weber's fundamental definitions of "action" and "sociology." Sorokin was certainly influential in the United States in this respect. He argued that sociology must be concerned with actions that have "meanings" to the social actors themselves; and in clear, plausible examples, such as the case of sexual intercourse, he argued that the same externally perceptible phenomena can be interpreted in very different ways by different members of a culture and that these different interpretations can be evaluated by them as indicating that certain very different responses should be made to the phenomena which seem so "alike" to a cultural outsider.[3] And, more recently, the "action theorists," most especially Talcott Parsons, have emphasized the necessity of studying social action as "meaningful" action (though this is normally made more restrictive by defining "social action" as action that is "motivated," rather than more generally as action that is "meaningful").

There is, however, a difference between what Weber was calling for and what these later sociologists interpreted his work as calling for. Weber was concerned with obtaining the "inside story" or "meaning" of events as the actor himself saw or interpreted it. These later, semi-Weberian sociologists have, on the other hand, been quite unconcerned, in the particular when not in the abstract, with determining the meaning of things from the standpoint of the actor.[4] For example, in the considerations of "motivation" these works give almost no consideration to the imputations of motivations made by the social actors themselves,

[3] See Pitirim A. Sorokin, *Society, Culture, and Personality*, New York: Harper and Brothers, 1947.

[4] There are some very important exceptions. The Chicago School in the 1920's produced some important semi-ethnographic works in which there were attempts, however inadequate, to get at the meanings of things from the standpoint of the actors. And, as we shall see below, the development of subculture theories has been a beginning in the move back to a purer Weberian goal.

nor to the many problems of determining how "sincere" such imputations are, etc. Instead, these sociologists have relied on various measurement techniques developed by behavioristic psychologists and similar methods. (Freudian methods of interpreting "motives" are included under this designation because there is no concern on the part of the sociological analyst with showing how one can go from the "meanings" of the social actors to the abstract, subconscious or unconscious motives of the Freudians. Though Freud himself was very much concerned with the fundamental problems of interpreting or measuring meanings,[5] the sociologists who have used Freudian analysis to arrive at conclusions about the meanings of things to the social actors have almost universally avoided such considerations themselves and have simply imposed the Freudian formulations upon the actors.)

The fundamental reason for this difference between Weber's goal and the work of the contemporary sociologists has probably been the subjective nature of Weber's approach to the problem of measuring "subjective meanings." Weber's theory of "understanding," involving the various nineteenth-century ideas of "empathy," "imaginatively reconstructing" for oneself the situational meanings of the actors one is studying, was very much in opposition to the strong tide toward highly "objective," formalized methods in American sociology. It is, indeed, rather clear that there was a fundamental, unresolved conflict between the "understanding" method and more formal, externalistic methods in Weber's own work, presumably resulting in most part from his conviction that the actions of men cannot be explained entirely in terms of what they think they intend—since the best intentions often lead men astray. Most especially, his analysis of the "ideal types" of authority seems to have served as a general model for the most abstract forms of *typologizing* completely divorced from any considerations of how the things look to the social actors involved in the situations—precisely the kind of typologizing that was already firmly fixed in the sociological studies of suicide

---

[5] For a careful consideration of Freud's contributions to the study of meanings, see Hugh Dalziel Duncan, *Communication and Social Order*, New York: The Bedminster Press, 1967, pp. 3-18.

because of the typology of suicide proposed by Durkheim.

The "typological" approach was only one of the two dominant approaches to the determination of cultural meanings stemming from Weber's work; the other approach was that of the *average building-block approach*. As much as Weber emphasized the need to study meanings concretely and in their "complexes" (i.e., what we would call their *contexts*), such approaches did not *seem* to lend themselves to objective, externalistic methods of analysis and measurement. First, Weber himself seems not to have resolved the conflict between his demand for studying meanings concretely, which, presumably, would call for the study of individual meanings, and his concern with very generally shared patterns of meanings.[6] Second, for all his concern with the subjective meaning of events to the individuals involved, Weber did not conceive of these meanings as being constructions of the individuals: quite to the contrary, he looked at the statements, actions, etc., of individuals only to discover the underlying, causal, general (or "average") patterns of meanings which he considered to be the basic components of cultures.

The major sociologists who have been fundamentally concerned with the analysis of "subjective meaning" since Weber's work have relied almost exclusively upon the *average building-block approach* to the analysis of meanings.[7] Sorokin's work on socio-cultural systems is fairly representative of this strong tendency: in spite of his knowledge of the history of Western culture, Sorokin's analysis of "meanings" focuses on the analysis of volumetric measures, rates of transmission of different types of meanings, etc.[8]

[6] For a brief discussion of Weber's failure to solve the problem of relating the general to the particular, see Nicholas S. Timasheff, *Sociological Theory: Its Nature and Growth*, New York: Random House, 1961, pp. 176-180.

[7] To avoid giving the impression that this is the only approach that has had any significant currency since Weber's work (other than the very recent works which we shall consider below) I would mention that there have been significant alternatives proposed. Spengler's *prime symbol* theory of socio-cultural phenomena is one clear example that involved neither an *averaging* of meanings nor a building-block *principle of aggregation*. (Benedict's approach to the analysis of cultural meanings in terms of an *ethos* was similar to Spengler's approach in fundamental principles, though quite independently arrived at.)

[8] See, especially, Pitirim A. Sorokin, *Social and Cultural Dynamics:*

Yet this work of Sorokin's on socio-cultural systems of mean-ings is the only sociological work since Weber's to thor-oughly consider the many fundamental problems involved in the analysis and study of meanings. Almost all other sociological works have apparently assumed that there are no particular problems involved in specifying what the meanings of things are to the social actors, or they have been concerned only with the "general," "abstract," "average," "patterned," etc., meanings of whole socio-cultural systems and *have not attempted to show how it is that one would infer cultural patterns of meanings from the particular, con-crete, observable phenomena any science must deal with.*[9]

The development of research and theories on "subcul-tures," especially of "deviant subcultures" where the dif-ferences between the things members of such subcultures do and the things generally done in "similar situations" by members of the more encompassing culture are very clear, has been the most noteworthy exception to this general failure to consider the problems of measuring and theo-retically dealing with meanings; and this exception is only partial. In most of these works on subcultures there are the usual assumptions that one can adequately understand what the members of the subculture mean when they say something, even when the language is quite different from that of the observer,[10] and that one knows what things mean subjectively to the actor. For example, in one of the best works on delinquency Albert Cohen has argued that the actions of "delinquent boys" are clearly "non-utilitarian." This statement involves an implicit assumption, possibly

---

Basic Problems, Principles, and Methods, vol. IV, New York: The Bedminster Press, 1962.

[9] Harold Garfinkel pointed out to the author that even Talcott Parsons implicitly assumes in his essays on symbolism that the social actors face no problem in deciding what specific situations *mean* in terms of some generally shared set of symbols of situations—there is an implicit assumption that the symbolic meaning of situations (i.e., what meanings are relevant to what situations) is "automatically" given.

[10] Differences in language are especially clear among certain ethnic and racial groups in the United States. For example, the language of the Negro subculture (if one can usefully speak of it as being fundamentally a unitary phenomenon) is clearly distinct from that of the other subculture groups in the United States for whom English is a native language.

unseen by Cohen, that what is "utilitarian" and what is "non-utilitarian" is no different for these boys from what it is to a sociologist: i.e., a sociologist can look at the actions committed by these boys and tell right away from his understanding of such things as a member of the culture that these actions are "non-utilitarian" for the boys themselves. The same assumption is made concerning the criteria of "rationality": "There is no accounting in rational and utilitarian terms for the effort and the danger run in stealing things which are often discarded, destroyed or casually given away."[11]

A few of these subculture studies or theories, however, do take some of the meanings of things to the actors being studied to be problematic and do devote some consideration to the ways in which the social actors actually communicate with each other about the things that are significant to them. For example, in his study of a maximum security prison Sykes was concerned with determining the linguistic categories in terms of which the inmates communicated with each other about inmates, guards, and others of significance within the prison.[12] Unfortunately, however, Sykes was primarily concerned with the linguistic categories as providing a kind of "map" to the *assumed* "system of social roles," so that there is actually relatively little attempt here to deal with the subjective meanings of such things to the social actors themselves: their language is simply used as a *representation* of some underlying "meanings" which the sociologist assumes to be there, though the specific contours of the underlying meanings are themselves partially inferred from these representations.[13]

---

[11] Albert K. Cohen, *Delinquent Boys: The Culture of the Gang*, Glencoe: The Free Press, 1955, p. 26. (On this same page Cohen does make a reference to what the boys say about such things: i.e., that they do it "just for the hell of it." But he prefaces this reference with the note that the informant is using "homelier language.")

[12] Gresham M. Sykes, *The Society of Captives: A Study of a Maximum Security Prison*, Princeton: Princeton University Press, 1958.

[13] In a study presenting a greater wealth of material and focusing far more on linguistic categories of social types, Orrin E. Klapp has quite clearly put the whole matter in the context of this "action frame of reference": "But the typing process is more than just pigeonholing people. It is a vast collective undertaking to be studied with the social system as the focus. In this sociological aspect, we are concerned with

There are some good reasons why the *representational* (or "denotative") theory is inadequate as a general approach to the study and interpretation of meanings;[14] but the use of such an approach in this specific way (i.e., going from the linguistic categories used in communications to some inferred, "underlying things," such as eidetic images) is clearly far better than not bothering to *empirically* study the "subjective" social meanings at all. But my particular criticism of this type of representational analysis of meaning is that it *infers* that the "things" or "meanings" lying behind (or under) the linguistic categories (or whatever they take as their data) are the grand abstractions of some sociological theories, though the nature of such concepts as "social role" is more that of an *ad hoc* assumption than of an abstraction. (What are the rules for "abstracting" such concepts from the observable phenomena of everyday life?) These sociologists do not infer from linguistic categories any images, thoughts, feelings, beliefs, etc., which one might actually observe or experience indirectly by communications with the actors or directly as a social actor himself. Rather, they simply assume that the observable phenomena are representations of their theoretical categories. Such analyses of social phenomena really tell us nothing of a scientific nature: they consist primarily of merely imposing upon the immediately observable phenomena (of linguistic categories in this case) an abstract set of assumptions about the nature of society, assumptions which can be applied anywhere to any social phenomena.[15]

---

a stock of images and symbols, as part of a culture, and the way this stock changes and works in the system." (*Heroes, Villains and Fools*, Englewood Cliffs, New Jersey: Prentice-Hall, Inc., 1962, p. 7.) In this passage Klapp clearly presents the dominance of the "social system" in such analyses of everyday social meanings. He also clearly assumes the *building-block approach* to the study of meanings, though the reference to a concern with how such categories "work" might indicate *some* concern with the *construction* of meanings.

[14] See Gilbert Ryle, "The Theory of Meaning," in *The Importance of Language*, edited by Max Black, Englewood Cliffs: Prentice Hall, Inc., 1962, pp. 147-171.

[15] Let us take note of the somewhat overdrawn nature of this argument. It is, of course, not true that sociologists do not give any consideration to the specific details of meanings in our culture(s). They do in fact do so in many places; and certainly Sykes has done so at various places in his work. (One of the reasons I have chosen his

At this point we are clearly faced with the question of what alternative approach to the study of social meanings can be followed. It is not my intention to argue that general or abstract theoretical propositions are irrelevant or necessarily bad in such work. On the contrary, I shall be quite concerned with *certain* general propositions and arguments concerning the nature of suicidal meanings and the way one should study them. But, if my position is not one of extreme nominalism, neither is it one that admits of the normal excesses of sociological "realism." I definitely shall not be much concerned with arguing from general propositions about the nature of social systems, the nature of social actions, the nature of social meanings, etc., down to the specific, concrete details of suicidal meanings. I *shall*, however, be concerned with *certain* ideas concerning the general dimensions of suicidal meanings and of the general properties of suicidal processes. In fact, my whole method of analyzing social meanings leads us to try to see the general in the particular and the particular in the general; and certainly one of the fundamental ideas of this (*"Zirkel im Verstehen"*) method is that the particulars are frequently comprehensible only in terms of the general context in which they occur, so that one must have some idea of the general context in order to understand the particular. (We might call this *the principle of the contextual determination of meanings.*) And this general context is not something that is necessarily part of the *meanings* available to the social actors themselves: they may be, and almost certainly are most of the time, quite unaware of such general dimensions as we shall be considering. But it is of the greatest importance that these fundamental dimensions of suicidal meanings are intended to be directly relatable to concrete, observable suicidal phenomena in this culture. (Some of these are arrived at by a process of logical abstraction, but it would seem clear that "intuitive" creation has been more important as the method by which the ideas have been first obtained.)

---

work as an example to criticize is that it is one of the best in recent years: it is very much the opposite of a straw-man example.) The argument is simply directed at the structure of these works, the dominant tendencies, the aspects of these works which their authors seem clearly to have taken as the most important aspects.

The statements, cries, actions, and whatever other real-world phenomena one can come up with are the data that one must use to study and analyze meanings; and *in the initial stages* some of these phenomena must necessarily be the experiences and observations of the sociological observers themselves.

In line both with this fundamental orientation in the direction of studying the concrete phenomena and with my many earlier arguments concerning the value for such studies as this of using open-ended concepts, especially on the most fundamental level, it is not our intention in this work to propose any general definition of the concept of "meaning." The position taken here is very similar to that expressed by Sorokin on this question:

> Some of the critics . . . and some of the contemporary addicts of so-called semantics (behaviorism, logical positivism, etc.), raise an objection to the term "meaning," and indicate again and again the vagueness of the *meaning* of the meaning. Yet, like all the ultimate terms—such as "consciousness," "mind," "thought"—it cannot be defined more clearly by any other term. But its essential meaning is clear to anyone who has mind and thought, while to those who do not possess them it will remain a mystery—just as colors are a mystery to the blind, or love to those who never have been in love. When, however, these critics of the terms "meaning," "mind," "thought," "consciousness" and the like try to replace them by such terms as "verbal reflex," "verbal stimulus-response articulation," "articulated verbal reflex," "symbolic verbal sign," "mind is minding," "science is sciencing," or "logical syntax of language"; or when they define thought, meaning, consciousness as "an electron-proton association" as "a complex integration and succession of bodily activities closely related to or involving the verbal and gestural mechanisms" as "stimulus-response relationship," and so on, they certainly do not improve but enormously aggravate the situation. Such supposedly better definitions of "meaning," "mind," or "thought" do not describe them at all, do not touch in any way these phenomena, and do not indicate any of their characteristics. On the other

hand, such definitions can be applied to thousands of phenomena having nothing in common with meaning or mind or thought or consciousness. As such, these pretentious efforts are excellent examples of the barbarian atrocities of thought and logic. See the criticism and literature on them in my *Contemporary Sociological Theories*. . . .

As to the fashionable mode of replacing the terms "meaning," "thought," "mind," "consciousness," by such terms as "verbal sign," "verbal symbol," "symbolic behavior," and the like (R. Carnap, A. J. Ayer, and a crowd of "semanticists" and vulgarizers like S. Chase, G. Lundberg, and others), and as to their belief that by such a substitution they escape the vagueness of the terms "meaning" or "thought" and improve the meaning of "meaning," the fashion as well as the belief is perfectly childish. To be meaningful, the terms "symbol," "sign," "language," presuppose and convey their meaning, while the meaning does not need them. It is both primary and ultimate, while "symbol," "sign," or "language" are derivative from meaning and hence secondary. "Symbol" symbolizes a meaning different from the symbol's empirical form; "sign" signifies a meaning of which it is the mere "sign" or "substitute." If they did not symbolize or signify meanings, they would not be symbols or signs. Meaning is the *conditio sine qua non* of any symbol or sign or word or language (in contra-distinction to meaningless jibbering or noisemaking). "Symbols" are worth studying on account of what they symbolize (that is, mean); the cultivation of symbols for their own sake is a philosophical form of worship of the sign instead of the thing signified."

For these reasons, the criticism of my use of the term "meaning" is superfluous. It displays mainly the deficiency of logic and the baseless pretentiousness of the critics themselves. It certainly is a good example of a definition of *clarum per obscurum*.[16]

The concept of "meaning" is so fundamental to any consideration of human action that it is exceedingly difficult

[16] P. A. Sorokin, *Social and Cultural Dynamics*, Vol. IV, p. 12, fn. 10.

to define it in terms of other factors. This is not to say that an attempt to define the concept is not worthwhile. It is simply to admit that the endeavor is far too much of a job in itself to make it part of such a work as this. The literature on the subject is immense and terribly involved.[17] Consequently, I shall simply rely upon a cultural understanding of the term.

From my standpoint the important problems of method are not problems of defining the "meaning of meaning" or any such thing, but, rather, those of how to go about studying and analyzing meanings. We have, of course, been considering such problems throughout this part of this book and will do so far more in the specific attempts at studying and analyzing communications involving suicidal phenomena; but there is one more general point that should be considered here.

Comparisons are, as Durkheim so well realized, the fundamental method of any study of meanings. The difference between the comparisons to be considered here and those usually made by sociologists is a primary attention to the actual statements and actions of people in everyday life;[18] and a concern not with simply comparing the linguistic categories or any other such immediately, externally observable phenomena, but, rather, with comparing these and any unseen (though not unstudiable—since various indirect means can be used, such as inferences from the nature of the language, which we shall give an example of) phenomena as well.

The comparative approach has recently been more highly developed by anthropologists who have been especially con-

---

[17] It is my suspicion that the problem is so fundamental that considering what "meaning" is is very much like considering what gravity is. The problem might eventually become "solvable" (just as gravity might someday be explainable in terms of weak forces or some such thing), but it seems likely that for a long time it will be best for sociologists and those in similar disciplines, unlike linguistic philosophers, to concentrate on doing studies and analyses of "meaning" rather than trying to show what causes meaning or what "meaning really is."

[18] Thus, our comparisons are in direct conflict with the various Durkheimian statements made by the students of suicide, such as that made by Gibbs: "Only a rate of suicide is suited for comparisons . . ." ("Suicide," in Robert K. Merton and Robert A. Nisbet, editors, *Contemporary Social Problems*, p. 232.)

cerned with the study of social action that clearly has associated with it highly developed systems of linguistic categories—the study of kinship has been especially amenable to such an approach. Some of the ideas developed by these anthropologists, such as that of "criteria of relevance" in Conklin's "ethnogenealogical method," are of value, at least in terms of stimulating thought, in such a study as this.[19] But, as I shall shortly argue, the meanings of suicidal actions are not neatly organized into systems with systems of linguistic categories carefully associated with them. Consequently, such techniques of analysis as this are not very appropriate to the study of suicidal meanings except as analogies or suggestions. The general properties which suicidal meanings seem to have call for a special approach which we shall now examine.

[19] See Harold C. Conklin, "Ethnogenealogical Method," in *Explorations in Cultural Anthropology*, edited by Ward M. Goodenough, New York: McGraw-Hill Book Company, 1964, pp. 28-29.

14 THE CONSTRUCTION OF SOCIAL MEANINGS

A generally shared principle in the study of the meanings of actions (or of any meanings) is that one can safely assume a direct relation between the patterning of language and the patterning of meanings. One of the implications of this is that the more the shared linguistic terminology for dealing with some social actions, the more the shared meanings of such phenomena. (Leo Spitzer quoted the following to illustrate the principle: "Wortwandel ist Kulturwandel.") Though we have previously observed the invalidity of this representational interpretation as a general principle, still it is a useful tool when one has little other empirical data than the linguistic categories themselves; and we shall at this point make some use of it.

In the Western world there has clearly been an increase in the last few centuries in the degree of shared language for treating suicidal phenomena. (The very word "suicide" and its closely related equivalents in the non-English languages is an example.) There are also many shared, associated terms: despair, unhappiness, life is not worthwhile, escape from the harsh realities, etc. And there do seem to be certain basic dimensions of meaning for which these are slightly variant means of expression. But these terms are also clearly not *sui generis* to the phenomena themselves. On the contrary, they are terms from many other areas of experience. They are terms adopted from various spheres of experience for the purposes of *constructing meanings* for these suicidal phenomena. (The line of influence is similar to that found in much of the language of rocketry today. Rockets are called birds, but birds are not yet called rockets.) Moreover, there seems to be no very clear set of rules either for *ordering* the linguistic terms or *applying* them to specific phenomena: i.e., *there is variability, ambiguity, and conflict in the imputations of the linguistic cate-*

gories, including the fundamental category of "suicide," (or "suicidal") itself.

The implication of this ambiguity in the language of "suicidal" phenomena is simply that there is a high degree of ambiguity in the *meanings* of suicidal phenomena to the social actors within Western culture. Such phenomena, then, are not very clearly defined for the social actors *in the concrete situation.* There is also some further linguistic evidence to suggest this is the case. The linguistic expressions are not very *detailed.* On the contrary, they are generally abstract, common-sense theoretical terms. Since specific actions are not based on abstract theories, even those of a common-sense nature, the common language of suicidal phenomena (and, inferentially, the common, culturally-shared meanings) cannot provide a base for interpreting specific, concrete suicidal phenomena that one is involved in (at least as long as one is involved in them—one might well become abstract in retrospect).

There is, of course, far more evidence than simply the linguistic that the *concrete, situated meanings* of suicidal phenomena are *not* very detailed or well ordered—i.e., not very *adequately defined in everyday meanings,* in spite of the adequacy of definitions in abstract, non-situated communications. Of greatest importance is the evidence from the statements and actions of the actors and the members of the audience (the involved, significant others). First, the significant others who get involved in the suicidal phenomena by having suicidal threats made against them, or by having suicidal actions committed in such a way that they are socially defined as implicated or involved in some other way, are frequently confused and helpless. They frequently express feelings of inadequacy in dealing with the whole matter, feelings of being at a total loss as to what to make of these actions, feelings that this just can't be "real," can't be happening to them, etc. And they often take the action defined as appropriate for dealing with something that one cannot adequately deal with: i.e., they turn the "problem" over to those socially defined as the experts or specialists in dealing with such "abnormal" phenomena. Even the definitions of these statements and actions as those calling for specialist treatment may come about only after a long, complex sequence of events and feelings of uneasiness, "despair," etc. In some cases one can even find a "crescendo of suicidal acts" leading up to the definition of this as something requiring specialist care.[1]

The specialists themselves are under great pressure to make some standardized, meaningful whole out of suicidal phenomena: it is their social responsibility to do so. But they also frequently find it extremely difficult to know what to make of suicidal phenomena. Even with a general tendency to impose categories of sickness, Freudian theories, and so on, upon such phenomena, they still frequently express the belief that the whole thing is not very clearly defined or understood. For example, in the case of Virginia Arlington, reported by Kobler and Stotland, there are many instances of statements by various "specialists" that the whole thing was not very clearly defined. After a suicidal attempt by the patient one of the psychiatrists said that it was a "messed up picture,"[2] a member of the ward staff believed that the ward staff was generally "confused about whether she was sick or not, suicidal or not";[3] a member of the ward staff reported that after a sequence of events involving suicidal threats the ward staff was "thrown off balance";[4] and, as a good indication of the conflict over how the patient should be defined, the director of nurses stated that "the whole time I had the feeling that nobody really knew how sick this woman was."[5]

Finally, suicidal phenomena often are not generally clearly defined for the individuals who are initiating them. There are many instances of suicidal action in which the individuals seem quite "sincerely" (to the interviewers) unable to understand what they did or why they did it; they do not seem able to make any particular "sense" of it—i.e., to give an "adequate" meaning from their own standpoint. (This inability to understand is, quite likely, the fundamental

[1] As an example see Case 23 reported by Stengel and Cook, *Attempted Suicide: Its Social Significance and Effects*, New York: Oxford University Press, 1958, p. 77.

I do not, of course, want to imply that there are no cases in which the participants feel certain that they understand the whole matter and know just what to do: there are such cases.

[2] Arthur L. Kobler and Ezra Stotland, *The End of Hope: A Social-Clinical Theory of Suicide*, p. 171.

[3] *Ibid.*, p. 195. [4] *Ibid.*, p. 201. [5] *Ibid.*, p. 195.

reason for their common inability to communicate some adequate meaning of the act to others, such as the specialists to whom they have gone for help.[6]) This lack of clear, shared meaning is very likely a general cause of the feeling of "losing control," "losing contact with reality," "going out of my mind," etc., that one finds in individuals with suicidal tendencies (as well as with non-suicidal, "schizophrenic" individuals): *if one cannot determine the meaning of something, then he does not feel that he can control it.* In the case of Virginia Arlington, for example, this theme of not understanding herself and not being able to control herself ran through her communications with others for weeks or even months and seemed to increase toward the end of her life (ended by suicide in a mental institution).[7] The case of Virginia Arlington also shows the interdependent nature of meaningfulness and meaninglessness (in the particular sense in which we are considering "meaning" here): as others came to consider her statements and actions to be inadequately defined, except insofar as they could be defined as lacking any adequate meaning in everyday terms—i.e., as "insanity" or "sickness,"—so she came increasingly to see her statements and actions as lacking any adequate meaning in everyday terms:

> "It doesn't seem like my behavior makes any difference to you people. When I do something or say something, do you regard it or do you just say to yourselves, she's sick." ['Our business is to regard patient's behavior.'] "Well, why don't you respond; like when I'm angry, have you ever tried to get angry with a brick wall?" ['Because we don't say anything does not mean we don't regard it.'] She continued by talking in her hopeless fashion, saying that if she was going to be the worst one here, why didn't they strap her down and be done with it. She was desperate inside, etc. Some of it had a threatening quality (toward hospital).[8]

[6] Kobler and Stotland reported that "Mrs. Clift and Dr. Lyle both felt strongly at that time that Mrs. Arlington's inability to communicate what was wrong to Mrs. Clift was frightening her further, aggravating the anxiety and the 'shattering.'" (*Ibid.*, p. 157.)

[7] *Ibid.*

[8] *Ibid.*, p. 179. This quote was taken from a statement made by some member of the ward staff; but Kobler and Stotland did not give de-

All of this does not, of course, mean that suicidal actions do not have specific meanings to the individual committing them or to the significant others involved. In many instances suicidal actions seem clearly to have very specific and certain meanings for the individual and for the others involved.[9] These instances seem to be a minority of the cases of suicidal actions, but they do exist and are by no means rare. In most instances of suicidal actions several meanings are imputed to the actions by the several people involved. Sometimes there is simply a disagreement among those involved about what the action means, so that any ambiguity of meaning would have to be considered to exist only *as a whole* (or on the average). Rarely is there one meaning imputed to suicidal actions by each person involved. There are, presumably, a number of reasons for this, one probably being the relatively unusual nature of the phenomena and the recency with which men in the Western world have seen them as worthy of serious study. But the most important reason is very likely an intrinsic ambiguity, one resulting from the conflicting meanings in Western culture of two fundamental dimensions of the meanings of such actions. As I shall argue in the next chapter, suicidal actions almost always mean something fundamental both about the person and about the situation of the person: each of these is seen as a "cause" of the suicidal action. This means that on the most fundamental level it is always possible to argue that the action is either the result of the situation of the individual or, from the opposite side, to argue that the action is the result of something inside (something "wrong with," etc.) the individual; and, of course, one could also argue that it is the result of some interaction of these two things.[10]

---

tails on how the conversation was reconstructed. As noted in our later consideration of psychiatric case reports, this is one of the frequent problems in dealing with such reports.

Goffman has described many of the specific patterns of behavior that seem to have this effect of destroying the feeling of *adequate meaning*, but has not dealt with it in these terms. See his *Asylums*.

[9] The examples in the section below on "revenge" suicidal actions are sometimes very specific and certain in their meanings for those involved.

[10] Kenneth Burke presented just such an analysis of the *ambiguities*

Now, we have said that it is "always possible" to argue either or both ways. This is true as long as one is considering suicidal actions in the abstract; but it is clear as soon as one considers actual cases that, though in any given case there might actually be someone who, for some reason or other, does argue either side of the case, there is generally one side of the argument that seems to most of those involved to be more likely (more plausible) than the other. This is not simply the result of chance. Rather, the particular events, previous imputations of selves to the person who commits the action, and many other aspects of the particular case are the fundamental determinants of what the meanings will be to those involved. *In very general terms we could say that the meanings of this particular event (or a sequence of events coming in one time and situation, as seen by those involved) are determined by their* contextual relations *with many other meanings.*[11]

Now, a *social constructionist theory of meanings* clearly differs from the usual building-block approach in its emphasis on the fundamental significance of the ways in which specific events, symbols, etc., are *related* by individuals to each other to determine the meanings of something to those individuals. But such a formulation leaves open as a possible interpretation the usual *mechanistic approach* to interpreting the meaning of specific things in terms of a number of "building blocks" such as values. In terms of this interpretation the specific meanings of specific events is supposed to be given in some unspecified manner by the *structure* of

---

of suicide motives in Western literature; and it was this beautiful analysis which was so important in leading this author to see the relevance of rhetoric to all suicidal actions. See Kenneth Burke, *A Rhetoric of Motives*, New York: The World Publishing Company, 1962, pp. 527-537.

[11] Alternatively, one could say that meanings are *functionally* determined. The use of functional in this sense has some clear precedent in the study of language. (See, for example, André Martinet, *A Functional View of Language*, Oxford: The Clarendon Press, 1962.) But there does exist an obvious, superficial similarity between our approach to meanings and the functionalist approach to the analysis of "systems of social roles," as first clearly developed by Radcliffe-Brown. To avoid any unfounded arguments about these being "really" the same theories, the approach to meanings used here shall be called the *social constructionist theory of meanings.*

meanings shared by the members of the culture being considered.

I would argue, on the contrary, that such an approach can work only on some sociologistic level at which one does not have to show how the specific meanings of specific events come about: one could only talk about non-observable "average meanings" which can not in any specific way be shown to be derived from observable phenomena. One would have to do as Durkheim did: that is, show that there exists some statistical correlation between the official suicide rates and some type of group and then simply impute some meanings to that group so that the relative rate of suicide appropriate (in terms of one's theory) to that group will be seen to be the one found.

As soon as one looks at the specific meanings imputed by those involved in suicidal phenomena, one can see that, though there is a great complexity to the various considerations made by the social actors and no specific structure inherent in some patterns of meanings, still there is some agreement on the specific meanings of these specific events. I would argue that the structure one finds in the meanings of specific suicidal phenomena is not given by the transmitted culture, though some of the specific meanings and criteria that make this structure possible are so given, but that the individuals involved *construct this structure of meanings.* Though the possible (or plausible) meanings of these phenomena are primarily determined by the *shared, cultural meanings* which are culturally defined as relevant to these phenomena (including the criteria of various sorts) and by the *shared context of meanings given to the individuals involved by their past interactions,* the specific, actualized meanings of these phenomena will be in large measure determined by the intentional actions of the individuals involved. Moreover, I would argue that the only way one can go about scientifically studying the meanings of suicidal phenomena (or any other social phenomena) is by studying the specific meanings of real-world phenomena of this socially-defined type as the individuals involved construct them: we must work from the clearly observable, concrete phenomena upward to abstractions about meanings in any culture (though, I would argue, it is generally necessary to see the whole in some way in order to know how one should go about studying the particulars and abstracting from them); and the abstractions must be the results of comparisons made by sociologists of the concrete meanings of these phenomena defined as *similar* by the members of the culture. It need hardly be added that the meanings being compared must be those constructed by the actors involved in their "natural cultural habitat" rather than those constructed by the actors in response to some "unnatural" instrument with its own implicit assumptions about the structure of meanings being studied.

SOURCES OF INFORMATION AND THE CONSTRUCTION OF A THEORY OF SUICIDAL ACTIONS AS SOCIALLY MEANINGFUL ACTIONS

15

I have gone to great lengths in Part III to show the fundamental inadequacies of the data on suicide that have been used by sociologists and, consequently, the inadequacies of the sociological theories that have been developed out of and tested by that data. This critical work brings into serious question the very possibility of constructing at this time any worthwhile theoretical approach to suicidal actions as social actions. It seems appropriate, then, to briefly consider the present sources of information on suicide that are relevant to my theoretical approach, the relative adequacies of these data, and the consequences of these considerations for the construction of theories of suicidal actions as socially meaningful actions. We shall first consider the general problems involved and then take up two sources of information that are of greatest importance to the theoretical approach to be proposed here.

There are, first of all, those types of information which might normally come to mind when one thinks of "meaningfulness": that is, information which deals with individuals as individuals. The most common kind of information of this sort would be "psychological" information, such as information on the life histories of individuals who commit some form of suicidal action or information of a "depth" nature. We shall consider the whole problem of the "biographical approach" of psychologists and psychiatrists below, but we should first consider the relevance of "depth" psychological information here. The fundamental approach of most psychologists when dealing with such phenomena as suicidal actions is to try to show that certain "personality factors" are the basic causes by trying to show some significant (generally statistical) relations between depth measurements of individuals and the suicidal actions. More specifically, psychologists have normally been concerned in the twentieth century with depth information on the "dynamic" or motivational factors. (The recent increase in concern among the psychologists of personality with cognitive factors has hardly had time to influence the psychological studies of suicidal actions.) Psychologists have, therefore, concentrated their efforts on getting information such as is obtained from the analysis of Rorschach tests of individuals who have attempted suicide (in comparison with various kinds of "control groups"); and this information has normally been concerned with the "motives" (or "needs") *presumed* to be associated with the suicidal actions because of an association found between the individuals involved and measurements of these individuals' "motives."

The underlying assumption of this whole approach is that individuals have certain properties which are the causes of their actions over very long periods of time; and that these causal links between motives and actions can be inferred independently of the real-world situations in which the actions are performed.[1] This monadic conception of the actions of man is just the opposite of the fundamental conception lying behind the theoretical approach proposed here. We propose to study human actions and their "meanings" from the bottom upward, at least in some good part. (The idea proposed here must, of course, be modified by our considerations below of the *Zirkel im Verstehen* approach to the analysis of meanings.) The *ideal* of this approach is to go from what people say and do in the real-world situations upward toward an analysis of the patterns that can be found in their actions and the meanings of their statements and behavior; then, only when the problems of these levels of investigation have been solved, to proceed to develop theories of the social meanings. Moreover, it is a strong expectation lying behind this particular approach that the *situation* of fundamental importance in determining the meanings of suicidal actions for the real-

---

[1] Some psychologists have doubted the value of such an assumption, but the specific works on suicide and similar behavior have largely overlooked such doubts.

world participants will be *social* in nature: that is, that the meanings will be determined by the actual processes of meaningful social interaction in the situation in which the suicidal actions occur. This does not mean that information on non-situated meanings is not relevant. Clearly, such information is important. There are probably stable patterns of meanings of such phenomena, both of a shared-and-transmitted nature and of an individual nature; and these patterns of meanings are probably fundamentally important in determining what specific forms of meanings can be constructed in specific social situations by the social actors. (They form the materials which largely constrain the possibilities of the social actors.) But, again, if such patterns are there and are of fundamental importance, it will be proposed here to analyze them *out of* the specific information that one can gather from the real-world phenomena, rather than imposing them upon the real-world phenomena because one happens, for whatever reason, to believe that these are *the* important patterns of meanings in his culture.[2]

The implication of this approach for an appraisal of the value of "depth" psychological information seems rather clear. Such information might prove of value once one has systematically studied the real-world patterns of constructed meanings and has been able to analyze them; but such information is not relevant, and can hardly be based on anything other than false assumptions until these early stages of work have been accomplished. An example can be given. A psychologist studying the causes of suicide will generally try to show that certain kinds of intervening variables which he calls "motives" and gives an abstract definition to are the causes of suicide.[3] The approach proposed here would lead on to study "motives" first only as they appear in the statements of social actors involved in sui-

[2] Again, the actual method of analyzing meanings used here is to go from the particular to the general but also from the general to the particular. The strong statements here are intended largely to emphasize the need to keep as close to the real-world phenomena as possible at this early stage of development and work up to more abstract conceptions and then theory only at the rate that seems justified by the information on real-world phenomena.

[3] There are, of course, a great number of these abstractly defined "motives": e.g., need for security, need for achievement, fear of failure, etc.

cidal phenomena: that is, one would study the imputations of motives made by the actors themselves. These "imputed motives" would then be analyzed to attempt to determine what importance the meanings of such statements have in the whole suicidal process. Only at a very advanced stage of investigation might it prove valuable to try to get as abstract as to say anything about individuals' needs for "security," etc., in relation to *suicidal* actions.

Psychiatric and Psychological Sources of Information on Suicidal Phenomena

The psychiatric and psychological literature on suicide is extensive. There are three general types of information to be gotten from this literature. First, the most important source of information on suicidal phenomena now available are the transcriptions and reconstructions of what individuals who made suicidal statements or committed suicidal actions said and did, in what sequence, etc. Second, there are the descriptions of what the psychiatrists and others did and said toward the individuals who made suicidal statements or committed suicidal actions. And third, there are the various interpretations (i.e., the imputed meanings) of these phenomena by the psychiatrists.

Since we shall be examining the psychiatric case studies throughout the rest of this work, there is little need for detailed treatment of them here, but there are certain basic points that need to be considered. The last two forms of information to be gotten from these case studies and the rest of the psychiatric literature are of much less importance than the first, so we can easily deal with them. The interpretations of suicidal communications and actions by the psychiatrists can, like the sociological literature, be treated as a source of information on common-sense ideas about suicidal phenomena. These psychiatric interpretations are, however, much closer to the actual, real-world phenomena and have taken into consideration far more of the actual communications of the individuals committing the suicidal actions. This has resulted in more complex interpretations which contain some significant similarities to the proposed approach to suicidal actions as socially meaningful actions. These interpretations, however, have generally not been made in the context of such an orientation. They have been done specifically in the context of theories *sui generis* to the psychiatric discipline and within (or from the standpoint of) common-sense interpretations of social phenomena. The interpretations of suicidal phenomena by the psychiatrists assume a great importance in the whole suicidal process when they become part of the communication of psychiatrists dealing with suicidal phenomena or when they determine the actions of psychiatrists dealing with suicidal phenomena. (We shall consider these problems at great length in our treatment of the suicidal process.)

The first general problem to be dealt with in analyzing the value of psychiatric reports of particular cases of suicidal phenomena is the method of recording what was observed. Psychiatrists have rarely used any recording devices (such as tape recorders or sound films) until quite recently to record their encounters with cases. Nor have they generally used note-taking during the encounter, though this has very likely been done in a rough way in many cases to provide memory cues. When this has been done, however, it is generally not possible for the reader to tell that this was the case, since the nature of the encounter is not treated as part of the determination of what is observed by the psychiatrists. The dominant means of recording what happened is reconstruction from memory shortly after the actual encounter. The evidence that can be gained by comparing the memories of psychiatrists with recordings of what actually went on would seem to indicate that there is a good deal of difference between what they remember was said and what was recorded as having been said.[4] The interpretation normally given to this finding is that their reconstructions have distorted or selectively presented what went on in fact, presumably to fit the motives, self-conceptions, etc., of the psychiatrists. It is entirely possible that this is the best explanation of such differences. On the other hand, it could also be simply that the memory is selectively retentive not of specific statements or actions but, rather, of socially and personally *meaningful units and complexes*. If

[4] Probably the best study of such matters is that reported in Robert E. Pittenger, *et al., The First Five Minutes: A Sample of Microscopic Interview Analysis,* Ithaca, New York: Paul Martineau, 1960.

this is so, and such an explanation is very much in line with the general theoretical orientation of this work, the verbal reconstructions of an observer would then be seen not as exact replicas of the verbal statements made, but, rather, condensations of the over-all meanings that were communicated by verbal statements, facial expressions, hand and body motions, eye movements, etc. In this case one would definitely expect that there would be differences between what in fact was spoken and what was remembered as spoken. This would lead one to expect that the psychiatric reconstructions (i.e., the "case reports") are better presentations of what went on than it would seem from recordings. But such an interpretation remains questionable. These are all speculations and, even if these reconstructions were good representations of what went on, they would still be from the standpoint (i.e., the imputed meanings) of the specialist and might actually be very different from the meanings of the whole process to the case. This brings us to the next basic problem involved in using the case reports of psychiatrists.

Psychiatric case studies do not generally involve any specific consideration of the effect of the multi-faceted definitions of the relationships involved on the nature of the communications that take place. There are, of course, considerations of such phenomena as lying, sincerity, speaking indirectly, etc.; but the specialists almost always treat these matters within the context of common sense: that is, they are concerned with these primarily as part of their endeavor to find out what the person "really means," "what he's resisting," etc. They do not consider the way the specialist-case relationship, which can be defined in many different ways by different individuals in different relationship processes, is itself a determinant of such things as lying and the specific content of one's communications. (To take an obvious example, consider the matter of the psychiatrists' tendency to "turn what you say against you." Individuals being interviewed by psychiatrists know more or less what kinds of things will seem irrational, illogical, and insane, to the psychiatrists; and they know that the psychiatrist is evaluating them in the most fundamental way. Is this not exactly the kind of relationship in which the individual being interrogated will distrust the interrogator and communicate with him in a very special manner?).[5] That this makes the case reports of psychiatrists much less valuable is clear, but it does not mean that they cannot be used. It simply means that one must try to take such factors into account and rely on direct quotation from the case as much as possible.[6]

There is, however, an additional problem involved in dealing with the psychiatric case reports that sometimes makes it quite difficult to deal with the above problem by taking into account the nature of the relationship. Frequently these case reports do not present any significant information on how the interview was conducted. The cases reported in *The End of Hope*, for example, are presented with very little detail on how the information was collected.[7] It is clear from various statements that much of it was collected long after the suicides from interviews with staff members of the hospital; but it is generally not made clear just how the interviews were conducted, how the *post facto* nature of many of the interviews might very well have produced specific forms of communications in itself, etc.

Besides these problems of knowing what was communicated and how the process was significant in determining the types of communications, there is the problem of determining from the psychiatric case reports the influence of preconceived theories on the reports. Since one cannot present descriptions of everything, or even a very large part, it is always necessary to restrict what one reports; and such restrictions are very stringent in the mass of case reports. There are certain strong assumptions made by most psychiatrists about what phenomena are "related," "important," etc., in the study of suicidal phenomena; and these assumptions strongly influence the things they choose to describe in their case reports. Farberow, for example, in his

[5] Much of the discussion here of specialist-case relationships is influenced to some degree by Erving Goffman's *Asylums: Essays on the Social Situation of Mental Patients and Other Inmates*, Garden City, New York: Doubleday and Company, Inc., 1961.

[6] The fundamental problem involved in interviewing of any sort is considered below in the section on "Uninformed and Informed Experiences."

[7] Arthur L. Kobler and Ezra Stotland, *The End of Hope*, New York: The Free Press of Glencoe, 1964.

discussion and presentation of the "Case History of Mr. A. S." has pointed out the impossibility of presenting a very large part of the information available about a given case and has argued that certain assumptions about the nature of the phenomena generally do—and must—underlie the choice of what one will present.[8] A specific example of such assumptions is that made by most psychiatrists to the effect that the "biography" of the case is one of the most important areas of information. In case reports by psychiatrists one frequently finds, as a result of this assumption, a great mass of information on the infancy of the case, his troubles in school, etc., while the whole process of interactions and events just preceding and involved in his suicidal action or communication may be almost totally neglected. (This is true of the case report of the attempted suicide of Mr. A. S.) This assumption (i.e., the "historical personality" or "biographical" assumption) is in conflict with the general argument to be presented here[9] and will have to be allowed for in the approach which we take to these case reports.

An additional assumption of great concern to us is the "culture free theory." Psychiatric theories, and psychological theories in general, are often assumed to be culture free. Such theories do not consider the possibility that cultural or subcultural differences will make any difference in the nature or causation of suicidal phenomena. There are some valuable exceptions to this, especially of very recent origin,[10] but the great majority of psychiatric case reports of suicidal phenomena do not consider cultural differences.

This last problem might prove to be especially important for a theoretical orientation such as that adopted here—the study and explanation of suicidal phenomena as meaningful phenomena. Such case reports can hardly provide us with sufficient information on cultural differences in the meanings

[8] See *The Cry For Help*, edited by Edwin S. Shneidman and Norman L. Farberow, pp. 155-166.

[9] "Biographical" information is, however, of importance in the approach to suicidal phenomena as meaningful phenomena in that such information provides, at least in some cases, an important part of the meaningful context out of which the individual must construct the meanings of his specific actions in specific situations.

[10] The best of these exceptions is Herbert Hendin's *Suicide and Scandinavia: A Psychoanalytic Study of Culture and Character*, New York: Grune and Stratton, 1964.

of suicidal phenomena. The same is more or less true of the other sources of information on suicidal phenomena.

Thus, we cannot at this time develop very worthwhile theories (or, at least, test theories) which involve any fundamental ideas about cultural differences. This, however, does not mean that we cannot use the psychiatric case reports to develop worthwhile theories of suicidal actions as meaningful actions. First, there are certain generally shared patterns of meanings to suicidal communications and actions in the various subcultures of the Western world;[11] and, second, there are subcultural variations on these patterns, *specific* meanings that are largely restricted to one or a few subcultures.[12] It is primarily these latter, specific meanings that one must beware of, since the present information is so inadequate to deal with them. The former, general patterns of meanings of suicidal phenomena can, however, be clearly distinguished in many of the case reports. Even when the specialist reporting the case is fundamentally concerned with using the case report to show that some theory of irritability, for example, is the fundamental cause of suicidal actions, it is still frequently possible to use the report to study the meanings of the suicidal action, even from the standpoint of the individual who committed the action, since the psychiatrists frequently report what the case has said about it.[13]

Using the cases to get at the fundamental patterns of meanings of suicidal phenomena involves several obvious

[11] It is entirely possible that certain parts of what are normally considered to be inside the Western world culture, such as Eastern Europe and the extreme southern part of Europe (especially Spain), do not have these patterns of meanings of suicidal actions so common to the central part of Europe, Scandinavia, and the United States. For the most part there is almost no information on real-world cases of suicide in these peripheral areas, so we shall not normally, if ever, be considering them; and we shall certainly not be taking any of our cases from these areas.

[12] The idea of "Death" as an "eternal, sweet, soothing, rest" is common to some extent to the whole Romantic Movement, regardless of cultural limits; but it seems most distinctive of German Romantics; and the theme can be found in actual cases of German suicide in recent days. (See, for example, the note on p. 60 of W. Morgenthaler, *Letzte Aufzeichnungen von Selbstmördern*, Bern: Verlag Hans Huber, 1945.)

[13] As an example of this, see G. Deshaies, *Psychologie due Suicide*, pp. 114-115.

problems. First, how can one be sure that these patterns of meanings found in such reports are not entirely artifacts of the interviewing relationships or of the theoretical preconceptions of the specialists doing the reporting? Our primary checks against such problems are both the information available on suicidal phenomena in the Western world from other sources (artistic sources, etc.) and, perhaps most importantly, the uninformed and informed experience with suicidal phenomena of the theorist in everyday life. Second, there is the problem of knowing what is generally shared when the study is not statistical: that is, how can one be sure that he is not merely focusing on patterns of meanings that are peculiar to a few cases? This problem is not so difficult as it might at first seem for the simple reason that the patterns of meanings that we shall be concerned with are not rare; they are quite frequent and can generally be found in many different sources, including different types of sources. The all important thing is to determine what the fundamental nature of suicidal actions is in the Western world—*if* there is any fundamental patterning of such phenomena throughout the Western world; and to determine how such phenomena must be studied to arrive at increasingly adequate information for the construction and testing of theories about such phenomena. In pursuing such a goal the case studies are important—especially the statements, patterns of actions, etc., of the suicidal individuals themselves. The case studies should be taken from the English-speaking subculture as much as possible, but the relative paucity of good case reports of suicidal phenomena makes it necessary to use case studies from other parts of the Western world as well.[14]

[14] Since most of the subcultures, just in terms of linguistic and national differences, are well represented in the United States, any study of American cases already involves the use of such diverse sources; and, most unfortunately, this is generally not taken into accounts at all in the case reports by American psychiatrists. (Sometimes subcultural differences seem to be very important, but the psychiatrists have left out all such details. For example, the study of the suicides in Crest Hospital seems to have involved beliefs about being in death camps, all of which would indicate that in some way the subculture of American Jews was important; but only the pseudonyms of the cases gives one clear evidence that this was the case. See Kobler and Stotland, *The End of Hope.*

Uninformed Experience and Informed Experience as Sources of Information on Suicidal Phenomena

One of the strongest characteristics of the dominant positivistic approach in recent sociology has been the demand for "objectivity"; and one of the factors most frequently supposed to be necessary for objectivity has been that of non-involvement. The man who is involved in a social experience is presumed to be unable to objectively observe, describe, or analyze that experience.[15] The ideal kind of information for sociological purposes has been considered to be information that is "thing-like"—i.e., presumably, external to the observer, an object not cathected by the observer, and easily quantifiable. (All of this is implied in Morselli's statement that "A corpse is a corpse.")

We have previously observed that even Durkheim, one of the foremost proponents of this kind of sociological positivism, did in fact make use of his own common-sense ideas about the "meanings" of the rates he was analyzing. This *actual* method of analysis, however, did not lead Durkheim to modify the *ideal* of positivistic analysis which he had previously proposed in strong terms,[16] nor did it prevent his rejecting the common-sense imputations of motives and similar information often given credence by earlier students of suicide as totally useless for "explaining" suicide.[17] Given the great influence of Durkheim's *ideal* method, the general consequence has been that his work on suicide has strongly reinforced the suspicion of any information gained from actual experience, either of a common-sense or informed

[15] This is not to say that sociologists do not use their own experiences as sources of information (especially as examples). They do in fact use such experiences, most frequently in "teaching" but also in publications; and they generally do so without any consideration of the problems involved in observing one's own actions.

[16] See *The Rules of Sociological Method*.

[17] One might argue that Durkheim's imputations of meanings was not common sensical in the same way that such imputations of motives are; for, after all, he was imputing meanings in the light of already established facts of statistical relations. (One would then, however, be able to criticize him for taking *ex post facto* explanations of statistical associations as the most valid.) But, then, one could also argue that the expert officials, who have often worked most directly with such things for many years, would be acting non-common sensically in imputing such motives in the light of expert knowledge.

nature. (As we noted earlier, there is hardly a reference in the sociological literature on suicide to any case of suicide or any form of suicidal phenomena actually observed by the sociologists doing the work.)

To an important degree the increasing use of questionnaires and case studies by sociologists in other areas of sociological interest has helped to counteract the extreme assumptions (or arguments) of Durkheim's sociologistic methods. The emphasis has still been on the "experimental approach," which has generally meant using the hypothetical-statistical approach, so that all important decisions about the subjects and methods of observation and analysis are made before the study (or following some preparatory pretesting) to insure "objectivity" and quantitatively analyzable and comparable results. The case-study and case-report methods of clinical psychology and psychiatry have given much greater consideration to the common-sense (or "insider") understandings that the scientific observer has of the actions of the subjects, but even here the ideal of "objectivity" has tended to strongly limit the use of "insider" experience as a scientific tool, as a source of information and insights.

In general, where sociologists and psychologists have made use of their experience as cultural insiders they have *taken the standpoint* of common sense: i.e., they have acted *from* or *within* common sense. They have taken their own particular common-sense meanings as being valid and nonproblematic and have then integrated these common-sense meanings with those positivistic methods of analysis peculiar to the social science disciplines.[18]

[18] Levi-Strauss has argued that it is just this insider knowledge of a culture which constitutes the greatest advantage of sociology over anthropology. "The subject extends beyond the purview of the observer, but it is always *from the observer's point of view* that the sociologist tries to broaden it. In his attempt to interpret and to assign meanings, he is always first of all concerned with explaining *his own society*; what he applies to the generality are his own logical classifications, his own background perspectives. If a French sociologist of the twentieth century works out a general theory of social life, it will inevitably, and quite legitimately, reveal itself as the work of a twentieth-century French sociologist; whereas the anthropologist undertaking the same task will endeavor, instinctively and deliberately (although it is by no means certain that he will ever succeed), to formulate a theory

The fundamentally important point, however, is that sociologists have acted *within* common sense to provide themselves with the meanings of social actions to be analyzed by the specialized methods of the discipline, but they have not normally taken common sense itself to be a subject of investigation. They have, especially when studying suicide, taken their own particular common-sense standpoint and their discipline standpoint as *givens* in any study of suicidal phenomena. They have generally used common-sense explanations (and meanings) of suicidal actions as the bases of their explanations, *rather than treating such common-sense explanations as phenomena to be studied by sociologists (or psychiatrists) because such explanations are themselves likely to be part of the suicidal processes.* It is from this latter standpoint that we propose to *make use of*, rather than *take the standpoint of*, common-sense understandings of suicidal phenomena.

In this respect we are simply using our everyday experiences and our "cultural knowledge" as a source of information on what it is like to view and deal with suicidal phenomena as a member of this culture. But it is precisely such information that the positivists reject as unobjective (even when in fact they use it). How, then, is one to justify using such information?

First, there is simply the matter of *availability* of information. It is not so terribly difficult for sociologists and psychiatrists to *study* cases of suicidal actions *after the fact* of such actions has been brought to the notice of officials. To

---

applicable not only to his own fellow countrymen and contemporaries, but to the most distant native population. . . .

"We see therefore why sociology can be regarded, and rightly regarded, sometimes as a special form of anthropology (this is the tendency in the United States) and sometimes as the discipline which occupies first place in the hierarchy of the social sciences; for it undoubtedly occupies not merely a particular position but a *position of privilege*, for the reason, with which we are familiar from the history of geometry, that the adoption of the observer's standpoint makes it possible to discover properties which are apparently firmer in outline and certainly easier to employ than those involving an extension of the same perspective to other possible observers. Thus Euclidean geometry can be regarded as a privileged case of a metageometry which would also cover the consideration of spaces with different structures." (Claude Levi-Strauss, *Structural Anthropology*, New York: Basic Books, 1963, pp. 362-363.)

study the processes of such actions under these circumstances it is necessary to use interview methods involving reconstructions of events that were very confusing, unusual, etc.[19] Such techniques of gathering information have been extensively used by psychiatrists to gather what is presently the best source of professionally collected information on suicidal actions. Such techniques have thus far been primitive when applied to suicidal phenomena. (They have rarely, for example, involved systematic comparison of informant statements.) Much more can be gotten from them if they are properly developed. But the various interview relationships are themselves socially defined (or meaningful) and, as socially meaningful relationships, they themselves are fundamental determinants of the nature of communications that will take place within their province. Hopefully, in time such meanings of interviews will become well known and their effects on interview communications determinable; but at this time there is little that is actually known about such matters.[20] Given this situation, the *uninformed* and *informed* experiences of everyday suicidal phenomena had by the student of suicide (or by others who communicate them to him) become a vital *check* on the information gathered by the case study methods.[21]

But there is another, related reason why such uninformed

---

[19] One could, presumably, use seemingly informal interviews to gather reconstructed memory information about suicidal comments and thoughts. This author has, in fact, done this with some degree of success. But, given the problems of dealing with memory reconstructions and the definitions of interview relations, these interviews have mainly served to assure the author that *some* other individuals in this society have had thoughts and encountered suicidal comments and actions similar to those of the author.

[20] The methodologists in sociology who have been fundamentally concerned with the validity of interview results have, of course, long been aware of various effects (generally considered as "biases") of the interview situation itself on the communicative content of interviews; but most of the specific work done by those concerned with this problem has been to demonstrate that specific biases do exist and should be corrected for (racial effects, agreement effects, etc.). The most important consideration of the problem has been developed by Harold Garfinkel.

[21] By *uninformed* experience is meant experience of everyday suicidal phenomena that came before one was a student of suicidal phenomena. By *informed* experience is meant the experience of everyday suicidal phenomena that came after one was a student of suicidal phenomena.

and informed experience of everyday suicidal phenomena is of crucial value at this time to anyone concerned with constructing theories of such phenomena. It is, of course, not only possible but almost unavoidable for a medical specialist dealing with mental illness to encounter all forms of suicidal phenomena—i.e., threats, death wishes, pseudo-cides, suicides, etc. But all of these are within one realm of cultural meaning—that of specialist-mental-patient relation-ship. Now, one must expect that in different culturally meaningful contexts one will not only find different phe-nomena (e.g., different ways of talking about such matters) to some degree, but that the same factors will be used to build different meanings. One needs, therefore, not simply a check on the meanings of suicidal communications within the realm of specialist-case relationships, but a knowledge of the different situated meanings: *one needs some reasona-ble knowledge of the whole complex of situated and non-situated meanings of such phenomena before he can adequately determine the meanings of any particular phe-nomena of this sort in any particular situation; and this is so simply because of the contextual nature of any particular meaning—i.e., the meaning of any particular cultural (or personal) communication is determinant only if the context is known.* Now, this does not mean that one could not pro-ceed by studying one particular phenomenon in detail, then proceeding to some similar phenomenon, and so on. Such a procedure might well work. But this would restrict one at this time to the most picayune type of study, since there has hardly been a start made in the direction of studying such phenomena as culturally and personally *meaningful*. Moreover, if one does not look at such phenomena as a whole as well as in particular, it seems quite unlikely that it would occur to the researcher to study them as meaningful phenomena at all: looking at them as particular types of phenomena (such as is delineated by Durkheim's definition of suicide) it is not at all clear that they are given specific *functions* in specific situations by cultural participants. The best strategy would seem to be one making use of extensive uninformed and informed experience of everyday suicidal phenomena of as wide a variety of types as possible to form a general map of the nature of the meanings of such phenomena, then proceeding to deal with specific aspects of such a web of cultural meanings, and then going back from these particulars to the general: one weaves back and forth between the general and particular, each determining the other as one proceeds.[22]

The last fundamental reason for using one's uninformed and informed experience of a given realm of cultural meanings as a basic source in a scientific treatment of that realm is, perhaps, the most important. The simple, obvious fact is that there are not yet any scientific means of measuring meaning. One simply *has to* rely upon his own vast experience in his culture to understand the meanings of the phenomena he observes within a given realm of experience. But one does not have to act *within* common sense. He can and should treat his own experiences and understandings of meanings as something to be investigated. And he must not simply assume that his understandings are the understandings of those involved. The use of his own *insider* understanding to understand what things mean to someone else is a fundamental necessity, but it is a fundamental mistake to assume that it is not problematic to understand what things mean to the other person or group. The meanings of specific, situated phenomena are not only necessarily problematic to a scientific observer, but they are also problematic to the participants—and this is fundamental to gaining any scientific understanding of the nature of social phenomena.

[22] The strategy for studying meaning which is proposed here is the one first clearly stated by Schleiermacher and named "Zirkel im Verstehen" by Dilthey:

And the circle . . . is not a vicious one; on the contrary, it is the basic operation in the humanities, the *Zirkel im Verstehen* as Dilthey has termed the discovery made by the Romantic scholar and theologian Schleiermacher, that cognizance in philology is reached not only by the gradual progression from one detail to another detail, but by the anticipation or divination of the whole— because 'the detail can be understood only by the whole and any explanation of detail presupposes the understanding of the whole.' Our to-and-fro voyage from certain outward details to the inner center and back again to other series of details is only an application of the principle of the 'philological circle.'

(Leo Spitzer, *Linguistics and Literary History: Essays in Stylistics*, Princeton, New Jersey: Princeton University Press, 1948, pp. 19-20.)

16

GENERAL DIMENSIONS OF THE MEANINGS OF SUICIDAL PHENOMENA

It is not, of course, my contention in this work that suicidal phenomena have clear and distinct definitions or meanings that are generally applicable to any suicidal phenomena. In fact, the *building-block approach* to the meanings of suicidal phenomena is quite contrary to the general orientation and the specific theories of this work. There are, I have previously argued, general, common-sense, theoretical meanings normally imputed to suicidal phenomena *in the abstract*. This is seen especially in the "Unhappiness Theory" of suicidal phenomena. And these abstract meanings can be found to some extent in the specific meanings imputed to concrete instances of suicidal phenomena, but these abstract meanings do not seem to be *determinants* of these concrete, situated meanings. Rather, the abstract, theoretical meanings seem to be complex derivatives of the dimensions of meanings that one normally finds imputed to concrete suicidal phenomena.

By *dimensions of meanings* I do not mean specific, concrete meanings imputed to concrete instances of suicidal phenomena, such as one would find in specific statements concerning such concrete instances. Rather, I mean the properties (or patterns) that seem to be generally found in instances of suicidal phenomena[1]; and our analysis of the dimensions of meanings is intended to be analogous to analyses such as Gilbert Ryle's analysis of the concept of mind.[2]

[1] Normally we are concerned only with "suicidal phenomena" that are actually "taken seriously" or are "intended to be taken seriously," so that the term "suicidal phenomena" must be understood to refer only to such a realm of phenomena. But the dimensions of meanings of such phenomena can sometimes be found in the non-serious—i.e., humorous or fictional—instances of suicidal phenomena as well.

[2] The most significant difference between the two is simply that

These dimensions of meanings of suicidal phenomena are, then, in no way to be taken as building block meanings: i.e., they cannot be combined with each other in some set ways to construct increasingly complex units of meanings. They are, rather, general orientations (or "sets") of actors in Western culture when they are faced with specific, concrete instances of suicidal phenomena. These dimensions constitute the minimal, generic meanings of such specific, concrete phenomena. Whether these generic, meaning "boundaries" determine the existence of some specific, concrete meanings of a given type or whether the particular meanings can simply be seen to have such generic dimensions of meanings, without any causal relation existing between the type and the concrete instance, is hardly possible to say for sure at this time. But, in line with the general ideas concerning the relation of the whole to the part in the determination of meanings, we would expect that the dimensions of meanings or the "meaning boundaries" are of importance in determining the specific meanings.[3] In any event, these general dimensions of meanings of suicidal phenomena serve to indicate that in each suicidal phenomenon certain types of meanings will be found, so that these are very likely the types of meanings that the individuals involved must work with in order to construct a meaningful whole for themselves.

Suicidal Actions are "Meaningful"

Perhaps the most fundamental dimension of meaning of suicidal phenomena is that of "meaningfulness." By meaningfulness is meant that the individual members of this

---

the analysis done here is meant to be scientific, so that in time one might well use more formal methods of analysis to determine the adequacy of this analysis. (See Gilbert Ryle, *The Concept of Mind*, London: Hutchinson, 1949.)

[3] By "meaning boundaries" or "dimensions of meanings" we mean more or less the same thing Harold Garfinkel has meant by the term "constitutive set," except that he has included the idea of the determination of the particular meaning by the generic meaning, which we take to be a strong assumption when one is dealing with something as unclearly defined as suicidal phenomena. (See Aaron Cicourel, *Method and Measurement in Sociology*, New York: The Free Press, 1964.)

culture consider the phenomena to be "meaningful." Something is considered to be "meaningful" in our culture when it can be interpreted or explained in some way considered by the members to be adequate. What constitutes an "adequate" interpretation is by no means clear and is not our fundamental concern here: we are concerned only with the "things"[4] considered to be relevant to an "adequate" interpretation of suicidal phenomena. The "things" considered to be relevant in this respect are, as should already be reasonably clear, certain "motives," certain "situations," "intention," and, perhaps, some other specific "things." But it is only *certain* motives in certain situations that are relevant for giving an "adequate" interpretation of the suicidal phenomena—such motives as depression, escape, etc. Most important in this respect, as the most frequent dimension of meaning relevant to the imputation of the category of "suicidal," is "intention." If the observers (or the actor himself) cannot adequately determine whether the individual intended to commit the actions, or intended the consequences of the actions, then the actions are not seen as very "meaningful," except insofar as categorizing some phenomena as being "accidental," "strange," "mysterious," "weird," "meaningless," etc., does communicate a certain meaning—at the least, they say that the thing is not adequately interpretable or explicable and that clearly tells others something about how the phenomenon is to be treated.

There seem to be few cases where the death of an individual or actions with dangerous consequences for his physical well being are not clearly categorized as "accidental," due to "natural causes," "suicidal," "homicidal," etc. (There are, of course, many careful distinctions made in everyday discourse concerning the modes and causes of death; but just what these are has not been investigated

---

[4] The word "thing" is used here because it is the term normally used in our culture to refer to "motives," etc. Sociologists, psychologists, etc., generally use such terms as "variables," "factors," etc.; it simply seems preferable when talking about everyday "meanings" to use everyday ways of talking about it. (Just what the term "thing" means in general is clearly one of the most difficult questions concerning the English language.)

sufficiently for us to be sure.) Even official categorizations leave relatively few in the ambiguous categories—the categories of "accidental-suicide," "unknown"; and it seems likely that in everyday treatments of deaths there are even fewer ambiguous categorizations. In general, then, it seems that there are not many cases where individuals feel uncertain as to whether the individual who committed a given action that had dangerous or fatal consequences, for himself, actual or potential, intended the action. (There are probably far more cases of disagreements among individuals on intention than there are cases of individual uncertainty.)[5] In this sense, then, suicidal phenomena are clearly meaningful (or unambiguously defined)—there is rarely a case of death in which the everyday definition of the action or the consequences is "maybe suicidal" or "accidental-suicidal."

But this is true only of those actions where the intention is of a certain or specific type—the *intention to die*. If there is little doubt that the individual intended the actions and/or the consequences of the actions, but there is doubt that his intention was to die, then the action might well be seen to be less meaningful, especially if the individual dies *in spite of* his intentions, or if there is any clear contradiction between the intention and the consequences. The common-sense expectation is that there will be a clear, direct, linear relation between an individual's intentions and the outcomes of his actions, at least in the realm of suicidal phenomena.

[5] It might be suggested here that the reason for this relative lack of uncertainty concerning intention is that actions that can be interpreted as suicidal at all receive their specific meanings in some good part from the meanings of the situations and the substantial self of the individual involved; if these are of the types that can be interpreted as suicidal in nature, or conducive to suicide, then the actions of the individual will be seen to be "adequately interpretable" as suicidal. (For example, if an elderly woman dies from an overdose of sleeping pills, it might well be thought that this was an accident. But if one knows that her son committed suicide a few hours earlier, that she was deeply attached to this son, and that she was "brooding" for several hours before her death, then it seems unquestionable to the observers that this was a case of suicide. Exactly such a case was reported in the *Los Angeles Times*, October 2, 1964, p. 3.) This is another small example of the way parts of the whole phenomena determine the meaning of other parts of the whole, so that what each part means is clearly dependent on the meaning of everything else—that is, on the context.

Suicidal Actions Mean That Something is Fundamentally Wrong with the Situation of the Actor.

To say that a suicidal action has a general dimension of meaning to the effect that something is wrong with the situation of the actor at the time he commits the suicidal action is almost humorous.[6] This is such a fundamental meaning of just about any suicidal action that it is hard to seriously consider it. But it is precisely this taking of the obvious for granted that has, presumably, led to the general failure to see the many implications of this fundamental meaning of suicidal actions.

It is this *reflexive dimension of the meanings of suicidal actions* which makes suicidal actions such effective social weapons. Psychiatrists, psychologists, sociologists,[7] and men with cultural wisdom have long realized that suicidal actions are frequently "acts of aggression." But the idea of hurting yourself in order to hurt someone else has also seemed to be a "strange," "bizarre," "irrational," "insane," thing to do, at least to Western men.[8] Consequently, these "abnormal" expressions of "aggression" have been explained in terms of some "identification with the hated individual," "catalogic," "hypereridism," "regressive fantasy," etc. All of these theories have failed to take into consideration the cultural meanings of the actions they were intended to explain. It is, in fact, quite clear that suicidal actions are interpreted as being *situationally determined actions*: they are actions believed to be directly dependent upon the situation in which the individual existed at the time of the action. There

[6] The definition of the term "situation" is by no means a simple matter. It is, of course, as is the normal practice, used in its everyday sense; but the specification of what that sense is is not a simple matter. Roughly, the term means "those parts and aspects of the external world that are relevant to the internal world of the actor at the time and place under consideration." The term is, then, roughly equivalent to the terms of *Umwelt* and *Mitwelt*, as used by existential psychologists, with an emphasis on the aspect of "relevance."

[7] We have, of course, dealt with these various theories in many places in this work; but the most detailed consideration to them has been in the section on the Henry and Short theory of Suicide.

[8] The various ideas of committing suicide upon the head of another man, etc., have been much clearer to Western observers of primitive societies. See, especially, M. D. W. Jeffreys, "Samsonic Suicide or Suicide of Revenge among Africans," *African Studies*, xi (1952), 118-122.

are also important meanings concerning the individual himself (such as the biographical element) and various ideas concerning the importance of an overall summing-up of his life situation;[9] but in almost all cases the individuals involved in suicidal actions see the short-run situation of the individual as in some way causing him to cause injury to himself. Normally, the significant others are considered of greatest immediate importance in the causation of this type of action so that quite frequently some significant others are seen to be the fundamental "causes" of an individual's suicidal actions or statements.[10] Moreover, the "cause" of a suicidal action is considered to be "wrong," or "bad," or "immoral." It is a fundamental normative assumption that no one should do something which "pushes a man too far," so that he commits some suicidal action. It is, on the other hand, completely possible for the action to be seen as an "over-reaction," or "going too far." The specific meaning is determined by the complex of situations believed to be typically associated with suicidal actions, so that if an individual commits suicide because someone refuses to do some little favor he will hardly be seen as the "cause" of the suicidal action. Rather, the cause will be seen to be primarily internal to the individual himself (see below). The individual who is seen as having done something that plausibly "caused" the suicidal action is, however, held to be "responsible," at least to some extent; and, given the normative judgment that causing suicidal actions is "bad," this individual is partially "to blame" for the suicidal action. The reflexive nature of the suicidal action, then, makes it possible to "rationally" (in terms of everyday, common-sense criteria of rationality) use suicidal actions as weapons or acts of aggression that can be quite effective.

[9] It seems likely that the rationalistic, summing-up idea is one that is considered almost entirely in the abstract, rather than by individuals actually involved in the concrete instance of suicidal action, where the concrete, immediate phenomena are seen to be dominant. However, some few individuals about to commit suicide do themselves write notes that involve some summing-up. (As an example of such summing-up suicide notes see Case 18-B in "Genuine and Simulated Suicide Notes," in Edwin S. Shneidman and Norman L. Farberow, *Clues to Suicide*, p. 208).

[10] The whole matter of the "imputation of causality" will be discussed somewhat further in the discussion below of "Revenge Suicide."

We shall not go into the details of how one can do such communicative work successfully (or fail to do so) until later when we discuss "revenge suicides"; but let us consider two brief case reports that clearly show the reflexive meaning of suicidal actions for the situations of the actor at the time of the action:

Case 7.

Mr. F. B., born 1902, had for several years before his admission to hospital shown increasing irritability, suspiciousness and lack of inhibition. In 1945 he became openly paranoid and depressed, and at the same time made excessive sexual demands. He was afraid of committing suicide (three members of his family had killed themselves), and threatened his wife and child. When his wife started separation proceedings he became extremely depressed and self-accusatory. One evening he drank acid with suicidal intent and told his wife that he had done so. He was immediately admitted to a general hospital and thence transferred to the observation ward and finally to a mental hospital. His paranoid and depressive symptoms remained stationary and he settled down to a dull retarded state. There was no suicidal attempt in hospital. His wife did not continue with the separation proceedings, but visited him regularly, and said that she would not divorce him as he might try again to take his life. At the time of the follow-up interview, seven years after the suicidal attempt, he was still in hospital. . . .

Case 10.

Mrs. F. I., born 1910, was unhappily married to a brutal psychopath. They separated in 1944. In 1946 she learnt that he had taken divorce proceedings which, though she wanted a divorce, greatly upset her. She had some time previously started a love affair with a colleague, a married man with one child. Soon after she learnt of her impending divorce, her lover told her that he did not intend to leave his family to live with her, as she had hoped he would. She became acutely depressed and tried to poison herself with aspirin. She was taken to the observation ward whence she was sent to a convalescent ward after two weeks. Three months after the suicidal attempt she resumed work. Her lover left his family after all and at the time of the follow-up six years after her suicidal attempt they were living together and both declared that they were thoroughly happy. She thought that her suicide attempt "had brought him to his senses." Her family, who had been against this relationship, had become reconciled, and finally approved of it.[11]

In the first of these two cases (Case 7) we can see that the wife interpreted her husband's suicidal actions as being a direct result of her separation proceedings[12]: that is, it was clear to her that this particular, immediately preceding situation was a "cause" of his suicidal actions. In line with her interpretation of his suicidal actions and her desire that he not commit suicide, she changed the situation back to what it had been before the "causal situation."[13]

In the second of these two cases (Case 10) we can only indirectly infer from the actions of the lover that he could see that her suicidal actions were caused by the situation which he was largely responsible for, the situation in which he was the most significant part to her. (See below the brief discussion of "seriousness" as one dimension of meaning in suicidal actions.) But, at least *post facto*, we can see that she herself saw her suicidal actions as being caused by what the lover did *and*, quite importantly, her interpreta-

[11] From *Attempted Suicide* by E. Stengel and N. Cook, Copyright © by Institute of Psychiatry 1958, Basic Books, Inc., New York.

[12] It should become clear to the reader after the treatment below of "pointing out" phenomena in the suicidal process that the husband's calling the wife to tell her of his suicidal action was of fundamental importance in determining this specific meaning of his actions for her: that is, he was pointing out to her that his suicidal action was directly relevant to her, to their relation, or, as seems true in this specific case, to something specific that she had done to him.

[13] Again, I do not believe that we can validly take anything in case studies as "clear." In this particular case, I certainly think it possible that this woman was using the whole suicidal incident and her particular interpretation of it to further some "ulterior" motive (she might have discovered that he had suddenly inherited a great fortune). I would generally agree—indeed, I have insisted!—that human beings are sly and wily creatures; and I would argue that the investigators of these cases have generally not taken this into account adequately even on a common-sense level. But we shall normally be forced to overlook things that don't seem plausible in terms of what is presented or in terms of what we know about such things from other sources. Moreover, in this particular case, as in others, such an interpretation would still be assuming that her interpretation was a culturally plausible one.

tion of what he did as "wrong" in some way, and her interpretation of her suicidal action as having had such a meaning to him so that he then corrected his wrong—seeing the effect of his actions, he "came to his senses" and did the right thing. (Since aspirin was used and she was later so articulate about the effect of the suicidal action in bringing about a preferred situation, it is quite possible that we have here a clear case of manipulation by actions that are only marginally, in terms of the shared categories of our culture, "suicidal": that is, her actions *might* have been interpreted as being pseudo-cidal, "she didn't really mean it," "just a sympathy play," etc. We do not have enough detail on what she did after taking the aspirin to see why her action was categorized as "suicidal" by the significant others—if in fact it was—rather than something else. Presumably, had she called for help and done it in public she would have had much more of a chance of having her actions categorized as something other than suicidal.

Suicidal Actions Mean Something Fundamental about the Actor Himself

Generally, when an individual is thought to have committed a suicidal action the communication of this news to those who knew him produces "shock," "bewilderment," "disbelief," etc. This shocked response is, presumably, due partially to the lack of expectation in everyday life that any individual, even one who has talked about suicide or committed a suicidal action in the past, will actually commit suicide.[14] And it is probably due in part as well to the fear or anxiety that news of death tends to elicit in our culture, at least when the death is of someone not expected to die. (The same sort of shock is experienced when news of accidental death is received.) But there is *some* of this same shock experienced when the individual did not die, but simply made an abortive attempt—i.e., is believed by the communicator to have done what he categorizes as "attempted suicide." Moreover, even after the initial shock has passed, individuals very generally find it "hard to be-

---

[14] For an attempted explanation of this phenomena see the section below on the initiation of suicidal communications in the suicidal process.

lieve," "disturbing," etc.; and there is generally a good deal of discussion concerning the suicidal action of this particular person in this particular situation. In some instances it is so clearly a situation considered to be typical of suicidal actions (such as a confluence of great personal losses with a lack of hope for any change for the better) that the entire conversation about the instance might be concerned with the *situation*—sympathy expressions, using of the suicidal action as a commentary upon this type of situation, blaming of those seen to be responsible for this action in this situation ("If her lousy daughter hadn't deserted her at this time she never would have done such a crazy thing"[15]), and so on. If we look at the historical records on interpretations of suicidal phenomena we see that this emphasis on the situational factors has strongly increased during the last century. In the beginning of the nineteenth century it was rare, though not unheard of, for individuals to *write* about suicides in such a way that the situation was seen to be of fundamental importance. (Whether they spoke of it in this way in everyday life we cannot say, but must surmise that they did not do so with any great frequency.)[16] Rather, the emphasis was almost always on interpretations that assumed that something must be fundamentally "wrong" with the person committing the suicidal action. It is this idea about the nature of suicidal persons that was so clearly expressed in the psychiatric theory that all individuals who committed suicidal actions must be "insane," "crazy," "unbalanced," "disequilibrated," etc.

It has been commonly accepted in sociology, especially since the work of George Herbert Mead, that there is a fundamental distinction that must be made by sociologists between the "I" and the "me," the "I" being largely the "self" independent of any particular situations, what the

[15] Whenever possible I shall use reconstructions, as close as memory will allow, of actual events observed by the author (or by other sources properly documented where that is appropriate). This quasi-quote is from one of the instances of attempted suicide heard about by the author long before his interest in studying suicide developed.
[16] The shift in emphasis in interpreting suicidal actions has probably been just one aspect of the general shift toward an increasing *externalization* of the self in the culturally shared conceptions of persons, which is probably the most fundamental cultural conception behind the development of sociology in the Western world.

individual considers himself to be at all times, the seat of consciousness, while the "me" is the "selves" of the individual resulting from his involvement in and commitment to certain types of socially defined patterns of action.[17] This distinction is not important here except that it does roughly approximate a very important distinction in the everyday meanings of social actions—that between the *substantial self* and *situated selves*; the distinction made by Mead merely represents the disciplined form of the everyday meanings.

Though the subject is fundamental to any thorough consideration of the meanings of social actions, it can hardly be dealt with in more than a cursory fashion in this work, but it is necessary for an understanding of the meanings of certain types of suicidal phenomena to go briefly into the subject of the *substantial self*.[18] (I hope the reader will understand that the argument on this abstract level is offered quite provisionally.)

In the Western world there is a general, implicit, non-theoretical assumption made in everyday communications (with oneself and with others)[19] that each individual has,

---

[17] We are not concerned here with the complexities and difficulties of Mead's particular theories. (These can be easily seen in a recent collection of essays on "symbolic interactionism," in which the concepts of "self" are given various definitions—as is "symbolic interactionism" itself. See *Human Behavior and Social Processes: An Interactionist Approach*, edited by Arnold M. Rose, Boston: Houghton Mifflin Company, 1962, especially pp. vii-xii and 3-179.) Mead's theoretical ideas on the subject of "self" are more or less representative of most sociological approaches to the subject.

[18] The idea of the *substantial self* has been previously used by Harold Garfinkel in his work on "Conditions of Successful Degradation Ceremonies" (*The American Journal of Sociology*, LXI (1956), pp. 420-424); but he used the term "essential self" rather than "substantial self." The reason for using the term "substantial self" is simply that the soul (i.e., the ultimate, fundamental self) was for centuries specifically considered to be a "substance," in the Aristotelian sense, by the philosophers of the Western world; and it is my hypothesis that this philosophical principle was a rough approximation of the view of this matter in everyday life. For considerations of these philosophical ideas see Anton C. Pegis, *St. Thomas and The Problem of The Soul in the Thirteenth Century*, Toronto: St. Michael's College, 1934; and Risieri Frondizi, *The Nature of the Self*, New Haven: Yale University Press, 1953.

[19] The whole problem of defining what a "communication" is in general is not too much less difficult than defining what "meaning" is; and, in fact, it hardly seems worthwhile defining "communication"

or is, a *substance*. This substantialist meaning of persons leads to judgments of persons as wholes,[20] judgments which are fundamentally (though not necessarily entirely) independent of time, place, and situation; and this substantialist meaning of persons is of the nature of a unitary complex of meanings—or characteristics—which are imputed to a person as a whole (as a substance), not as a player of special roles in special scenes and times. (The most universal "characteristics" are those concerning trustworthy-non-trustworthy, sincere-insincere, and honest-dishonest qualities.[21]) The imputations of substantial selves, which generally involve specific linguistic categories (such as "rat," "louse," "heel," "jerk," "angel," etc.), seem generally to be the result of a whole series of imputations of situated selves, though this is not any additive process; but once a person is understood substantially (i.e., once one knows what a person "really is") the imputations of situated selves become largely dependent on this substantial self. (It is these situated selves which are seen to involve the characteristics of substantial selves that at first determine and then are determined by the imputation of the substantial self.)[22]

---

unless one has already defined "meaning." Consequently, no general definition of "communication" will be given here.

[20] As noted above, the substantial self used to be called the "soul" in everyday communications; but this term is used today almost entirely in religious discussion, ceremonies of death, etc. The terms "character," "whole man," "personality," "real self" (in such injunctions as "Be your real self"), are the ones most frequently used today in everyday communications to deal with these meanings of the person; but it should be clear that each has a special meaning and each is different from the term "soul," which comes closest to meaning what is meant here by "substantial self."

[21] These are the fundamental aspects of the meanings of "persons," so that any adequate study of the meanings of persons will have to deal with them. They are clearly not independent of each other and they are clearly related to such other aspects as "serious-non-serious," etc. But other than this general structure of the meanings of persons in everyday life, nothing much is clear about the subject. (For a beginning analysis of "trust" and its importance in social interaction see Harold Garfinkel, "A Conception of, and Experiments with, 'Trust' as a Condition of Stable Concerted Actions," in *Motivation and Social Interaction: Cognitive Determinants*, edited by O. J. Harvey, New York: The Ronald Press Company, 1963, pp. 187-239.)

[22] There is, of course, an area of social psychology in which there has been significant work on the problems of the common-sense meanings of persons and social actions—that normally called "Person Perception and Interpersonal Behavior."

I have argued that generally the imputation of a substantial self to a particular person is the result of a long process of imputations of situated selves that are implicitly seen to involve the various characteristics of the substantial self that is then imputed in an all or nothing way;[23] but there are specific complexes of phenomena that occur that are believed to tell us immediately about the nature, the substantial self, of the person. Everyone experiences such "sudden revelations" about their friends and acquaintances, and there are clearly set ways of saying that a *transformation* in one's imputation of substantial self to someone has taken place: "I never thought she was that type," "I was shocked to hear that he had done such a thing: he seemed like such a nice person," "I just couldn't believe it—not him" (the implication here being that now one has changed his entire opinion of the other, so that he does believe it).

When properly performed, suicidal actions can be used in just this way to transform the substantial self.[24] We shall be considering the ways individuals go about transforming their substantial selves by using suicidal actions in the next chapter.

[23] The process of imputation which seems to be involved in the imputation of substantial selves is something like what is normally called "insight" or an "aha experience."

[24] It is still not infrequent for the substantial self of an individual to be seen as being transformed by the suicidal action in a way common in the nineteenth century—i.e., the individual is now seen as being possibly or certainly "insane." In one of Shneidman and Farberow's genuine suicide notes one man even seems to have been attempting to deride such an imputation, presumably to offset its effect:

> Mary: The only thing you never called me was crazy. Now
> you can do that. I loved you so.
> Signed.

(Quoted in "Appendix," *Clues to Suicide*, p. 212.)

17

COMMON PATTERNS OF MEANINGS CONSTRUCTED IN WHICH THE MEANINGS OF SUICIDAL ACTIONS ARE OF FUNDAMENTAL IMPORTANCE

As we have noted, there is insufficient data on suicidal actions and their meanings to permit us to study meanings statistically, even if that were what we wanted to do. One must, in fact, be highly selective in the use of what evidence there is about suicidal actions and their meanings: there is so much that is bad that it is very easy to be misled. One must, then, seek to use the best evidence. But one must use that material which is reasonably common to this culture if he is to arrive at sound conclusions about suicidal actions as socially meaningful actions. I propose to do this by concentrating our attention on the analysis of those patterns of actions and meanings which seem, from a general survey of the literature in the Western world on suicide, to be most frequent. These are very likely those patterns of meanings which are distinctive of suicidal actions.

I shall first present the patterns of meanings that seem most common and then attempt to analyze the ways individuals go about constructing these patterns of meanings for themselves and for others.[1]

Suicide as a Means of Transforming the Soul from this World to the Other World

I have argued that one of the fundamental meanings of suicidal actions is that of indicating what the *substantial self* of the one who commits the act is, that suicidal actions have the possibility of *transforming* the substantial self of the

---

[1] As a method of presentation this seems preferable, but for doing research on suicidal actions it would seem best, once one has thoroughly reviewed the literature on the subject so that he has some vague overall picture of suicide in the Western world, to generally work from the specific descriptive material up to the patterns—i.e., the abstractions.

actor.[2] Involved in this transformation of the substantial self is the meaning of "death" or "dying." One of the fundamental meanings of "death" in general, whether from suicide or any other process, is that of "transformation." In the Western world death is thought and felt[3] to be a permanent transformation of the substantial self from the realm of the time-bound, space-bound, worldly, everyday meanings to the realm of the timeless, infinite, other-worldly meanings. Death, then, is fundamentally (i.e., substantially) meaningful in itself; and any actions performed within the realm of the complex of *death meanings* take on these meanings.

Suicidal actions, by social definition, necessarily involve, though to varying degrees, this complex of meanings called "death": if the actions are not seen to involve an association with death, then it is not really an attempted suicide, a sincere communication of intention of killing oneself, etc. Moreover, suicide is generally believed, in terms of one of the most common shared *images* of suicidal actions, to follow an individual's *summing up* for himself of his whole life, its worth to him, etc. Consequently, this summing-up process gives to suicidal actions the meaning of a statement

---

[2] It might be noted here that one of the most important meanings of suicidal actions for the "situation" of the actor is that of transforming the substantial selves of some significant others—i.e., the action can so "blame" them as to make them appear to be substantially other than what they had previously been considered to be.

[3] It seems important at this point to make it clear that the use of such terms as "thought" in this work are not meant to imply that one is concerned only with "symbolic meanings"—i.e., meanings that are well articulated in words. Especially when one is dealing with "death," those experiences we normally call "feelings" are a very large and fundamentally important part of the experience. In such situations one has a far greater awareness of the way feelings can affect verbal meanings. In such realms of semiconscious (or subconscious) experiences, it does seem to make sense to speak of "feeling that something terrible will happen" (which is expressed by such terms as "ominous") or "feeling that something is true though it doesn't make sense (rationally)," etc. (This idea does, of course, have a significant history in the Western world. Among its greatest and most recent exponents is one philosopher of some particular relevance to our work—Miguel de Unamuno. See his *Tragic Sense of Life*, Dover, 1954. For a general treatment of the relations of feeling to symbolic thought in ways more akin to the usual ways of thinking of social scientists see Eugene T. Gendlin, *Experiencing and the Creation of Meaning: A Philosophical and Psychological Approach to the Subjective*, New York: The Free Press, 1962.)

by the individual about his whole self—i.e., his substantial self. But this latter effect is not nearly as important as that produced by the association of suicidal actions with "death," at least where considerations of the meanings of the suicidal actions for the substantial self of the actor are concerned.

The implication for this study of suicidal actions should, then, be clear: individuals in the Western world *can* make use of suicidal actions to transform the meanings of themselves, of what they fundamentally *are*.[4] This is not to say that one can make use of suicidal actions in order not to exist, which seems to be one of the popular ideas *in the abstract* about suicidal actions. Quite to the contrary, my studies of case reports on suicide indicate that when an individual is thinking and acting in the realm of *death meanings*—i.e., when his dominant mode of meaning is "mythical"—then the individual can "see" that death is a way of transforming his substantial self, of producing a new mode of being, not of doing away with his "self." Thus it is that one finds many clearly *religious suicides*. It is this meaning of suicidal actions also that has very likely led to the frequent finding of individuals attempting suicide with the specific intention of "escaping," something which seems so clearly irrational or foolish in terms of the normal, everyday criteria of rationality, but which is very rational when one understands the relation of the meanings of death to the substantial self *within* the context of the mythical mode of death meanings. Children seem especially prone to this mode of meaning, since they have been taught to think that way and have not yet been taught to think in terms of the everyday criteria of rationality; and it is in children's suicidal actions that Bromberg and Schilder, in one of the few

[4] This parenthetical suggestion is part of a much longer speculation which seems a bit too unsupportable at this time to make a part of this work. My suggestion is simply that there is a "dominant mode of meaning," equivalent to what Cassirer called a "symbolic form," which determines the general structure of all meanings associated with the meaning of "death"; and that this mode of meaning is what we normally associate with the term "myth." Under this mode of meaning what we might normally call "fantasy" becomes "real," so that the person is very liable to be classified as "psychotic" in some form in our society today, which would account for the generally high percentage of attempted suicides who are so classed by psychiatrists.

good studies of the meanings of death, found the *escape theme* so very frequent.[5] In the studies of adult suicidal actions one also commonly finds this theme, though by no means as often as in children. There are two lines of information which support the argument that this particular meaning of death is found frequently in cases of adult suicidal actions. First, Shneidman and Farberow have shown that in suicide notes one frequently finds a reference to the self as being still able to experience things after death.[6] Second, this same meaning seems to be implicit in the language that one uses to talk about "life" and "death" in situations involving suicidal actions in fact or potentially. Let us consider a highly stereotyped question: "Is life worth having?"[7] Again and again throughout suicidal communications one finds such statements, declarations, and questions: "Is life worth living." "What good is life to me?" "What is life worth without him?" "Is life such a precious thing?"

In all the statements of this type "life" is treated as a thing or an entity outside the speaker. It is spoken of as a property of the person or subject of the statement, not as part of the person, as some essential or substantial quality of the person which is necessary before one can even speak of a person as existing. (In the same way, people speak of taking or destroying a life, not a person or a soul or whatever.)

This habit of treating the physical being, the thing which has existence, as something separate from the self, as some-

---

[5] W. Bromberg and P. Schilder, "Death and Dying," and "The Attitudes of Psychoneurotics toward Death," *Psychoanalytic Review*, 23 (1936), 1-28.

[6] Edwin S. Shneidman and Norman L. Farberow, "The Logic of Suicide," in *Clues to Suicide*, pp. 31-41. See also Charles William Wahl, "Suicide as a Magical Act," *Ibid.*, pp. 22-31.

[7] It is hardly necessary to give a reference to such statements as this; everyone has surely heard them. But this was taken verbatim from Thomas Cooper's *The Purgatory of Suicides: A Prison Rhyme* and it might be worthwhile to add a bit more of the poem to put the question in context:

Is life worth having? Or, is he most wise
Who, with death-potion its fierce fever slakes,
And ends, self-drugg'd, his mortal miseries? (1852)

The similarity of such a statement to Hamlet's soliloquy is quite clear, so that such statements have certainly seemed plausible in the English-speaking world for centuries.

thing, therefore, separable from the self, is a fundamental aspect of the meaning of suicide.[8]

One might think that man can commit suicide because he has foresight (while animals cannot because they do not have foresight) which enables him to relate the present state of affairs to some imagined future state of affairs— that is, man is able to commit an intentional act. One might think that this is the only necessary, *human* aspect of the actions of this sort. But I would suggest that it is quite necessary for man to be able to treat the physical being as something different, quite outside the *self* or person. (In this sense, suicide is a spiritual action.) In a culture, if there is such, where this total distinction is not made, one should not find suicide. Or perhaps I should say that such external actions as suicide will be culturally meaningful in very different ways if they are found in such a culture.

The idea that individuals are motivated to die in order to live is clearly nothing new. St. Paul's statement that he wished to die in order to be with Christ is an example that has been quoted for centuries;[9] and Unamuno has given a beautifully clear statement of this idea in the twentieth century:

> . . . Our hunger for God, our thirst of immortality, of survival, will always stifle in us this pitiful enjoyment of the life that passes and abides not. It is the frenzied love of life, the love that would have life to be unending, that most often urges us to long for death . . . we chant the praises of the never-ending rest because of our dread of it, and speak of liberating death. . . . The greater part of those who seek death at their own hand are moved thereto by love; it is the supreme longing for life, for more life, the longing to prolong and perpetuate life, that urges

---

[8] The problem is, of course, quite complex. It is, for example, quite possible to treat the "body" as being identical with the "soul," at least for some purposes. An example of this is the not infrequent request, by suicides and non-suicides, that a loved one's body be buried with them in order that they might "be together once again." Just how one is to systematically treat all such communications about "death" ("body," "soul," etc.) is not at all clear.

[9] Montaigne, for example, gave St. Paul's statement as an example of seeking death not as an escape from worse things but because of love of it.

them to death, once they are persuaded of the vanity of this longing [for unending life in this world].[10]

Remembering how honored (and how frequent?) self-initiated death[11] was in the early centuries of the Christian West and remembering that Augustine began the centuries-long attack against self-initiated death specifically, according to his account, because of the great number of "would-be martyrs" who courted death by insulting the Romans, it seems quite likely that for many centuries men and women killed themselves largely with the *intention* of "going to heaven." Indeed, it seems that the dispute over whether certain kinds of self-initiated deaths were justifiable lasted for many centuries since Bede clearly considered some of the classical suicides to be honorable (and since we must suspect that the Church suppressed or opposed this view). Thus, the very severity of the punishment for actions injurious to one's own body may have been a result of the need to counter this great temptation of hastening one's departure from this world for the other world.

In the last century, however, it seems that "the other world" has been more divorced from our everyday lives, primarily in that it has become increasingly less "real"— most importantly, it does not have the "feeling of reality" in most of our life.[12] But there are some realms of meanings in which the other world (and God, more than any other aspect of the other world, though there is still talk about heaven in some suicides) is felt to be very important and "real."[13] In the realm of "death" this is overwhelmingly the

[10] Miguel de Unamuno, *Tragic Sense of Life*, pp. 44-45.

[11] I have used this terminology because we must avoid any implication that their social definition of suicidal actions was in any way similar to that definition most shared in our culture today. It must be remembered here that even the word "suicide" (or its equivalents in the non-English-speaking cultures of the West) has been generally shared for only the last few centuries.

[12] Whether this can be seen as the result of any general "secularization" of Western culture is not an issue here.

[13] The "feeling of reality" is certainly one of the fundamental phenomena in our everyday interpretations of anything; but it is also one of the most complex and difficult to deal with (probably because it is so fundamental that, like "time" and "space," it can hardly be talked of in other, less fundamental terms). I do not intend to attack the problem here.

case; and, as they are associated in varying degrees with death, feelings of fear, anxiety, and depression are also associated with a strong feeling of the reality of the other world. It is primarily with these negative feelings, then, that *death as a way to the other world* has become associated in our culture in the last century or so. One almost never finds a suicidal action in which the individual speaks of wanting to go to heaven simply because it is a great "good." Almost always there is a strong indication that there is first something wrong with this world; and it is in these terms that the desirability of dying to go to the other world (to God) is normally presented.[14] But the self-presentation of motives in these terms is very frequent indeed.[15]

There are many case reports that demonstrate the validity of this analysis. But the one I shall use is that taken largely from the diary of a young woman who, as far as could be told (especially from her own testimony), did kill herself after killing her lover. This is one of the two cases treated extensively by Cavan, but her treatment of the case bears little relation to this analysis. First, let us consider those parts of the case and her diary that deal with "death" or "suicide":

From material not contained in the diary the following background has been obtained. Marion was a high-school graduate, the daughter of a well-to-do tradesman who was divorced from her mother. Marion apparently lived with her mother and sister until the time of her marriage, and also maintained a correspondence with her father. Her home before her marriage was in a middle-class residential neighborhood in Chicago.

Marion met a young clerical worker, Thomas Whitford, at a high-school dance one spring and five months later

---

[14] Even those literati of the West, especially the Romantics, who "romanticized death," generally presented death as a good thing when one is at the height of happiness *because this happiness can not last and will be spoiled in retrospect* or reflectively. (This was true even of Leopardi's work, which became for the literati the *ne plus ultra* of works extoling death.)

[15] Clearly this whole discussion is quite contrary to the nineteenth-century idea, still presented in most sociological works as being true, that religious people do not commit suicide. The evidence is just the opposite, though it could well be that there is not a statistical relation between church membership and suicide.

was married to him. She was nineteen at the time of their marriage. They moved into a neighborhood very different in character from the well-organized communities in which both had lived. Their apartment near Forty-Fifth Street and Wabash Avenue was in a mobile neighborhood where roomers were common, and the South Side vice district with its cabarets and dance halls was near.

The first entry in the diary is about two months after Marion's marriage. . . . The first few entries in the latter part of 1912 are concerned with Marion's craving to be loved, with the need of herself and Tom for money, and with their quarrels. . . . In the early part of 1913 Marion had an abortion, accepted in a very matter-of-fact manner both by herself and by Tom. (difficulties continue . . .)

"I asked Tom what he wished to do, if we could go on, and he suggested that we separate. . . . All of a sudden I seemed really to know what that would mean for me and I thought I would go mad. I certainly am an unhappy woman with him now sometimes; how should I feel without him?"

(tensions continued. . . .) 1914-15. On her birthday in February, 1915, married about two and a half years, Marion wrote, "I hope that next year I won't be here to write."

Early in January, 1916, came a period of particular difficulty for Marion, with many death wishes. Tom confessed to her that he had spent a certain night with another woman.

". . . For the first time in my life I had the desire to kill, to plunge a dagger in her (the other woman's) heart. She's innocent. She didn't know he was married, and even so, she is not to blame. He is all wrong. I wonder if what I feel is jealousy. I think not. It is simply repugnance for the whole human race and their ideas, their unjustness. . . . How can the world go on? Oh, God, tell me. Let someone explain. . . . Is there any answer but the one. 'Man makes it so?' Doesn't a woman count for anything: Is she nothing? What is there a woman can do that a man cannot do? Bearing a child is the only thing I can think of. All this is killing me, but thank God, I want to go. I want and beg to go home, to drop out of this earth where there is no place for me—where I don't want a place. . . . I wish to God I could drop off the earth and just end my life, but it is not so."

Two days later:

" 'Bichloride of mercury, cyanide of potassium, either will kill a dog.'

"I am not jealous. I am tired of living, of fighting and arguing. . . . Oh, God, if anyone needed me, was dependent upon me, if even I had work to do, I would never think of death. But I have always thought of that since I've been ten or twelve, and I certainly am not made to be happy. If I had anything to do, I'd leave here and get a room and if I could I'd live decently, and if not, I'd go the limit or jump in the lake. Which is the worse? I prefer the lake. . . . They say it is only a coward who commits suicide. There once was a race in Julius Caesar's time, the Romans, his race, who thought it honorable death. I think it is not cowardly, and I know many people who have not nerve or bravery to do it. Myself is one, otherwise, I would have been dead long ago, long ago. I lack either courage or despair. I believe it is the former which will show to what extent I pity myself."

Several weeks later her mind was still in a turmoil: "The last rest is all I pray for now. Oh, God, how many times have I asked you to take me, take me, take me. Either I shall go mad from the thought I have, or I shall change my mind when I find an answer to the question I ask. Why should I be made to suffer for what Tom does?"

She no longer blamed herself for their difficulties. "He is so discourteous that I feel I hate him; He is so small and mean. A man with a big heart would never act as he does."

More than a year passed, until November, 1917, before a final separation came.

". . . Oh, God, how lonely. I am starving. Oh, God, I am ready for the last, last chance. I have taken two already and they are not right. Life was the first chance, marriage the second, and now, I am ready for death, the last chance. It cannot be any worse than it is here.

". . . I wonder if another year will see us together.

Would to God I could die first. I am too great a coward to kill myself.

"Oh, God, what a night I am having and no sympathy. No understanding, no words of approval. . . . This AM when I came home from swimming I had a queer idea, I burned. I know I would be happier with Tom off the earth. . . . Now just as I write this I wonder if this book will be found some day *after* and used against me? . . . If I go it will be most interesting for these people near me. I can almost hear Tom saying to himself that he never thought it was as bad as that. Well, it is; it is unbearable. I must go, I want to go, and by God, I shall go, I shall go; I will thrust myself upon him; I want to be in peace, to rest quietly, and I have no words for Tom but these: Make yourself a worthy man before you marry again, and watch her heart so you will not break it unknowingly or willfully. . . . October 7, 6 P.M. Alone all day, sick in mind and body. The day is dying. I wish I was, and I am sad, lonesome, and forgotten. . . .

". . . New men friends, cabarets, shows filled her time. Always short of money, she expressed during this period no wishes for death. The entries are filled with the trivialities of uneventful days.

". . . After Tom left it seemed as though the world would end, or as though there would be no end to my pain. . . . I'll be happy to have my things out of storage, and Bert and I will have such a lovely little home. Oh, God, I wonder what I'll be writing about Bert a year from now. Tom's 'little girl' is surely having her fling. God help me, I am weak and contemptible, but I'm so alone. . . . Oh, God, have mercy, comfort me. Take me—and keep me.

"November 9 . . . I leave in a few minutes now to meet him. Suffered dreadfully from despondency, ennui, and loneliness. Oh, I long to throw myself into some sort of dissipation, something to make me forget—forget myself, my troubles, my very life. Why can't it end—am I so unfit that God can't take me?

"November 16, Sunday, 11 A.M. . . . No word from Bert yesterday. I hardly thought he would come. It's all right if I never hear from him. My heart can't break any more.

But the pieces left will drop out. They must. Again I am beginning to wish I was dead—through, put away—it must be a fall disease. It is a dreadful one, more agonizing, than any physical ill. Life is a burden. I was born in vain, a restless one.

"January 17, 1 P.M. . . . Bert is going, Bert is going! That is all I can think of now. My heart hurts. I am miserable. Nothing is right. I don't wish to live longer. There is nothing to live for. Everything—every object in the house—makes me think of Bert, his little dog on the table, the dear violets in the living-room that I wouldn't allow my mother to touch. . . . Am I weak, that I cry continually? I am miserable. I have the utmost contempt for myself, I pity myself. But the lake is cold and soon it will be warm. Oh, God, to rest in your arms—to rest and have peace.

"Bert swears he will find out if I have lied about the past and if I have, all will be over. He has a presentiment that the end is near, and I, oh God, I see only death or life without my Bert ahead of me. So many things are preying on my mind, destroying my peace—killing me slowly.

". . . He never has cared much. He is with me simply because I do everything for him. This week and last I had a woman do washing and cleaning, and he said it cost too much. . . . I just wanted to die, and to rest, rest forever in peace.

"September 11. I've been reading all the foolish things I have been writing for the last two years about Bert. This book is filled with moans—just one moan after another. It is surprising how I can remain untired of it all. I have written many times that I cried because Bert did not kiss me good night. I don't cry now. That's something, anyway.

". . . I'm ill, thin, worn out—how can I even hope for any future life with Bert? It is all that keeps me from taking the last final leap into darkness, just the thought, not even hope, that some day maybe something will happen that will bring us together never to be separated. And so I go on, existing from day to day, that sole thought keeping me from the arms of God. . . . It is strange how little I care for anything. It is only Bert, Bert. My love for him oppresses me. It is consuming me. And the few happy moments I have are terrible ones in their emptiness, for I know that Bert does not care. I have work to do. Oh, God, I must make him care, or at least have some interest in me. . . . Bert is driving me crazy. He will kill me yet. I have done my best to please. I am ill, I think, worn out, and he cares not at all for me. . . . I've gone the limit. I see there is no use trying to gain Bert's affection, and I may as well go now, or very soon. He is giving me much courage."

December 10, while Marion was away from the apartment Bert packed his clothes and left, but returned after a few hours.

"The next time he goes like that, I won't be alive when he returns, if he ever does. What is the use of being unhappy? He hardly spoke this morning, never touched me, just nothing. If only I had the ambition to take care of myself, or eat, but I can do nothing.

"December 12, Sunday, 1 P.M. Bert left an hour ago to go north. He kissed me last night in a spasm of passion. . . . I am ready to collapse. Sometimes I think I can go on, but always in my mind is the thought of going, of leaving this world. Just two days ago I thought of taking Bert with me. I am writing this deliberately, while my colored Fanny is near me, cleaning the floors. . . . I'm the goat and I'm tired. This is all written for others to read after—wonder if I will do it." (The foregoing entry is the first mention of killing Bert.)

". . . January 16 . . . We had a talk this morning and Friday night and he said he'd rather be here all the time, but has a duty to perform. . . . He said . . . he does not intend to spend the rest of his life with me. I told him he would be very sorry when he gives me up. Oh, God, the end seems very near.

"January 21 (Marion caught Bert in a lie about his whereabouts on a certain night and she suspected that he was with another woman.) He lay on the lounge, and I sat and looked at him. He told me it was none of my business what he does. Oh, God, I'm miserable. This is the last straw, to have him untrue, and to lie about it . . . I told Bert he is playing with fire, but he will not take seriously anything I say . . . I know now that Bert has been untrue right along.

"Bert just phoned and is not coming tonight either. He is going to B's to board. Have a care, Bert. I am mad, mad. I have held myself in for so long. Not a tear, not a sigh, not a spark of anger—only quiet despair, and madness. I can feel myself slipping—my mind is—is going. It is blank, except for the tormenting thought I have. If only I could forget—complete oblivion would be a blessing. . . . May 6, Saturday, 9:40 A.M.? Thursday A.M. Bert phoned, swore at me furiously about phoning the night before. Marjorie raised Cain, he said. I listened to nothing but oaths and hung up. I did not phone yesterday, nor did he. I thought I'd let him cool down, and he knew I had only $6 Tuesday night. Just now he phoned and said he wanted to send me some money, and I said I was going downtown and would meet him for lunch. I'm glad I didn't phone first. I am all broken up about Bert. My sense of honor (Oh, God, how ridiculous that sounds, for me) tells me to leave my Bert, who belongs to another. Some day I will have the strength."

The foregoing is the last entry in the diary. What happened between Marion and Bert when they met is not known, but Bert stayed with her the night of May 6 and sometime while he slept Marion shot and killed him and then killed herself.[16]

Before I note what seem to me to be the most important aspects of this case study, it might be well to note a few important rules for analyzing such reports. First, given the complex, quickly changing nature of human communications, it seems unwise to place too much importance on any single statement. We must look primarily for basic, recurring patterns. And, in close relation to this, we must not emphasize particular words or phrases *unless* the communicator himself uses them in such a way as to indicate by a consistent pattern that they have a particular meaning and importance to the communicator. The words must be seen

[16] This has all been quoted in summary form from *Suicide* by Ruth S. Cavan with the permission of The University of Chicago Press.

in their context, above all in the context which the communicator purposefully put them. We must also be wary
of assuming that a word or phrase used by the communicator means the same for him that it means for us. For
example, in Marion's first use of the term "go the limit" it
is not at all clear to this author what she meant by the term.
She could have meant that she might have sexual intercourse with other men, presumably as a way of getting even;
and later uses of the term by her might support this interpretation, as would current usage in the United States. But,
on the other hand, she might well have meant that she
should either kill herself or kill Tom, where killing Tom is
equivalent to going the limit. This would seem to account
for her balancing the two as being of nearly equal moral
weight; and it would be in accordance with the evidence
from later entries which show that for a long time, as much
as a year, she was quite seriously intending, or wishing, or
thinking about, killing Tom. The reasonable thing in such
instances would seem to be simply not to assume any meaning for this, to go around it unless it is one of those parts of
the communication which seems critical.

The one pattern of meaning that keeps reappearing in
Marion's diary and seems so clearly to have gotten stronger
and more frequent and lengthier is *dying in order to go
home to rest at peace with God*. At no point is there any
doubt expressed that her death will lead to a peaceful state
of rest with God and that the feeling state associated with
this will be that of being where she belongs, at home with
God. She, then, had no doubts, as far as one can tell from
her detailed diary, that death would result in a transformation of her soul from this world to another world. (There
are some individuals who do have such doubts; and they
have actually used suicidal actions to "test" the existence of
God—if one lives through the attempts, then God must
exist.) Moreover, she did not consider it to be a possibility
that her actions would result in her going to some undesir-
able other world—"hell."[17] (Some individuals seem to have

[17] Her statement that death was her last *chance* and that it could
not "be any worse than it is here" seems to be the one significant
indication that she might have had some small doubts in this respect;
but it is so weak a statement that it hardly seems likely that she was
considering it to be possible that the after life might be horrible.

such fears, so they take some action, such as prayer, to offset this possibility. But this seems infrequent in the Western world today, presumably because suicide itself is not seen as being very immoral.)[18] Marion did, however, think it desirable to consider whether suicide was immoral because it might mean that one was "cowardly," an idea very generally prevalent in the Western world today, but only as an *abstract* idea and possibly as part of the *rhetoric* against suicide intended to prevent significant others from committing suicide. And she uses the rhetorical device of comparing her actions with a "race" who considered it honorable, thereby making her own actions seem honorable. There are, then, certain implications, as she sees it, of suicidal actions which she must successfully deny. This is one of many subordinate considerations relative to the idea of committing suicide; and these meanings of her proposed action were, presumably, important to her so that she had to manage her statements and actions so that she would not be blamed by her audience (that is, the readers of the diary, for she specifically intended it to be read) for her actions.

But the central, ever-recurrent meaning of her actions to herself, that of *going* to God, was not something that needed presentation to the audience.[19] This was not a meaning of suicide of which she felt others needed to be convinced. It was not even a meaning that they would have to be told about, except that by telling them that she must die and go to heaven she is telling them how miserable she is in this world, hence, how much she is deserving of their *sympathy*.[20] This *going to God* is the meaning of suicide to her

[18] Hendin found that his cases of Scandinavian suicide attempts did not see anything very immoral about the act; certainly they did not think they might go to hell for it, though some, especially one man, thought it desirable when questioned to argue that God would forgive such a transgression, especially if one prayed for forgiveness before the action. (See *Suicide and Scandinavia*.) It would seem, as others have suggested, that suicide is considered much more immoral among members of Catholic, especially Spanish, subcultures.

[19] One could, conceivably, argue that she was trying to show her audience how histrionic or dramatic she could be. But surely there would be some easier ways to do it.

[20] Since we shall consider the pattern of sympathy below, there is no reason to go into it in more depth here. And, since we shall go into the matter of multiple meanings of suicidal actions in our analysis of another case of suicide below, we shall not go into depth in the consideration of it here.

and that is sufficient, so that any external communication about this is not called for except as it has other meanings as well. The implication of this in general terms is that she can do this meaningful thing, or commit this action with this meaning, independent of what anyone else thinks about it; it isn't something that needs to be presented, argued about, etc. And when argument does seem to her to be called for, it is always argument with *typical audiences* who make *typical responses*. We have almost no evidence that she ever talked at significant length with anyone about this whole problem. (Her reticence could have been because of the combined actions of suicide and homicide.)[21]

One of the things she is continually presenting to convince her audience is the idea that she is "being killed" by others, that the situation is unbearable. Such a clear *pointing-out of the situation* could be, and very frequently is, used to blame the situation, especially the significant others involved, for one's death. (See the discussion of Revenge Suicide below.) But Marion did not do this: that is, she did not construct the meanings so that others would be blamed for her death after she was gone and continue to suffer for it after she was gone. The reason is obvious: she intended all along to take "him" with her if she ever got the courage to do it. Consequently, any blame of him was intended to show that he deserved what she intended to do—that is, murder. But the striking thing is that Marion does not seem to have been concerned with specifically, *explicitly* pointing out the blame of the men for her actions. She might, of course, have simply expected that it was so obvious that she did not have to bring it up explicitly; and the evidence seems to make this clear, *if* one is a member of this culture so that he can see when someone is being considered to "blame" for something. But there seems to be another reason why she did not even emphasize the blame meaning of her communications and actions; that is, she was pri-

---

[21] Marion clearly saw homicide as something that had to be morally justified in itself, so she spent much time arguing with her imagined typical audiences about the justification of this part of her action. Normally I have not gone into her communications concerning the murder because it is not generally relevant to her communications about her own suicide. (Her suicide, for example, is not presented as an *atonement*.)

marily concerned not with punishing the man, but with having him as her own, all her own, in the only way she could see to do this—*taking him with her to God.* Consequently, though the other meanings (of justification for murder by showing blame, etc.) are there, they seem to be dominated by the central, core meaning of going to God, with the man, by means of suicide (and homicide).

Marion's suicide is, then, a form of substantial-self escape from this world. But it also shows a common *specific* meaning that is given to this transformation by means of suicide: that of a *reunion* with a loved one. Marion's specific idea seems to have been to reunite herself with her lover after having left this world by means of suicide and homicide. The theme is common in many suicides. (It seems even more common for mothers to kill their children and then themselves in order to be together in heaven.) But there is also a common pattern of committing suicide in order to join a loved one who has already died from natural or accidental causes. Various psychoanalysts have reported cases in which the actor will actually commit suicide in the same way as the loved one died (e.g., rolling off a bridge) so that the identification with the loved one is made perfectly clear even by the pattern of actions one uses to die—therefore, one must go to the same place as the dead loved one.

Suicidal Actions and the Transformation of the Substantial Self in This World or in the Other World

There is another and fundamentally different way in which the individual can transform his substantial self: he can perform actions and make statements in such a way that they have the meaning of changing what he fundamentally is in terms of the meanings he expects will be imputed to him as a result of those actions and statements by some significant audience, either of this world or of the other world (i.e., God). The matter of fundamental importance here is that *his substantial self must be changed for others.*

He might simply try to show that he is not really (i.e., substantially) what he has been thought to be by some significant audience. He might, for example, use the suicidal action to show that he is Christ. Indeed, this particular meaning of suicidal actions has been observed in some detail many times.[22] This use of suicide to change the meaning of the substantial self is, however, meant to transform the self by showing that it really (i.e., substantially) is something else and you have merely been mistaken in your past identifications. There is a second, though related, way in which one can transform the meanings for others of his substantial self—that is, in general, by showing that the significant audience has been mistaken in its interpretations of the meanings of his actions, hence, of his substantial self, but not in their imputations of personal identities to him. For example, since the usual answer to the question of whether life is worth anything is simply that it is (and it might well be that many people stop thinking about suicidal actions when they arrive at such an answer), the killing (or attempted killing) of oneself can be used as a *general indication of how serious, sincere, committed one is.* What it is that one is serious, etc., about must be communicated by the specific actions, statements, and situational contexts in which one commits the suicidal action or makes the suicidal statement. Saying something such as "I'll kill myself if you leave me" may, given the specific context, mean that the individual is so devoted to the one he is speaking to that "life would be worthless" without that person, so that it *can* be simply a statement of devotion without being a threat of suicide. However, the context is usually such that such a statement is a way of pointing out of the other as being potentially responsible for the death of the speaker, so that it is a "threat" and not simply a statement of devotion. It seems likely, in fact, that in order to avoid the communication of the meaning of "threat" the individual must say more specifically that "life would not be worth living" but not indicate that this means that he intends to take the action of putting an end to it—this is only one of the plausible

[22] The story written by a man who did later commit suicide, a story which we shall consider later, includes a specific reference to this meaning of the suicidal action for the "imagined" (but very realistic for this man) suicide. Dahlgren even reports a case of a woman who made very symbolic hangings of herself with a piece of thread around her neck; she believed that she was to be a second Virgin Mary and bear a Messiah-Swedenborg. (See *On Suicide and Attempted Suicide,* p. 100.)

implications of such a statement and need not be realized or actually communicated unless the individual wants to.

The power to convince which suicidal actions have seems clearly to be related to their meanings of "sacrifice" or of "risking" or giving what is defined in everyday life as the thing of highest value—one's own life. Throughout our culture there are many different ways of showing how very much one *means* something—that is, how committed one is to what he says or promises, or how sincere he is about what he says or promises. (There are such statements of commitment and sincerity as "I'll bet you that . . . ," "I'm willing to lay you any odds that . . . ," "Cross my heart and hope to die," ". . . with all my heart," "I really mean it this time," "I swear that I shall tell the whole truth," etc.)

But the power to convince significant others that one's substantial self is other than what they thought it was, frequently because you can show them by your suicidal action that you are not the *type* of person who would do such a thing, is only partly the result of sacrificing what is considered to have the highest value. One must, generally, combine the sacrifice with certain other fundamental meanings that must be imputed to him if his communicative work is to be successful. Let us consider the case of *atonement suicides*.

If the individual makes it clear that he is giving up something dear (his life), that he is doing this by his own will, and that he is doing it *because of* something that he did which in some way he or some designated audience (e.g., God) considers to be "bad" (or in some way reprehensible), then his suicidal actions can be an act, frequently ceremonialized, of *atonement*; in accord with the *talion principle* (of worth for worth—eye for an eye) he gives his life to make up for what he has done; and he shows what he is making up for by the way in which he commits suicide.[23] All of these principles of action are well represented in the following case of suicidal atonement:

[23] Our ultimate goal must be to specify just exactly what the components of meaning are: i.e., just what *types of things* the individual must do in what ways (such as the *sequences*) to produce what particular meanings in what types of audiences with whom he has what types of relations.

WIFE READS BIBLE AS SLAYER DIES

Police Killer Says Good-By to Son Before Suicide

The man who killed two New York detectives early yesterday had his estranged wife read to him from the 51st Psalm while he put a gun to his head and killed himself.

Donald B. Guyette, a 35-year-old ex-convict and former mental patient, shot the two detectives at 12:15 A.M. when they went to question him about an assault on his wife and a threat on her life.

Guyette ended his own life 45 minutes later at his wife's apartment, but not until he had telephoned his 6-year-old son in Illinois to say good-by and his minister to tell him of the slaying. Guyette's wife was apparently too dazed and frightened to prevent the suicide.

The detectives who were killed were sent to investigate after the Rev. William H. Lothrop, who had given marriage counseling to the Guyettes, had alerted the police to the assault upon and threat to Mrs. Guyette.

Mr. Lothrop, of the Calvary Baptist Church, at 23 West 57th Street, said Guyette had told him that he had had enough of institutional life and that no policeman would ever take him alive. The minister also said he and Mrs. Guyette had previously been threatened by Guyette with death if they talked to the police about him.

The chain of events, as reported by the police and the minister, began at 9 P.M. on Wednesday, when Mr. Lothrop called the police about Guyette, a steeplejack who collected guns as a hobby.

The minister told the police that Guyette could probably be found at his basement apartment at 1632 Hendrickson Street, in the Flatlands Section of Brooklyn, where for the last two months, according to the police, he had been living with an unemployed waitress.

Two detectives, James A. Donegan, 38, and Salvatore Potenza, 35, went to the neat, middle-class neighborhood . . . (both were shot). . . .

(Guyette) then proceeded to the apartment of his wife Edith, 37, about 2½ miles away at 210 Hawthorne Street.

There, he forced his way in but assured his wife he would not harm her.

"You know what these are?" he asked his wife as he held up the detectives' guns. "I just killed two detectives. They didn't have a chance." He told his wife to get his son, Dan, on the phone in Chicago, where the boy was taken by his mother last weekend for protection.

Guyette said good-by to his son and made one more call—to Mr. Lothrop. "Well, I've done it," the minister quoted him as saying, "and there will be one more life going out tonight." The minister said later: "I frankly thought it was mine."[24]

Suicidal Actions as a Means of Achieving Fellow-Feeling

There are many specific patterns of meanings to certain types of suicidal actions which involve some form of "fellow-feeling" or "sympathy." The whole subject of "feeling with or for" other individuals or for or with oneself is a vastly complex realm of meanings which has hardly been investigated, with the singular exception of Scheler's penetrating work on the subject.[25] Members of our culture make a fundamental distinction between "sympathy" and "pity," but it is not clear just what that distinction is. We cannot attempt to go into the complexities of the subject here, but it is important to note the well-patterned ways individuals actually make use of suicidal actions to gain some form of "fellow-feeling," even "pity," for themselves.

First, let us consider a story written by a young psychiatric patient who repeatedly threatened and then attempted to commit suicide. His threats had been denounced by his father, who at one time dragged him to a window and told him to go ahead and jump. He did die soon afterwards as a result of having taken too many barbiturates while on a weekend pass which his parents had insisted upon. (While we must refrain from definitely calling this a suicide, since

[24] Walter Carlson, from *The New York Times,* Friday, October 16, 1964. © 1964 by The New York Times Company. Reprinted by permission.
[25] Max Scheler, *The Nature of Sympathy,* London: Routledge and Kegan Paul Ltd., 1954.

there is no evidence reported on what the parents and others defined it as, how he took the pills, etc., it seems unlikely that this would have been socially categorized as an "accident.")

This is the best story I have ever told in my life. He's very mentally depressed, he's a self-pity victim. This is the George Washington Bridge in New York City, and he's in a mental depression. He figured he got a raw deal from life. He's an isolationist. He leaves his home and thinks, I'm going to find a priest. He's not going to tell the priest he's going to jump off the bridge. He'd made up his mind before to jump off the bridge. He's going to seek counsel from the priest. He doesn't eat any lunch, he wants to drink on an empty stomach. He's afraid of people stopping him from jumping off. He finds a bar away off from the bridge. He's afraid of people reading his thoughts. Afraid they'll stop him. He has a guilt complex. Feels he's already committed the murder in his own mind. Dejected, nervous, upset, scared stiff. He gets off the bus, he figures he'll have to spend the money for liquor. So he buys the most expensive cigar in the store. He's afraid if he buys something cheap, he'll receive the greater condemnation. Afraid if he doesn't give money to the poor he'll be punished for all his sins. He leaves enough to get three or four drinks under his belt. Then he thinks, well, what am I going to do now, he needs a cigarette. He has a pack in his pocket. He smokes one and gives the pack away. He's all through with his drink at the bar. Cheap, powerful stuff. He leaves the bar and walks out, kind of cockeyed. He imagines he's Christ, that he's also murdering Christ. He walks up to the bridge. He won't take the short cut, he takes the devious way, so no one will spot him. He actually makes things twice as suspicious. He thinks someone is following him. He's afraid his father might show up and stop him, or brother might drive by and recognize him. He starts to run. He's pursued by his mind. He starts running up the ramp. He looks back, trips, and falls, and hurts himself real bad. Picks himself up and starts walking again. He hurt his knee and walks with a limp. He figures the left hand side is no good because he's right handed and had to jump off the right side. He's suspicious, superstitious. If he doesn't jump off the right side, he wouldn't die. He crosses the street to the right and almost gets killed by a car. The fenders hit him on the leg—gives him a shock. Like a shock. He's in a state of actual terror. He's something to be pitied because he's frustrated by fear. He's not the master. He gets on the right. By this time it's 4:00 in the afternoon. Daylight saving time. He brought his prayer book with him. He sees all these benches and realizes he's tired. He sits down, gets out his religious book and searches the scriptures. Starts praying. He preaches to the world but they can't hear him. He gets up and says I've got to cut this short, the longer you wait the harder it seems. He walks over, still feeling his liquor, still full of self-pity, now he's up ready to jump off. Says, "Gee whiz, this is quite a drop," and his mind answered him, "Yes, it is." And he has quite a battle with himself. Says he's got to stop now, I've invested money in this. I've given away my cigarettes, spent my last money for drink and all that. Keeps goading himself, thinking how his girl friend broke faith with him. He grabs the railing, gets up on it and with a mighty heave of energy he makes it. He's on the rail. Says he's not going to dive, he's going to jump. Like a dope he says some prayers and some cars come along and some guys come along and he doesn't even hear them. Somebody touches him in the shoulder, and a voice says something, and he connects them, says they must be together. He jumped, he was about this far over and a pair of capable hands caught him under the armpits. They asked him all kinds of questions. He was humiliated and insulted. He was convinced he was the son of God. Didn't think humans could interfere with him. Drove him off the bridge, sent him to the hospital, put him in a ward there. Then he was taken out and taken to court and there was a sergeant sitting there, pompous, behind a desk, and the sergeant says, "Don't you know you had no right to try to kill yourself," and I say "I am a law unto myself." I got him around to my way of thinking actually. But it didn't work.[26]

[26] Edwin S. Shneidman and Dorthea M. Lane, "Psychologic and

The story teller began the story with an indication of how excellent he thinks the story is, then a statement that he, the subject of the story, who is clearly the teller himself, is a "victim" of "self-pity." In line with my previous suggestion that one should not seize upon an isolated word as an indication of the fundamental, patterned meaning of a whole sequence of events and/or statements, we should note that the story teller once again said, at the peak of the story, when the subject of the story climbed up on the bridge to jump off, that he was "still full of self-pity." Just in terms of his own statements concerning the matter, then, it seems clear that he felt and thought that "self-pity," a special form of "feeling with or for," was a central meaning in the story, a fundamental meaning of the whole suicidal drama.

But the turning point of the story is the thwarting of his attempt to kill himself. Throughout the earlier part of the story the subject is alone and clearly intends to kill himself. He shows many forms of the idea discussed at great length above, that he must commit suicide to leave this world, that this is possible because his soul or mind is something outside of himself,[27] that he is in some way identical with Christ whom he is going to kill; moreover, he carefully performs certain magical or "superstitious" actions (some of a sacrificial nature) to ward off any evils that could result from "murdering" himself, he seeks to justify the action in various ways (and is especially concerned with how the representative of God will judge the act), etc. But included in the story is an account of his being almost killed by a car, an event which fills him with terror. It seems clear from this, as from his references to alcohol as necessary to rid him of fear, that he is quite ambivalent about dying. Then, when he does come to the point of killing himself, he is stopped by some unseen, unknown person who unexpectedly saves or rescues him from his own intention to die.

It is clear from repeated statements that the general,

Social Work Clues to Suicide in a Schizophrenic Patient," in E. S. Shneidman and N. L. Farberow, *Clues to Suicide*, Copyright © 1957 by McGraw-Hill, Inc. Used by permission of McGraw-Hill Book Company.

[27] When tested with the MMPI he agreed with the statement that "My soul sometimes leaves my body."

external situation is a threat to him ("raw deal from life," car nearly kills him, etc.). He's afraid of the things outside of him, maybe even of God, and one feels that these external things are partly responsible for what he is doing; but, at the same time, it is clear that what he is doing is primarily the result of his own intentions, his own thought-out, intended actions. He is both a victim and a perpetrator: both an effect and a cause. But by the end of the story he is stopped, the outside takes over and stops him from killing himself. A pair of "capable" hands rescue him at the last minute; he is humiliated, but he is saved from what he has earlier expressed terror of—killing himself or dying.

The high point and end of the story is a dramatization of the world's suddenly saving him from actions intended by himself because of the world. Rather than killing him, as the car almost did, the world, in the form of a specific person,[28] now *rescues* him. This does not mean that the world has been totally transformed by his action; to the contrary, from his not very pleasant relations with the police, it is reasonably clear that his relation with the outside is still poor; but he no longer expresses the terror of them. He simply gives in to their insistence that he not kill himself.

It has long been recognized by psychiatrists that in many suicidal actions, especially in "attempted suicide" where the danger does not seem to be great, there is an "appeal" meaning involved: that is, the suicidal action *means* to the individual and to the significant others that he needs some form of social help. Such an appeal meaning of suicidal actions is, of course, a perfectly clear meaning because all suicidal actions *mean* that something is fundamentally wrong with the individual's situation (i.e., there must be a "bad" situ-

[28] The father "symbolism," in terms of usual Freudian analysis, is quite profuse here and throughout the whole story. In view of the boy's great, conscious preoccupation with his father and his having previously specifically chosen his father as his target for threats of suicide and his father's response of humiliating him for it, it seems highly likely that all of this had something to do with his father, that much of it has the indirect meaning of a desire to be saved by his father—i.e., that he specifically wanted an expression of love, concern, pity, or some "fellow-feeling" from his father. But we shall try to stay clear of indirect, subconscious meanings of this sort: it is not even possible to deal very well with the direct meanings, to say nothing of the very much more uncertain, indirect ones.

ated motive to produce this "desperate" action); and, consequently, because an indictment involves an implicit call for redress, these actions call for help—for a redress of the "bad" situation which has caused this bad effect. Just what is wrong can be *pointed-out*[29] by the specific context of his actions, specific statements about what the cause is, etc.[30]

Such appeals can result in drastic changes in the life situations of the individuals who commit the suicidal actions; and, though things sometimes don't go the way they want them to, the general tendency seems to be for the significant others to give in to their desires and demands.[31] In such cases as this, the blaming of the actions on the situation, the condemnation of the situation by the meanings of suicide, and the use of "sympathy" as a motive for doing what is necessary to change the situation for the better all seem to be involved.

But in the case of suicide being considered here the "fellow-feeling," which the suicidal action is in some way intended to elicit, is not something to be "used" or have an effect on the situation. The individual seems concerned with the "fellow-feeling" for its own sake. Now, it does seem possible for an individual to be unambivalent in his intention to die to achieve sympathy, so that, as in the case of transforming the substantial self by committing suicide, the meaning of the action could, presumably, be complete in the suicide itself—i.e., the suicidal action makes the meaning of "sympathy" (or "how pitiful" or "how sympathetic") *complete*. If there are such cases, however, they must be

[29] We shall discuss the pointing-out meanings below. Here let us just note that we mean by this the various forms of "blaming" people, things, etc. Such meanings can be communicated even by the timing of one's actions with respect to a sequence of events, because "time" is of fundamental importance in the imputation of *causality* (which includes motivations).

[30] The most important psychiatric works which attempt to show this appeal meaning of suicidal actions are those of Shneidman and Farberow, *The Cry for Help*, and Stengel and Cook, *Attempted Suicide*.

[31] Case 13 reported in Stengel and Cook, *Ibid.*, pp. 59-60, is a case in which the suicidal action resulted in the rejection of the individual by his family, the opposite of what he wanted. Such outcomes are the result of the whole communicative process, which we shall consider directly in our later discussion of the *suicidal process*.

rare; few cases seem to this author to fit this pattern.[32] On the contrary, most cases seem to involve a very clear meaning of wanting to be rescued while at the same time wanting to die, so that being rescued actually provides a *proof of fellow-feeling*, while dying can either mean that one gets sympathy, perhaps from others than those from whom one specifically wants it, or, as seems more likely, one gets some form of revenge upon those who were given the chance, by communications of intention to commit suicide, to prevent it. In our case we can actually see that at the same time that the story teller was indicating a desire to avoid detection of his intention to commit suicide he was also making people all the more suspicious of him.

The social meanings of the rescue situation, then, provide the individual with an excellent opportunity for the expression of ambivalent intentions—either to be loved or to take revenge (i.e., express "aggression"). The outcome of such an ambivalent sequence of actions is dependent on just how the individuals involved go about constructing their meanings and what it is that they want from each other. For example, the way significant others respond to a suicide threat can be of fundamental importance in determining which way the balance is tipped. Consequently, suicide in such cases must be looked at in terms of a whole sequence of meaningful actions and statements, each link in the sequence being of fundamental importance in determining those which come after it. We shall return to this problem in the section on the suicidal process after we have considered revenge suicidal actions.

Suicidal Actions as a Means of Getting Revenge

As we have previously noted, the idea that suicidal actions are some form of expression of "aggression" is one of the most common interpretations of suicidal actions as "meaningful" from the standpoint of the social actor himself.[33] The

---

[32] The type of case that might be construed to fit this pattern is that type well represented by Case 1 reported in Stengel and Cook, *Attempted Suicide*, pp. 51-52.

[33] The bibliography of "revenge" suicide, some of which has been presented at various points in this work, is extremely large and it

common use of "violent acts" to produce a physically injurious state, the "fury" obvious in the actions of some suicidal individuals, and similar observable phenomena have,
presumably, been partly responsible for this treatment of
suicidal actions as aggressive actions. But, probably of equal
importance, has been the recognition that suicide can cause
great pain to others—the pain of mourning, loss of money,
etc. These are, in fact, some of the things that some suicides
seem to have in mind. But the idea that suicide can be used
to "blame" others for your death is not a very common idea.
It is my argument here, however, that this is in fact a common intended meaning of suicidal actions; and, further, that
suicidal actions frequently have just that consequence for
the significant others involved. Let us start by considering
a blatant case; that is, a case of suicide in which the blaming
meaning of the action was made completely clear:

A young clerk twenty-two years old killed himself because his bride of four months was not in love with him
but with his elder brother and wanted a divorce so that
she could marry the brother. The letters he left showed
plainly the suicide's desire to bring unpleasant notoriety
upon his brother and his wife, and to attract attention to
himself. In them he described his shattered romance and
advised reporters to see a friend to whom he had for-
warded diaries for further details. The first sentence in a
special message to his wife read: "I used to love you; but
I die hating you and my brother, too." This was written
in a firm hand; but as his suicide diary progressed, the
handwriting became erratic and then almost unintelligible
as he leaps into unconsciousness. Some time after turning on the gas he wrote: "Took my 'panacea' for all human
ills. It won't be long now." An hour later he continues:
"Still the same, hope I pass out by 2 A.M. Gee, I love you
so much, Florence. I feel very tired and a bit dizzy. My
brain is very clear. I can see that my hand is shaking—it

would serve little purpose to reproduce any significant part of it here.
But, for a recent, brief review of the important anthropological ideas
on the subject see A. Giddens, "Suicide, Attempted Suicide, and the
Suicidal Threat," *Man.* LXIV (July-August, 1964) 115-116; and for a
recent, unusually valuable psychiatric treatment of the subject see
H. Hendin, *Suicide and Scandinavia*.

is hard to die when one is young. Now I wish oblivion would hurry"—the note ended there.

Another note regretted the inconvenience to the landlady for using her premises as a death-house. Still another read: "To whom it may interest: The cause of it all: I loved and trusted my wife and trusted my brother. Now I hate my wife, despise my brother and sentence myself to die for having been fool enough to have ever loved any one as contemptible as my wife has proven to be. Both she and her lover (my brother) knew this afternoon that I intended to die tonight. They were quite pleased at the prospect and did not trouble to conceal their elation. They had good reason to know that I was not jesting."

The brother who is twenty-three years old spoke frankly to the police about his friendship with his brother's wife. Though separated in childhood when the parents had drifted apart, the two brothers had later on become inseparable companions until shortly before the tragedy, when both fell in love with the same girl. The younger man attempted suicide when his love was not returned and upon his recovery, the girl agreed to marry him out of pity—but later on she found she could not live up to her bargain. After a few weeks of married life, the husband discovered the relationship existing between his wife and his brother. He became much depressed and threatened suicide. The day before his death, there was a scene and when assured that the two were really deeply in love with each other, the clerk retorted: "All right, I can do you more harm dead than alive."[34]

This case shows very clearly the general structure of meanings that suicidal actions are often intended to construct in the minds of others and in the mind of the individual committing the suicidal action. First, and strikingly clear in this case, is the importance of *pointing-out* the person one thinks is to blame, the person whom one intends be held responsible for the suicidal action by others, *including the person blamed*. The general problem of analyzing such

[34] Louis I. Dublin and Bessie Bunzel, *To Be or Not to Be: A Study of Suicide*, pp. 294-295, as quoted in Marshall B. Clinard, *Sociology of Deviant Behavior*, New York: Rinehart and Winston, Inc., pp. 423-424.

meanings is that of determining how it is that individuals in our culture go about imputing *causality* of social actions and what it means (normatively, especially) to be the cause of this type of action.[35] In the present case the pointing-out of whom the actor takes to be to blame and whom he thinks should be blamed by others (and by themselves) is very clear: he left many notes and made many statements so that those whom he blamed would be perfectly clear. But the pointing-out of these he wants to be taken as the culprits is not enough: to have them defined as the causes by others (or by themselves) he has to show that there exists some typical situation which is typically believed to cause a typical motive, which in turn is believed to cause certain typical actions, such as suicide. He tried to show that he had been betrayed by the immoral action of his brother and his wife.

Now, since the construction of such a meaning is clearly dependent upon much more evidence than simply his own statements, the meaning that is created in other minds is partly dependent upon the meaningful responses to this blaming by those pointed-out by him as to blame. In this case they tried to appear sincere (freely talking with the police) and show that she never *really* had loved him, was simply doing a kind deed, and could not help herself from betraying him because of the force of love (i.e., it was not really a betrayal at all, though it might be admitted that it looked that way from his standpoint). The problem which such strategies face is that the committing of a suicidal action means that one is highly committed to what he says (that he is serious and sincere, as this action of ultimate commitment shows) and that he is deserving of "sympathy" because of what the external situation has forced him to do.

[35] Hendin has tried to show that in Denmark persons are believed to be not only a fundamental cause of the actions of others, as they are in the whole Western world, but that they should be held "responsible" for the actions of others far more than is the case in most of the United States. It would thus seem that the fundamental difference, a difference which makes it far more possible to use suicidal actions as a threat (thus to achieve whatever one wants to achieve) and as revenge, is due to a difference in the social definition of "responsibility" for the actions (welfare, etc.) of others, rather than in any difference in definitions of the causality of such events. (See Hendin, *Suicide and Scandinavia*, pp. 28-29.)

In such a situation those who are blamed have a difficult time trying to define things in a way more acceptable to themselves (especially if they "know" that what he says is "true"). And they can hardly argue that they are more right or more sympathetic. They would seem to have only two courses of action that promise exoneration: that of redefining what happened (it wasn't "really" the way he said it was), which is the path chosen by the brother and wife in this case, and that of redefining the person who committed the suicidal action—he was "crazy" or he was just trying to harm us, so that he is not so sympathetic after all. This might well help to explain why it is that so many individuals who attempt suicidal actions are treated as "crazy" (sent to psychiatrists, etc.) by their significant others and why individuals who intend their suicidal actions to blame others often use less direct means of blaming (i.e., so that they won't be clearly *just* "aggressive").

The more subtle ways of blaming someone else are very complex: and it would hardly be possible to analyze the problem adequately until a much clearer picture of how individuals impute causality for social actions is arrived at. We can, however, give a few illustrations of how individuals seem to impute blame to others. One way is to use the theory of motivation that is generally shared in our culture, at least on the level of fundamental considerations. The more immediately an action follows upon some other action, situation, etc., the more it is seen to be a response to (that is, caused by) that action. (Naturally, evidence of deliberation, etc., all have effects on such imputations.) Consequently, if one wishes to blame another for his suicide, he can act just after the other individual has done something that is typically defined as being associated with the typical motives of suicidal action—e.g., betrayal in love leads to the state of despair which is believed to be a motive of suicide.

This case which we are considering here involves a second form of blame which reinforces the first blame: the suicide "victim" clearly said that he had told his brother and his wife that he intended to kill himself and that they did nothing to stop him. Given the normative rule that one should always do what he can to rescue a would-be suicide, a norm so important in the *public drama of suicide rescues,* anyone who does not try to stop a suicide is clearly to blame for an immoral action.

Now, as we noted at the beginning, this was a blatant case of using suicide as a means of getting "revenge." We shall now consider a case that is somewhat more subtle; and which also has the virtue of introducing our last major topic, the *suicidal process*. (In this case report on the suicide of Marguerite S., one of the many lengthy reports constructed by Deshaies, it is also instructive to note the lack of any indication by the psychologists of how or where he got the reconstructed conversations between the actors. The general quality of this work, which is surely one of the finest works ever done on suicide, can be taken as some evidence in favor of "objective" treatments of the cases, but the lack of any precise consideration of such matters is, as we noted much earlier, characteristic of almost all works on suicidal actions.)

Thirty-eight years of age, divorced for several years, Marguerite S. had lost her parents and a child. She lived alone and worked as a saleswoman in a Parisian department store. Very pretty, refined, well-balanced, not at all emotional, she had never had the least psychopathic trouble. Of normal intelligence, she was very affectionate, obliging, gentle, devoid of all aggressiveness, on the whole passive and somewhat listless. She had a coquetry, self-confidence, and the simpering, slightly childish manner common to pretty women. She scarcely exploited her charms, and lived rather turned in upon herself, waiting for events instead of preparing for them.

In 1938 there occurred an event. Chance linked her with an engineer, Guy, two years younger than she. She became his mistress. Their liaison was not interrupted by the war, on the contrary—it reinforced it, at least on Marguerite's part. And then, these were the sad years of the occupation, with their anxieties and common hopes. Even though they didn't live together, Marguerite strained her ingenuity to better Guy's existence; their sexual understanding was perfect. Marguerite was happy and loved passionately, without reserve, without afterthought, with no eye to the future—even though their liaison was without a formal engagement. (Guy, a methodical and prudent fellow, had taken care to make this clear from the beginning.)

For Marguerite, Guy represented the universe. He was at the same time child and lover, family and master, the reason for living and the aim of living. He had bound up all her capacity for affection, filled the emptiness of an incomplete existence, and made the ideal teacher around whom her deeper personality could develop. It was not a matter of a thunderbolt, but of a slow, steady, building up of layers which united her indissolubly to her object. The hold of the object manifested itself in everything though without being anything of an obsession, for the self had no place to struggle, its adhesion was complete. To give oneself body and soul is not a vain image, the oblative form of love, the purest perhaps, the proof, as in the present case. A fortunate passion, a normal passion. Why must it be so rarely given out?

A November evening in 1943 produced the catastrophe. With consideration, but with decision, Guy announced to her the end of their liaison. Marguerite experienced an intense emotion, with cardiac pain, facial congestion, tears, asthenia. "It's impossible, oh! no, it isn't true! Tell me it's a nightmare! My Guy, my Guy, you are everything for me, you are my God, you are my soul! Can one live without his soul? It's not possible. You're all my life, everything. . . . To whom will I tell my troubles, my thoughts? It's horrible! You are my sole reason for living, without you I no longer have anything. I feel as if my head will burst. Must I pay with all the tortures of the heart and mind for the few hours of joy I've known? My darling, if you go away it's either madness or death for me. . . . I don't wish it, but I wouldn't have the strength to bear. . . ."

Destroyed, poor Marguerite stopped working, stayed inside, and lost interest in everything that wasn't the object of her passion. Her disarray was total, a veritable cataclysm in which, at one blow, all the affective organization of her life foundered, all her attachments were broken, all her interests vanished, her whole future dissolved. The duration stopped at the threshold of the present, burdened with a past which could no longer lead to anything. The weeks rolled by, their alternating hope and despair determined by the attitude of Guy, who was sometimes softened and charitable, sometimes hardened and pitiless according to the predominance of his tender feelings or his rational will to carry out his plan.

. . . Meanwhile Marguerite had gone back to work and was striving to reconquer her lover. She was calm, with a normal deportment, no longer emotional; nevertheless, her passion remained unchanged. After a sad Christmas-time, cruelly nourished by the tender memories of the past, she appeared for the first time animated by an aggressive tendency which gave to the idea of suicide the character of vengeance. "I am suffering, I can't stand it any longer, I wish to die. I wish I were able to hate you! I have given you everything and you have given me a hard heart. Why haven't I met another man who had a heart less hard? Why do I love you so much? I would like to hate you, I would like to kill you and then myself. . . . Have pity!" "But I know what I will do: it isn't you who will leave me, it is I. I shall die before you, under your eyes, I want you to see me die. I want you to see me dead and I want the image of me always between that woman and you." Jealousy explodes and works against the unknown rival: "I will scratch that woman's eyes out. I will kill her. I will kill her. She has no right to marry you. You are my whole life, without you it's the end of the world, without you I can't go on living." This aggressiveness was transitory and suicide continued to be seen as a liberation from suffering and also a way to free Guy from the problems and boredom she had created for him.

The idea of suicide was active and accepted, but Marguerite still hesitated, perhaps from a lack of courage, but especially because a vague hope persisted, since Guy continued to see her. Her sleep was troubled by expressive nightmares: train accidents, falls down precipices; she is going to hide herself under the water, deeper and deeper and she suffocates; she throws herself out the window of Guy's building; Guy suddenly appears at her home and she tells him: "I shall remain with you always"; sometimes some sexual dreams, exceptionally dreams of war (bombing at which she is impassively present).

Then all hope disappeared. Guy definitively maintained his decision and told her to "remake her life" without him. And then since she could no longer live either with him or without him, she decided to kill herself. She still loved Guy as much, and in a letter which she addressed to him on April 29, 1944, she told him again all her love, and very tenderly, with neither irony nor complaints, she wished him happiness before telling him adieu. The next day they took her body from the Seine.[36]

The one thing that seems most striking about Marguerite's suicide is the great difference in the general "tone" or over-all meaning (that is, the context of meaning determined by the dominant meanings) of the last communication with her lover, her "farewell" letter, from the earlier communications about her intention to commit suicide. In the earlier stages of the struggle it is clear that she was fighting and that suicide was being used as a "weapon," a threat of making the other responsible for the grave and immoral injury to herself. In the last communication, which, most unfortunately, Deshaies did not reproduce, she was, providing Deshaies' interpretation is correct, not at all aggressive; quite to the contrary, she was kind and loving toward him. It is, of course, quite possible on the surface of it to believe that she had a change of heart and decided not to blame her lover for her death. But, even if this were what she had intended, this is not the meaning of such a communication, or not the sole meaning, to someone, such as the lover himself, who looks at it. The meaning to an observer, especially one involved with her in such a way as to be somewhat sympathetic, is that she has at the very end expressed her deepest love for him and has been so forgiving as to wish him only the greatest happiness. This not only makes her more dependent upon him, because of the great love, and, therefore, makes him more the cause of her suicidal action; but it also makes her far more sympathetic. The overall

---

[36] This case was translated by the author. It is taken from *Psychologie du Suicide* by G. Deshaies, Paris: Presses Universitaires de France, 1947. It is translated and reprinted with the permission of the Presses Universitaires de France.

result of her change in tone is to make her lover even more "guilty" or to "blame" for her terrible action, probably even in his own eyes. (It is, however, entirely possible that her lover, being subjected to blame, might still see it in terms of the first tone of her communications, especially since the first parts of a sequence of communications tend to strongly determine the context of the latter parts of the communications.[37] If so, then he would quite possibly interpret her "farewell" as being just such an indirect form of aggression.) The expression of sympathy can itself be an action intended, or in fact, even if not intended, to produce the greatest injury: and it seems especially possible to do this when one commits a suicidal action, so that the only aggression expressed is that turned upon oneself in such a way as to make the other, whom one expresses only love for, appear to be the one really responsible for the injury.

Now, there are many instances of similar indirect "revenge" achieved by suicidal actions. One form that seems especially common is the explicit denial that some specific person, such as one's husband, is to be considered responsible for one's suicide. Such denials of responsibility can be a pointing-out of who is clearly responsible combined with a presentation of oneself as more sympathetic than someone who overtly blames the guilty one. But, without knowing the specific context of such a communication, we cannot say that the communication does not have the meaning of simply being a denial.

The important point is that one must know the context of the communication to know its meaning. This general proposition, which we have taken up at many points in this work, would mean, in this case and in many others, that one would have to know the local (or neighborhood) meanings that have been constructed by a number of individuals interacting with each other over time. It is such micro-cultural meanings that give a determinate (or highly plausible) meaning to the communications of the individual committing suicide.

[37] This suggested "primacy effect" is one of the many properties of communications which one would have to understand quite well before he could give any nearly definitive interpretations of the meanings of suicidal phenomena.

In this work there has been relatively little said of the significance of other individuals in the process of communications which leads to the construction of specific meanings for different individuals of suicidal actions of some one (or few) of the individuals involved in the communication process. This has been due to the paucity of information on such matters. Because of their theoretical preconceptions of such matters, psychiatrists have generally recorded just the meanings to the individuals who commit the suicidal actions. Sociologists, on the other hand, where they have even considered these actions to have meanings or to be appropriately studied from the standpoint of meaningful actions, have been almost entirely concerned with general, abstract, culturally shared meanings. Consequently, there is simply very little evidence to adequately deal with suicidal actions as meaningful actions in the right way—that is, as a whole process or sequence of meanings that lead to the construction of meanings of suicidal actions of a specific sort by a few individuals, one of whom is led to commit some suicidal action because of the specific construction which seems plausible to him and in some way fits his intentions.[1]

If, however, we cannot extensively analyze the construction of meanings of suicidal actions in the whole suicide process, we can at least consider the analysis of a special problem that demonstrates the way such analyses should develop over time. To do this we shall study both a subject about which there is some significant information and one which has obvious value as a starting point: the process by which meanings are constructed in the initial suicidal communications.

[1] We have, of course, given some consideration to the problems involved in analyzing suicidal meanings and actions in terms of communication processes in our earlier considerations of the *categorization process*.

The everyday meanings and theories of suicidal phenomena are important for more reasons than simply that
they *might* give us insights into the immediate, time-and-
situation bound meanings of real-world suicidal phenomena.
They are important primarily because they are an integral
part of the social processes that lead to suicidal actions or
which are stopped before the suicidal actions are committed.

If one conceives of suicidal actions as being merely actions
committed at a given point in time, then the everyday
meanings and theories of suicidal phenomena would very
likely be seen to be important only to the extent that such
meanings and theories become part of the decision-making
process of the individual deliberating upon suicide. If, on
the other hand, one considers suicidal actions to be the end
product of a whole process of thoughts, actions, *and* interactions over a prolonged period of time, then the everyday
meanings and theories of suicidal phenomena are seen to be
important determinants of the whole process. Investigations
by Robins, *et al.*,[2] by Shneidman and Farberow,[3] and by a
number of others[4] have shown that in at least 75% of the
completed (or "successful") suicide attempts, the individual
communicated to significant others his intention to commit
suicide. An excerpt from a case description by Stengel and
Cook (Case 12) is representative of the more clearly developed forms of such communication:

> At the time of the attempt his wife was again pregnant
> and had declared her intention of leaving him. For a
> fortnight before the attempt he spoke to her of ways of
> committing suicide but this did not change her attitude.
> He was discovered making an attempt by hanging, but
> even this had no effect on anyone in the household and
> elicited no sympathy or action. After further threats and
> suicide notes the police were called.[5]

[2] E. J. Robins, *et al.*, "The Communication of Suicidal Intent,"
American Journal of Psychiatry, 115 (1959), pp. 724-733.

[3] Edwin S. Shneidman, *et al.*, "The Suicide Prevention Center," in
The Cry for Help, edited by Norman L. Farberow and Edwin S.
Shneidman, p. 13.

[4] Cavan, Vail, Pokorny, Schmid (in St. Louis), and Rado.

[5] E. Stengel and Nancy G. Cook, *Attempted Suicide: Its Social
Significance and Effects*, p. 59.

The lack of "sympathy or action" could, of course, be the result of a desire to have the person die. But even a contention of that sort involves an implicit assumption that the individuals involved have something in mind, some goal in mind for the other person *and* that they believe his communications about suicide are related to such goals. More generally, the communications about suicide by this person in this situation to these individuals mean certain things to them which, when combined with some orientations or intentions towards that person in such matters, lead them to do certain kinds of things. In this case their interpretations of what he was saying and doing led them to "no sympathy or action." Frequently this is because the individuals involved *do not believe* that the person will actually commit suicide. And this lack of belief is directly related to the common-sense theories of suicidal communications and actions. There seems to be a general belief that individuals who talk about suicide will not commit suicide. Shneidman and Farberow have even considered this one of the most common beliefs (they call it a popular "myth") about suicidal communications and one of the most important determinants of the interaction process preceding suicides. Specifically, they have argued that because people do not take such communications seriously they do not do what is necessary to stop the suicide, so the suicide occurs.[6] Moreover, in psychiatric reports of cases of suicide it is quite common to find that the significant others said things about not being concerned with the communications of suicidal intention because this person had said such things many times[7] or because they simply didn't think he would possibly do such

[6] Edwin S. Shneidman, *et al.*, "The Suicide Prevention Center," in *The Cry for Help*, edited by Norman L. Farberow and Edwin S. Shneidman.

[7] Some individuals seem to make suicidal remarks frequently and in such a "non-serious" manner that the significant others may not believe them *even* if they have previously committed some suicidal action. This is suggested, for example, in the following case in which the man had attempted suicide before:

> In such moods he would sometimes remark that one day he would end his life. When she returned from a two days' holiday the patient was missing. He was found dead in the shop, having taken an overdose of sodium amytal.

(E. Stengel and Nancy G. Cook, *Attempted Suicide: Its Social Significance and Effects*, pp. 74-75.)

a thing. Often, it is precisely the suicidal attempt that makes the verbal communications plausible: the actions convince the significant others that the communicator "really means it," that he isn't "simply talking."[8] The explanation of this common-sense belief about the meanings of suicidal communications does not seem too difficult. Psychiatrists have tried to explain it in terms of motives or needs. They have, especially, argued that individuals seek to repress the meanings (or implications) of such communications because they produce fear or anxiety. It is possible and even likely that this is partially true, at least for many individuals. After all, the thought of the possible death of a loved one, or anyone with whom we can identify, is generally anxiety-producing. But there is a far simpler explanation than this, one which does not involve so many difficult inferences about what is conscious or unconscious and what one does or does not feel. Suicidal communications are extremely common. One can encounter them at just about any time anywhere, at least when people are intimate enough to allow the communications of such an intimate nature. (Just as one feels embarrassed about being present when a family fight is going on, so one feels embarrassed when a non-friend communicates his lack of "reason for living," etc.)

[8] In the same way an actual suicide can make it seem clear that what was once seen as possibly an accident was "really" a suicide attempt. A striking example of this appears in Dahlgren's presentation of his Case 58. This man was an epileptic who not infrequently "got lost" and had seizures. Dahlgren first presented the details of the case, which included the following events:

In the night before his admission there had been a scene at the patient's home because his foster-son had come home late and made a noise. In the morning the patient was despondent. Because of some trifle the patient lost all control of himself, took a razor and threatened everybody present, and then ran away from home. Some hours later the family was informed that he had got in front of a tram. According to the statement of the tramway conductor it looked as if the patient had thrown himself purposely in front of the tram. Afterwards the patient himself did not remember much of the event.

Then Dahlgren later concluded, without any consideration of whether this was actually an accident related to a seizure, that "The follow-up investigation showed that the patient committed S about 3 years after his AS by means of strangulation." (Karl G. Dahlgren, *On Suicide and Attempted Suicide*, p. 126.)

This is simply one small example of the way an action categorized as suicide reflexively changes the meanings of previous events, presumably *by changing the meanings of the person involved.*

Suicidal thoughts temporarily occupy the consciousness of most individuals at some time in their lives, perhaps especially during childhood and adolescence. Most such thoughts are "just thinking what it would be like," "playing with the thought," or "turning the thought over in one's mind." (William James once remarked that "I take it that no man is educated who has never dallied with the thought of suicide." Clearly, those who have the kind of classical education and education in the literature of nineteenth-century Europe, the kind of education James must have had in mind, would dally with the thought because of its great importance in the deaths of famous Romans and figures of literature. But there is no need to restrict it to the educated of that sort or even simply the educated.) We must, however, distinguish between the thoughts of oneself being dead, of the "wishing" oneself never born or dead and thoughts of "dying by one's own hand," etc. The former kinds of thoughts about being dead or dying are embodied in the Tom Sawyer death theme ("Oh, how sorry they'd be then"). Thoughts of this sort are extremely common, perhaps universal, at least during childhood or adolescence.[9] Whether such thoughts of dying or being dead, thoughts which are primarily concerned with a state of affairs or with the consequences rather than with the *doing* something, ever proceed to the point of becoming a *considered project*[10] in the minds of most people is quite another thing. It would seem likely that most individuals do not go that far in their thoughts about dying and about what one might do about dying. Still, the number of people who go as far as stating

[9] Cavan reported this to be the case on the basis of a questionnaire study she did of it. (See "The Wish Never to Have Been Born," *The American Journal of Sociology*, xxxvii (January, 1932) 547-559.) Others such as Wahl have expressed the opinion that the Tom Sawyer death theme is "ubiquitous among children." (See "Suicide as a Magical Act," in *Clues to Suicide*, edited by Edwin S. Shneidman and Norman L. Farberow, p. 25.)

[10] By "considered project" is meant "a series or set of thought-actions" (or imagined actions as long as one does not take "imagined" to mean "dreamed about" or autistic) ordered according to some everyday criteria of rationality in the direction of attaining some specific goal. This concept is specifically related to Schutz' concept of "project," but is distinct in not including the core factor of "intention" to bring about the goal.

out loud, at least to themselves,[11] that they would be better off dead and that perhaps they should do something about it, must be great, especially in view of the high proportion of people who admit to interviewers that at some time they have "attempted to commit suicide."[12]

Given a high frequency of such complicated, ambiguous, ambivalent, and rapidly alternating statements about suicide on the part of a high percentage of the population, many by the individual to himself and many heard by him, and given the relative rarity of actual attempts and the far greater rarity of actual (or successful) suicides, one can only expect that individuals, judging a given statement of suicidal nature in terms of their past experience in such matters, will decide that such statements are not seriously intended, are meant to "con," are "mere talk," and so on. (The same would seem to be true of such statements as "I'll kill you for that." Indeed, there is even an obvious bias in favor of discounting *statements of intention* in much of American culture, as is shown in various aphorisms such as "Talk is cheap," "Deeds speak louder than words," etc.)

My treatment of suicidal communications, the meanings of such communications, and the actions related to such meanings has so far implicitly assumed that the individual who makes a suicidal statement is, at least in the initial stages of such a process, making a statement about himself. That is, the first communications of a suicidal nature in some on-going interaction will be in some way expressions meaning that the individual doing the talking (or gesturing in

[11] Lichtenberg made a very relevant statement of this nature: "Often I have wished myself dead, but well under my blanket, so that neither Death nor Man could hear it." (Quoted in J. P. Stern, *Lichtenberg: A Doctrine of Scattered Occasions, Reconstructed from his Aphorisms and Reflections*, Bloomington: Indiana University Press, 1959, p. 8.)

[12] The relatively great number referred to is about 2 to 3 per cent, as found by Mintz in an as yet unpublished report of a series of interviews done in Los Angeles. It must, of course, be expected that it is very much a problem to individuals asked such questions to decide for themselves whether the taking of many aspirins with intentions, more or less, to do harm to themselves, or driving very rapidly in fog, etc., is to be so classified. I am assuming here that there must be many times more such actions and even more seriously intended talking about such things than there are what most psychiatrists would call "attempted suicides."

some way) has an intention, wish, thought, vagary, etc., about the death or suicide of himself. But this assumption has been made purely for expository reasons. The truth is quite different and much more complex.

In the great majority of cases where suicidal phenomena occur this assumption that the statement (or gesture) is *self-referent* is clearly true. Presumably because of the *relative* rarity of suicidal communications that lead to dangerous actions, not many individuals *initiate* suicidal statements (or gestures) about other individuals. (Such statements would be of the form of "He's the type of guy who'll kill himself if she leaves him.") Moreover, the thought or consideration of the possibility that someone in particular might commit suicide is quite rare. This is an important determinant of the very usual *experience of shock* that results from being informed that someone known to the communicators has committed suicide (or attempted suicide, etc.). (This *shock experience* is, very likely, quite important in producing—or facilitating—the reinterpretation of the substantial self of the person who commits suicide and of the nature of the situations and persons he was involved with at the time and in the past.) There are, however, certain important exceptions to this "rule of initiative" and we shall briefly consider each one of the major categories of exceptions.

Previous Communications of a Suicidal Nature

In many cases of suicidal phenomena someone imputes suicidal wishes, intentions, projects, and so on, to another person without any clear (or even unclear) suicidal gesture or communication on the part of that person. Frequently, the person doing the imputing is acting in terms of some previous gesture or communication that was taken by him to mean that the person would do suicidal things in just such a situation as now seems to exist (i.e., when he is doing the imputing). If a person is known to have said "I'd kill myself if I ever got cancer," and then comes to believe that he has cancer and communicates this to someone who knows of the previous statement, then suicidal intentions, etc., might well be imputed to him by that person. Similarly, a man's suicide can be explained as rational and foresightful by pointing out that he once said he'd commit suicide in such a situation.[13] In the same way, it is not too infrequent for a highly devoted married couple to have a kind of generally understood agreement that without the other life is "meaningless" or "worthless"; and sometimes there are even agreements not to go on living without the other. In such situations, those aware of the understandings or suspicious of such agreements will watch them closely and sometimes clearly impute suicidal intentions to the person.[14]

Suicidal History

There are some social relationships, most especially some family groups, in which suicidal phenomena are more frequent than usual. One of the cases reported by Stangel and Cook had a very high frequency of suicidal actions and communications:

> Case 30. Miss S. Y., born 1912, came from a family in which suicide had played a considerable part. Her father and his father had committed suicide. Her mother had often threatened suicide. Father's sister had attempted suicide.[15]

In such groups one would expect that suicidal communications would become everyday matters and that suicidal intentions would be initiated by various members of the group regarding other members simply because everyone in the group is well aware of this historical characteristic of the group. But even in such groups one would expect that such imputations would be made primarily in terms of certain expectations regarding *typical suicidal situations*; but

---

[13] This is a specific case encountered by the author long before his work on suicide began.

[14] It is possible that there are certain types of non-suicidal actions and/or communications that generally lead individuals to impute a substantial self to the actor which includes some idea that he is the type of person who would kill himself in the typically suicidal situations, so that they impute such intentions, etc., to him when he is in such a situation. (We have already noted that a suicidal action can lead to such an imputation, though it might well be that simply a situated self is involved.) Such imputations might be made in terms of categories such as "a born loser," a man with a "tendency to ground level," a man with an evil fate, and so on. But, if this is so, it does not seem too common.

[15] E. Stengel and Nancy G. Cook, *Attempted Suicide*, p. 80.

this is an independent source of imputations of suicidal intentions.

Typical Suicidal Situations

There are, as we have previously observed, many situations considered to be *typical* of suicidal communications and actions. But such typicalities are almost always made use of only *after the fact* of suicidal communications or actions.[16] The question here is whether there are any situations in which suicidal phenomena are seen to be a relevant consideration *before* any such phenomena are observed and categorized as being of a suicidal nature. (Such phenomena would be seen to be *relevant* to suicidal phenomena but not themselves suicidal in nature.)

The one clear case of a typical situation, very generally defined, which does lead at times to the imputation of suicidal intentions to an individual before he has himself initiated any suicidal actions or communications is that of *sudden, great personal loss*. Perhaps any sudden, great personal loss (of money, job, reputation, loved one) can lead to such considerations on the part of the significant others. But it is the loss of a loved one that seems most frequently to lead to such considerations. Great personal loss here is not simply sharp, painful loss; but also a loss that is all-engrossing, encompassing, or involved, because of an assumed high degree of *identification* of the bereaved with the dead. (In common sense terms identification is spoken of as "being so much a part of each other," "like one person," "inseparable," etc.) Such loss and grieving[17] is sometimes seen to involve

[16] This statement is not meant to imply that the "fact" of the suicidal nature of any phenomenon is not problematic. I am simply concerned here with clearly distinguishing between situations or phenomena seen to be relevant to suicidal phenomena and those seen to be suicidal in nature. The argument here is that such apperceived relevancies come generally only after some actions or statements by the individual have been categorized as suicidal.

[17] The "grieving" is very likely a determinant of the "danger" seen to be involved. Not all "grieving" is treated the same in our culture. It is, for example, very important to the observers to know whether the griever is expressing his grief or brooding over it. If the loss is such as to be seen as a *great* loss (i.e., there was high identification, etc.), then a lack of outward signs of grief (i.e., a lack of visible grieving) is believed to be the most dangerous kind. (In recent years various psychologists have "discovered" this "truth," but it is almost certainly

a distinct "danger" that the griever might commit some suicidal action.[18] (Sometimes such thoughts would hardly even be expressed to oneself in terms of "suicidal," but the general meaning would be communicated in terms of "the danger," "rashness," etc.) Depending on their understandings of the persons and situations, the significant others will carefully watch the griever at all times, refuse to let him go off by himself, and, probably gradually, encourage him to "get over it," "let yourself go," and so on.[19]

Specialists' Communications

In a complex and highly "rationalized" society *special contexts of meaning* almost inevitably develop. Such a specialized context has developed in the United States around the whole complex of actions and meanings roughly named "mental health" (or "mental illness"). Presumably because of the very old, basic belief that suicidal individuals are in some way "insane" (or, more recently, "mentally abnormal") and that insane individuals are likely to be suicidal,[20] this complex of meanings and actions has come to be closely associated with suicidal phenomena: that is, suicidal phenomena are seen to be *relevant considerations* in the mental illness context, even in the absence of previous suicidal talk.[21] This particular context of meanings is not so much

---

a very old, very basic part of everyday understandings of grief and grieving.)

[18] In many primitive cultures there are elaborate precautions taken to prevent the living from seeking to follow the dead. In our culture this wish to join the loved one who has died is rarely verbalized, but it is assumed to be there and is a major reason for such imputations of "danger" to situations involving grief.

[19] The author has had a specific example in mind while writing of these communications. Especially valuable in analyzing such phenomena are family experiences in which the sociologist knows all of the people involved, including himself, quite well.

[20] Historically, it would seem that first suicidal actions were associated with insanity and, only later, insanity was then seen to make suicidal actions a possibility.

[21] One would even expect that, in accord with some principle of *cognitive balance*, once an individual who was categorized as mentally ill did commit a suicidal action, then the specialists associated with the case would reconstruct their memories of what he said and did in the past in such a way that it would be seen that he had made previous suicidal statements or actions. This is one of the problems in using any reconstructed information.

a part of general common sense as it is of the "understand-ings" shared by the specialists entrusted with dealing with such matters—i.e., the psychiatrists and psychologists (and, thence, the nurses, orderlies, etc., associated with these specialists in performing their tasks in the special context of the mental hospital).

As a consequence of this generally perceived relevance of suicidal phenomena in this context, *any individual who gets involved in this context as a "patient"* (or, more gen-erally, anyone "needing" the help of "experts") *is subject to suspicions of suicidal intentions*. These suspicions may be initiated by the patient or by the specialist. Because the patient to some extent shares the definition that the spe-cialist has of him, just being in such a situation (i.e., being defined as a "mental patient" by the specialists) has a high potential of meaning to him that he is the sort of person who might kill himself. Therefore, though one of the reasons for his getting defined as a "mental case"[22] might well be some form of suicidal communication or action initiated by him against himself, his becoming so defined for other rea-sons might just as well be the reason for his initiating suicidal communications about himself.[23] There is an addi-tional reason why the specialist might initiate suicidal sus-picions and, thence, suicidal communications on the part of the patient: one of the fundamental responsibilities of all medical specialists is to prevent patients from doing any harm to themselves.[24] And it is believed that the risk of

[22] To be quite specific we should distinguish between a "mental case" as one who is properly the subject of "expert help" and a "mental patient" who is both the former *and* is actually hospitalized (or in some other way controlled by the "experts") for reasons of his "mental illness." These are very important social distinctions that make a great deal of difference to the individuals involved. (Being a "patient" means that one is "unable" to be anything else, etc.)

[23] There are, of course, many examples of the kinds of suicidal communications that go on between "patients" and "specialists." It seems common for "patients" to "express the wish to 'go to sleep and just not wake up—or step in front of an automobile. It's the only solution I can see. Nobody really cares whether I live or die. It doesn't make any difference. I don't see any use to keep trying—I should never have been born.' " (Quoted in Theron Alexander, *Psychotherapy in Our Society*, Englewood Cliffs: Prentice-Hall, Inc., 1963, p. 124.)

[24] Among American specialists the *practical concern* with saving lives is so fundamental an assumption of the whole medical-specialist enterprise that even those who are fundamentally concerned with sui-

suicidal actions is to some minimal degree present in all therapeutic relations, but especially in cases of depression.[25] (Since some depression is found in such a high percentage of cases, this is hardly much of a restriction.)

While the specialists see suicidal intentions and actions as relevant to the situation, they also believe that they have the responsibility of not suggesting such ideas to the patients.[26] There is, then, a patterned conflict between the obligations and expectations that a specialist is subject to in this situation: suicidal phenomena are seen as relevant considerations, they are seen as important to the whole therapeutic relationship and process, and yet the therapist must avoid giving suicidal thoughts to the patient.

---

cide take this as a determinant of how they will go about studying suicide. The author observed a group of specialists discussing a previous presentation of some of Jung's ideas regarding suicide. Since Jung treats at least some suicides as having positive meanings to the suicide, it can easily be seen that his ideas can be interpreted as potentially supportive of suicide or, at least, as not viewing suicide as a basic evil to be fought against. This interpretation did occur to these specialists in their discussion. Their response to such an idea was almost that of outrage or even disbelief.

[25] Earlier in this century, largely because of the influence of Freud's theory of suicide, therapists tended to see depression as almost a necessary component of any serious suicidal action. But, largely because of the influence of Zilboorg's articles on suicide and various later studies, therapists today tend to believe that any kind of case can involve suicidal actions.

[26] This belief that talking about suicide with a psychologically "unbalanced" (or whatever expression is used) person might precipitate suicidal thoughts, intentions, actions, etc., is frequently extended by the specialists to cover just about anyone. Consider, for example, the following statement:

The simulated suicide notes were obtained from *non-suicidal* individuals contacted in labor unions, fraternal groups, and the general community. Recognizing the moral, ethical, and taboo overtones associated with suicide, several precautions were exercised in eliciting these pseudosuicidal notes. Each individual was given a personality questionnaire and was interviewed briefly. If he indicated any signs of personality disturbance or tendencies toward morbid content of thought he was diverted by being asked to write about 'the happiest experience of his life,' and he was not given the suicide-note task; however, if he indicated that he was reasonably well adjusted, not depressed, not concerned with suicide, and would not be upset by thinking about suicide, he was instructed as follows . . .

(Edwin S. Shneidman and Norman L. Farberow, "Appendix: Genuine and Simulated Suicide Notes," in *Clues to Suicide*, p. 199.)

What is the solution to this conflict in this type of situation? It seems unlikely that there is any general, abstract solution of the problem that is applicable to most cases. (A very frequently invoked rule of thumb is "proceed with caution when the situation arises." But proceeding with caution can be one way of communicating "suspicion" or "importance" of a subject. See below.) Quite to the contrary, such situations must be handled largely on a specific, concrete basis. (It is quite possible that some specialists meet such structurally or culturally conflictfully defined situations by imposing some general policy on it, such as "never discuss it"; but, if so, there is little or no evidence of such general policies in the literature on suicide.) It is up to the participants to make of the situation a *specific, meaningful whole* by means of their communicative process. But, since this is a communicative situation that is relatively *asymmetric*, the meaningful whole must be determined largely by the communications and actions of the specialists involved. (It is not necessary that the meanings created in the communication process be *shared* meanings. The sharedness is an independent factor of some importance in determining "misunderstandings," "empathy," "confusion," etc.[27])

This is why it is especially important to know what the specialists initiate with respect to suicidal communications. The general indications at this time suggest that specialists are wary of *directly* initiating any statements about suicidal communications, past or present, presumably because of their belief that such initiation might well be *suggestive* to the patient. The use of standardized tests to determine "mental balance" (or whatever it is called by the particular specialist) does, however, frequently involve direct initia-

[27] In any communications where a "psychotic" is attempting to communicate with a "non-psychotic," especially with a specialist who has a set of categories and standard operating procedures already worked out that have nothing directly to do with the understanding of the situation on the part of the "psychotic" himself, it is almost inevitable that the "psychotic" will feel "confused," "misunderstood," "persecuted," etc. He is at a tremendous cultural disadvantage in imputing meanings (by definition no one can take his words as representing reality; and he himself shares these meanings to some degree). Moreover, he is experiencing phenomena quite distinct from those ever experienced by the specialists (or so the specialists believe) so that, though he can partially know by empathy what things mean to the specialists, they can hardly know what things mean to him.

tion of such statements. The MMPI, perhaps the most frequently used of such tests in the United States, includes a number of statements (to be judged true or false by the case) that have culturally defined relevance to suicidal thoughts and actions. One of these statements is very direct: "Most of the time I wish I were dead." (Number 339.)[28] Many others are less direct, but must serve to indicate to the patient that he is considered the type of person in the type of situation who is considered to have, at least potentially, suicidal ideas and actions.

It is also possible that some specialists think it desirable to "feel out" a case about any suicidal ideas or actions he might have had or committed in the past, especially if the case is depressive, to avoid the possibility of there being hidden ideas or intentions that might lead to suicidal actions for which he, as the responsible specialist, might be held responsible. (Moreover, given the assumptions of medical specialists, the specialists would see any injury done by the patient to himself to be "bad" for the patient.[29]) But there is little or no direct evidence that this is the way they treat the matter. Rather, the indications are that they are circumspect, cautious, and even silent about such matters until the patient mentions something about it. But, as indicated above, being cautious may well *mean* to the patient that such suicidal matters are not only relevant to him in general (because of now fitting the type) but that he specifically at this time is suspected of having such ideas, intentions, etc. There are as yet no adequate studies of how individuals impute "suspicion" of a specific sort to other individuals, though Glaser and Strauss have recently made a start in this direction (in specific considerations of how patients

---

[28] A list of statements from the MMPI considered to be relevant to suicidal thoughts and actions was reproduced by Shneidman and Lane in their report of "Psychologic and Social Work Clues to Suicide in a Schizophrenic Patient" (in *Clues to Suicide*, pp. 170-186). They are most especially relevant in terms of the *generally shared cultural definitions* of suicidal phenomena, so that it should be clear to the patient what is being talked about.

[29] This interpretation of suicidal actions as "bad" for the "victim"— a term that includes the evaluation itself—and the assumptions that underlie it are in no way thought to be *sui generis* to the medical disciplines. They are part of generally shared cultural meanings of suicidal actions in Western, and, especially, American societies.

become suspicious of the "awareness context" of doctors).[30] But individuals clearly do so and such considerations are of tremendous importance in relationships, especially those where "trust" is as central as in the specialist-case relationship. The individuals already categorized as "mental patients" are either *already* suspicious of themselves (or distrustful of themselves) with regard to such "abnormal" types of things as suicidal intentions, etc., or else they can easily be made so by the cultural definition of their situation; and the medical specialist is the man culturally accredited with the greatest knowledge (hence, by definition, power) of such matters. Suspicion imputed to the specialist about such matters will lead to suspicion of the self. The suspicion that one might kill himself is not merely disturbing or anxiety producing, though it certainly is these.[31] These suspicions, like the general suspicions that arise from being socially and/or self-defined as a "mental patient" (or "abnormal") give rise to general feelings of self-alienation, to the feelings that what is happening to the situated selves is not directly related to—most importantly, not dependent upon or caused by—the substantial self. The initiation of such suspicions by a specialist (or, to a lesser degree, by anyone else) could, then, provide part of the basis for looking at the self as a physical, living body that can be acted upon to produce "death" by "suicidal actions": such suspicions help to widen the feeling of difference between the "inner" and the "outer" selves (the soul and the body).

But the communication in any way by the specialist to the patient that suicidal intentions are relevant serves also to point out to the patient other meaningful possibilities of this situated relationship. Most important, it can indicate that this is a way to gain the concern, sympathy, and under-

[30] Barney G. Glaser and Anselm L. Strauss, "Awareness Contexts and Social Interaction," *American Sociological Review*, 29 (October, 1964) pp. 669-679.

[31] Perhaps the one experience that is not so uncommon which this feeling is like is that of "seriously" contemplating suicide or any form of "death" to the self while looking at oneself in the mirror. The mirror image tends to give one a feeling of being outside of oneself, so that this contemplation or disjunction between the "I" of experience or consciousness and the "me" of object (to use the Mead terminology) can have more of an objective, "reality feeling" to it.

standing of the specialist. And it can help to indicate that an injury to himself is an injury to the specialist, especially if he sees clearly that in some way it is a cultural (or medical-discipline) obligation of the specialists to prevent such suicidal actions by their patients.

These latter meanings, however, are rather specific and can be managed by the specialist in his interaction with the patient once the initial suspicion of suicidal intentions has been brought up. This management of the meanings can have the effect of *focusing* their relationship around suicidal phenomena; and can provide the basis for using suicidal actions to achieve sympathy, revenge, etc., whereas a turning aside of such communications *might*, depending upon the specific context of the communication, have prevented suicide from becoming clearly significant enough in the relationship to make it plausible to "blame" the specialist (or whomever the communication was made to) for the suicidal action.

There is clear evidence from some case reports that such focusing might well take place and provide the meaningful basis for the first suicidal actions. Let us consider, for example, the following report, in which the psychiatrist, toward the end of one session clearly indicated how glad he was that the patient had brought up the whole subject of suicide and which led to a *reported* abortive attempt the next day, which the patient then began to tell the psychiatrist about at the beginning of the next session:

> I asked how the operation had gone. He said, "I really didn't want to take all that time, but my 'stream-line' was so bad that it sprayed all over. I had to sit on the toilet in order to take a leak."
>
> He said, "I get self-conscious," and I asked what it was that made him feel this way. He said, "It's my short penis, my big nose, and when I walk, I bounce along. It's my blond eyebrows and my light beard." I asked what these, put together, meant he was afraid of, and he said he was afraid of life. I asked what it was, specifically, he was afraid of, and he replied, "Probably I'm afraid I'm not man enough, but I don't want to believe that.

"Lately, I've lost all my sexual drive with my wife. I've heard that this means a guy's going to have a nervous breakdown." I told him this was not true. I stated it was possible to have a lot of anxiety and still be able to function. I also told him that people frequently lose their sex drive when they are very anxious. He said he had thought of committing suicide, and I told him I was glad he had come in to see me first, and was talking about it with me. He went on, "I'm so anxious, I can't hear the questions that other people ask me. I feel guilty because another fellow is doing my work."

Arrangements were made to see him the next day.

Therapy Interview

The patient came in very slowly. "I didn't go to work today because I've been feeling very bad. I think I'm going crazy. Is there something I can do about it? Maybe I ought to go to the hospital." I asked what was making him feel bad and he said, "These pains in my head and this tension. It's as if bands are pulled real tight around my head. I can't sleep and I can't eat. I can't do my job, I can't go to the store, I can't do anything. I know I'm worse than before. When I went to see the doctor, I was afraid to sit in the reception room. I've been making my wife nervous, moping around the house. I was really going to commit suicide today. First, I took all my pills and then I went for a long ride up the Boulevard. I was going to get a hose but couldn't find any. I went to the drugstore and got a quart of beer and a scratch pad to write my wife a note. I parked on a deserted street and started writing the note and then my pen ran out of ink. I had to laugh. I drank some more of the beer and felt a little bit better, and then felt that I just didn't have the guts to go through with it. When I went home, my wife gave me a list of things to get in the store, and I took some films into the drugstore. Afterwards, the lady across the street came over and played with the kids."

I asked what the reason was for this wanting to kill himself. He said, "It was my shattered childhood. I didn't have a father to instill any confidence. I want my wife to remarry to someone who likes children. Then the thought came that no one likes a child as much as his own folks. When I kissed my wife and child good-bye this morning, I really hated to go. Then I thought, 'I've got to hang around to take care of my boy and wife.' He began to cry again. "When I was young I had asthma and I was oversensitive. The war worried me a lot. Being cooped up in that house for five days, I couldn't eat or sleep. I can't relax, I can't concentrate, I'm thinking only of myself."

I asked what it was right now that everything seems so terrible. He said, "I can't do my job, I'm a failure," and I pointed out how he was seeing everything in black and white, and that he was feeling that if he couldn't do his job, he was worthless. He said he felt like an outcast. I pointed out all of the things that he had been able to do—how well he actually had been able to function despite the tension he had been feeling. I mentioned his house, his wife, his child, his job, but the patient was unconvinced. "At work, even if you're half dead, you're supposed to go in at this time. Other times I can call in if I'm sick and it's okay, but I'm afraid of what others will think now."[32]

We would expect that the communication process would follow similar lines outside of the specialist-case relationships—i.e., in the everyday world; but until we have collected the information on many suicidal processes, so that the *comparative study* of the constructions of suicidal meanings is possible in more than this quite hypothetical form, we shall not be able to go beyond what now seem to be *plausible arguments*.

[32] Norman L. Farberow, "The Suicidal Crisis in Psychotherapy," in Shneidman and Farberow, *Clues to Suicide*, pp. 125-127.

19 GENERAL CONCLUSION

> . . . *Profound considerations of this sort*
> *belong to a higher science than ours. We*
> *must be satisfied to belong to that class of*
> *less worthy workmen who procure from the*
> *quarry the marble out of which, later, the*
> *gifted sculptor produces those masterpieces*
> *which lay hidden in this rough and shapeless*
> *exterior.*
>
> Galileo, Dialogues and Mathematical
> Demonstrations Concerning
> Two New Sciences.

The general argument of this work has been directed at what seem to me to be the fundamental problems of sociology, but these general implications of the work have been left largely implicit. It has seemed best to approach such general issues through the particular problems involved in building a specific theoretical approach to a specific form of social action. At this point, however, it seems appropriate to attempt to summarize a few of the more important of these general implications.

Throughout this work I have tried to show that a long tradition has led sociologists to make certain largely implicit, unexamined assumptions concerning the ways we should go about empirically investigating and theoretically explaining suicidal actions and, more generally, all forms of social actions. (I have called the general approach involving these assumptions the statistical-hypothetical approach or, alternatively, the positivistic approach. The same approach is found equally in the works of the structural-functionalists and social system theorists.) I have tried to make these assumptions explicit, especially in the long consideration of Durkheim's work on suicide. I have then tried to show that this whole approach to social phenomena involves certain fundamental misconceptions about the nature of social phenomena.

Most important, I have tried to show that the statistical-hypothetical approach fails to take into consideration the fact that *social meanings are fundamentally problematic, both for the members of the society and for the scientists attempting to observe, describe, and explain their actions.* It is this failure to see that social meanings are fundamentally problematic that has led sociologists to ignore the actual nature of the official statistics on suicide; and it is this failure, combined with the consequent reliance on the official statistics, that has led to the failure to see the need for careful observations and descriptions of suicidal phenomena before attempting to explain the phenomena. And the failure to see social meanings as problematic has led sociologists to read into statistics whatever forms of meanings fitted their preconceived explanations.

One of the most abstract and important generalizations that we have considered in this work is that the meanings imputed to suicide independent of concrete situations in which the communicator is involved are different from the meanings imputed to concrete situations in which the communicator is involved. In general terms this means that the *situated meanings* are significantly different from the *abstract meanings.* This finding has two fundamental implications for all investigations and analyses of social meanings and, therefore, for all of sociology. First, it is not possible to predict or explain specific types of social events, such as suicide, in terms of abstract social meanings, such as abstract values against suicide. This generalization is a denial of the fundamental assumption of most general theories in sociology today. Second, it is not possible to study situated social meanings (e.g., of suicide), which are most important in the causation of social actions, by any means (such as questionnaires and laboratory experiments) that involve abstracting the communicators from concrete instances of the social action (e.g., suicide) in which they are involved. Both of these implications would seem to demand a fundamental revision of the methods and theories of sociology. But the emphasis here has been on the careful demonstration of general principles through very specific, empirical investigations and analyses of the social meanings of suicidal phenomena. Having tried to show that the previous approaches to social actions such as suicide are inadequate, I have then tried to show how sociologists might more successfully go about doing empirical investigations and constructing theoretical explanations of such social actions. Some of the best available descriptions of suicidal phenomena have been used to demonstrate how we must approach the problems of determining social meanings and how we can then proceed to explaining social actions as meaningful actions. The serious shortage of good descriptions has prevented us from advancing very far toward our general goal of explaining suicidal actions as meaningful actions.

All the past examples of sociological theories of suicide have demonstrated the dangers involved in constructing theories without a firm foundation of careful, detailed descriptions of real-world events. The immediate goal before us, therefore, must clearly be that of providing such careful, comparative descriptions of many forms of social action. Only then can we get on with the general task of constructing more abstract theories to explain social actions.

APPENDIX I

Durkheim's Theory of the Relations between the Individual and Society and Suicide

As Mauss has said, the fundamental concern of Durkheim's scholarly work was that of the relations between the individual and society.[1] There was, of course, nothing new in Durkheim's concern with the problems involved in relating the individual to society: at least since Plato, some form of the problem had been central to most Western thought on ethics. But Durkheim's specific ideas about the *substantialist* distinction between the individual and society[2] and about the epistemological problems resulting from this distinction were in some good part innovations of his own.[3]

In any event, it is the specific forms given to these ideas by Durkheim which have had such fundamental influence in determining the directions of sociological research and theory, especially research and theory on suicide and the

[1] See Edward A. Tiryakian, *Sociologism and Existentialism: Two Perspectives on the Individual and Society*, Englewood Cliffs: Prentice-Hall, Inc., 1962, pp. 47, 65.

[2] The term "substance" is used here in the Aristotelian sense, precisely because it seems most likely that this is the way Durkheim thought of it at first, though by the time he wrote *Suicide* his ideas had been partially changed to meet the criticisms that had been made of his works on this ground.

[3] In his first serious work Durkheim referred to very clear statements involving such a distinction in Rousseau. After having quoted several passages from Rousseau, Durkheim concluded that "this remarkable passage proves that Rousseau was keenly aware of the specificity of the social order. He conceived it clearly as an order of facts generically different from purely individual facts. It is a new world superimposed on the purely psychological world. . . . In his view, society is nothing if not a single definite body distinct from its parts." Emile Durkheim, *Montesquieu and Rousseau: Forerunners of Sociology*, Ann Arbor: University of Michigan Press, 1965, pp. 82-83. However, it seems reasonably clear that Rousseau was concerned primarily with the ancient ethical problems (above all with freedom and authority) and that his distinctions were made primarily in those terms, rather than in terms of the epistemological and ontological distinctions Durkheim was concerned with making.

statistical nature of so much of sociological research and theory. Since many sociological works, especially works on suicide, have simply *assumed* that Durkheim demonstrated the necessity of such a distinction (primarily in *Suicide*) and because they have built on this distinction, it is of some importance to present-day research and theory to thoroughly investigate Durkheim's theory of the relations between individuals and society, especially within the context of his *Suicide*.[4]

It is first necessary to recall that Durkheim was fundamentally concerned with the problems of the "nature of man" as a concrete—i.e., individual—being and with the problems of the science that studies the concrete human being—psychology. He was a serious student of the psychology of his day, especially of the "structuralism" of Wundt. Durkheim, for example, was seriously enough concerned with the problems of the psychology of his day to argue quite energetically against the pragmatic theory of James and in favor of Janet's theory of the unconscious.[5] Indeed, it seems obvious that many of Durkheim's fundamental ideas about human action, especially the idea of "representations," and his methods of *studying* human action were greatly influenced by the theories and methods of the structural psychologists,[6] as is seen most especially in his strong tendency to assume that introspection (say, of the

[4] For an excellent general statement concerning Durkheim's demonstration of the need for such a distinction see H. Alpert, "Explaining the Social Socially," *Social Forces*, 17 (March, 1939) pp. 361-365. For a detailed discussion of the importance of this assumption in recent sociological works on suicide, see Part II.

[5] See Durkheim's discussion of these matters in his essay on "Individual and Collective Representations," in *Sociology and Philosophy*, translated by D. F. Pocock, Glencoe: The Free Press, 1963, pp. 1-35.

[6] In his influential essay on "Personality and Social Structure" (in *Sociology Today*, ed. by Robert K. Merton, *et al.*, New York: Basic Books, 1959, pp. 249-275), Alex Inkeles has strongly implied that Durkheim is inconsistent in this respect in *Suicide*. One needs only to put *Suicide* in the context of Durkheim's earlier studies, especially his appreciative study of Wundt's work during his stay in Germany, and his later work, especially "Individual and Collective Representations," to see that this psychologizing is not inconsistent or surprising. Indeed, it should be noted, as Sorokin has, that Wundt's general theory of society (especially as proposed in his *Völkerpsychologie*) was very similar to Durkheim's general sociologistic theory of society. (See P. A. Sorokin, *Contemporary Sociological Theories*, New York: Harper and Brothers, 1928, p. 458, fn. 46.)

trained sociological observer) is an adequate means of determining the *meanings* of social relations. Our major concern with Durkheim's psychological arguments must, however, be with his disagreements with most of the psychologists of his day concerning the nature of man.

Durkheim's fundamental assumption about the nature of man was that the self or personality of an individual is plural or multidimensional rather than singular or unidimensional as had been generally assumed by Europeans for centuries.[7] Durkheim's next assumption about the nature of man was that in each man there is a "biological self," derived from the body, and a "spiritual self," or "soul," derived from, leading to, and being the repository of "society." Durkheim believed that this duality of "body" and "soul" involved not merely a coexistence of separate parts of the self, but, rather, that it involved a "polarity." The "body" and the "soul" of the individual were inevitably in "conflict," in the sense that each opposed (at least, potentially) or restricted the effect (or forcefulness) of the other on the actions of the individual.[8] Durkheim considered it obvious that in all cultures men assume that there is a "soul" that *exists* independently from the "body" and that is eternal and (at least, potentially) is in conflict with the body. Because of his fundamental epistemological assumption that "social belief implies (proves?) existence,"[9] Durkheim be-

---

[7] See Durkheim's essay on "Individual and Collective Representations." This idea was rather clearly stated in the latter parts of *Suicide*. See, for example, p. 320.

[8] Durkheim's most extensive discussion of this whole matter is contained in his essay on "The Dualism of Human Nature and Its Social Conditions," in *Émile Durkheim, 1858-1917*, edited by Kurt Wolf, Columbus: The Ohio State University Press, 1960, pp. 325-340.

In his "Introduction" to Durkheim's *Sociology and Philosophy* Peristiany has argued that "The Durkheimian individual is a *homo duplex*, both *I* and *We*. This is a polarity, not an antithesis, which is deeply rooted in his conception of society and of its moving forces." (*Sociology and Philosophy*, p. viii.) Unfortunately, Peristiany did not specify just how a "polarity" differs from an "antithesis." But it would seem that he is denying that Durkheim believed there exists a conflict between the dual aspects of man. Durkheim's essay on this polarity should, however, dispose of any such counterarguments.

(Durkheim's conception of man as "double" is clear in *Suicide*. See, for example, *Suicide*, p. 213 *et passim*.)

[9] The similarity of this fundamental assumption of Durkheim's epistemology and the "principle of correspondence" of the early

lieved that this supposedly universal social belief in the independent, eternal existence of a soul that is in conflict with the body meant that there must really be such a "soul" so related to the "body." He further believed that introspection clearly shows us that there is a difference and (at least quite frequently) a conflict between feelings, which he assumed to be due to the biological drives of the body, and thinking (especially evaluating), which he assumed to be due to the functioning of the soul.[10]

The only major step that remained for Durkheim's reasoning was to identify the "individual" (or ego or "I") with the body and the social (or "we") with the soul. He believed this to be a perfectly valid and natural identification both (1) because introspection shows us that the drives of the body are self-centered (or "egoistic") while the thoughts of the soul are other-centered (or "altruistic") and (2) because the universal definitions of the body and soul are such that the body is defined similar to the observable nature of the individual (i.e., mortal) while the soul is defined similar to the observable (?) nature of society (i.e., eternal).[11]

It would, however, be a gross oversimplification of Durkheim's theory to consider "society" to be *merely* the sum of all individual souls. Durkheim considered "society" to be that which has resulted from the past interactions (or communications) of souls and which causes future interactions of souls. Its "existence" is, presumably, in the souls of individuals but its components make up only part of each man's soul and its totality or wholeness transcends the soul of each individual both (1) ontologically in that it exists as different parts in different individuals[12] and (2) epistemologically in

---

phenomenologists is striking. (See W. Stark's "Introduction" to Max Scheler's *The Nature of Sympathy*, London: Routledge and Kegan Paul, Ltd. 1954, especially pp. xviii-xiv.) It must be expected that there is some direct, common source.

[10] See both "Individual and Collective Representatives" and "The Dualism of Human Nature and Its Social Conditions."

[11] *Ibid.*

[12] See *Suicide*, pp. 319-320.

"We refuse to accept that these phenomena have as a substratum the conscience of the individual, we assign them another: that formed by all the individual consciences in union and combination. There is nothing substantial or ontological about this substratum, since it is merely a whole composed of parts. But it is just as real, nevertheless,

that one can causally explain the *shared or similar* actions of individuals only by reference to all the different parts of society in all the different individuals. One cannot, therefore, understand or explain social phenomena in terms of the properties of individual souls. One must explain such phenomena in terms of the observable products or effects of the operation of all parts of society (such as the "juridical norms").

Now, in *Suicide* Durkheim assumed that the degree to which the actions of individuals are determined by society can vary from one society to another or from one time to another, depending on the nature and/or strength of the society (i.e., the collective representations?). That is, the society (the collective soul forces) may "restrain" the individual (both body and individual soul or representations) *more or less.* An increase in restraint on the individuals results from an increase in the social force (collective representation?) of altruism (i.e., the social aspects of the souls of the individuals is stronger). A decrease in the restraint on individuals (which Durkheim considered to be the tendency in nineteenth-century European societies) results from an increase in the social force of egoism.[13] Altruism, then, is a "soul" force *or* a force increasing the effect of the "soul" on individual actions, while egoism is a "body" force *or* a force increasing the effect of the body on individual actions. Fatalism and Anomie are forces with analogous causes, effects, and existence in the body and soul aspects of individuals.

---

as the elements that make it up; for they are constituted in this very way." (p. 319.)

". . . We clearly did not imply by this that society can exist without individuals, an obvious absurdity we might have been spared having attributed to us. But we did mean: 1. that the group formed by associated individuals has a reality of a different sort from each individual considered singly; 2. that collective states exist in the group from whose nature they spring, before they affect the individual as such and establish in him in a new form a purely inner existence." (p. 320.)

[13] Egoism is both a positive and a negative cause of suicide; excessive individualism not only results in favoring the action of suicidogenic causes, but it is itself such a cause. It not only frees man's inclination to do away with himself from a protective obstacle, but creates this inclination out of whole cloth and thus gives birth to a special suicide which bears its mark. (*Suicide*, p. 210.)

Durkheim believed that the well-being of individuals, which will be reflected in their feelings (e.g., hope versus despair and joy versus depression), is the result of a proper balancing of the body and soul forces. A lack of well-being or pathology results from the loss of proper balance or equilibrium (i.e., integration) between the opposing forces of body and soul. The well-being and pathology of the society of individuals result from the analogous equilibrium and disequilibrium on the level of the social soul (i.e., the collective representations of egoism-altruism, and anomie-fatalism). As the pathology of society (or of the individual) goes up the tendency to commit suicide will also go up and conversely. Hence, we get all of the relations between the integration of society (i.e., the equilibrium of the four forces) and suicide rates.

For the consideration of Durkheim's theory of the relations of individual and social factors to suicide it is most important to remember that for Durkheim both the individual and the social factors were of causal significance for explaining suicide, but only the social factors were thought to be of fundamental importance for explaining the "suicide rates."

We do not accordingly intend to make as nearly complete an inventory as possible of all the conditions affecting the origin of individual suicides, but merely to examine those on which the definite fact that we have called the social suicide-rate depends. The two questions are obviously quite distinct, whatever relation may nevertheless exist between them. Certainly many of the individual conditions are not general enough to affect the relation between the total number of voluntary deaths and the population. They may perhaps cause this or that separate individual to kill himself, but not give society as a whole a greater or lesser tendency to suicide. As they do not depend on a certain state of social organization, they have no social repercussions. Thus they concern the psychologist, not the sociologist. The latter studies the causes capable of affecting not separate individuals but the group. Therefore among the factors of suicide the only ones which concern him are those whose action is felt by society as a whole. The suicide-rate is the product of these factors. This is why we must limit our attention to them.[14]

Deshaies and Inkeles have both argued that Durkheim implicitly assumed that individual factors are important in the causation of suicide.[15] But they failed to note that the society and individual factors were considered by Durkheim to be causes in different senses—Durkheim assumed there were different *types of causality* involved. He implicitly assumed that Aristotle's distinctions between different types of causes were important for this problem, while at the same time he adopted the nineteenth-century scientific view that "efficient causes" are the only "real" causes.[16] It is obvious that this is largely a linguistic problem.

First, it is obvious that the individual, both as body and as the vehicle of individual (soul) representations, is necessary

[14] *Suicide*, pp. 51-52.

[15] Deshaies' statement concerning the psychological elements in Durkheim's and Halbwachs' works on suicide is based on a misinterpretation of Durkheim's fundamental theory, though Deshaies is probably correct in his criticisms of Halbwachs' theory: "In truth, suicide escapes sociology. This is already apparent in the doctrine when Durkheim admits a tendency on the part of man to kill himself, although he makes it the expression of a collective force, when he speaks of excess or of insufficiency of individuation as if the force of the individual self should count in itself, when Halbwachs describes the anguish and terror, the sentiment of solitude. Are those not expressions which have only individual and psychological meaning? Is this not to recognize implicitly, we could say subconsciously, that the causation of suicide extends to the individual and that ultimately it is understood only in terms of him." (Gabriel Deshaies, *Psychologie du Suicide*, Paris: Presses Universitaires de France, 1947, p. 320.)

For Inkeles' similar criticisms of Durkheim, which are based partly on a misinterpretation of Durkheim's ideas about causality, see his "Personality and Social Structure."

[16] Unfortunately, Durkheim does not seem to have directly mentioned Aristotle's conceptions of causality. The one statement in which he *most* obviously was referring to one of Aristotle's fundamental distinctions between causes is the following: "Just as the science of physics involves no discussion of the belief in God, the creator of the physical world, so the science of morals involves no concern with the doctrine which beholds the creator of morality in God. The question is not of our competence; we are not bound to espouse any solution. Secondary causes alone need occupy our attention." (*Suicide*, p. 318, fn. 14.)

It seems quite clear from this statement that Durkheim simply assumed that his readers (nineteenth-century Frenchmen) would know immediately that he was referring to Aristotle's distinctions between "primary" and "secondary" causes. He must also have assumed that his readers would easily see that "active causes," etc. were "efficient causes" and so on.

for suicide. Durkheim *defined* suicide in terms relevant only to individuals. But this means nothing more than that the individual has to be considered a "material cause" of suicide. Without knowledge states of individuals and actions by individuals, one cannot possibly have suicides. Durkheim explicitly believed, however, that the individual is a cause of suicide, or, rather, of non-suicide (but not, thereby, of suicide rates?), in that an individual will not commit suicide if it is against his nature (or "essence"), regardless of what happens to the social factors.[17] The individual can, then, choose *not* to commit suicide. This means that he can have a negative causal effect because the individual body and soul is an "essential cause" as well as a "material cause." But it is only "society" that is a positive "effective cause" of suicide.[18] (The individual may veto, but society proposes.) And it is the "efficient cause" that is the "active" and only "real" cause of suicide,[19] both (1) ontologically in that these are "things" acting on other "things" and (2) epistemologically in that one can only explain the "general" scientifically

[17] *Suicide*, pp. 102-103 and 322-323. "We are thus referred to the conclusion of the preceding chapter. Doubtless, suicide is impossible if the individual's constitution is opposed to it. But the individual state most favorable to it is not a definite and automatic tendency (except in the case of the insane), but a general, vague aptitude, which may assume various forms according to circumstances, permitting but not necessarily implying suicide and therefore giving no explanation for it." (pp. 102-103.)

[18] Durkheim was somewhat inconsistent in his arguments regarding the individual factor of "insanity." In a number of places he stated specifically that "insanity" is an "efficient" (i.e., determining, etc.) cause of suicide.

"But though there is no individual state except insanity which may be considered a determining factor of suicide, it seems certain that no collective sentiment can affect individuals when they are absolutely indisposed to it." (*Suicide*, pp. 322.) (See also pp. 103, 145, and 181.) But on p. 323 he contradicts this and makes insanity a predisposing factor (i.e., material or essential cause?): "Neuropathic conditions only cause the suicides to succumb with greater readiness to the current." The psychiatric case evidence seems to have been too strong to deny, yet his general theory *seemed* to demand such a denial. So Durkheim vacillated and made contradictory statements.

[19] Durkheim used at least four different terms to refer to the concept of "efficient cause": (1) "active cause," (2) "generating cause," (3) "determining cause," and (4) "productive cause." ("Positive cause" is probably a fifth term.) The clearest statements concerning the distinction between society as efficient cause and individual as material and essential cause can be found on pp. 102, 104, 141, and 149 of *Ibid.*

—the individual phenomenon being inexplicable except insofar as it is a member of the general class of phenomena.

Most of Durkheim's considerations of the interrelations of individual and social factors to suicide are either little more than linguistic confusions or they are made to seem unnecessarily complex by such linguistic confusions. It is important, however, to note that Durkheim's contention that only the social factors are "efficient causes" or the "really active causes" does not say anything about *observable* phenomena. What it does say, in a roundabout way, is that only the social factors can be used to give a scientific explanation of suicide. The general idea here is that only efficient causes can be used in scientific explanations, but there are also more specific ideas involved, the most important of which has been very clearly formulated by MacIvar in his interpretation of the epistemology of *Suicide*.

In their contentions that Durkheim *did* use individual factors to help explain suicide, Deshaies and Inkeles seem for the most part to have been referring to Durkheim's various statements concerning individual "motives" (such as despair and unhappiness) for committing suicide. Durkheim knew, of course, that these were the usual "causes" given by common sense to explain individual cases of suicide. And he assumed explicitly that these are the individual phenomena to be observed when one looks at an individual case of suicide. Indeed, though Durkheim thought it nearly impossible to get reliable evidence on such matters, he seems to have assumed it to be so obvious that these motives are the individual "reasons" why individuals commit suicide that he hardly considered such individualistic explanations to be problematic.[20] He did *not* attempt to collect evidence to show that one could *not* get such reliable evidence: he simply assumed this most implicitly and most emphatically. Just as he assumed he knew the meanings of the social relations he was considering, so he assumed he knew the meanings of suicidal situations and the individual "reasons" for committing suicide.

[20] Durkheim's numerous statements on the despair, sadness, etc., of the suicides is clear evidence of this. At one point he even went so far as to say that "Of course, suicide is always the act of a man who prefers death to life" (*Suicide*, p. 277), even though this seems to be in complete contradiction to his earlier statement that "intention" is too "intimate" to determine—how less intimate is preference?

The Formal Definitions of "Suicide"

Suicide is clearly a subject of considerable interest to many of the disciplines concerned with human behavior. As long as this is simply the immediate, practical interest of preventing individual deaths, the problem of defining "suicide" and any related terms is either unrecognized or, if it is recognized, can be handled relatively simply: the definition can be given ostensibly (i.e., in terms of the real-world cases that concern the definer). However, as soon as one becomes concerned with the more abstract problem of *explaining* suicide, he immediately faces the problem of giving some reasonably clear and distinct definition to the term.

Even the most cursory survey of the vast literature on suicide will quickly lead one to conclude that the students of suicide have not very often been able to agree on how to define the term. Probably the basic reason for this continual disagreement over the definition is the complex family of meanings given to the term in Western culture by everyday usage and, consequently, by all the forms of literature. There are, in fact, certain arguments over the meaning of suicide that have not changed much throughout the entire history of Western culture.[1]

There are, presumably, many other reasons as well for the proliferation of different definitions of suicide in the literature. But the important point is that these many definitions exist and that significant progress in this field of study will continue to be greatly hampered until the students of

---

[1] For example, the arguments of Augustine and his opponents concerning whether "martyrs" were "suicides" involved almost the same disagreements found in the arguments between Durkheim, Halbwachs, and others over whether "self-sacrifices" are to be considered "suicides." (On Augustine see W. E. H. Lecky, *History of European Morals from Augustus to Charlemagne*, New York: Braziller, 1955. For a résumé of the twentieth-century dispute see G. Deshaies, *Psychologie du Suicide*, Paris: Presses Universitaires de France, 1947, pp. 4-5.)

suicide become clearly aware of the many different potential meanings of the term "suicide" and of the empirical and theoretical justifications normally given for each fundamental dimension's being included in the definitions. The following is an attempt to present these fundamental dimensions of meaning and to analyze the justifications given for using "suicide" in each sense.

Fundamental Dimensions of Meanings in the Definitions of Suicide

When one considers the many different conceptual treatments of suicide it becomes reasonably clear that there are several fundamentally independent but related dimensions that are included in different combinations and to varying degrees in most, if not all, of the definitions:[2]

(1) the *initiation* of an act that leads to the death of the initiator;

(2) the willing of an *act* that leads to the death of the willer;

(3) the willing of self-destruction;

(4) the loss of will;

(5) the *motivation to be dead (or to die)* which leads to the initiation of an act that leads to the death of the initiator;

(6) the *knowledge* of an actor that actions he initiates tend to produce the objective state of death.

These dimensions are not entirely "pure": some of them do overlap. But, they also seem to cover most of the important dimensions of meanings found in formal definitions of suicide in the Western world. They do not, however, completely cover such definitions. It is possible to give at least three other dimensions that have been given in formal defi-

---

[2] Karl Menninger (*Man Against Himself*, New York: Harcourt, Brace, and Company, 1938) has tried to show that *every* suicide has (to different degrees) a desire (a) to die, (b) to kill, and (c) to be killed. Such attempts to deal with the most *fundamental* necessary and sufficient dimensions of all suicides are rare in the literature on suicide. Frequently the most fundamental dimensions of *description* and *decision making* are thrown into a pastiche of factors that includes supposed causes such as "loss of a family member at an early age" or "unresolvable conflict." (See, for example, Ruth S. Cavan, *Suicide*, Chicago: University of Chicago Press, 1928.)

nitions: (1) The degree of central integration of the decisions of an actor who decides to initiate an action that leads
to the death of the actor; (2) the degree of firmness or
persistibility of the decision (or willing) to initiate an act
that leads to the death of the initiator; and (3) the degree
of effectiveness of the actions initiated by the actor in producing his own death. The first of these is, in fact, of considerable historical importance because it covers most of
the argument over whether or not "insane" individuals can
commit suicide.[3] I have, however, chosen to exclude it from
consideration for three reasons: first, the subject is immense
in itself; second, modern students of suicide have largely
agreed that it is not a worthwhile argument; and, third, we
have considered some parts of the argument in our considerations of whether an individual can ever be rightly said to
kill his "self." The other two are not given separate consideration because they occur infrequently and because they
have been largely dealt with under the major dimensions.

(1) *Suicide as the initiation of an act leading to one's own
death.* The act initiated need not be an act that leads
directly to one's death. Indeed, the act may simply be an
act that *objectively* places the actor's life in danger, whether
he wills it or not, whether he knows it or not.[4] There are
varying degrees of *objective indirection* or *uncertainty*[5] possible in the sequence of actions initiated by an actor that
objectively places his life in jeopardy, whether the end
result is death or not.

This dimension covers about the broadest range of referents of any of the dimensions used in the definition of suicide. In some ways it would certainly seem on *prima facie*
grounds to cover too much to be of much value in a theory
of suicide. The *initiation of the act* may well be a *necessary*
dimension in the definition, but it does not distinguish be-

---

[3] This was the major concern with the definition of suicide in the
nineteenth century.

[4] The popular use of "suicide" is frequently of this sort. See, for
example, H. W. Rose, *Brittany Patrol: The Story of the Suicide Fleet,*
New York: Norton, 1937; and W. Westover, *Suicide Battalions,* New
York: Putnam's, 1929.

[5] This *objective* uncertainty must be distinguished very clearly
from the *subjective* (decisional) uncertainty of number (6), the sort
of decisional uncertainty that Durkheim recognized in his considerations of the definition of suicide (see below).

tween something called "suicide" and phenomena called "accidents" and "mistakes." Such a general definition would hardly seem useful for any theory other than one that is concerned with the cosmological forces leading to an individual's blind fulfillment of his fate.[6] But, on more careful consideration, it would seem that there are three excellent reasons for retaining this most general conceptual dimension for at least potential use in the theory of suicide.

First, there are many cases of *ego-initiated death* (or near death) in which it would be very difficult, if not impossible, to show that the individual had *intended* consciously to kill himself or had *decided to die* by his own actions; yet it can be shown that the individual has nearly killed himself many times by deadly acts; and, furthermore, that the individual has many motives toward death. Consider, for example, a case of attempted "suicide" (i.e., ego-initiated deadly acts) studied by Zeckel. This twenty-four-year-old girl almost succeeded in killing herself with gas, yet "when conscious she said she could not remember intending to commit suicide." She does remember, however, several previous experiences of fugues and amnesias. Her deadly act occurred after a (psychosomatic?) coughing spell which seems associated with her guilt feelings about an attack of asthma that sent her fiancé to the hospital. This guilt response is very similar to certain very strong guilt responses she learned as a child in her relation to her father.[7] Such guilt feelings might well have produced the fugue state in which she initiated the act that nearly killed her. Such a fugue state might, indeed, be a necessary factor in her initiation of a deadly act against herself; for, while conscious, her values and fears might have effectively blocked the act. A definition of suicide (and attempted suicide) as necessarily being the result of a *con-*

[6] Some students of suicide have, to be sure, been largely concerned with just such a factor as "fate," though generally it is a natural-selection mediated "fate." See, for example, N. D. C. Lewis, "Studies on Suicide," *Psychoanalytic Review*, xx (July, 1933) 241-273; and *Psychoanalytic Review*, xxi (April, 1934) 146-153.

[7] A. Zeckel, "Hypnotherapy in a Case of Amnesia with Suicide Attempt," *Psychiatric Quarterly*, 25 (1951), pp. 484-499. It is an unanswered question as to whether this girl was conscious when turning on the gas and has since repressed the memory or was unconscious at the time of the act. I have inferred, contrary to Zeckel's unsupported assumption, that this was a fugue state, not merely amnesia.

scious or *intentional* or *knowledgeable decision* would immediately exclude such extremely interesting phenomena as found in Zeckel's case. Such phenomena may, of course, be quite anomalous; but it is precisely these extreme and rare phenomena that frequently add most to our understanding.

The second justification concerns the age-old argument as to whether animals commit suicide or any form of "self destruction." Some students of suicide have maintained that only man can commit suicide because, as Montaigne said, "Only man can hate himself." Most have maintained that animals cannot commit suicide because they cannot *know* of the relations between their acts and the consequences of their acts.[8] Such arguments may well hold in considerations of lemming marches to the sea or of mythical, incestuous horses; but there are some extremely well-documented (even experimental) cases of animal "self-destructive" behavior. Consider, for example, the case of the Macacus Rhesus Monkey named Cupid.[9] Cupid was conditioned to be dependent on Psyche (a Macacus Cynomologus monkey) and to have a monogamous sexual relationship with her. He was then conditioned, though with some and only partial success, to have a sexual relationship with Topsy (a Macacus Rhesus). Then Psyche was returned to Cupid, who resumed their sexual relation, but with a good bit of attention to the nearby Topsy. When Topsy and Psyche were once again switched Cupid almost immediately began biting his foot and lacerating his body. This "self-destructive" behavior seems very definitely related to a high degree of conflict, possibly even "guilt"; and there can be no doubt that he quickly learned the relation between biting and torn (painful) flesh. That this response is similar to many "appeal" attempted suicides[10] of human beings is seen in the fact

[8] See, for example, Durkheim's argument against the "suicide" of Aristotle's incestuous horse (*Suicide*, p. 45).

In a similar vein, Hegel has said, "I possess my life and my body only in so far as my will is in them; *an animal cannot maim or destroy itself, but a man can.*" (T. M. Knox, *Hegel's Philosophy of Right*, Oxford, 1942, p. 43.)

[9] This case is reported in O. L. Tinklepaugh, "The Self-Mutilation of a Male Macacus Rhesus Monkey," *Journal of Mammology*, 9 (1928).

[10] See E. Stengel and N. G. Cook, *Attempted Suicide*, London: Oxford University Press, 1958; and N. L. Farberow and E. S. Shneidman, *The Cry for Help*, New York: McGraw-Hill, 1961.

that Cupid would only bite and lacerate himself when being *looked* at by Topsy or the experimenter. There is further evidence, of an even more carefully controlled experimental nature, that animals do, both partially and wholly, destroy themselves in situations very similar to those in which human beings destroy themselves. The Russian psycho-physiologists, for example, have found that as the degree of neurotic conflict (and consequent neurotic disorganization) increases in animals subjected to neurosis-inducing conditioning, the tendency to "self-referent" behavior, which is largely "self-destructive," increases.[11] Such behavior is remarkably similar to hypereridism[12] in human beings. Since such animal behavior is more subject to experimentation than similar human behavior, there is excellent reason for attempting to determine precisely the similarities rather than defining such data on animals out of consideration of the theory of suicide.

It should be noted, of course, that the *failure* to *initiate acts* that are objectively necessary to life is as important to this definitional dimension of suicide as the *positive* initiation of acts.[13] Simone Weyl's refusal to eat enough to keep herself alive during World War II was intended to heighten her identification with the suffering people of her homeland, France. But this negative act, this not eating, is certainly an initiation of acts that indirectly lead to her death, especially since she initiated acts against the acts of attending doctors.[14]

(2) *Suicide as the willing of an act that leads to the death of the willer.* The conceptual dimension of willing a deadly act, which is more or less equivalent to the *intention* to kill the self, is certainly one of the most frequently given as a

[11] L. N. Norkina, "The Production of Experimental Neurotic States in the Lower Apes," in Reprinted, Translated from Russian: *The Central Nervous System and Human Behavior*, U.S. Department of Health, Education, and Welfare, 1960, pp. 718-727.

[12] See P. M. Yap, "Hypereridism and Attempted Suicide in Chinese," *Journal of Nervous and Mental Disease*, 127 (July, 1958), pp. 34-41.

[13] See Durkheim's discussion of *positive* and *negative* acts in *Suicide*, p. 42.

[14] Some students of suicide have called this negative initiation of acts "physiological suicide." See G. N. Raines and S. V. Thompson, *Suicide: Some Basic Considerations*, U.S. Naval Hospital, Bethesda, Md., 1950.

necessary and (less frequently) sufficient definition of suicide. Halbwachs' definition, for example, includes the dimension of *intention* as necessary (though not sufficient).[15]
The justification for this definition lies in the conception of
the *self* or the individual's *being* as essentially *volitional*.
The argument has generally been vague, but the fundamental line of reasoning seems simple enough:

(1) suicide is synonymous with "the destruction of the
self by the self";
(2) the *self* is the *willing* or *volitional* factor of mind
(-body);
(3) therefore, suicide is synonymous with "the destruction of the will by the will" (or the intentional destruction of one's self).

Of course, since the will was generally considered to be distinct from the body, it would be necessary to add the factor
of willed *acts* and to speak of suicide as the *willing of a
state of the world* that acts back upon the will to destroy it:

No entity can lose a character by virtue of a reflexive act
which presupposes the presence of that character. It is
thus incorrect to speak of a man taking his own life; one
should rather speak of his putting himself in a state so
that his life can be taken from him. . . . By itself (a living
being) forms a closed system. . . . It cannot by an act of
its own produce the Relative Nothing which is its nega-
tion.[16]

In these conceptions of suicide as the willing of acts that
lead to the willer's destruction, we are presented with the
problem of *unity* of the self. Since the will was normally
considered to be *unitary*, conceptions of suicide as *willing*
the destruction of the *will* (i.e., *self*) run into the problem
of explaining how a unity can be against itself. But these
problems will be considered later, especially under the section concerned with the *degree of central integration*.

In considering the dimension of *intention* (or willing) in
the initiation of acts that lead to one's death (or near death)

[15] M. Halbwachs, *Les Causes du Suicide*, Paris: Felix Alean, 1930,
pp. 451-480.
[16] P. Weiss, *Reality*, Princeton, New Jersey: Princeton University
Press, 1938, p. 167.

it is most important to note that there are specific cases of self-initiated death in which the victim is, in a very real sense, the *victim of himself*. In these cases the individual *knows* that he is killing himself and *wills*, as far as can be determined, to stop himself from killing himself, but to no avail. Consider, for example, the case of a young English mother who continued to suffer intermittent attacks of depression even after a prefrontal leucotomy. She initiated deadly but unsuccessful acts against herself three times during depression. She realized (or *believed*, if one wishes to be sceptical) that she had strong impulses to kill herself and fought against them. She expressed confidence that she would be able to stop herself in any new attempts because she had in the first three attempts. But in a fourth initiation of a deadly act against herself (aspirin consumption) she died.[17] Such cases frequently involve *compulsion* and/or *hysteria*.[18] Compulsion especially seems to be a very important factor in producing the non-intentional, *partial and progressive* initiation of acts over a number of years that lead to one's death. Arthur Rimbaud is an example of a man who spent a lifetime doing a great number of things that progressively destroyed him; yet his sole (conscious) *intention* in all of these acts was to find security for himself. He seems to have realized after, and sometimes during, the acts that they were destroying him, yet he could not seem to stop himself from performing them.[19] At its greatest intensity a compulsion may turn reason to its support and certainly when a man is in the full possession of his compulsion he wills to live the compulsion even if it should result in his death. But it cannot be said that he has willed or intended the actions associated with the compulsion. He may fight these actions, may consider them utterly abhorrent and will to oppose them at all cost. Only when he has been swept up by the ecstasy of the doing does the will turn to the complete support of the compulsion:

[17] See Case 20 in E. Stengel and N. G. Cook, *Attempted Suicide*, pp. 73-74.

[18] See G. Zilboorg's discussion of compulsion and hysteria in cases of "suicide" in "Differential Diagnostic Types of Suicide," *Archives of Neurology and Psychiatry*, 35 (January, 1936) pp. 270-291.

[19] See Henry Miller, *The Time of the Assassins*. This work is a brilliant critical biography of Rimbaud and his work. Miller specifically maintains that Rimbaud spent his adult life destroying himself.

Pure reason advised him to take this step. But pure reason has its sophistries; in this case it was in league with his lurking passion. The hope of winning a return to Russia at roulette may well have been the immediate pretext that brought him to the casino again; but what held him there afterward was the irresistible attraction of gambling itself. For once he had begun, it did not matter whether he won or lost; every incident, every circumstance at the gaming table served him equally as a fresh stimulus to go on gambling. If he won, his winning was a sign to go on; if he lost, he could not rest until he had won back his losses. "The principal thing is the game itself," he confessed.

To his three afflictions—exile, poverty, and illness—there was added a fourth: the obsessive passion for gambling that had its source in the depths of his own nature. It was this that completed the doom of his life in exile.

As in a Greek tragedy, from then on all evil hazards intertwined, all the conflicts mounted inexorably toward disaster. As though the hostile goddess of fate, Ate, were punishing him for the *Hybris* with which he attempted to bend fortune to his will, his pursuit of a coup at roulette carried him headlong to destruction. . . .

He had already passed through many an inferno; but this moral hell into which he was driven by his "cursed vice" and his "all to passionate nature" was worse than anything else. Tormented by shame and repentance, he resolved again and again to leave off gambling, that "diabolical possession, that self-poisoning" by his own imagination, and to live at Anya's side for his work alone. "I shall have only the one goal in view; to finish the novel swiftly and successfully. I will put my whole soul into the work. If it succeeds, we are saved."

But he could not escape.[20]

There are, then, cases of ego-initiated acts that kill ego (with varying degrees of *directness*) without ego's willing or intending to perform the acts, nevertheless willing to kill himself. These cases seem of potentially great value for a theory of suicide and self-destruction. It would seem, there-

[20] Rene Fueloep-Miller, *Fyodor Dostoevsky*, New York: Scribner's, 1950, pp. 25, 28, 29.

fore, that the dimension of *willing* or *intending* an act that
leads to the death of the willer should not be considered
a *necessary* dimension of suicide; yet it would be unwise to
overlook the significance of this dimension for the theory
of suicide.

Some students of suicide have assumed that there exists
some continuum relationship between the most fleeting
thought or image of suicide and the act of committing suicide.[21] The continuum relationship is generally thought to
be determined by lesser and greater degrees of *intent* to kill
oneself. Other students have tried to show that attempted
suicides are further or closer to the act of suicide in terms
of the *degree of lethality of the attempt,* which is thought
to be determined by the degree of *intent* to act in a manner
that will lead to one's death.[22] Such a very close relation
between intention and action has not actually been found
in studies of ego-initiated deadly acts. In their study of
English mental patients, for example, Stengel and Cook
found that:

(1) only among the (medically determined) "absolutely
dangerous" attempts is the degree of intent maximal
in a majority of cases;

(2) in one-fifth of the "absolutely dangerous" attempts
there is only medium intent;

(3) serious intent is frequently associated with only a
medium danger;

(4) lowest danger is generally associated with medium
to low intent;

(5) degree of danger in attempt varies (partially independently of degree of intent) with respect to mental disorder syndrome.[23]

[21] For a discussion of such factors see P. B. Schneider, *La Tentative
de Suicide,* Paris: Delachaux, 1954, pp. 9-43.

[22] See, for example, C. Catalano-Nobili and G. Cerquetelli, "Il
Suicido: Studio Statistico e Psicopatologico," *Rassegna di Neuro-
Psichiatr.,* 4 (1950) pp. 22-87.

[23] E. Stengel and N. G. Cook, *Attempted Suicide.*
It might be noted that from a study of six hundred "attempted
suicides" at Bellevue H. Hendin estimated that one-third of the men
and one-half of the women had a minimum *actual intent* to kill themselves. ("Attempted Suicide: A Psychiatric and Statistical Study,"
Psychiatric Quarterly, 24 (1950), pp. 39-46.) But the basis for
Hendin's estimates is unclear.

But, at the same time that intention and danger of attempt cannot be shown to vary with respect to each other in more than a roughly monotonic fashion, there is, nevertheless, ample evidence to suggest that intention, as determined by the previous *expression* and *demonstration* of intention, is generally present to some degree in those who initiate actions that kill themselves.

But, if there is no proof of a strictly monotonic relation between degree of *intent* and degree of danger of the act initiated by ego against himself, there is, nevertheless, some evidence that those who die by their own acts have most frequently given previous *expressions* of *intention* to kill themselves:

(1) in a retrospective study of suicide in a VA hospital from 1949-1959, Pokorny found that only eleven of the forty-four had given no previous *expression of intention* to commit suicide; of the thirty-five, seven had attempted suicide before;[24] eight gave indirect "hints," and eight very direct expressions of intention to commit suicide;[25]

(2) in a study of 152 New Hampshire mental patients who committed suicide in 1955-56, Vail found that fifty-three per cent had made either overt expressions of intention to commit suicide or had made previous "attempts."[26]

Of course, it is most important to note that the studies of Pokorny and Vail do not contain controls so that there may be an equally large (or even larger) population who *express an intention* to commit suicide, to initiate deadly acts against themselves, but do not actually do so. Indeed, in a study of "attempted suicides" and "suicide threats" in a VA Mental Hospital Farberow found both great personality differences between the two populations and great differences in their *actions*. Most of those who threaten to commit suicide do not actually do so. Some, however, very definitely do.[27]

---

[24] From the above discussion, of course, it is obvious that an attempt to "commit suicide" cannot be used directly to infer any intent—unless one is being merely tautologous.

[25] A. D. Pokorny, "Characteristics of Forty-Four Patients Who Subsequently Committed Suicide," *American Medical Association Archives of General Psychiatry*, 2 (March, 1960) pp. 314-323.

[26] D. J. Vail, "Suicide and Medical Responsibility," *American Journal of Psychiatry*, May (1959) pp. 1006-1010.

[27] N. L. Farberow, "Personality Patterns of Suicidal Mental Hospital Patients," *Genetic Psychology Monographs*, XLII (1950) 3-79.

We are, then, left uncertain as to the relations between expressions of intent, actual intent, and actions. In such matters it seems best to take the counsel of Schneider: "We see it as dangerous to try to establish at all cost any straight agreement between the act of suicide and the thoughts and motives of suicide.[28] Gaupp and others had previously established the necessity of distinguishing between "motives" ("the reasons which appear in the consciousness of the person in question") and "causes" ("the driving powers behind the act which very often do not become conscious").[29] We have seen here that we must distinguish not only between "subjective estimates" and "objective estimates" of the *causes* of suicide, but also between "subjective estimates" and *actions* and between actions and *consequences* (degree of danger, etc.). Some researchers have, indeed, considered intention to be most generally characteristic of suicide, but have implied that the term "suicide" is actually descriptive of actions rather than intention itself: "Some people undoubtedly commit suicide by 'accident,' i.e., as the result of a suicidal gesture that miscarried."[30] This conceptual approach is quite different from that of the researchers who consider *intention* a necessary dimension of suicide. These latter researchers would exclude any such phenomena as "accidental suicide," though they might consider them to be "pseudocides."[31]

To distinguish between intended suicide and accidental suicide that results from dangerous actions initiated by ego with the intention of eliciting a response (e.g., sympathy or

[28] P. B. Schneider, *op.cit.*

[29] See K. G. Dahlgren, *On Suicide and Attempted Suicide*, Lund, 1945, pp. 19-20. It is very interesting to note what Lichtenberg said concerning these matters as early as 1799:

If suicides gave their reasons for the act in set terms, not much light would be thrown on the matter. But this is precisely what everyone who hears of a suicide tries to do. All he really accomplishes is to reduce the case to his own language, thus making it something different from the reality. G. C. Lichtenberg, "Reflections."

[30] P. G. Daston and G. A. Sakheim, "Prediction of Successful Suicide from the Rorschach Test, Using a Sign Approach," *Journal of Projective Techniques*, 24 (December, 1960) pp. 355-362.

[31] F. Lendrum ("A Thousand Consecutive Cases of Suicide," *American Journal of Psychiatry*, 13 (1933), pp. 479-500), for example, excluded seven "pseudocides" from his study of Detroit "attempted suicides."

control) not only involves the assumption that the *meaning core* of "suicide" is the intention to die by one's own (positive or negative) actions, but also the assumption that *intention* is not merely a *willing* but a *decision* involving more or less *effective expectations*, both social and non-social.[32]

The students of suicide and attempted suicide have come increasingly to realize that suicidal phenomena can not only be *meaningful* in the Durkheimian sense (see below), but also in the sense that *the individuals performing these acts expect that their acts will not only have consequences upon their bodies but upon their relations to significant others as well—individuals committing dangerous acts against themselves are not only concerned with the past, with the loss of social ties or of a hated love object,[33] but also with the future.*

In a study in St. Louis of individuals who had committed dangerous acts against themselves Schmidt found that approximately 35% of them had previously communicated their *intention* to commit suicide. But, whereas Vail and Pokorny stopped with determining the "expression of intention," Schmidt determined the social targets of these communications to be friends and relatives in the vast majority of cases.[34] In an even more specific set of studies Jensen and Petty have tried to show that those committing dangerous acts against themselves very frequently intend a specific significant alter to save them. For example, one man who did succeed in killing himself by carbon-monoxide asphyxiation

[32] It is of interest to note here that Kant maintained that the mind is reducible to three fundamental faculties: (1) the faculty of *knowledge*, (2) the faculty of *feeling* pleasure and pain, and (3) the faculty of *desire*. (See *Critique of Judgment*, Oxford: Oxford University Press, 1952, pp. 4 and 15.) Most of the fundamental definitions of "suicide" consider the operation of one of the faculties to be critical: (1) Durkheim favored "knowledge," (2) Lendrum, *et al.*, "desire," (3) Schilder, *et al.*, pleasure and displeasure. It is only with the introduction of *decision* or choice that "monistic-faculty" theories are transcended.

[33] Almost all psychoanalytic theories are as deficient in this respect as Durkheim's theory, but Sandor Rado is a great exception: see his discussion of the "appeal" nature of "melancholia" and "suicide" in *Psychoanalysis of Behavior*, New York: Grune and Stratton, 1956, pp. 40-46.

[34] E. H. Schmidt, *et al.*, "Evaluation of Suicide Attempts as a Guide to Therapy," *Journal of the American Medical Association*, 155 (June 5, 1954), pp. 549-557.

had left many notes around the house indicating the need to check the insurance and had left a Chekhov book open at a case of suicide. Jensen and Petty hypothesize that this man's "plans for rescue" failed because his wife failed to respond to all of the obvious cues.[35] Such cases would seem to indicate that many individuals who die by the acts they intend to perform may intend something very different from dying.[36] They may have decided to run the *risk* of dying from their acts in order, by their destructive actions, to produce certain responses on significant alters.[37]

(3) *The willing of self-destruction.* The intention to destroy oneself as opposed to the intention simply to initiate actions that lead to the (objective) death of the individual (body) involves far more of the problem of the *unity of the self*. If the self is considered to be *unitary*,[38] then the objections of Hegel, Weiss, and others to the idea of a *self negating itself* becomes far more significant. Most men who have considered *ego-initiated* deadly acts have considered the "self" to be, in some way, unitary, and have almost always agreed in some way that "there can be no possible suicide of our being." There were a few who considered the possibility that a unitary self might have death as its unitary (and, thus, "natural") end. Spinoza was one of these few:

If it agreed better with a man's nature that he should

---

[35] V. W. Jensen and T. A. Petty, "The Fantasy of Being Rescued in Suicide," *Psychoanalytic Quarterly*, xxvii (1958) 327-39. Jensen and Petty have even given a detailed description of a chronic paranoid schizophrenic who "committed suicide" only after having made three unsuccessful "attempts to be rescued."

[36] Actually, of course, this has long been recognized by many observers. Consider, for example, the statement by Ximenes Doudon, a French Romantic: "I do not say that it is cowardly to kill oneself, because that moral antithesis has always made me laugh, but I do say that there is a desire to create an impressing, personally experienced justification." Quoted in O. Brachfeld, *Inferiority Feelings*, New York: Grune and Stratton, 1951, p. 130.

[37] See J. M. A. Weiss, "The Gamble with Death in Attempted Suicide," *Psychiatry*, 20 (1957), pp. 17-25.

[38] Quite obviously, few men who have considered the "self" (or the "soul" as many earlier students called it) to be unitary have considered the "self" to be *monolithic*. They have considered the "self" to be made up of many parts, but of parts which in some way make up a whole, a unity.

hang himself, could any reason be given for his not hanging himself? Can such a nature possibly exist? If so, I maintain (whether I do or do not grant free will), that such an one, if he sees that he can live more conveniently on the gallows than sitting at his own table, would act most foolishly, if he did not commit suicide.[39]

Yet even Spinoza came to the conclusion that the unitary "self" cannot actually destroy itself, cannot will its own end: "All persons who kill themselves are impotent in mind, and have been thoroughly overcome by external causes opposed to their nature." The assumptions and reasoning behind Spinoza's conclusion that "self-destruction" is against the nature of man are very similar to those of Hegel: "Spinoza would see a death instinct as inadequate: the very nature of man is appetite (unconscious) and desire (conscious) . . . a death urge, an urge to return to no desire, is self-contradictory."[40] As previously intimated, then, the reason for considering "self-destruction" to be impossible was not simply that the "self" was considered to be unitary, but that the "self" was considered to be *essentially will or willing.* "Self-destruction" on the most fundamental level would mean, then, that the will had willed non-willing, that intention had produced non-intention. This clearly seemed logically absurd as long as the "self" was assumed to be unitary over time. Of course, the denial of the logical possibility of "self-destruction" did not necessarily lead to a denial of the logical possibility of "suicide." As long as "suicide" was defined as an act against the body that objectively produced (body) death, it was quite logically possible, perhaps even most logically correct, to maintain that "suicide," rather than being a "self-destruction," is actually an affirmation of the self: "Suicide is a strong affirmation of the will to live, not a denial of will." (Schopenhauer)[41]

"Self-destruction" could, however, be shown to be logically possible (1) by denying that the "self" is essentially the "will" or "willing," or (2) by denying that the "self" is

[39] Spinoza, *Correspondence with Blyenbergh*, xxxvi.

[40] L. S. Feuer, *Spinoza and the Rise of Liberalism*, Boston: Beacon Press, 1958, p. 213. That Spinoza's view is still held by some can be easily seen from a few statements by O. Lodge in a recent *Fortnightly Review*: "Surely no one wishes to injure his essential self. . . . Self injury is unnatural though in certain moods it is possible."

[41] Quoted in J. Sully, *Pessimism*, London: Henry and King, 1877.

unitary over time, or (3) by denying the "self" to be fundamentally unitary.

Western thinkers found it almost impossible to escape the
assumption that a man will not "will" what he knows to be
"bad" for himself, i.e., in terms of the balancing of his own
pleasure and pain expectations. To the Greeks and Romans
suicide was preeminently a "rational" action intended to
either increase one's happiness[42] or decrease one's unhappiness. There was hardly any thought of self-destruction.[43] As
the "will" assumed an increasingly central position in the
conception of the "self," the concept of "self-destruction"
became increasingly logically contradictory.

The development of psychology and sociology in the
nineteenth and twentieth centuries contributed a great deal
to the unseating of the "will" from the core of man. The
extreme "willfulness" of Faust, the Romantics, and the early
nihilists has largely given way to an *externalized conception
of man*, of which the *oversocialized* conception of man is
only one type.[44] Some of the early sociologists, especially
Max Weber, saw man as a *chooser* (and, thus, a "willer") in
a pluralistic social universe;[45] but this partially-internal-and-
partially-external conception of man has given way before
an increasingly externalized conception of man by sociolo-

[42] Cleombrotus is probably the best example of a Greek's killing
himself to increase his happiness: "And he who, to enjoy Plato's
Elysium, leaped into the sea, Cleombrotus." (Milton, *Paradise Lost*,
Bk. III)
"Suicide is *unlawful* when committed for the sake of the body, but
rational when committed for the sake of the soul, since this is sometimes advantageous to it." (Plotinus, *First Ennead*, Bk. 9.)

[43] It is of interest to note that even the Apostle said that "No one
ever hated his own flesh." (Discussed by A. Girard *et al.*, in "Justice"
in *The Virtues and States of Life*, ed. A. M. Henry, Chicago: Fides,
1957, pp. 360-361.) That many Christian thinkers continued to see
"suicide" as essentially a "rational" act and, if intended to help others,
as morally right, is demonstrated by the fact that St. Jerome and the
Venerable Bede even included Christ among the Suicides. (See H. R.
Fedden, *Suicide: A Social and Historical Study*, London: Davis, 1938,
p. 10.) For a full treatment of the tremendous conflict that raged
among Christian thinkers concerning the descriptive and moral nature
of "suicide" see W. E. H. Lecky, *History of European Morals from
Augustus to Charlemagne*, New York: Appleton, 1869.

[44] See Dennis H. Wrong, "The Oversocialized Conception of Man,"
American Sociological Review, 26 (April, 1961), pp. 183-193.

[45] "Weber saw social life as a polytheism of values in combat with
one another, and choices were possible among these values." (Talcott
Parsons, "Introduction" to *From Max Weber: Essays in Sociology*, New
York: Oxford, 1946, p. 70.)

gists. This externalized conception of man has quite naturally led to a conception of the "self" in terms of "complementary expectations" which are considered to be "constitutive rather than merely regulative of human nature."[46]

Once the "self" has been divested of "will" and made over in the image of a social structure it can quite *logically* be hypothesized that "self-destruction" not only exists but is *directly* related to "status integration" or to "status deprivation." But such an approach cannot even leave conceptual room for the question as to whether "status disintegration" is the *cause* of "self"-destruction or itself merely one possible outcome of personality developments that also produce "suicide."

Many psychologists and psychiatrists, especially psychoanalysts, use the term "self" as a core term in their theories; but they have come to use "self" to mean very much the same thing the externalizing sociologists mean by it.[47] An alternative term used to mean much the same thing is "identity," which is what Erikson has called a "psychoanalytic sociological" term.[48] Used in this sense "self-destruction" (or "identity-destruction") becomes not only logically possible, but is frequently considered to be the primary factor in suicide:

. . . the "wish to die" is only in those rare cases a really suicidal wish, where "to be a suicide" becomes an inescapable identity choice in itself.[49]

[46] D. Wrong, *op.cit.* This conception of the "self" is not only central to the Durkheim-Parsons line of sociological theory. It is also central to the line of theory and research that has developed from the theories of "self" (and "self concept") of Cooley and Mead: see, for example, the recent work of W. R. Rosengren, "The Self in the Emotionally Disturbed," *The American Journal of Sociology*, LXVI (March, 1961), pp. 454-463.

[47] See, especially, H. S. Sullivan's theory of the "self-system" (*The Interpersonal Theory of Psychiatry*, New York: W. W. Norton, 1953) and P. Schilder's theory of "fluctuating self-experiences" (*The Image and Appearance of the Human Body*, New York: International Universities Press, 1951).

[48] "It has not escaped the reader that the term identity covers much of what has been called the self by a variety of workers. . . ." (Erik H. Erikson, "The Problem of Ego Identity," in *Identity and Anxiety*, M. R. Stein, *et al.* (Eds.), Glencoe: The Free Press, 1960, pp. 37-88.)

[49] *Ibid.* Erikson gives an example of a young woman whose mother had conditioned her to feel both that death is better than prostitution

These psychological theorists did not, however, discard "will." "Will" has been increasingly incorporated into the concept of "ego,"[50] which has been considered to be the fundamental "choosing" factor that produces the "self" or the "identity":

> In this paper, we are concerned with the *genetic continuity* of such a self-representation—a continuity which must lastly be ascribed to the work of the ego. No other inner agency could accomplish the selective accentuation of significant identifications throughout childhood; and the gradual integration of self-images in anticipation of an identity.[51]

The psychoanalysts do not consider "ego-destruction" to be any more logically possible than the philosophers and psychologists who used "self" to mean approximately the same thing as "ego" considered "self-destruction" to be logically possible. Their fundamental (largely implicit) assumptions concerning the *adaptive* nature of human choice have prevented their considering "ego-cide" or "ego-destruction" to be possible.

One type of psychological theory that has a great deal in common with psychoanalysis but which has partially broken through this *conceptual barrier* is *existential analysis*. In existential analysis an individual's *existence* covers not only *will* (or the fundamental *choice* functions) but also "self" (or "identity"); yet ego-initiated death, is considered to be not only possible but quite frequently actual:

> Existential analysis cannot be content with the psychological judgment that the suicide of Ellen West is to be explained by the motive of her suffering of torture and the wish arising therefrom to end this torture; nor can we be

---

and that she herself had strong tendencies in that direction. When (falsely) arrested for prostitution she hanged herself, closing her suicide note with the words: "Why I achieve honor only to discard it. . . ."

[50] It is best to consider this incorporation as still an on-going process. In the beginning Freud conceived of the ego as entirely cognitive. Only later did he consider the ego to have "drive energy" of its own, which was necessary for ego to take over entirely the functions of "will."

[51] E. Erikson, *op.cit.*

satisfied with the judgment that her festive mood in the face of death is to be explained by the motive of her anticipating the certain end of this torture and the joy over this end. These judgments fall back on the motive as a final basis for explanation, whereas for existential analysis the motives too are still problems. For us it remains a problem how to understand that these motives become effective, in other words, how they could become motives at all.

From the standpoint of existential analysis the suicide of Ellen West was an "arbitrary act" as well as a "necessary event." Both statements are based on the fact that the existence in the case of Ellen West had become ripe for its death, in other words, that the death, this death, was the necessary fulfillment of the life-meaning of this existence. This can be demonstrated by existential analysis, but conclusive evidence calls for insight into the kind of temporality which this existence engendered.[52]

There is no conceptual contradiction involved in "existence-destruction," in part because the existence included not only "will" or "choice" but also the ongoing situation as experienced by the willer. This brings in the possibility (and, in the case of Ellen West, the actuality) of changes in the "self" (or "identity") over time, which brings us to the consideration of the logical status of "self-destruction" when the self is not *unitary over time*.

[52] Ludwig Binswanger, "The Case of Ellen West," in Rollo May, *et al.* (Eds.), *Existence*, New York: Basic Books, 1958, pp. 294-295. Binswanger's analysis of Ellen West is both one of the best documented and most brilliant analyses of an individual's suicide. Though Binswanger's analysis of Ellen West's "suicide" is very creative in that it goes so far beyond most of what has been done in this direction before, it should, nevertheless, be noted that his analysis has a great deal in common with the German view of "oceanic suicide": ". . . the desire to escape from one's individuality, whether through love, through death, or through music—a tendency which has led to tragic consequences in the German history of the nineteenth and twentieth centuries—is an essentially formless and nihilistic desire to succumb to the chaos of the universe." (Leo Spitzer, "Three Poems on Ecstasy," in *A Method of Interpreting Literature*, Northampton, Mass.: Smith College Press, 1949, p. 56.) "Aus dem Leben, wie aus seinem Keime, Wächst der ewige Würzer nur." (Schiller, "Melancholie an Laura," quoted in J. R. Frey, "Schiller's Concept and Poetic Treatment of Death," *Journal of English and German Philology*, LVIII (October, 1959), pp. 557-588.)

Jung is one of the psychologists who conceives of the "self" as unitary by definition. The "self" is the directive *mechanism* of the personality that holds together the many different and even conflicting tendencies of the personality. This "self" may even be one or a few dominant motives.[53] But Jung maintains that this "self" *may not be unitary over time*, that this unitary mechanism may be destroyed or may simply change (especially "oscillate") over time; and that this dissolution or change of the "self" over time may lead to suicide.[54]

Jung maintains that this tendency to suicide results largely from an internal conflict within the "self" (especially a conflict involving a *slight* predominance of introversion over extroversion), a conflict which tends to produce a very great deal of tension which, in turn, produces an "equivalence of alternative paths" of which suicide is one. Jung considers suicide to be the result of following a *decision-path* made up of links connected by critical junctures (decisions) which are determined by "feeling-values" that approach each other as the tension (affect) level increases.[55]

But, though Jung's *dynamic* conception of the "self" makes it logically possible for ego-initiated deadly acts to be the result of a destruction of one "self-concept" by another "self-concept," it would not seem that Jung's conception of the "self" would give rise to the logical possibility of a *"self"*

[53] See C. G. Jung, *Psychological Types*, New York: Pantheon Books.
[54] The anguished feeling of lacking unity that results from radical, rapid changes (or oscillations) in one's "self" has been excellently expressed by Virginia Woolf in *The Waves*: "I have no face . . . other people have faces. . . .Their world is the real world. The things they lift are heavy. They say Yes, they say No; whereas I shift and change. . . ." Virginia Woolf seems to have suffered precisely such shifts in "self" and she committed suicide in a manner that might reasonably lead one to believe that she was seeking an "oceanic unity" of self:

> She walked out into the sea until she became a part of the river and sea. She was tired of the land. And being tired of the time, too, she turned her back on it and walked into a timeless beyond named eternity.

(Carl Sandburg, "Virginia Woolf's Personal Decision," in *Home Front Memo*.)
[55] C. G. Jung, *Psychiatric Studies*, New York: Pantheon, 1957, pp. 120-124.

that decides against itself, that decides in favor of a loss to itself.[56]

Alfred Adler's theory of suicide offers little more hope in this direction. Adler considers the individual personality to be dynamic, ". . . a unified and unique whole, at all times directed by one over-all striving . . . a striving for a goal of success."[57] Adler does consider suicide to be "a striving on the useless side,"[58] but this is an objectively determined "uselessness," not a subjectively realized loss to the "unified and unique whole." Indeed, Adler maintains most explicitly that the individual commits suicide to increase his gains, to win over significant others, especially the most significant other.

Freud's theory of suicide is both *instinctual* and *psychosocial*. On the instinctual level he conceived of suicide as a result of the triumph of the "death urge" (*Thanatos*) over the "life urge" (*eros*). On the most fundamental level the ego is involved in a conflict between these two opposite urges; should the "death urge" win out, the *id* becomes directed toward death and suicide is the end result.[59] On the most fundamental level this death-directedness was even conceived of as a natural process of organic running-down, a process truly beyond the pleasure (and displeasure) principle.[60] Yet this does not mean that Freud considered "self-destruction" (i.e., "ego-destruction") to be an actuality.

---

[56] Jung was probably partly prevented from conceiving of suicide in such terms because of the close relation between his conception of "self" and the earlier (see above) conception of the "will." He even quotes the following excerpt from Schopenhauer in his discussion of "suicide": "Man ever does what he wills, and does so by necessity; that is because he *is* what he wills; for from what he is there follows by necessity everything he will ever do." (*Ibid.*) Such an approach is not only partially tautologous; it is also completely opposed to the decisional approach that synthesizes across the *personality-situation* nexus (see below).

[57] Alfred Adler, "Suicide," *Journal of Individual Psychology*, 14 (May, 1958) pp. 57-62.

[58] H. L. Ansbacher, "Suicide: The Adlerian Point of View," in Shneidman and Farberow, pp. 204-220.

[59] See S. Freud, *Beyond the Pleasure Principle.*

[60] See J. C. Flügel, "Death Instinct, Homeostasis and Applied Concepts," *International Journal of Psychoanalysis* (Supplement), 34, pp. 43-74; and L. Saul, "Freud's Death Instinct and the Second Law of Thermodynamics," *International Journal of Psychoanalysis*, xxxix (1958) 323-325.

The instinctual death-directedness is confined to the libidinal level, the level "below" the "self" (or "ego").

On the psycho-social level Freud considered suicide to be the result of an *introjected conflict* between the libidinal motivation to kill a loved-and-hated object and the super-ego-founded guilt resulting from this motivation to kill, a guilt which is made ineluctable by the death of the loved-and-hated object.[61] Suicide is simply a self-initiated death that is either unconsciously or consciously drive-determined. Suicide is not seen as a decision by the ego or self to act destructively toward the self or ego. Rather, suicide involves the ego or self only insofar as the ego or self fails to resolve the conflict between the id and the superego.

Otto Rank's treatment of suicide is both quite similar and quite dissimilar to Freud's. Rank maintained that self-initiated death is the result of a fundamental conflict within the self or ego, a conflict between the fear of living and the fear of dying that is inborn as fear but learned as fear of:

> It seems, therefore, as if fear were bound up somehow with the purely biological life process and receives a certain content only with the knowledge of death. . . . The individual comes to the world with fear, and this inner fear exists independently of outside threats, whether of a sexual or other nature. It is only that it attaches itself easily to outer experiences of this kind; but the individual makes use of them therapeutically since they objectify and make partial the general inner fear. Man suffers from a fundamental dualism, however one may formulate it, and not from a conflict created by forces in the environment that might be avoided by a "correct bringing-up" or removed by later reeducation (psychoanalysis).[62]

Rank believed that this "ambivalent conflict of life fear and death fear" produced, in neurotic extremes, an *action strategy* based on the bargaining of life for *non-death*: the neurotic individual inhibits his life and, thereby, slowly kills himself *in order to avoid death*. The basic goal which is the primary determinant of the individual's willing (or deciding) to inhibit life is that of *non-death*. The decision to

[61] See S. Freud, "Mourning and Melancholia."

[62] Otto Rank, *The Myth of the Birth of the Hero*, New York: Vintage Books, 1959.

seek this goal by this means may *incidentally* produce the individual's death, but death is not his goal. Moreover, the decision is quite in agreement with the pleasure or, rather, with the displeasure, principle. It would, then, seem that Rank's theory does not even go *beyond* the pleasure principle, to the extent that Freud's theory does; and Freud's theory merely circumvents the pleasure principle by hypothesizing most instinctual *tendencies*—though not individual behavior—to be independent of the pleasure-displeasure principle.

Most depth-psychological theories, then, lead one necessarily, by definition, to conclude that the individual cannot will the destruction of the self (or ego). Freud's theory allows for the destruction of the self as a result of willing in favor of the instinctual tendencies other than *eros*, which is the tendency to pleasure and away from displeasure. But even Freud believed that man decided fundamentally in favor of *eros*, if only he can come to know what will gratify *eros* and what will not. In going "beyond" the pleasure principle, Freud did not go against it: he did not believe that man could will self-displeasure or fight against self-pleasure for its own sake. Masochism led Freud and others to believe that men can and frequently do will suffering for the self, but they have seen this willing of self-suffering as being the result of expectations of "secondary gain," either through "victory through defeat"[63] or "less defeat through preemptive punishment."[64]

The identification of the self (or ego) with willing and the basic assumption (or theoretical principle) that willing is in the direction of pleasure and away from displeasure (or pain) have been two fundamental factors in the development of the theories of suicide. The identification of self with willing has made many definitions of suicide illogical and has led, as well, to narrowly restrictive "willful" definitions of suicide. The opposite—to exclude will from the determining factors of human action has led to externalized definitions of suicide or the failure to give any definition of suicide other than "that which officials are supposedly counting when they make estimates of suicide rates." The

[63] Theodore Reik, *Masochism and Modern Man*.
[64] Sandor Rado, *Psychoanalysis of Behavior*, New York: Grune and Stratton, 1956.

tendency to assume, either explicitly or implicitly, that suicide involves willing and willing is determined by pleasure and pain has produced a strong hedonic strain in most theories of suicide, a strain which seems to grossly underestimate the complexity of human action.

The evidence clearly shows both factors to be of significance in determining actions initiated by an individual that lead to his own death. But there seems little justification for *defining* suicide in terms of them.

(4) *The Definition of Suicide in Terms of the Loss of Will.*

There have been many reported cases of death resulting from a simple "giving up the ghost" or losing of the will to live:

> Death and all that belongs to it is full of significance to these people. They are not afraid of it *per se*, they have no dread of its approach; in fact, given provocative reasons, they welcome death. I have seen several young men and women lie down and die as anyone lies down and sleeps. It was not suicide by poison and they committed no violent act nor did anyone else; they just died.[65]

Cannon even attempted to explain voodoo deaths in terms of a psychic giving-up that results in physiological giving-up (i.e., endocrinological stress-response breakdown).[66]

The important question here, however, is the degree to which suicide is defined in terms of a loss of will as opposed to the degree to which the loss of will is hypothesized to be a cause of suicide: in general, it seems that there has been little tendency for theorists to slip into *defining* suicide in terms of the loss of will, though, as usual, there certainly exists a tendency for some theorists to misuse their terms in such a manner that they at least seem to be using such a definitional identification.

Theorists such as Kennan have suggested that there are some individuals who are quitters and that these quitters account for many suicides.[67] Bergler has hypothesized that

[65] Reported by J. H. Holmes and quoted in G. Zilboorg, "Suicide," *American Journal of Psychiatry*, 92 (May, 1936) pp. 1347-1368.
[66] W. B. Cannon, "Voodoo Death," *The American Anthropologist*, 44, no. 2 (1942) pp. 169-182.
[67] George Kennan, "The Problem of Suicide," *McClure's Magazine*, 31 (1908) pp. 218-229.

inner passivity, masochistically tinged, is the primary causal factor producing suicide.[68] But such approaches do not lead to any definition of suicide in terms of a loss of will.

Davidson goes a bit further toward the identification of suicide with the loss of will, but he is really stating a theoretical relation between the two.[69] He maintains that at the point of suicide the individual has reached the limits of his resources and has lost his goals. The immediate situation acts as a "dominant" that restricts the field of consciousness to such an extent that there is inattention to life itself. Organic depression sets in and prevents the higher nervous system centers from complying with and controlling the incoming impulses in order to choose an action. The individual ceases to will, giving way to imagination, with the result that normal, automatic rejection of what is unhealthy fails.

Durkheim very briefly considered such giving-up suicides in a footnote.[70] He considered them to be a special *type* of suicide and called them *fatalistic suicides*. He was not delineating *giving-up* or *loss of will* as a potential causal factor in suicide. He was *defining* a special type that involved a failing to will that was known by the individual to be fatal. Death from ego-initiated acts that are fatalistic in nature were subsumed under the term of suicide.

The work of Lewis is an example of those theories which come close to *identifying* all suicide with the *loss of will*.[71] This tendency, especially in the case of Lewis, is largely the result of a biological approach to suicide in terms of the failure of the will to self-preservation. Such approaches seem to suffer from a simple inability to clearly recognize (or state) the difference between a *statement of identification* and a *statement of cause*. When Achille-Delmas says that suicide *is* "the perversion of the instinct of self-preservation" we can be rather sure from the context that he does not mean that they are synonymous, one and the same

[68] Bergler, *Inferiority Feelings*.
[69] G. M. Davidson, "The Mental State at the Time of Suicide," *Psychiatric Quarterly, Supplement*, 15 (1941) pp. 41-50.
[70] *Suicide*, p. 276, fn. 25.
[71] N. D. C. Lewis, "Studies on Suicide," Parts I and II, *Psycho-Analytic Review*, xx (July, 1933) 241-273 and xxii (April, 1934) 146-153.

thing.[72] But when Lewis makes a very similar statement it is not clear from the context that he does not mean that suicide and the loss (or failure) of the will to live are the same thing.

There has been no adequate justification given thus far by any theorist for a definition of suicide in terms of a loss of will (to live or to anything). Efforts to do so largely slip into a definitional solution to the problems involved in explaining deaths resulting from ego-initiated acts. It is, of course, possible that the loss of will is important in causing suicide, but there is at present no reason to make the two synonymous.

(5) *Suicide Defined in Terms of the Motivation to be Dead Which Leads to the Initiation of Acts that Lead to the Death of the Initiator.*

Such a definition of suicide is very similar to the colloquial conception of suicide as death resulting from a wish or desire to be dead. This definition is obviously very similar to the treatment of suicide in terms of the intention to die and the resulting acts and their consequences. The main difference is that a definition of suicide which involves the factor of motivation involves a postulated *affective association* between the expected consequences and the acts, whereas a definition simply in terms of intention may involve only the postulation of the *cognitive relation* between expectations and actions. It is important to recognize the clear distinctions between intention and motivation.[73] The distinction is at least of analytic and probably of concrete significance. For example, O'Neal's findings of greater "in-

---

[72] F. Achille-Delmas, *Psychologie Pathologique du Suicide.*

[73] In general the distinction is not even recognized. Prisco, for example, seems to include both under the term "voluntary": "Suicide is the voluntary action by which one takes away his own life." (Quoted in "Suicidio," *Encyclopedia Universal Ilustrada,* LVIII, pp. 559-574.) The failure to make any such distinction can clearly be seen in the following quotation from Dublin and Bunzel: "An immense resistance, both objective as well as subjective, must, however, first be overcome. Yet in spite of all the safeguards provided by instinct and social sanctions, the death motive does often gain the ascendancy. There are many people who voluntarily seek death, sometimes on apparently slight provocation, even though they would seem to have every incentive to live." Louis Dublin and Bessie Bunzel, *To Be or Not to Be,* New York: Harrison Smith and Robert Haas, 1933, p. 5.

tention" to die by one's own acts in the aged[74] may be quite compatible with the hypothesis that the young are more motivated to die in their deadly acts but, as Yap has suggested, fail more because of the behavioral disturbances produced by the high affect involved.[75]

In general, many of the same criticisms may be made of the definition in terms of intentions. It should be noted, of course, that both are multi-dimensional definitions: each involves an internal state, external action, and the externally perceived consequence of death. Consequently, they both suffer from the disadvantage of any multi-dimensional definition: it is almost impossible to use it in a fundamental theory since the dimensions may covary independently of each other with respect to other variables.

Both Deshaies and Schneider recognized the theoretical necessity of considering the factor of *motivation to die* in their definition of suicide. They decided to include the dimensions of *act, consequence,* and *consciousness* in their definition, but specifically excluded any dimension of *motivation to die* as necessary: "Suicide is the act of killing oneself in a continually conscious manner, taking death as a means or as an end."[76] Schneider definitely does believe that *motivations* are of great importance in leading to suicide. He does not, however, believe that any *motivation to die,* any desiring of death as a goal in itself,[77] is involved in producing or leading to suicide. To include the dimension of the *motivation to die* in the definition of suicide would actually eliminate Schneider's entire theory.[78] But there is a more

[74] P. O'Neal *et al.,* "A Psychiatric Study of Attempted Suicide in Persons over Sixty Years of Age," American Medical Association *Archives of Neurology and Psychiatry,* 75:3 (March, 1956) pp. 275-284.

[75] P. M. Yap, "Suicide in Hong Kong," *Journal of Mental Science,* 104 (April, 1958) pp. 266-301; and "Hyperiridism and Attempted Suicide in Chinese," *Journal of Nervous and Mental Diseases,* pp. 34-41.

[76] G. Deshaies, *Psychologie du Suicide.*

[77] In discussions of this sort one runs into the problem of the distinction between what one *chooses* or *wants* (given reality) and what one *prefers* or *would like to have* (if only reality were amenable). For a recent theoretical treatment of the definitional problems involved here see Francis W. Irwin, "On Desire, Aversion, and the Affective Zero," *Psychological Review,* 68 (September, 1961) pp. 293-301.

[78] Such a definition would also exclude from suicide all cases of "appeal suicide" and "escape suicide."

basic reason for their rejection of the dimension of motivation from the definition of suicide. Suicide is the variable to be explained, the dependent variable. It must, therefore, be easily observable, easily measured by sense perceptions. To Schneider, as to almost all theorists, the *actions* are *givens* (or *easily gottens*) by sense perceptions; and one seeks to explain these givens by finding unseen variables, or *inferred variables*, that come before the givens, the *act-states*.[79] It can be objected, of course, that the inclusion of the factor of consciousness in the definition of suicide largely vitiates this purpose; and there seems to be a good bit of truth to this charge. Surely the specification of consciousness (or of knowledge) is already the first step in giving an explanation in the above sense. The justification, of course, lies in the greater definitional purity achieved by cutting away unconscious or accidental acts, presumably with the expectation that this greater definitional purity will lead to a more valid theory. The inclusion of the factor of consciousness has many of the same difficulties as the factor of intention—such as the exclusion of phenomena that very clearly involve the other two dimensions (of deadly act and deadly consequence) but only minimally or not at all the factor of consciousness. But it should further be noted here that the inclusion of any factor that links the individual's acts and their consequences to an internal state has already set the stage by definition for a theory in terms of motivation[80] and, of course, especially in terms of motiva-

[79] The belief that science should start from the most easily observable and/or measurable variables and proceed to explain these variables in terms of less easily (or less immediately perceived and/or measured) variables is related to, and is probably largely derived from, the widely-held belief that ". . . Science begins with what is most obvious . . ." (Bernard Bosanquet, *A History of Aesthetic*, New York: Meridian Books, 1957, p. 5.) It is important to remember that this approach in scientific theory is a *strategy* for doing research and theory, not a criteria of validity. The difficulty is that the immediacy of perceptibility is to some degree at least a first-stage criteria of reliability in scientific theory and, thereby, tends to come to seem a full-fledged criteria of validity.

[80] The precise definition of motivation is, of course, problematic; but the best definition for our general purposes seems to be that of McClelland: ". . . a strong affective association, characterized by an anticipatory goal reaction and based on past association of certain cues with pleasure or pain." (Quoted from David C. McClelland, *Studies in Motivation*, New York: Appleton-Century-Crofts, Inc., 1955, p. 226.)

tion to die or to be dead. Such definitional stage setting is, of course, an integral part of any highly developed theory applied to a highly worked-over field of phenomena; but it is most important that the highly differentiated and complexly integrated field of observations and the developing theory related to this field of observations be the guides to the definitions and not the definitions the guides to observation and theory.

(6) *The Knowledge of an Actor that Actions he Initiates Tend to Produce the Objective State of Death.*

In the twentieth century most psychiatrists and psychologists who have studied suicide have tended to define the term in terms of intention, motivation, willing, or similar terms. Sociologists, on the other hand, have tended to assume, either implicitly or explicitly, that Durkheim's definition was the only correct one. Like the psychiatrists and psychologists, Durkheim assumed that suicide must be limited to deaths which are in some way meaningful to the social actors initiating the actions that result in their deaths. However, whereas the psychiatrists and psychologists have been primarily concerned with volitional or affective meanings, presumably because of their conviction that suicidal actions are the result of one's volitional or affective state, Durkheim and sociologists have generally tried to limit the meanings entirely to the cognitive meanings:

> Suicide, we say, exists indeed when the victim at the moment he commits the act destined to be fatal, knows the normal result of it with certainty. This certainty, however, may be greater or less. Introduce a few doubts, and you have a new fact, not suicide but closely akin to it, since only a difference of degree exists between them. Doubtless, a man exposing himself knowingly for another's sake but without the certainty of a fatal result is not a suicide, even if he should die, any more than the daredevil who intentionally toys with death while seeking to avoid it, or the man of apathetic temperament who, having no vital interest in anything, takes no care of health and so imperils it by neglect. Yet these different ways of acting are not radically different from true suicide. They result

from similar states of mind, since they also entail mortal risks not unknown to the agent, and the prospect of these is no deterrent; the sole difference is a lesser chance of death. Thus the scholar who dies from excessive devotion to study is currently and not wholly unreasonably said to have killed himself by his labor. All such facts form a sort of embryonic suicide, and though it is not methodologically sound to confuse them with complete and full suicide, their close relation to it must not be neglected.[81]

Durkheim had three major reasons for defining suicide in terms of knowledge and it seems worthwhile to give some brief consideration to each justification.

First, and probably most important for Durkheim, there was the methodological reason: Durkheim believed that intention (and, presumably, any factor of will or emotion) is much too subtle to infer on any large scale. This argument had some very serious consequences for Durkheim's whole work on suicide,[82] but he is clearly right in arguing that intention and willing are more difficult to infer than is knowledge of consequences. In fact, it seems clear that most definitions in terms of emotion or will or intention involve both the assumption that knowledge of consequences can be inferred and an additional assumption that willing or feeling about the consequences can be inferred. On the other hand, Durkheim seems to have been clearly wrong in thinking that the difficulty in inferring knowledge of consequences is of a different order from inferring the other kinds of information. It simply involves less information of the same type (information about what is "in the head" of the social actor), so that it has what Durkheim otherwise considered to be a grave disadvantage: it was highly inclusive. Durkheim's implicit assumption in his argument seems clearly to be that the act of suicide must be treated as something very rational, so that the student of suicide can simply reason about whether or not any man of average rationality would know that certain actions lead with a high

---

[81] *Suicide,* 45-46.

[82] For example, he made it impossible for himself to reasonably make use of official statistics to test his theory of suicide as defined by himself, simply because officials who collected the statistics generally define suicide in terms of intention or volition.

degree of certainty to death. If one actually considered only cases of self-initiated death in which the individual was acting quite "rationally," there would be relatively few cases to consider, so that one would have *defined* the problems out of existence.

Second, Durkheim was very concerned with eliminating accidental deaths from consideration, while including all other self-initiated deaths. Durkheim believed that all knowledgeable "renunciations of life" constitute a class of phenomena for scientific investigation:

> Whether death is accepted merely as an unfortunate consequence, but inevitable given the purpose, or is actually itself sought and desired, in either case the person renounces existence, and the various methods of doing so can be only varieties of a single class. They possess too many essential similarities not to be combined in one generic expression, subject to distinction as the species of the genus thus established. Of course, in common terms, suicide is pre-eminently the desperate act of one who does not care to live. But actually life is none the less abandoned because one desires it at the moment of renouncing it; and there are common traits clearly essential to all acts by which a living being thus renounces the possession presumably most precious of all. Rather, the diversity of motives capable of actuating these resolves can give rise only to secondary differences. Thus, when resolution entails certain sacrifice of life, scientifically this is suicide; of what sort shall be seen later.
>
> The common quality of all these possible forms of supreme renunciation is that the determining act is performed advisedly; that at the moment of acting the victim knows the certain result of his conduct, no matter what reason may have led him to act thus. All mortal facts thus characterized are clearly distinct from all others in which the victim is either not the author of his own end or else only its unconscious author.[83]

Such a rationalistic argument as this tends to be confusing: on the surface it might well seem reasonable, yet it is not satisfying. The fundamental problem is simply that Durk-

[83] *Suicide*, pp. 43-44.

heim did not give any justification for treating the "knowledgeable renunciation of life" as the only boundary determinants of a class of phenomena. Why not argue with
Halbwachs that an action that takes death as a means is
categorically different from one that takes death as an end
in itself? Durkheim's method of determining what constitutes a class of phenomena seems to have been simply
choosing whatever seemed to him reasonable, without specifying why it seemed reasonable. This is not a very valuable
method of defining a theoretical variable.

Third, Durkheim seems to have believed that common
usage of the term suicide was in agreement with his definition and that this constituted a reason for rejecting any
definition in terms of intention:

> Indeed, if the intention of self-destruction alone consti-
> tuted suicide, the name suicide could not be given to facts
> which, despite apparent differences, are fundamentally
> identical with those always called suicide and which
> could not be otherwise described without discarding the
> term.[84]

This seems to be an assumption that the term has a *necessary
meaning* that the scientist must get at, rather than a meaning which he gives it, and that Durkheim's definition is the
only one that has gotten at the necessary meaning. As we
have already noted, officials in the nineteenth and in the
twentieth centuries have generally thought that intention
or volition is a part of the everyday meaning of the term and
they have used it in that way. Most people in everyday life
probably use the term similarly. Consequently, it is hard
to see what Durkheim could mean in arguing that those acts
always called suicide have the properties he has attributed
to the term suicide but not the property of intention. Presumably, he simply did not look carefully enough at the
way in which the term is used.[85]

[84] *Ibid.*
[85] Halbwachs used precisely the same sort of "verbal realism"
argument to arrive at a conclusion in opposition to Durkheim's conclusion: "If we do not allow one thus to separate the collection of
suicides into two types so different from each other that one does
not see how and why one would reunite them into one type, it is,
first of all, because we do not believe that, if they were naturally and

Thus, using "suicide" to mean self-initiated death with knowledge of consequences but without the constraint of establishing intention is not satisfactory. On the other hand, it should be clear that knowledge and intention (or will, etc.) can vary independently and must be treated independently. This brings us to the conclusion of our whole argument.

Conclusion

Most students of suicide who have taken the problem of defining suicide seriously have tried to specify some *fundamentum divisionis* of the phenomena *which they have already implicitly accepted as being the relevant phenomena on the basis of everyday usage of the term*. Their failure to recognize that their definitions are thus already partially determined by the everyday meanings has led to a great deal of confusion. Instead of recognizing that their realm of phenomena has been primarily determined by the everyday, *concrete* meanings of the term (especially as used by officials and doctors), with the consequence that their attempts to specify a *fundamentum divisionis* is partially predetermined by these everyday, concrete meanings, the students of suicide have tried to analyze these predetermined phenomena in terms of *ad hoc, abstract criteria (e.g., homogeneity) of what constitutes a* fundamentum divisionis *in any science*. The *ad hoc* nature of the selection of these criteria has been largely unrecognized by the students of suicide; each student has felt that there is something *inherently, necessarily* correct about his own criteria. The result has been endless, confusing, unresolvable arguments over defining suicide.

Moreover, the students of suicide have usually ignored the question of the *theoretical value* of their definitions (except insofar as the whole idea of a *fundamentum divisionis* is seen to constitute, or reveal the way to *the* most theoretically valuable definition of terms). They have not apparently considered the possibility that even if they were able to arrive at some systematic set of pure (or disjunct) defini-

essentially different, one would give them the same name and that society would react in the same way in the presence of them." (Halbwachs, *op.cit.*, pp. 406-407.)

tions to cover the "relevant" phenomena, these definitions could still prove quite useless in building any worthwhile theories. It would seem instead that *the best strategy in such scientific work is to develop observations, descriptions, definitions, measurements, and theories simultaneously, each molding the other.*

Making use of our discussions of the many attempts to define "suicide," applying the strategy just proposed to the matter of defining "suicide," and accepting as we have argued in this work that the everyday meanings of "suicide" are not merely *implicit* determinants of our definitions of "suicide" (as in earlier works) but are themselves information of the first importance, we can arrive at some conclusions about the definitions of "suicide" that should prove useful in studying "suicide."

First, a student of suicide should not expect to *begin* with a clear and distinct definition of what he is studying: he must begin with open-ended, largely unexpressed definitions (or meanings) of suicide. He must begin with his own (and other's) common-sense or everyday understanding of the term.

Second, he must attempt at once to determine just what these everyday meanings are; but he must try to determine these *concretely*, that is, the way the term(s) is used in the treatment of actual cases.

Third, his increasingly formal definition(s) of suicide (i.e., his attempts to close this open-ended approach to defining the term) must be made within the context of attempts to explain the suicidal phenomena: explanation and definition must modify each other.

BIBLIOGRAPHY

There are two previously published bibliographies of material on suicide which, taken together, provide an almost complete bibliography on the subject up to 1961. The first of these, a truly magnificent bibliography by H. Rost (see the complete reference below), includes over 3700 references up to the year of 1927. With a few significant omissions, the second, published in *The Cry for Help* by Shneidman and Farberow (see the complete reference below), covers the period where Rost left off up to 1961. The existence of these two extensive and, on the whole, correct bibliographies makes it unnecessary to present anywhere near a complete bibliography on suicide in this work. Instead, only those works are presented which are clearly of direct relevance to the major arguments of this work.

Bibliography

Achille-Delmas, F. *Psychopathologie du Suicide*. Paris: Felix Alcan, 1932.

Alpert, Harry. *Emile Durkheim and His Sociology*. New York: Columbia University Press, 1939.

Bayet, A. *Le Suicide et la Morale*. Paris: Felix Alcan, 1922.

Benoit-Smullyan, E. "The Sociologism of Emile Durkheim and His School," in Harry E. Barnes, Editor, *An Introduction to the History of Sociology*. Chicago: University of Chicago Press, 1948.

Bergler, E. "Differential Diagnosis between a Calculated Risk and a Masochistic Action," *Diseases of the Nervous System*, xxi (January, 1960) pp. 30-32.

Binswanger, Ludwig. "The Case of Ellen West," in Rollo May, *et al.* (eds.), *Existence*. New York: Basic Books, 1958.

Bohannan, Paul. (ed.). *African Homicide and Suicide*. Princeton: Princeton University Press, 1960.

Boismont, Brierre de. *Du Suicide et de la Folie Suicide*. Paris: Bailliere, 1856.

Breed, Warren. "Occupational Mobility and Suicide," *American Sociological Review*, 28 (1963) pp. 179-188.

Buckle, Henry T. *Introduction to the History of Civilization in England. Revised Edition*. London: George Routledge and Sons, Ltd. (no date given).

Cavan, Ruth S. *Suicide*. Chicago: University of Chicago Press, 1928.

Cavan, Ruth S. "The Wish Never to Have Been Born," *The American Journal of Sociology*, xxxvii (January, 1932) 547-559.

Crocker, L. G. "Discussion of Suicide in the Eighteenth Century," *Journal of the History of Ideas*, 13 (January, 1952) pp. 47-72.

Dahlgren, K. G. *On Suicide and Attempted Suicide*. Lund, Sweden: Lindstadts, 1945.

Davidson, G. M. "The Mental State at the Time of Suicide," *Psychiatric Quarterly Supplement*, 15 (1941) pp. 41-50.

Deshaies, G. *Psychologie du Suicide*. Paris: Presses Universitaires de France, 1947.

Devereaux, G. *Mohave Ethnopsychiatry and Suicide*. Washington, D.C.: U.S. Government Printing Office, 1961.

Douglas, Jack D. *The Sociological Study of Suicide: Suicidal Actions as Socially Meaningful Actions*. Unpublished Ph.D. Dissertation, Princeton University, 1965.

Douglas, Jack D. "The Social Aspects of Suicide," in *The International Encyclopedia of the Social Sciences*. New York: Crowell-Collier, forthcoming.

Dublin, Louis I. *Suicide: A Sociological and Statistical Study*. New York: The Ronald Press Company, 1963.

Dublin, Louis I. and Bessie Bunzel. *To Be or Not To Be*. New York: Harrison Smith and Robert Haas, 1933.

Durkheim, E. and Marcel Mauss. *Primitive Classification*. Chicago: University of Chicago Press, 1963.

Durkheim, E. *Sociology and Philosophy*. Glencoe, Illinois: The Free Press, 1953.

Durkheim, E. *Suicide*: A Study in Sociology. New York: The Free Press, 1951.

Durkheim, E. *The Division of Labor in Society*. New York: The Free Press, 1954.

Durkheim, E. *The Elementary Forms of the Religious Life*. Glencoe: The Free Press, 1954.

Durkheim, E. *The Rules of Sociological Method.* Glencoe: The Free Press, 1938.

East, W. N. "On Attempted Suicide, with an Analysis of One Thousand Consecutive Cases," *Journal of Mental Science,* 59 (July, 1913) pp. 428-478.

Ellis, E. R. and G. N. Allen. *Traitor Within: Our Suicide Problem.* Garden City: Doubleday and Company, 1961.

Farberow, N. L. "Personality Patterns of Suicidal Mental Hospital Patients," *Genetic Psychology Monographs,* XLII (1950) pp. 3-79.

Faris, Robert E. *Social Disorganization.* New York: The Ronald Press Company, 1955.

Fedden, Henry R. *Suicide: A Social and Historical Study.* London: Peter Davies, 1938.

Feifel, H. (ed.). *The Meanings of Death.* New York: Mc-Graw-Hill Book Co., 1959.

Fenton, W. N. "Iroquois Suicide," in *Anthropology Papers,* no. 14, Washington, D.C.: U.S. Government Printing Office, 1941.

Ferri, E. *Homocidio-Suicidio.* Madrid, Spain: Editorial Review, 1934.

Firth, Raymond. "Suicide and Risk-Taking in Tikopa Society," *Psychiatry,* 24 (February, 1961) pp. 1-18.

Ford, R. and A. L. Moseley. "Motor Vehicular Suicides," *Journal of Criminal Law, Criminology, and Police Science,* 54 (September, 1963) pp. 257-259.

Freud, S. "Mourning and Melancholia," *Collected Papers,* vol. IV, London: The Hogarth Press, 1925.

Gargas, S. "Suicide in The Netherlands," *The American Journal of Sociology,* XXXVII (1932) 697-713.

Gibbs, Jack P. "Suicide," in R. K. Merton and R. A. Nisbet, Editors, *Contemporary Social Problems.* New York: Harcourt, Brace and World, Inc., 1961.

Gibbs, Jack P. and Walter T. Martin. *Status Integration and Suicide.* Eugene, Oregon: University of Oregon Press, 1964.

Gibbs, Jack P. and A. L. Porterfield. "Occupational Prestige and Social Mobility of Suicides in New Zealand," *The American Journal of Sociology,* LXVI (September, 1960), 147-152.

Gold, Martin. "Suicide, Homicide, and the Socialization of

BIBLIOGRAPHY

Aggression," *The American Journal of Sociology*, LXIII (1958), 651-661.

Halbwachs, M. *Les Causes du Suicide*. Paris: Felix Alcan, 1930.

Hendin, H. *Suicide and Scandinavia*. New York: Grune and Stratton, 1964.

Henry, Andrew F. and James F. Short. *Suicide and Homicide*. Glencoe: The Free Press, 1954.

Hillman, James. *Suicide and the Soul*. London: Hodder and Stoughton, 1964.

Hopkins, F. "Attempted Suicide," *Journal of Mental Science*, 83 (1937) pp. 71-94.

Hurlburt, W. C. "Prosperity, Depression, and the Suicide Rate," *The American Journal of Sociology*, XXXVII (1931-1932) 714-718.

Jeffreys, M. D. W. "Samsonic Suicide or Suicide of Revenge among Africans," *African Studies*, XI (1952) 118-122.

Jensen, V. W. and T. A. Petty. "The Fantasy of Being Rescued in Suicide," *Psychoanalytic Quarterly*, XXVII (1958) 327-339.

Kobler, A. L. and Ezra Stotland. *The End of Hope*. New York: The Free Press, 1964.

Kruijt, C. S. *Suicide: Sociological and Statistical Investigations*. Door: Van Gorcun and Company, 1960.

Lecky, W. E. H. *History of European Morals from Augustus to Charlemagne*, 2 vols. New York: D. Appleton and Company, 1869.

Legoyt, A. *Suicide Ancien et Moderne*. Paris: A. Drouin, 1881.

Lendrum, F. C. "A Thousand Cases of Attempted Suicide," *American Journal of Psychiatry*, 13 (1933) pp. 479-500.

Lunden, W. A. "Suicides in France, 1910-1943," *The American Journal of Sociology*, LII (1946-1947) 321-334.

Meehl, P. E. and A. Rosen. "Antecedent Probability and the Efficiency of Psychometric Signs, Patterns, or Cutting Scores," *Psychological Bulletin*, 52 (May, 1955) pp. 194-216.

Meerloo, J. A. M. *Suicide and Mass Suicide*. New York: Grune and Stratton, 1962.

Menninger, Karl. *Man Against Himself*. New York: Harcourt, Brace and Company, 1938.

Miner, J. R. "Suicide and Its Relation to Other Factors," *American Journal of Hygiene, Monographic Series*, no. 2, 1922, 72-112.

Morselli, H. *Suicide: An Essay in Comparative Moral Statistics*. New York: D. Appleton, 1903.

O'Neal, P., *et al.* "A Psychiatric Study of Attempted Suicide in Persons over Sixty Years of Age," *Archives of Neurology and Psychiatry*, 75 (1956) pp. 275-284.

Palmer, D. M. "Factors in Suicide Attacks: A Review of 25 Consecutive Cases," *Journal of Nervous and Mental Diseases*, xciii (1941) 421-442.

Parsons, Talcott. *The Structure of Social Action*. New York: The Free Press, 1949.

Piker, B. "1817 Cases of Suicide Attempts: A Preliminary Statistical Study," *American Journal of Psychiatry*, 95 (1938) pp. 97-117.

Pokorny, A. D. "Characteristics of 44 Patients who Subsequently Committed Suicide," *A.M.A. Archives of General Psychiatry*, 2 (March, 1960) pp. 314-323.

Porterfield, A. L. "Indices of Suicide and Homicide by States and Cities," *American Sociological Review*, 14 (1949) pp. 481-490.

Porterfield, A. L. "Suicide and Crime in Folk and in Secular Society," *The American Journal of Sociology*, lvii (1952) pp. 331-338.

Porterfield, A. L. "Suicide and Crime in the Social Structure of an Urban Setting: Fort Worth, 1930-1950," *American Sociological Review*, 17 (1952) pp. 341-349.

Porterfield, A. L. "Traffic Fatalities, Suicide and Homicide," *American Sociological Review*, 25 (1960), pp. 897-901.

Porterfield, A. L. and R. H. Talbert. *Crime, Suicide, and Social Well-Being in Your State and City*. Fort Worth, Texas: Leo Polisham Foundation, 1948.

Powell, Elwin H. "Occupation, Status, and Suicide: Toward a Redefinition of Anomie," *American Sociological Review*, 23 (April, 1958) pp. 131-139.

Quetelet, M. A. *Du System Social et des Lois qui le Regissent*, Paris, 1848.

Robins, E., *et al.* "The Communication of Suicidal Intent," *American Journal of Psychiatry*, 115 (February, 1959) pp. 724-733.

Robins, E. and P. O'Neal. "Culture and Mental Disorder: A Study of Attempted Suicide," *Human Organization*, 16 (Winter, 1958) pp. 7-11.

Rosen, A., *et al.* "Classification of 'Suicidal' Patients," *Journal of Consulting Psychology*, 18 (1954) pp. 359-362.

Rost, H. *Bibliographie des Selbstmords*. Augsburg: Haas and Grabherr, 1927.

Sainsbury, P. *Suicide in London: An Ecological Study*. London: Chapman and Hall, 1955.

Schilder, P. and W. Bromberg. "Death and Dying," *Psychoanalytic Review*, 70 (1933) pp. 135-185.

Schilder, P. and D. Wechsler. "The Attitudes of Children Toward Death," *Journal of Genetic Psychology*, 45 (1934), pp. 406-451.

Schmid, C. F. "Suicide in Minneapolis, 1928-1932," *The American Journal of Sociology*, xxxix (1939) 30-48.

Schmid, C. F. *Suicides in Seattle, 1914 to 1925*. Seattle: University of Washington Publications in the Social Sciences, 1928.

Schmid, C. F. and D. van Arsdol, "Completed and Attempted Suicides: A Comparative Analysis," *American Sociological Review*, 20 (1955) pp. 273-283.

Schneider, P. B. *La Tentative de Suicide*, Neuchâtel: Delachaux et Niestle, 1954.

Selvin, H. "Durkheim's *Suicide* and Problems of Empirical Research," *The American Journal of Sociology*, lxiii (May, 1958) 687-620.

Shneidman, E. S. and N. L. Farberow. (eds.). *Clues to Suicide*. New York: McGraw-Hill Book Co., 1957.

Shneidman, E. S. and N. L. Farberow. (eds.). *The Cry for Help*. New York: McGraw-Hill Book Co., 1961.

Simpson, G. "Methodological Problems in Determining the Aetiology of Suicide," *American Sociological Review*, 15 (1950) pp. 658-663.

Stengel, E. and Nancy Cook. *Attempted Suicide: Its Social Significance and Effects*. New York: Oxford University Press, 1958.

Strahan, S. A. K. *Suicide and Insanity*. London: Swan Sonneschein and Co., 1894.

Straus, J. H. and M. A. Straus. "Suicide, Homicide, and

Social Structure in Ceylon," *The American Journal of Sociology*, LVIII (1953) 461-469.

Tabachnick, N. "Countertransference Crisis in Suicidal Attempts," *A.M.A. Archives of General Psychiatry*, 4 (June, 1961) pp. 571-579.

Tabachnick, N. "Interpersonal Relations in Suicidal Attempts," *A.M.A. Archives of General Psychiatry*, 4 (January, 1961) pp. 16-21.

Teicher, J. O. "A Study in Attempted Suicide," *Journal of Nervous and Mental Diseases*, CV (1947) 283-298.

Tiryakian, E. *Sociologism and Existentialism*, Englewood Cliffs: Prentice-Hall, 1962.

Tosti, G. "Suicide in the Light of Recent Studies," *The American Journal of Sociology*, III (1898).

Trautman, E. C. "The Suicidal Fit," *A.M.A. Archives of General Psychiatry*, 5 (July, 1961) pp. 76-84.

Tuteur, W. "Statistics and Statisticians: A Timely Warning," *American Journal of Psychiatry*, 116 (September, 1959) pp. 263-264.

Verkko, Veli. *Homicides and Suicides in Finland and Their Dependence on National Character*. Kobenhavn: G.E.C. Gads Forlag, 1951.

Wechsler, H. "Community Growth, Depressive Disorders, and Suicide," *The American Journal of Sociology*, LXVII (July, 1961) 9-17.

Weiss, J. M. A. "The Gamble with Death in Attempted Suicide," *Psychiatry*, 20 (1957) pp. 17-25.

Westernarck, E. "Suicide: A Chapter in Comparative Ethics," *The Sociological Review*, 1 (1908) pp. 12-33.

Williams, G. W. *The Sanctity of Life and the Criminal Law*. New York: Knopf, 1957.

Wolff, Kurt H. (ed.). *Emile Durkheim, 1858-1917*. Columbus, Ohio: Ohio State University Press, 1960.

Wolfgang, M. E. "An Analysis of Homicide-Suicide," *Journal of Clinical and Experimental Psychopathology and Quarterly Review of Psychiatry and Neurology*, 19 (1958) pp. 208-218.

Wolfgang, M. E. "Suicide by Means of Victim-Precipitated Homicide," *Journal of Clinical and Experimental Psycho-

pathology and Quarterly Review of Psychiatry and Neurology, 20 (1959) pp. 335-349.

Wood, A. L. "Crime and Aggression in Changing Ceylon: A Sociological Analysis of Homicide, Suicide, and Economic Crime," in *Transactions of The American Philosophical Society,* 51 (December, 1961).

Yap, P. M. "Suicide in Hong Kong," *Journal of Mental Science,* 104 (April, 1958) pp. 266-301.

Yessler, P. G., *et al.* "On the Communication of Suicidal Ideas," *A.M.A. Archives of General Psychiatry,* 5 (July, 1961) pp. 12-30.

Zilboorg, G. "Considerations on Suicide, with Particular Reference to That of the Young," *American Journal of Orthopsychiatry,* vii (1937) 15-31.

Zilboorg, G. "Differential Diagnostic Types of Suicide," *Archives of Neurology and Psychiatry,* 35 (January, 1935) pp. 270-291.

Zilboorg, G. "Suicide among Civilized and Primitive Races," *American Journal of Psychiatry,* 92 (1935-1936) pp. 1347-1369.

INDEX

Achille-Delmas, F., 100, 171, 205n, 374
Adler, A., analysis of suicide, 370
aetiological definition of suicide, 26-29, 65
aggression, and suicide, 132-43
Allen, G. N., 222n
Alpert, H., 18n, 24-25, 31, 35, 43, 60, 61, 66
altruism, 37, 38, 39, 40, 42, 45, 50, 51, 53, 54, 55, 57, 58, 64, 66, 72, 129, 180, 345, 346
analytic induction, 104
animals and suicide, 354-55
anomie, 18-20, 37, 38, 39, 40, 41, 42, 45, 50, 51, 53, 54, 55, 56, 57, 58, 66, 71, 72, 92-94, 113, 129, 345, 346
Aristotle, 5n, 72n, 75, 347, 347n
Arlington, V., 249
atonement by means of suicide, 302-304
attempts to conceal suicide, *see* statistics on suicide
Augustine, St., 3n

Bayet, A., 60-62, 68, 79, 157, 181
Bendix, R., 30n
Benedict, R., 237n
Benoit-Smullyan, 180n
Bergler, E., 373
Berkowitz, L., 141
Bertillon, J., 21
Binswanger, L., 368n
biographic approach to case studies, criticism of, 262
Bock, K. E., 33n
Boismont, B. de, 14, 18-20, 25, 109, 110, 171
Bosanquet, B., 377n
Breed, W., 14; status-change theory of suicide, 120-23
Bromberg, W., 183n, 286n
Buckle, Henry, 9-10, 199
building-block approach to the

analysis of social meanings, 238-40
Bunzel, B., 150n, 195n, 311n
Burke, K., 216n, 250n
Burton, 6n

Camus, A., 4n
Cannon, W. B., 373
case studies of suicide, 164, 255-70
Cassirer, E., 29-30, 285n
Catalano-Nobili, C., 359n
Catholic suicide rates, biases in, 205-10
Catlin, G., 32n
Cavan, R. S., 164n, 169n, 221n, 223n, 226n, 323n; theory of suicide, 99-100, 103-108
Cerquetelli, G., 359n
Chateaubriand, 18-20
Christ, and suicide, 365
Cicourel, A., 163n
Cohen, A. K., 239n
collective consciousness, *see* collective representations
collective representations, 32, 45, 48, 51-52, 60, 62, 67, 75, 76, 126
common sense, sociologists taking the standpoint of, 266-67
communications of suicidal intentions, 321-23, 325-28
construction of social meanings (ch. 14), 247-54
contextual determination of meanings, principle of, 242-43
Cook, N., 248n, 277n, 320, 321n, 326n, 354n, 357n
Cooley, C., 366n
coroner's reports, California case, 186-88
Crocker, L. G., 4n
cultural homogeneity, assumption of, 155-58
culture, 28